Memoirs
of a Social Atom

W. E. Adams

MEMOIRS OF A SOCIAL ATOM

———◆———

BY

W. E. ADAMS
Author of "Our American Cousins," etc.

WITH PORTRAITS

1903

In grateful remembrance of many years of service and association, I dedicate this work to the memory of

JOSEPH COWEN, M.P.

whose influence in journalism, courage in politics, and commanding eloquence in the tribunes of the people, will ever be numbered among the inspiring traditions of Northern England.

PREFACE

THE greater portion of the matter composing these pages was printed as a series of articles in the *Newcastle Weekly Chronicle*, 1901—1902. The articles themselves were written in Madeira during a compulsory residence there in the winter of 1900—1901. Hearty thanks are due to the proprietors of the paper for permission to reproduce them in the present form.

CONTENTS

———————

ILLUSTRATIONS

———————————

INTRODUCTION

I CALL myself a Social Atom—a small speck on the surface of society. The term indicates my insignificance. I have mingled with no great people, been admitted to no great secrets, met with no great adventures, witnessed no great events, taken part in no great transactions. In a word, I am just an ordinary person: no better, and I hope no worse, than the ordinary run of my neighbours. Being thus so completely undistinguished in every way, why have I had the conceit or the impudence to intrude upon the attention of the public? The intrusion, I shall expect to be told, might have been understood, or at all events forgiven, in a younger man; but in one who has reached, perhaps has passed, the years of discretion, the offence, if not absolutely without excuse, is hardly slight enough to escape the general censure. But a word in explanation before sentence is pronounced.

It has been said that every man has in him the making of at least one good novel. The gentleman who first impressed this idea upon me was distinguished in science, but was yet desirous of trying the experiment of writing a novel himself. As the proposition was not accepted, we have no means of knowing how far the theory in his case would have stood the test of experiment. But if every man in certain given circumstances may be considered capable of writing (perhaps I ought to say of producing) one good novel, might we not assume with even greater reasonableness that every man of advanced age has seen and heard enough in the course of his career to enable him to write a book of recollections? Anyway, I think it may fairly be held that no man can go through the world with his eyes open for seventy years without seeing much that would, if intelligently explained and discussed, interest (and maybe instruct) the general public.

Holding this view, I hope to be pardoned for putting into some sort of literary form a few recollections of events and circumstances that have come under my own observation since 1832. The events and circumstances here indicated are not of high importance, although, as many of them concern the common people and the hopes and aspirations of the common people, they ought not to be the less appreciated, nor perhaps the less attractive, on that account. It is, after all, the common people who constitute society—society without the capital letter; for "the nation in all ages," as Mr. Bright once said, "live in cottages."

Books of recollections constitute what may be called a favourite class of literature. Though they cannot of course compete with novels, they stand as high in public favour, let us say, as poetry and the drama. And it is a wholesome taste—the taste for reading the records of actual occurrences and adventures. Actors, artists, authors, journalists, propagandists, politicians, and even statesmen, have from time to time told the world what they knew about themselves, what they thought of other people, what they remembered of the things that transpired in their day and generation. All these productions are more or less interesting—some because the writer is himself an interesting personage, others because he deals with incidents of stirring or tragic character, others again because he has light and agreeable stories to tell and a light and agreeable way of telling them.

I have read many such books, and have derived profit and pleasure from all. Maybe I can make a not unreadable contribution to that branch of literature myself. But I have already disclaimed any pretension to importance. My recollections, for the most part, will relate to the commonplace experiences of a humble worker in a humble sphere of life. I repeat, however, that they may not lack interest on that account. I recollect that one of the most entertaining books I ever read was the "Autobiography of a Working Man." It was published when I was still a youth. The character of the book may be judged from the title. It was simply the record of the trials and troubles, the joys and the sorrows, of a journeyman of the period. But the story was told intelligently and without pretence, and so it received, I remember, a cordial welcome from both the press and the public. A somewhat similar welcome—which, however, was perhaps less deserved in these cases—was extended to other works of the same complexion, the "Autobiography of a

Beggar Boy" and the "Autobiography of One who has Whistled at the Plough." The examples mentioned are at all events encouraging.

Another consideration has had much weight in inspiring the present enterprise. In the autumn of 1866, Mr. James Watson, an old Radical publisher who had been imprisoned in the days of the struggle for a free press, and who had been closely concerned in all the Radical movements of the previous forty years, was on a visit to Blaydon-on-Tyne. I had known Mr. Watson some years before, knew something of his history and his struggles, knew also that few men of my acquaintance could furnish the world with so graphic a narrative of the agitations in which he had taken part. The gentleman who entertained Mr. Watson at Blaydon, a still older friend than I was, urged him to write out his recollections. I added my own entreaties. Mr. Watson, who was then an old man, would promise nothing, and eventually did nothing. So was lost a wealth of memorable reminiscences that can never now be chronicled. Much the same thing happened later, when Mr. George Julian Harney was contributing articles to the *Newcastle Weekly Chronicle*. He, too, was urged to write down his recollections—particularly his recollections of the Chartist agitation, in which he had played a leading and important part. Mr. Harney promised to consider the proposal, and there the matter ended. It occurred to me at these times that I ought not to exempt myself from the pressure of my own exhortations, more especially as I also had had some small connection with the movements in which Watson and Harney had played conspicuous rôles. If I have taken my own medicine, it is at least good evidence that I had faith in its virtues.

One cannot be unmindful of the fact, even before putting a single line on paper, that personal memoirs or recollections cannot be recorded without an appearance of egotism that may be distasteful, not to say disgusting, to other people. The eternal "I" asserts itself in every chapter and in almost every sentence. This is naturally an enormous disadvantage, since it excites a prejudice against the writer. Yet there is no way out of the difficulty except by dealing with events in which one has personally acted as if one was merely a spectator of them. Such a process is all the more unsatisfactory because it creates the impression that the narrative is rather a work of imagination than a register of actual occurrences.

And then there is that other difficulty which confronts the faithful narrator—the difficulty of discriminating between what interests himself and what will interest the reader. A trivial incident may appear of considerable importance to the person who witnessed it, but of no consequence whatever to the person who did not. Matters that interest ourselves loom large in our own eyes, but contract to small dimensions in the eyes of others. It is as if one looked at an object from the right end of a telescope, while another looked at the same object from the wrong end. Besides, readers are of different tastes. What will please one class will not attract even the languid attention of another class. The best judges are often deceived in questions of popular likes and dislikes. Neither authors nor playwrights, however many their triumphs, are uniformly successful in gauging them. How, then, may a humbler scribe expect to fare? Well, he can only exercise his own judgment to the best of his own ability. The task is delicate, not to say perplexing. Whether success or failure attend the effort, the effort itself may be worth undertaking. The result is in other hands.

VOLUME I

CHAPTER I

A FASHIONABLE TOWN

THE town of Cheltenham has many distinctions, among the rest that of being the first to welcome the present writer. This interesting event occurred in the year of the great Reform Bill, and on the anniversary in that year of the birthday of General Washington. If the event had never occurred, the present history would never have been written. Maybe we have not much to be thankful for. Anyway, this bit of fooling, exquisite or otherwise, will serve to introduce "the birthplace of Podgers." Nothing further need be said on the subject, except that the statement can be verified, if anybody should want to verify it, by consulting the register of baptisms at the old Parish Church for February 11th, 1832.

Now that I have got over the preliminary difficulty of a modest narrator—cantered over it, as the late Mr. W. E. Forster, the projector of the Education Bill of 1870, thought he had cantered over the religious difficulty—I may perhaps profitably proceed to give some account of an old-fashioned fashionable resort. The account could be expanded into a volume; but as a policy of expansion in this case, whatever may be its effect on the future of the United States, would totally upset the author's scheme of proportion, the historical account at all events shall be restricted to a single chapter.

Cheltenham, as has been said, is a town of many distinctions. It owes its reputation—almost its very existence—to its mineral waters. These waters drew to the little resort which nestled under the spurs of the Cotswold Range the rank and fashion of an earlier age. Even Royalty, down in the doldrums, patronised it. Wherefore Cheltenham gave itself airs. Long before Scarborough was known as a rendezvous of health-seekers and holiday-makers, the town on the

Chelt claimed the title of Queen of Watering Places. It was a rival of Bath as far back as the reign of Beau Brummel. There were Pump Rooms in many quarters—the Old Wells, the Montpellier, the Pittville, all surrounded with lovely walks and gardens—besides the Cambray Spa, which was little larger than a Paris kiosk. Visitors of all sorts hobnobbed in the rotundas with lords and ladies of high degree. It was in the Old Well Walk—a magnificent avenue of elms long since displaced by villa residences—that old Mr. Coutts, the banker, fell in love with a pretty actress, made her Mrs. Coutts, and left her a large fortune. Harriet Mellon, the fortunate actress, was known afterwards as the Duchess of St. Albans. Owing to its sheltered situation, its pleasant environs, its soft and agreeable climate, the town became the favourite residence of so many retired veterans from India that it acquired the sobriquet of "Asia Minor."

It used to be said of a certain city in America that you couldn't fire a shot gun in any direction without hitting a colonel. Much the same joke might be made about Cheltenham. Half-pay officers abounded there. The place, so to say, was redolent of Eastern battles. Sir Harry Smith, the hero of Aliwal, was visiting it with his wife in 1847—the popular couple from whom are derived the names of three important towns in South Africa, Harrismith, Ladysmith, and Aliwal North. Even among the boys the almost exclusive subject of conversation at the time was the presence of the distinguished warrior. Fresh from his triumphs in the Punjaub, Sir Harry was presented with an address from the inhabitants by the Master of the Ceremonies—then the most important public functionary in the town, for his services were required to regulate and control the diversions of fashionable society. The great general is recorded as having delivered in reply a "stirring address" to the crowd that had assembled in the garden of his hotel. Cheltenham was associated, before and afterwards, with other famous Anglo-Indians. Lord Ellenborough, once Viceroy of India, had his seat in the neighbourhood. The two sons of the poet Burns, both military men, retired there to end their days in quietude and seclusion. Sir Robert Sale, who was killed at the battle of Moodkee, had been a resident in the town; and Lady Sale, the story of whose captivity in Cabul is one of the romances of Indian history, was still residing there when the news of her husband's death was received. And it was from the same place that Sir Charles James Napier, after the disastrous battle of Chillianwallah, was summoned to take command of the Indian army, the Duke of Wellington using on the occasion the memorable words—"If you don't go, I must."

The waters were supposed to be the chief attraction of the town. They were held in great esteem by the visitors; but by the poorer inhabitants they were not esteemed and hardly known at all. Companions of my youth used now and then to make Sunday morning excursions to an old shanty on Bay's Hill, there to make wry faces over draughts from a neighbouring spring, regardless of the consequences to health or comfort. But ailing people went to Cheltenham as they went to Bath, and as they still go to Harrogate and Llandrindod, to drink the waters. Old George the Third set the fashion in the last century. His Majesty, however, seems to have had faith in less orthodox agencies than mineral springs. A family of farriers known as the Whitworth Doctors were flourishing in Lancashire at the time. One of these, William Howitt tells us, was summoned to Cheltenham to attend the Princess Elizabeth, for whose complaint he prescribed pinches of his famous snuff!

The curative qualities of the Cheltenham springs have not escaped satire, as witness the well-known epitaph:—

> Here lie I and my three daughters,
> Killed by drinking the Cheltenham waters.
> If we had stuck to Epsom salts,
> We'd not been lying in these here vaults.

The graveyard surrounding the old Parish Church is credited with containing a stone bearing the celebrated inscription. But the stone and the inscription are alike apocryphal. At all events I never saw it myself, nor, I think, has anybody else. [1] There is, however, nothing in the absurdity of the epitaph to warrant the assumption that it would not have been sanctioned by the church authorities in less fastidious days than ours; for in the same graveyard may still be seen the tombstone of a pig-killer with this gruesome doggerel:—

Here lies John Higgs,
A famous man for killing pigs;
For killing pigs was his delight,
Both morning, afternoon, and night.
Both heat and cold he did endure,
Which no physician could e'er cure.
His knife is laid, his work is done;
I hope to heaven his soul is gone.

The town, however, had other attractions besides its waters. A Chartist orator, addressing a handful of adherents under a fine old willow in the Promenade, described the place as a Town of Gardens. The description was quite accurate. Every house, however humble, had ample space in front or rear for the cultivation of flowers or vegetables. Even the business quarters were not built up as they are elsewhere. There were trees everywhere—in squares and crescents, in walks and drives, in streets and roads. The Promenade, which starts from the very centre of the town, was a triple row of trees. Boulevards! When I first went to Paris, I found I had been familiar with boulevards from childhood—only they bore another name at home. Tennyson must have had Cheltenham in his mind (for, as we shall see later, he was once a resident) when he wrote the lines:—

A goodly place,
A realm of pleasaunce, many a mound
And many a shadow chequer'd lawn
Full of the city's stilly sound.

The great actor, William Charles Macready, who ended his days in the town, wrote thus to his friend Lady Pollock :—"I presume you, who have seen the cities and manners of many men, have not omitted Cheltenham in your wide survey. If so, you will not dissent from my opinion of its beauty. I do not think there is a town in England or out of it laid out with so much taste, such a continual mixture of garden, villa, street, and avenue." Macready speaks in the same letter of the hills that encompass it, "objects and interests of beauty observable from every point." One of the most ineffaceable memories of my boyhood is a view of the town from Cleeve Cloud shortly after dawn on a morning in summer. The white terraces and streets, embosomed in trees and shining like burnished silver in the brilliant sun, gave the place the appearance of an enchanted city. No prospect in fairyland itself could have presented a fairer picture than Cheltenham did then. And the same delightful vision is still at the command of all who take the trouble to ascend the heights to look for it.

The surroundings of the town are even more lovely than the town itself. Leckhampton Hill on the one side and the Cleeve Hills on the other, clothed with copse and verdure, except where broken into cliffs or scarred with quarries, are within an easy walk, while away in the distance may be seen the Malvern Range, with the silvery Severn creeping past Upton and Tewkesbury and Gloucester and many another old-fashioned settlement to the Bristol Channel. Beyond Leckhampton Hill, or rather on the further side of it, was one of the reputed sources of the Thames. It was called the Seven Springs; it was a favourite resort for excursionists from Cheltenham and Gloucester; and it was the Mecca of many a joyous and boyish pilgrimage of my own. A more delightful spot could not have been found anywhere. No description, however eloquent or graphic, could convey an adequate idea of its peaceful loveliness. Seven springs, bubbling up by the roadside, sent their pure and sparkling waters meandering through the undergrowth of a glorious wood. Near at hand was a charming dell or glen, called by the country folks Hartley Bottom, but christened in one of Charles Knight's publications the Velvet Valley. Nothing sweeter or more exquisite have I ever seen. The sward was softer even than velvet, while the trees and bushes which bordered its sloping banks made the whole place a dream of rural beauty. Hartley Bottom was open to the public in those early days. Anybody could wander through it on the way back over the hills to the town. A few years later, when, grown to man's estate, I visited the locality again, I was vexed to observe that a huge barrier was set up against the entrance, that trespassers were threatened with the "utmost rigour of the law," and that a veritable earthly paradise was closed to all but the proprietor and his gamekeeper. After the lapse of further years, I was still more vexed to learn that the landowner, annoyed at the popularity of his own lovely domain, had effectually destroyed the beauty of the Seven Springs themselves. Between the springs and the woods through which their limpid waters flowed he had erected an ugly stone wall! I have never visited the place since. The contrast between what I remembered and what I should have seen would have made me sad or—mad.

I have mentioned Leckhampton, and I have mentioned Macready. A brother of the tragedian, Major Macready, lies buried in the village churchyard. Attaching to the circumstance is a melancholy story. The widow of the officer adorned the grave with the choicest flowers, and made for herself a bower among them. There for years afterwards the poor lady used to spend long and frequent hours in fancied communings with the dead. The kindly villagers, sympathising with her distress, thoughtfully abstained from disturbing her sorrowful meditations. To this day the grave of Major Macready is an object of interest to visitors to the village of Leckhampton.

CHAPTER II

THE CLOSE SEASON

THE power of the Church was probably never more remarkably demonstrated anywhere than it was in Cheltenham during many years of the middle of the nineteenth century. As a matter of fact, the history of the town for all that period was the history of a single clergyman. The dominant authority in secular as well as religious affairs was a notable and imperious divine—the Rev. Francis Close, afterwards Dean of Carlisle.

The reign of the Rev. Francis—what may be called the Close Season—extended from 1826, when he was appointed to the Incumbency of Cheltenham, to 1856, the year in which he accepted the Deanery of Carlisle. During all these years, his presence so pervaded and his influence so dominated the town that little or nothing could be done there without his sanction. My recollection of him is still vivid. A singularly handsome man, he was adored by the ladies of the town, especially the fashionable ladies, matrons and maidens alike. The adoration, as is usual in such cases, took the form of slippers. It was stated at the time he transferred his labours to Carlisle that over 1,500 pairs of these articles, worked and embroidered by the hands of his fair adorers, were presented to Mr. Close in the course of his ministry at Cheltenham. Some of the more enraptured or more facetious of his admirers spoke of his fresh and comely countenance as "the beauty of holiness." [2] When he died in 1882, one of his contemporary biographers, writing of the earlier period of his life, described him as "the Pope of Cheltenham, with pontifical prerogatives from which the temporal had not been severed."

The description was not inaccurate, nor much exaggerated. The annual races or steeplechases on Cleeve Hill, far away from the town, were discontinued, and only fitfully resumed nearer at hand afterwards, owing to the incumbent's overpowering influence. But the most remarkable example of his authority in secular affairs was

7

the power he exercised in preventing the reconstruction of the theatre. Cheltenham had held an honourable place in the history of the drama. It was there that Mrs. Siddons appeared with a company of barn-stormers. The home of the drama was at that time situated in an obscure court. The tiring room was a hay-loft and the arena a stable. A party of titled people, among them the Earl of Ailesbury, thinking to get some diversion from the performance of "Venice Preserved," paid the place a visit. They went to laugh, but remained to cry. So powerfully had Mrs. Siddons acted the part of Belvidera that the ladies of the party were unpresentable next morning, owing, as Lord Ailesbury informed her husband, to their having wept so excessively the previous night. The report of the Ailesbury family induced Garrick to send an agent to Cheltenham with the offer of an engagement to the young actress. Thus did Sarah Siddons begin her triumphant career on the greater stage. The story is told at length in the poet Campbell's life of the illustrious mummer. Years afterwards a handsome theatre was built in the town. Lord Byron, at one time a resident, lent his aid in bringing down talent. All the great exponents of tragedy and comedy—Kemble and Kean, Macready and Anderson, Liston and Munden, Bannister and Grimaldi, Miss Mellon and Mrs. Jordan—strutted and mimed before succeeding audiences of fashion. But a great calamity befell the drama in 1839. The Theatre Royal, shortly after James Anderson had fulfilled an engagement in it, was totally destroyed by fire. I am not sure that the clergy of the period did not regard the occurrence as a manifestation of the anger of heaven. It is certain that the incumbent preached against the stage, published the sermon that he preached, and otherwise brought such pressure to bear on the community that no regular theatre was established while he held dominion over the town.

Many other evidences of narrow-mindedness were furnished by Mr. Close during the time that he was spiritual (and to a large extent temporal) master of the town. Some of these evidences may be found in the varied volumes of sermons, as well as the printed lectures and addresses, that were so highly treasured by his followers. When civil marriages were legalised in 1840, he stated from the pulpit that "he wished the canon law allowed him to refuse the sacrament to all persons married at the Registrar's Office." When infant baptism or some such subject was a burning question in the Church, he was credited with the declaration of his belief in the hyper-Calvinistic assumption that "there are infants in hell a span long." It was his custom for many years to preach a special sermon against the Roman Catholics on the recurrence of the 5th of November. Catholics and Unitarians were alike outside his pale; for all denominations save these were invited by him and his friends to join them when a Scripture Readers' Society was formed in Cheltenham. Mr. Close was perhaps a little superstitious too. Writing in a private letter about his relations with the Bishop of Gloucester, he said:—"Old Monk and I were very good friends. He never interfered with me in any one thing that I can remember. We had some difficulty about a special fast-day on occasion of the cholera. But he let me do what I pleased. And we held it—a wonderful day—and the cholera never visited Cheltenham, although it was all round us within four miles.

The worst instance of his bigotry was the part he was understood to have played in the prosecution of the now venerable George Jacob Holyoake. Mr. Holyoake was one of Robert Owen's social missionaries. In that capacity he came in 1842 to lecture to the Cheltenham folks. I was a boy of ten at the time. Hearing my elders talk of the new and strange doctrines that were being preached, I found myself in a meeting in the long room of the King's Head Inn— a room in the inn yard used for the annual dinners of Oddfellows and similar feasts and ceremonies. The lecturer was a young man, tall and slim, with dark hair and a thin, falsetto voice. I don't know whether my good friend will recognise the portrait; but it is my earliest recollection of him. What he said I can't in the least remember. Mr. Holyoake, paying a later visit to Cheltenham, lectured on "Home Colonization." After the lecture, in reply to a question, he made some remarks on the subject of religion which, though they would excite little notice now, at that time and in that town naturally aroused hostile attention. The *Cheltenham Chronicle* sounded the alarm. It published a paragraph in which Mr. Holyoake was called a "poor misguided wretch," and the audience was roundly abused for "applauding the miscreant," the editor appending a note to the effect that three persons in the employ of the office were ready to give evidence in case the authorities should institute a prosecution for blasphemy. One of these three persons was a man whom I came to know afterwards—a printer and local preacher of the name of Bartram, gifted with religious fervour, and not ungifted with a certain sort of eloquence. It was he, I believe, who wrote or suggested the incriminating paragraph. The authorities took the advice of the newspaper; Mr. Holyoake was prosecuted for blasphemy; and the result of the "last trial for Atheism," as he himself calls it, was six months' imprisonment in Gloucester Gaol. The prime mover in the proceedings was generally believed to be the Rev. Francis Close, who was for this or other reasons dubbed by Charles Southwell the "March-hare of the Church."

But Mr. Close, as was said at the time of his death, must be credited with eminent qualities to have founded so supreme and inquisitorial an empire over home and will as that which he established in Cheltenham. There can be no doubt of his energy and ardour. If ever there was a devoted Churchman, it was the incumbent of the parish of Cheltenham. Foremost in all "good works," he was instrumental in the erection of no fewer than eight new churches, while many charitable and educational institutions enjoyed the benefit of his support, some of them even owing their initiation to his commanding zeal. A commodious hospital was erected during his ministry. So also were the Cheltenham College [3] (now hardly second to Eton or Harrow or Rugby), the Ladies' College (commenced in a private house when I was a boy), and the Normal Training College for Teachers, of which the Rev. C. H. Bromby, afterwards Bishop of Tasmania, was made the first headmaster. Works of this kind ought properly to be placed to the credit of the distinguished Churchman. Nor was he, notwithstanding his serious and severe reputation, destitute of humour; for I recollect when he paid one of his frequent visits to the printing office in which I was engaged, and in which his occasional sermons and lectures were printed, how heartily he laughed as he told the old story of the Jew clothes-man who, when asked why he called out "O' clo', o' clo,'" instead of "Old clothes, old clothes," replied that his interrogator would be glad to cut the cry short too if he had to shout it through the streets all day long.

Among the new churches built in Mr. Close's time was Christ Church, on Bay's Hill, right away in the fields, with scarcely a house beyond it. Near at hand were clay ponds made by the brick-makers, where the boys of the lower part of the town (myself included) for want of a better place used to bathe among newts and frogs and slime. The first incumbent of Christ Church was an eloquent Irishman, who attracted crowded congregations to the new temple every Sunday—the Rev. Archibald Boyd. In pursuance of a half-fulfilled resolution to hear all the parsons in the town, I sometimes joined the congregations myself. Years afterwards, passing through Exeter, I attended service in the grand old cathedral. The edifice was crowded—so crowded that in the seat I occupied I could hear, but not see, the preacher. The sermon was a bitter denunciation of Mr. Bradlaugh, then engaged in his great struggle with the House of Commons. Some of the old fables about him were retailed from the pulpit. These being communicated to Mr. Bradlaugh, he contradicted them in his newspaper for the hundredth time. The preacher was my old acquaintance of Christ Church, then Dean of Exeter. Eloquence seems to be an endowment of the Boyd family, since among others who are distinguished for the gift is a nephew of the Dean of Exeter's, the Right Rev. William Boyd-Carpenter, Bishop of Ripon.

The curate of Christ Church in my time became afterwards even more celebrated than Archibald Boyd. This was the Rev. Frederick William Robertson—"Robertson of Brighton." One used to hear much in those days among the townsfolk about Captain Robertson, the father of the young preacher; a little, but very little, about his son, the curate; but a great deal too much about a rather harum-scarum brother of the curate's. It was only after he had obtained a living at Brighton that Robertson became famous. But he had literary tastes and longings even in Cheltenham. Tennyson was residing in the town at the time, and Robertson seems to have paid him a visit. The poet was not a man, either then or afterwards, but especially then, to welcome casual acquaintances. So, according to Mr. Knowles, fearing that his visitor was going to "pluck out the heart of his mystery," he talked to him about nothing but beer. [4] If they ever met afterwards, when both had become famous, we may be sure that they would have talked about something else. Robertson died young, but not before it had been demonstrated that he was one of the choicest products of the English Church. Dean Stanley called him "the greatest preacher of the century." When he died, he had published nothing but one sermon, two lectures, two addresses, and an analysis of "In Memoriam." But he had not been long dead before there arose an imperious demand for all he had said or written. No sermons have had so large a circulation as Robertson's; none have been so widely read, so warmly praised, so highly appreciated—not even Channing's, or Theodore Parker's, or Ralph Waldo Emerson's. Mudie found them as popular as novels, Tauchnitz added them to his foreign series, and at least one volume has been translated into German and another into Scandinavian. Within a brief period of the death of the author, says the Rev. Stopford Brooke in his biography of Robertson, fifteen editions of the first volume were published, thirteen of the second, and thirteen of the third. Even in America nine editions had been issued at the same period. Beyond question the fame of few preachers will live longer in literary history than that of the curate of Christ Church on Bay's Hill.

CHAPTER III

SOME CELEBRITIES AND OTHERS

ALFRED TENNYSON, the greatest poet of the century, was always a good deal of a recluse. It was his habit to shun the "madding crowd." Solitude and seclusion had more attraction for him than all the gaiety and glamour of what is called society. [5] This was certainly the case during the five years or so that he was often with his mother in Cheltenham. The period was the late forties. One used to hear of him as a sort of myth or shadow—the young poet whose books were in the booksellers' windows, and whose name was beginning to sound as familiar as that of Byron or Wordsworth. Frederick Robertson speaks of meeting him at the house of a physician; Sydney Dobell had a long walk with him and Carlyle at Malvern; other residents remember how he played in a game of blind man's buff at a Christmas party in 1848. [6] Beyond this little was known at the time, and not much more is known now, of the poet's life in Cheltenham. It is said that he was fond of taking his walks in Jessop's Gardens. Jessop [7] was a nurseryman, and his gardens covered a good many acres of ground. The gardens were pleasant and picturesque, and the little River Chelt flowed through them. But even in Tennyson's day they had begun to be despoiled; for the Great Western Railway set up a station therein.

"In Memoriam," the loveliest tribute any poet ever paid to a friend's memory, must have been written in Cheltenham. It was published in 1850, the last year of Tennyson's residence there. One can summon to the vision the scenery of the Cotswolds—the "high, wild hills, and rough, uneven ways" of Shakspeare—as one reads these stanzas:—

> Calm and deep peace on this high wold,
>   And on these dews that drench the furze,
>   And all the silver gossamers
> That twinkle into green and gold:

Calm and still light on yon great plain
  That sweeps with all its autumn bowers,
  And crowded farms and lessening towers,
To mingle with the bounding main.

The poet describes how he climbed the eminence and found in the landscape beneath no feature that did not breathe some memory of his friend:—

Nor hoary knoll of ash and haw
  That hears the latest linnet trill,
  Nor quarry trench'd along the hill
And haunted by the wrangling daw.

The quarries "trench'd along the hill" were happy hunting-grounds of local geologists. One of these—an eminent physician in the town, Thomas Wright, M.D.—had, in lectures at the Philosophical Institution and elsewhere, explained from the evidences he had gathered on Leckhampton Hill that the Severn Valley and even the Cotswolds themselves lay once in the bed of the ocean. Adding now the fact that Cheltenham, with its two miles of High Street, is built upon sand deposited by the sea which in distant ages spread over vale and wold, we can understand the perfect beauty and accuracy of these lines:—

There rolls the deep where grew the tree.
  O earth! what changes hast thou seen?
  There, where the long street roars, hath been
The stillness of the central sea.

The year in which "In Memoriam" was published was also the year in which another poem first claimed attention. This other poem was "The Roman," originally purporting to be the work of one Sydney Yendys. It was soon known to be the production of Sydney Dobell, the son of a Cheltenham wine merchant. George Gilfillan, who assumed at the time a sort of protectorate over new poets, described it with equal extravagance and enthusiasm as a "conflagration of genius." I and other young men in Cheltenham were all the more interested in "The Roman," because it had been inspired by the revolutionary ferment of the period, and had for its object the awakening of sympathy for the struggling patriots of Italy.

The Dobells were well known—at least by sight and name. I used to see some of them almost every day on the way to or from the counting-house and emporium of the firm. As a family, they kept themselves almost entirely to themselves. It may be said that they were more exclusive than Tennyson himself. There were balls and parties in the town; but they attended none of them. There were famous visitors to the town, as Sir Harry Smith or Sir Charles Napier; but they saw none of them. There were great political contests in the town, as between the Berkeleys and the Agg-Gardners; but they stood entirely aloof from them. The elder Dobell, married to a daughter of the founder of a church which claimed to be based on the primitive Christian model, was an old-fashioned merchant, much after the style one imagines Mr. Ruskin's father to have been. Connected with the Dobell establishments there were no outward attractions, no glaring lights, no flaring interiors, no insinuating barmaids. Even about the advertisements of the house there was an air of dignity and superiority which no other tradesman assumed. It was always "Mr. Dobell" who had this or that vintage, or this or that brew, to offer to the nobility and gentry. The religious tenets of the family seem to have been responsible for the peculiar mystery in which all the members of it enshrouded themselves. When Sydney married and brought home his bride, society people made the usual society calls, but were politely informed that mixing with the world was contrary to the strict requirements of the faith in which he had been nurtured!

The poet, the better to ensure the quietude and retirement his church enjoined and his own habits and studies dictated, pitched his tent in some of the isolated places of the neighbourhood. One of these was the village of Hucclecote, situated on the old Roman Road three or four miles from Gloucester. It was here that he commenced "The Roman." But Hucclecote is the locale of an anecdote which is perhaps even better known in Gloucestershire than the poem. Near at hand is Churchdown, shortened by common usage into Chosen.

Chosen Church stands on an isolated hill that commands so beautiful a prospect of field and wood, hamlet and town, for miles around, that it is a favourite resort of summer holiday-makers. To account for the situation of the sacred edifice, which necessitates a toilsome climb for the worshippers, the usual legend of impish intervention was invented. It was built in the vale, but was removed to the hill-top by the devil himself! But to the story. One Sunday the clergyman or clerk officiating in the parish of Hucclecote was making much of the appeal to the Lord—"And make Thy chosen people joyful." The appeal on this occasion was uttered with so much emphasis that a villager in the congregation, unable to stand what he thought was the marked preference for the residents of another parish, cried out aloud, "What have the Hucclecut folks done, then?"

Other members of the Dobell family have made their mark in literature. One of these is Dr. Horace Dobell, the author of many treatises on medical subjects, particularly an elaborate exposition of the salubrious qualities of Bournemouth, where for many years he was one of the leading physicians. If Dr. Horace was not a poet himself, his wife at any rate laid claim to the title; for she published one volume of poetical effusions and announced that seventeen more were to follow!

As there were brave men before Agamemnon, so there were poets connected with Cheltenham before the Dobells. Thomas Haynes Bayly, the author of an endless number of songs that everybody knew and sung in the earlier years of the century, lived and died in the town. Old people will have a lively recollection of the popularity of such sentimental ditties as these "She Wore a Wreath of Roses," "I'd be a Butterfly," and "Woodman, Spare that Tree." The inscription on a mural tablet to Bayly's memory in one of the churches was written by Theodore Hook. A later poet records in verse how he shed a tear over a brother poet's grave. This later poet was L. M. Thornton, author of the once familiar song, "The Postman's Knock," which was set to music by W. T. Wrightson. I knew poor Thornton passing well. The American humourist's definition of a poet as "a man who wears long hair and can't eat his vittles" would have suited him exactly. He hawked his own volumes, and, it was said, borrowed them and sold them again. It was a sad blow to the poet when a prosperous tailor of my acquaintance declined to part with the book he had purchased except on condition that the purchase money was refunded. Sad, too, was the poet's end, for he died in Bath workhouse after having been an inmate for many years.

A lady of some distinction in letters played a rather prominent part in one of the elections for Cheltenham. Daughter of the Earl of Lindsay, she married first Sir John Guest, the wealthy iron- master of Dowlais, who died in 1852. While she was Lady Charlotte Guest, she published two works of a totally different character—one a translation from the French of a treatise on the use of hot air in the manufacture of iron, the other a translation of fairy tales from a Welsh manuscript in the library of Jesus College, Oxford. Two years after she became a widow her portrait was painted by Mr. G. F. Watts. Next year, though she was forty-five and the mother of ten children, she was wooed and won by a young clergyman of less than thirty, the Rev. Charles Schreiber, son of an army officer well known in fashionable circles. Mr. Schreiber soon developed a desire to enter politics. Lady Charlotte was a mighty help in his contests for Cheltenham, which constituency and Poole he successively represented in Parliament. One of Lady Charlotte's daughters became the wife of Sir Austen Henry Layard, the explorer of Nineveh, and the British Ambassador at Constantinople during the troublous and critical period from 1877 to 1880. Mr. Schreiber and Lady Charlotte had tastes in common. Both were fond of collecting curious and out-of-the-way articles. The English part of a choice collection of porcelain, enamels, and ceramics, was, on Mr. Schreiber's death, presented to the South Kensington Museum. Another collection of the lady's—English fans of the eighteenth century—is now in the British Museum. Lady Charlotte continued the pursuit of her varied hobbies till she was considerably past her eightieth year. Nothing came amiss to this industrious antiquary. Glass and needlework and playing cards were in her line. She even collected and classified buttons! But enamels and fans, playing cards and buttons, are a long way from the Cheltenham election of 1859, which was the only reason for introducing Lady Charlotte Schreiber to the reader of these memoirs.

CHAPTER IV

HEROINES OF HUMBLE LIFE

NOBODY will be in the least interested in the writer's ancestry. Nor, to tell the truth, is he much interested himself—not because he couldn't rise to the occasion, but because there is nothing to be interested about. As far as I can learn, the only member of the family that ever did anything remarkable was a nephew of my grandmother's! It is true that one John Adams is reported in the *Newgate Calendar* to have been hanged for highway robbery; but I hardly think that he was any connection of ours—at all events I have never tried to establish the relationship. It is true, also, that another John Adams was President of the United States—no connection of ours either, though of course it would have been easy enough for a professional genealogist to trace a distant alliance. Pride of ancestry is not a failing or a fad of mine—for the reason, probably, that I can go back no further than two generations, and that only on one side.

We were poor but honest folks of Gloucestershire. It is necessary to make this statement, because otherwise, being poor, it might be inferred that we were not honest. A similar reason no doubt prompts a similar statement in all cases where people of humble origin are concerned: for the world at large seems incapable of associating poverty with even the negative virtues. We also, in the words of another old formula, did our duty in that state of life unto which it had pleased God to call us. I cannot find, after diligent inquiry, that any of us have ever been known to the police, not to speak of His Majesty's judges. Here at any rate we may claim some superiority over many aristocratic families. For these and all other mercies, as pious Scotch people say, the Lord be thankit.

My grandfather—he bore the name of William Wells—was a very old man when I was born. The only thing I remember about him was his shrewdness in telling me not to do a thing when he wanted me to do it—to bring him his walking-stick, for instance. My grandmother was a dear old dame, whose chief consolations in her last days were a pinch of snuff and half a glass of gin before bedtime. At that period the snuff box was always in her hand, but the glass was never seen except late in the evening. Anne Morris, to give her her maiden name, had a couple of personal peculiarities: she had only one leg, but, to make up for it, two eyes of different colours—one hazel, the other blue. The leg which she had not had been lost in a Worcestershire nail factory, where she had been employed as a girl, and where the constant standing on a damp floor had induced a disease that necessitated amputation. I well remember another feature too—the hard and unsightly corns on the old lady's knuckles, which were almost as large as the knuckles themselves. When she was left with a family of five girls, she and they set up a laundry—not a laundry in the modern, but in the ancient acceptation of the term. The corns were the result of the hard scrubbing and rubbing she used to bestow on the shirts and skirts of her patrons. It came to pass in her closing days, when her daughters, having embarked on other enterprises, were able to relieve her of the drudgery of the washtub, that her hands became as white and soft as a baby's. If my good old grand-dam had aught that could be described as a fault, it was that she too often saved her graceless grandson from the consequences of his escapades.

Concerning this laundry business, allusion to it would not have been introduced if there hadn't been a lesson to be drawn. It was an honest occupation—as honest, say, as stock jobbing. There was nothing in the whole episode of which any mortal need be ashamed. Yet dainty people would perhaps consider that it was a fact to be concealed. Let us understand each other. Work of any sort is honourable. It is idleness, and especially that form of idleness which is called loafing, that is disgraceful. Dickens never appeared to me so snobbish and contemptible as when he whined and whimpered about the degradation of having as a boy to earn a few shillings a week by pasting labels on blacking bottles. The thing is, however, not only to work, but to work well—to put the best that is in us into everything we do. Theodore Parker in one of his powerful sermons tells us that Michael sweeping round a lamp-post or Bridget sweeping out a kitchen, assuming that the work is honestly done, is as meritorious as Paul preaching on Mars' Hill. "Work is worship."

Honesty in work as in all things else. The same doctrine is taught by Emerson, Carlyle, Ruskin, and every great thinker who has expatiated on the subject. "All service ranks the same with God," writes Browning, whose ancestor was a footman. Well, the humble and industrious women who laboured amidst suds and steam carried into practice the precepts of the philosophers. The washtub and the mangle were dignified by what they did with them. As Cromwell's Ironsides put a conscience into marching and fighting, so did these poor women put a conscience into scrubbing and ironing. None of the gentry for whom they worked ever had reason to complain that their cuffs and collars, their flounces and their furbelows, were not returned without a sign of previous wear. Thus did widow and orphans earn the title to a place beside Paul on Mars' Hill. Mr. Ruskin proudly described his father as "an entirely honest merchant." I say as proudly of my grandmother that she was "an entirely honest washerwoman."

Of Anne Wells's daughters two only married—the eldest and the youngest. My mother was the eldest. She married a plasterer—one John Adams. My mother was a saint—not in piety, for she professed no particular faith, but in character and disposition. No tenderer or sweeter woman ever lived. I cherish her memory as that of one of the salt of the earth. The affection she bestowed on her children is delightful to remember. She worked for them, slaved for them, suffered for them. If she had affections, she had also intellect. Had she been born in less humble circumstances, with corresponding educational advantages, she would, as her letters testify, have been as accomplished as any lady in the land. She had courage against the world, too, this heroine of the poor. When, at a melancholy period of her career, she was driven to such straits that she had to persuade herself and her children that they were drinking coffee when the decoction was nothing but hot water poured on burnt crusts of bread, she never lost heart. Nor did she lose heart when, failing with all her industry to keep the wolf from the fold, she set out with four young children on a three days' journey in a waggon for London to search the great wilderness for her husband. A hard and laborious life in Cheltenham was followed by a hard and laborious life in London; but Sarah Adams bore both with the patience and resignation of a martyr, never whining or complaining, but always doing her best to turn an honest penny at the old calling. It was an intense delight to me years after, when I paid my first visit to London at the time of the Great Exhibition—for I had been left behind with my grandmother and aunts in Cheltenham—it was an intense delight to me to hear strangers address my mother as "Miss," and mistake her and her son for sweethearts.

John Adams, as will be inferred from what has already been said, was a bit of a wanderer. Even after he was married, he wandered to such widely separated places as Droitwich, Leamington, Ashby-de-la-Zouch, Gosport, and London, working at his trade the while. My very earliest recollection is of being carried on his back along the banks of a river or canal somewhere in the neighbourhood of Bromsgrove. As there were few railways in those days, wandering was a more tiresome business than it is now. But John Adams was a good workman. He used to point to a certain groined ceiling which he had completed in a private residence as the best bit of plastering in Cheltenham. Pride in his work was his weak point—if pride of that sort can be considered a weak point. It got him into many a squabble and scrape. Being somewhat quarrelsome in his cups, he would challenge anybody in the same trade to surpass his performance with the trowel—a challenge that was issued in so boastful a way that it generally ended in a fierce dispute. But my father, small as he was in stature, had the courage of his convictions: so it was that he found himself in more clashes and scraps than was pleasant for either himself or his family. His pugnacity, however, was not, like that of many cowardly men, reserved for home consumption. Except for the failings I have indicated, one of which at least leant to virtue's side, he was not a bad father or a bad husband. In his later years he was a great sufferer. And then it was that the heroism of my mother was shown again—such heroism as is, perhaps, shown only in the ranks of the poor and lowly.

I have mentioned that my grandmother's nephew was the only member of our family that had achieved distinction. His name was George Morris. I used to hear of him as connected in some undefined way with an insurance society in London. Little else was known, for never a letter came from him. What did come for years and years, as regularly as the week came round, was a weekly newspaper addressed to my grandmother—first the *Weekly Dispatch* and then the *Examiner*. The *Dispatch* was at that time the leading exponent of Radical ideas. It was, I think, still owned by Alderman Harmer, still numbered Eliza Cook among its contributors, still contained the stirring political letters of Caustic and Publicola—the latter supposed to be the production of W. J. Fox, the "Norwich Weaver Boy," afterwards member for Oldham, and one of the most notable of the Anti-Corn Law orators. The substitution of the *Examiner* for the *Dispatch* was not appreciated by the family; but we could not look a gift horse in the mouth, and, besides, we had no means of communicating with the giver. The *Examiner*, however, was a famous literary paper—Leigh Hunt's *Examiner*—then edited by John Forster, the "Gentleman John" of Newcastle, the "harbitrary gent" of the London cabman, the friend and biographer of Charles Dickens. Walter Savage Landor's "Imaginary Conversations" were then appearing in its columns, besides much else of a high literary value. I revelled as a boy in the politics of the *Dispatch*—as a youth in the criticisms of the *Examiner*. Many years later, when, at the end of a curious and disastrous experience with insurance societies, I took out a new policy in the National Provident Institution, I learnt that George Morris, the predecessor of Samuel Smiles [8] in the same office, had long been the secretary of that society. My grandmother's nephew was so highly appreciated that the directors voted him a handsome pension on his retirement, and even granted an annuity to his widow. George Morris's remote connection with our family does not deprive us of the right to claim that the insurance secretary was a credit to it.

My aunts were all estimable people too. Just, upright, honourable, considerate, thoughtful, industrious, they had all the best virtues. I was scarcely more than an infant when I was fetched from Droitwich on a stage coach to live under their roof for upwards of twenty years. The little imp who was thus introduced into the household was often a sad trouble to them, as may perhaps be shown later. When laundry work declined, they established a small trading concern—cultivating musk plants, and selling them; buying butter and crockery and odds and ends of all sorts, and retailing them at honest prices. The principles that had governed them at the washing tub governed them behind the counter. So at last by industry and frugality they acquired enough for their modest wants in a cottage. There they died one after the other at an advanced age, respected by all who knew them, and leaving behind a stainless and honoured name. It should be said also that they had minds of their own and capacity to exercise them, as we shall see when I come to write of certain public movements of their time. One of the sisters, who had gone forth into the world, while in service in Brighton, was a regular attendant at Trinity Chapel. It was from her that I heard of the wonderful sermons of Frederick William Robertson, long before the fame of his eloquence and of the beauty of his discourses had spread over the land. Proud indeed might any man feel of humble kindred such as mine.

CHAPTER V

THE OLD ORDER CHANGETH

IT is one of the commonplaces of conversation that the century which has lately closed has witnessed greater progress effected in all branches of human knowledge and activity, and indeed in all the affairs of human life, than all previous centuries put together. The statement may be said to be quite true in some things, partly true in most things, but not true in all things. We are wiser than the ancients, but not more virtuous. We know more, but we do not think more. Our dominion over the physical world is wider and more complete than ever before; but our dominion over the intellectual world is still as circumscribed as in the great days of Greece and Rome. Poets like Homer and philosophers like Plato are at least the equal of any poets and philosophers of a later time. But the progress we have in mind is the progress we see in the condition of society, the privileges enjoyed by the people, the application of science to industry, the discoveries and inventions in relief of labour. So far as mere comfort goes there is absolutely no comparison between the state of the humbler classes now and that of the same classes in my young days. I am speaking, of course, of the honest and industrious poor, not of the thriftless, the idle, or the evil-disposed. Some few of the changes that I have myself seen will answer the purpose of comparison.

Take, to begin with, the commonest of conveniences—matches. These little articles are cheap enough now. It was otherwise "when we were boys together." Matches, as we know them, were then unknown. If you wanted to strike a light, you had to make elaborate preparations to accomplish that end. A flake of flint, a strip of steel, and a box of tinder were all necessary before the brimstone sticks of the period could be ignited. Tinder was made by burning old rags, placing them half-consumed in a metal box, and pressing them tightly down with a metal lid. Then, with the steel held in one hand and the flint in the other, sparks had to be struck from them in such a way that they would fall on the tinder and ignite it. The application of a sulphur-tipped stick to the smouldering fire in the tinder-box produced the required flame. The process is easy enough to describe, but was not so easy to put in operation. It was often my duty in the old days, on early mornings, to strike a light with the aid of the clumsy implements just mentioned. And a dismal duty it was, especially before daybreak in frosty weather; for one often skinned one's shins in groping for the materials, and then skinned one's knuckles in using them. Moreover, if the tinder was either damp or exhausted by previous usage, it was impossible to get a light at all. But a better time for poor folks came when John Walker, the Stockton chemist, invented his friction matches. Great was the wonderment, I recollect, when they were introduced. Of course, they were poor things compared with the articles which are now supplied at a marvellously cheap rate. The earliest form of the lucifer match, as it was called, was a little strip of wood (dipped in a chemical substance) which (had to be drawn swiftly through a strip of doubled sandpaper. Small as his invention was, John Walker was one of the greatest benefactors of his time.

The light of other days was hardly more deserving of praise than the method of procuring it. Tallow candles were the illuminants of the poor—rushlights, long sixes, short sixes, and so forth—sold in bundles at so many to the pound. The wicks that were made of cotton required constant snuffing: hence snuffers and snuffer-trays, now as little known as tinder-boxes, were indispensable appurtenances to every polite household. Wax candles, which did not require snuffing, were the luxuries of the gentry, who alone could afford them. The light shed by the common illuminant was so feeble and dismal that it did scarcely more than make darkness visible. It was almost as well that the general body of the people could not then read; for persistent efforts to turn the advantage to account after sunset would most certainly have ruined half the eyes of the country. The candle factories—there was one in the very centre of our town—emitted, during certain parts of the process of manufacture, the most pungent and sickening stenches. Gas was a great improvement on candles—not, however, in the odours which issued from the works in the early stages of the novelty. When our streets were first lighted with gas, the lamp-lighters, like the new police, wore a special uniform. With white jackets and glazed hats, each shouldering a ladder, they marched up the middle of the main street together before branching off to their respective districts. The procession was not ineffective; but both it and the ladders have long since been discontinued as unnecessary.

Perhaps it is in respect to modes and facilities of locomotion that poor and rich alike have been most benefited. If the poor rode at all in pre-railway times, they had to ride in waggons, living and sleeping in them for days and nights even on comparatively short journeys. I remember them well, those great lumbering waggons, as big as haystacks, covered with tarpaulin, the wheels broad enough in the tyre to span a ditch, the six or eight horses apparently strong enough to move a mountain. Coaches were for those who could afford a more rapid transit. Between 1824 and 1839, which has been called the heyday of coaching, the High Street of Cheltenham presented as cheerful and picturesque a sight as could be seen anywhere. As many as thirty or forty coaches, chiefly four-in-hands, passed through it every day. The dashing steeds, the fanfaronades on the horn, the scarlet coats of the coachman and the guard, all combined to make the spectacle impressive and exhilarating. The ride, too, in warm, sunny weather, when the country looked its best, was intensely enjoyable. Two such rides are not likely to be effaced from my memory—one to Malvern, the other over the Cotswolds to Oxford. But in bad weather, at night, in storm, temperature below freezing-point, heaven help the unhappy passengers! The circumstances of the "insides," packed like herrings in a barrel, breathing the same air from the time they started till the time they stopped to change horses, was bad enough. Far worse, however, were the circumstances of the "outsides," perched on high without shelter of any sort, saturated by the rain or frozen by the cold. No wonder men made their wills before going long journeys in early days, for the risks of the road must have been at least as imminent from storm and snow as from bold highwaymen.

Railways superseded coaches, though it was not till the end of 1861 that the last of the highfliers between Cheltenham and Oxford— "Glover's Oxford Mail"-was driven off the road; but the new mode of locomotion did not all at once, as we shall see presently, greatly improve the conditions of travelling for the poor. The West of England was much behind the North in adopting the new system. And when it did, it made the mistake of laying down two gauges — the broad and the narrow. The Battle of the Gauges, begun in the thirties, was not finally and absolutely closed till the nineties. The Great Western line from Paddington to Plymouth was constructed on Brunel's plan; but the lines in all the rest of the kingdom were constructed on Stephenson's. It was a pity that the rivalries of companies and engineers did not permit of the choice, at the beginning of the locomotive era, of a gauge that would probably have been better than either the broad or the narrow. For many years a little stretch of line between Cheltenham and Gloucester was a sort of railway curiosity, for thereon trains belonging to both gauges were run till within very recent times. But the broad gauge had ultimately to succumb to the narrow. The revolution was effected at enormous cost to the Great Western Company. It was announced in the month of May, 1892, that the last of the broad gauge had disappeared, and that consequently there was then for the first time uniformity throughout the whole of our railway system.

When the Bristol and Birmingham Line (now part of the great Midland system) was opened in 1840, it was one day announced that a free trip to Bromsgrove would be offered to the inhabitants of Cheltenham. Great was the excitement among old and young. Along with a number of other lads I was anxious to share in the promised treat. Accordingly we assembled at a level crossing near the town (the station was, and is yet, about two miles away, nobody at the time the line was made wishing it nearer) in the expectation that passengers would be taken up there. Disappointment was general when the train was seen to steam past us. But we were fortunate after all; for many of the excursionists were left behind at Bromsgrove, thence to make their way home as best they could. The free trip was probably designed to remove the prejudices of the people. These prejudices were so great, especially among elder folks, that my dear old grandmother could never be persuaded to enter a railway carriage, and the dislike to the innovation extended even to some of her children. The distrust would perhaps have been justified if all passengers had been treated like a certain old lady in the North, who was pitched from the train in a collision, and who, when asked how she liked the new mode, replied that the riding was "no se bad," but that they had "a varry unsarimonious way o' pitting ye oot!"

The evolution of the railway carriage is interesting. The earliest of these conveyances was a mere truck, without seats and without cover. If you wanted to sit down on the journey, you had to provide yourself with a box or a basket; if you wanted to look at the country, you had to stand on tiptoe; if you wanted protection from the rain, you had to carry an umbrella! And this primitive accommodation was for years the only provision for the third-class traveller. Even as late as 1855 I rode from Manchester to Stockport in a coverless carriage. One of the first improvements on some of the lines was a kind of horse-box with seats and cover, but with shutters instead of windows. Of course, there were no lamps in these so-called carriages. Day and night at all seasons you had to sit in utter darkness if you did not care to run the risk of catching a chill. My first and last journey in a horse-box arrangement was between London and Brighton in the year 1862. Lords and ladies who wished to travel in comfort in the early days of the railway rode in their family coaches, which were fixed and wedged on the company's trucks. Old folks who now travel in third-class carriages with all the speed and in nearly all the luxury of first-class passengers will readily admit that progress—real progress—has been nowhere more marked than on the railway.

Real progress has been accomplished in many other directions also. I am not wrong in saying, I believe, that people who have been born in the latter half of the nineteenth century can form but a poor idea of the discomforts of life that their elders had to endure before the discoveries of science and the inventions of ingenuity placed within the reach of the humblest part of the community the thousand and one advantages we now enjoy.

CHAPTER VI

YIELDING PLACE TO THE NEW

MANY curious old customs that have now been discontinued and forgotten were in vogue when I was a boy. I shall here mention only a few.

New Year's Day, the greatest day of the year in Scotland, and always a jovial holiday in the North of England, was not observed at all in the South and West. Nor was much attention paid to Easter. May Day used to be recognised by the sweeps of the town, who exercised a sort of prescriptive right to dress up a Jack-in-the-Green (a wickerwork cage covered with ivy leaves, with a man inside to carry it), dancing round the figure in grotesque fashion, and collecting pence from the small crowds which witnessed the performance. Later in the month—the 29th—came Royal Oak Day, when the innkeepers decorated their premises with oak boughs, and the inhabitants, especially the lads, carried oak apples or oak leaves in their buttonholes. The lad who failed to adorn himself in this manner was an object of derision to the rest, who saluted him with cries of "Shick-shack." The precise meaning or origin of this contumelious expression I never knew, nor, probably, did any other of the youths who were in the habit of using it. If nobody now takes much notice of the anniversary, it is probably because people have begun to see that the nation, after all, had no great reason to be grateful for the escape of the Royal reprobate who found shelter in Boscobel Oak. Whitsuntide met with more general recognition. The Oddfellows and the members of other friendly societies, arrayed in all the glory of regalia, and accompanied by bands and banners, marched in procession on the Monday to the village of Charlton Kings, listened to a sermon in the parish church, and then, marching home again, dined sumptuously together in the long rooms of the different inns. Another feature of Whitsuntide was the appearance of the morris dancers. Antiquaries tell us that the morris dance was originally the Moorish dance, supposed to have been brought to England in the time of Edward the Third when John of Gaunt returned from Spain. The dancers were all men, though one, who played the fool to the rest, was dressed as a woman. Duck trousers and white shirts made up the costume, the sleeves of the performers being tied round and round with coloured ribbons, their legs below the knee bearing pads of tinkling bells. The dance they executed was curiously varied with the clapping of hands and the flirting of white handkerchiefs. Of course, after every dance, the "usual collection was taken." When Christmas came, the children went out carol-singing, while some among their elders organized parties of mummers. The mummers performed a kind of play, in the course of which, after deriding each other in rhyme, George the Fourth and Napoleon Bonaparte engaged in mortal combat. The carols sung by the children were of the most extraordinary character. Two lines of one of them ran thus:—

> It was the joy of Mary, it was the joy of one
> To see her infant Jesus sucking at her breast bone.

As a rule, the carol-singers closed their serenades with an appeal:—

> God bless the master of this house,
> Likewise the mistress too,
> And all the little children
> Who about the house do go,
> With money in their pockets
> And silver in their purse.
> Please, ma'am, to give us a ha'penny,
> And you'll be none the worse.
>   H-o-o-p!

What the "h-o-o-p " meant was unknown to us; but we always ended the appeal with the shout.

Among the old customs in which I had a hand was one that finally went out with us in 1845—"beating the bounds." Parish boundaries not being clearly defined, they were now and then perambulated by churchwardens and others for the purpose of keeping them in popular memory. The perambulation in 1845 was largely attended, as was likely to be the case when waggons laden with beer, cider, and penny loaves met the crowd at various points on the route. It was estimated that the followers, when the procession reached the Golden Valley, between Cheltenham and Gloucester, numbered not fewer than 2,000. Practical jokes were supposed to be permissible on these occasions. Boys were given "something to remember" at disputable corners of the boundary, while young men and old, regardless of age or infirmities, pushed each other into ditches and rivers and horse-ponds. Unhappy (and in some cases even fatal) consequences occasionally resulted from these pranks. Thus in the perambulation of 1845 a retired tradesman who was thrown into the deepest part of the Chelt died from the effects of the immersion. The young fellow who did the mischief was tried for manslaughter, but acquitted. The reason alleged for thrashing boys and larking with elder people was said to be that the parties concerned would recollect the boundaries and the time they were beaten if the facts of the matter in after-years should be called in question. It was alleged to be necessary that the bounds should be traced whatever the obstacles that stood in the way. Agg's House, a conspicuous mansion overlooking the town, was built in two parishes: wherefore a deputation from the crowd had to go through one window in the front and out of another at the back. An amusing account of "possessioning," as the custom was called in Berkshire, is given in an old diary of the parish clerk of Newbury. The possessioners (or processioners, to give them the name they bore in a neighbouring county) refreshed themselves with cakes and ale on the way, gave "three huzzas " at certain points, and sang psalms at others. "Stopt on the mount in the lane," says the diarist, "and cut X cross, put Osgood on end upon his head, and done unto him as was necessary to be done by way of remembrance." When the party "came to Mr. Daw's Mill, a shoemaker was pushed in and narrow escaped being drownded." The diarist ends with a note:—"Old Kit Nation was turned on end upon his head and well spanked in the corner of Northcroft and upon the Wash." Personal outrages of this description can only be perpetrated now at the risk of the perpetrator. A man who had been bumped according to custom at Walthamstow showed his assailants some years ago that he had not been bumped according to law, for he obtained heavy damages against them. Other actions in other parts of the country have put an end to practical joking at perambulations. And perambulations have themselves ceased almost everywhere. But the custom was discontinued at Cheltenham, not because a poor fellow lost his life, but because no provision was made for payment of expenses under the new Poor Law.

Fashions, which change every year, have necessarily undergone a complete revolution in half a century. Away back in the thirties and forties shaving was almost an obligatory process. It was rarely that one met an Englishman, no matter what the class to which he belonged, who did not sport the regulation mutton-chop whiskers—clean shaven otherwise. Anybody who was audacious enough to wear a moustache was taken to be a foreigner or an acrobat. No change in the fashion in this respect occurred till our troops—all bronzed and bearded— returned from the Crimea. The manly appearance of the warriors incited civilians to follow their example. Nevertheless, it needed a popular agitation to overthrow the tyranny of the razor. The Beard Movement completed what the veterans from the trenches had begun. Artists, authors, and journalists were among the first to adopt the new mode. A Royal Academician who did so (Mr. James Ward) published a pamphlet in explanation and defence, offering eighteen sound scriptural reasons why one might let the beard grow, and yet not offend his Creator. Still, lawyers and business men and ministers of religion long resisted the change. The first of the latter order whom I remember to have seen with a moustache—it was at a meeting of the Working Men's College in London—was the Rev. Llewellyn Davies, a famous Churchman in his day. If before the war with Russia a member of the Stock Exchange had had the temerity to present himself in the "house," I rather fancy he would have received attentions more personal than polite. When Edward Glynn, a Newcastle solicitor, paid a visit to London after he had adopted the new mode, the respectable lawyer upon whom he called first surveyed his moustache and beard with astonishment, and then pityingly remarked: "Well, Mr. Glynn, I hope you find that sort of thing pay down in the North." But the new order of things has so supplanted the old in the matter of shaving that every man who has tarried at Jericho can now do exactly as he likes.

Changes of costume are almost infinite. But a word about hats. Beavers, in the early years of the century, were almost the only wear. Some were bell-topped, some other shapes, but all were more or less fluffy. The material changed, but not the general outline for many years. Everybody who had arrived at man's estate—rich and poor, gentle and simple alike—deemed a high hat necessary to existence. It was part of the uniform of the new police, and it was part of the costume of the players in the cricket-field. If you take the trouble to examine the engravings of old Radical demonstrations— those of meetings on the Town Moor at Newcastle, for example— you will see that every man in the crowd is shown to be wearing a tall hat. The reign of the stove-pipe, as it came to be called, was, I think, first seriously challenged at the time that Kossuth and his compatriots appeared in England with the more shapely Hungarian chapeau. Partly out of compliment to Kossuth, partly on account of its better appearance, but chiefly on account of its greater comfort, young Radicals of my time began to favour the Hungarian hat. I have never returned to the old, hard, distressing mode since. Ten years after Kossuth's arrival, however, I was hissed, hooted, and followed by an unruly crowd in a remote part of Lancashire, for no other reason than that I happened to be out of the fashion in respect to headgear. Yet in that very same neighbourhood I saw disciples of Joanna Southcott—"Joanna men" as they were called by the factory operatives—wearing tall, white, fluffy hats that were even more conspicuous than my own. But mark the change. The soft, serviceable hat, altered but not improved in shape, is now the common wear of clergymen and ministers of all denominations.

It fell to the lot of a North-Country member to first break through the unwritten law of Parliament, which required that hon. gentlemen should wear nothing but high hats, unless on special occasions and for special purposes court or military suits were in order. The member in question, without intending or desiring it, caused a great sensation when he entered the sacred precincts with the style of hat he had worn for twenty years or more. A popular cartoon of the time represented Mr. Gladstone as declaring, when he saw the apparition, that he really must dissolve Parliament. The soft hat in this case had been adopted because the member concerned had in his younger days suffered from a peculiar tenderness of the skin of the temples. Nor had he ever seen any good reason to change. Indeed, a change to the regulation mode would have been inconvenient, disagreeable, even painful. Moreover, neither Parliament nor his constituents had any right to call upon him to make a personal sacrifice in the matter of costume any more than in the matter of the cut of his beard. There was in this case no touch of vanity or conceit, or desire to appear singular. It was otherwise in the case of a Socialist member, who, when he paid his first visit to the House of Commons, rode down to Westminster in a cloth cap, with a trumpeter blaring by his side. It was otherwise, too, with another member, who, according to a London correspondent, unbuttoned his coat in the Lobby, showed his working suit, and declared that he had come straight from the engine shop hundreds of miles away from London! Whatever the cause of the change, the old order has so given place to the new that men are now as free in the House of Commons as they are anywhere else to wear the hats and suits that suit them.

CHAPTER VII

THE LAWS OF THE STREET

PERHAPS a not uninteresting chapter might be made of the diversions in which the boys of the humbler classes were wont to find delight sixty or seventy years ago. "Boys will be boys," it is said, when any youthful escapade has to be excused. And the boys of the period named, grandfathers of the present generation, were probably no better—they were certainly no worse—than the boys of our own time. Fun and mischief are ineradicable from boyish nature. None but the sour and distempered would wish to eradicate them. At the same time, one might have expected—one undoubtedly hoped—that the training of School Boards would have resulted in obtaining from the young a greater respect for age and a greater consideration for infirmity than they seem disposed to render. A change in that regard, if in no other, is desirable for the comfort of society. But to the narrative.

Our street was in Lower Dockum—a locality that is unknown even by name to the genteel residents in the parades and squares and crescents of Lansdowne and Pittville. It had its laws and regulations, which were as rigidly enforced as the rules of social etiquette among the rich. Never a new boy came into it but had to find his level. If he submitted without fighting, he took rank below the least. If he fought and failed, he would most likely have to fight again till his exact position was discovered. Even if he fought and won, he would still have to go on fighting till he encountered the cock of the walk himself. Great was the rejoicing—secret, but none the less sincere— of the other boys if he conquered in this final contest for supremacy, for the cock of the walk was often the little tyrant of the street. I remember well what happened when a bully of the season, confident in his own strength and endurance, challenged a new boy to fight him with one hand. The challenge was accepted; the new boy by a sudden rush sent the old one staggering to the ground; and the crowd of lesser boys who had tremblingly assembled to witness the combat saw with gratification that they had now a new master. It was to some extent true then, as it is still, that the smaller and feebler lads in the street had to submit as best they could to the exactions and oppressions of the bigger and stronger. But a code of honour was not unknown. It was cowardly to use any other weapon than the fist, and it was still more cowardly to strike when your antagonist lay on the ground. Years afterwards, I recollect Mr. Bradlaugh giving this advice to his son: "Never hit a littler boy than yourself, and never let a bigger boy hit you." The general observance of that advice would help to put an end to the small tyrannies of the street.

Combats were not infrequent between boys of different schools and localities, as well as boys in the same street. Opprobrious nicknames were bestowed on each other by the scholars of the few schools in the town, such as "Capper's mice" or "Gardner's rats." These nicknames were shouted across the street when a Capper's mouse caught sight of a Gardner's rat, or vice versa, and there an end, unless the derided boy took offence, in which case the offender would probably seek safety in flight. But parties from the rival schools would sometimes meet by accident on neutral ground, when there would generally ensue a scrap of some sort, unless one side or the other exercised the better part of valour. Worse troubles would arise if a boy belonging to one locality should wander away to a neighbourhood whose youthful inhabitants he or his companions had done or said something to outrage. The lad in such an event could only avoid a buffeting by the free use of his legs, awaiting an opportunity for revenge when chance should place one of his tormentors in the same predicament. Boy nature, as may be gathered, is not much different from dog nature. Dogs and boys are both quiet enough till a stranger strays into what they think their territory.

No small part of a bad boy's enjoyment is derived from witnessing the irritation of elderly people. The more they can be vexed the more the bad boy is pleased. Though we were not bad boys in our street—at least, not all of us—we used occasionally to play tricks which could not in any manner be commended. Perhaps the worst was knocking at doors and then running away. An improvement on this annoyance was facilitated by a peculiar arrangement. Down the middle part of the street ran a dead wall. A string attached to a knocker and carried over the wall was operated by little imps who couldn't be seen in the darkness. How they chuckled and hugged themselves when the householder, shading a lighted candle with his hand, came to answer the knock! The trick couldn't be tried many times before it was discovered. Then the householder would appear, not with a candle, but with a thick cudgel. And then the ingenious tormentors would have to fly round all the corners that afforded the best cover and concealment. It was well for them if they were not caught. Among the residents in our street whom the boys took a special delight in teasing was an irascible old shoemaker. But "Old Jackson" had brought the trouble on himself, for he was in the habit of capturing and destroying the implements of the boys' play—their balls or their tops—when any of them came within his reach. The irate shoemaker would have saved himself many a bad quarter of an hour if he had recognized that the street was the only playground, and that the innocent games of the boys were no real cause of offence to anybody at all.

But the boys played tricks on each other quite as often as they did on their elders. One trick of this kind was called "shoeing the wild colt." It was never tried on anybody a second time, because the first lesson was sufficient for the dullest. A victim having been found, the next thing was to select a convenient door. The "wild colt," personated by the unhappy greenhorn, was tied to the handle; a pretence was made of shoeing him—sometimes his shoes were taken off; then, suddenly, there was a great banging at the door, and all the crafty little horse-breakers would scatter and disappear behind the shades of night. If the poor colt could not release himself before the householder came to the door, there was a trial of strength between the boy outside and the party inside. Of course the struggle ended in the triumph of the strongest. What happened afterwards depended on the disposition of the victor. If he had a spark of humour, a measure of kindness, or the least recollection of his own antics in boyhood, the fun was at an end. If not—well, the poor little victim had a double penalty to pay. The only consolation he had was that he would, some night later, assist in "shoeing a wild colt" himself.

As a rule, the games of the boys of our street were quite free from blame or blemish. There was nothing in the least wrong with marbles, peg-tops, whip-tops, kites, buttons, prisoner's base, rounders, shinney, foot-it, leap-frog, jump-a-jim-wagtail, and dozens of other modes of amusement. Marbles were played in various ways—ring-taw, knuckle-hole, etc. I suppose I must have been a bit of a dabster at ring-taw, since, when I got too old for marbles, I distributed among younger companions many hundreds of stone alleys with not a few agates. Prisoner's base was a splendid running game which it would take too long to describe, while foot-it and leap-frog were jumping pastimes that are all too seldom played in these days. Rounders was for poor lads what cricket was for the sons of the gentry. Base-ball, so much in vogue in America, is just rounders, with the element of danger and injury superadded; while hockey, now greatly in favour even among ladies in England, is just our old game of shinney—only the top end of a broomstick served us for a bat, and a stake from the hedge-side did duty for a club. The seasons for all games came in regular succession. How they were regulated or who regulated them none of the boys ever knew. But it was a law of the street that games could not be played at other than the appointed times without risk of forfeiting the materials of the pastime. If, for instance, a party of lads were seen playing at ring-taw or knuckle-hole out of season, it was considered perfectly legitimate for another party of lads to appropriate all the marbles they could seize. Whether the scramble became a scuffle depended, of course, upon which of the parties engaged in play or foray was the stronger. But the curious thing was that there was a code of honour regulating even the scramble. Raids occurred on the Borders whenever there was a deficiency in the larder; but raids on marbles or peg-tops were only legal when the season for playing with them had passed.

All our amusements were not quite as innocent as rounders or leap-frog. There was one which was considered the more successful the more mischievous the pranks played by the players. It was called "vamping." A single lad would challenge another to vamp him— that is, to do as daring feats, such as jumping from a high wall, as his challenger. But the usual plan—I think it was sometimes called "follow-your-leader"—was for a company of boys to select the most adventurous among them, and then follow his lead in all that he did. The tricks which this leader performed and which the rest repeated were often reprehensible, sometimes dangerous, nearly always annoying. It was the element of danger, indeed, that gave spice to the game. Perhaps, also, the vampers appreciated the fun because it almost invariably set some of the older people by the ears. The leader, followed by his string of companions, would begin with a few very ordinary performances, gradually rise in audacity, and perhaps end up by doing damage to somebody's property. Thus patting a lamp-post or running into a shop would be succeeded by knocking at doors and then knocking down tradesmen's goods. The length to which the lads would go naturally depended upon the immunity they enjoyed and the forbearance of their victims. A rush with a horse-whip or a walking-stick would probably disperse the vampers before they had done much mischief. If uninterrupted, however, they would proceed from bad to worse till they became as veritable a terror as the Hooligans of our own time; for, be it understood, the new police force, at the period of which I am writing, was only just beginning to supersede the old watchmen and constables. It ought to be said, even for the vampers, however, that the pranks they performed were merely a boisterous form of amusement, and that the annoyances which resulted from them were merely incidents of the play.

I have made no mention of football in these recollections of boyhood, for the reason that football, like golf and lawn tennis, was not numbered among the popular pastimes of the period. We used to hear of football, but only as a game that was played at the great public schools, such as Eton or Rugby. Nor did it come into general favour till many years after I had ceased to be a boy. Lawn tennis is in much the same case, except that it was not known even to schoolboys till the century had considerably passed middle age. The pervading popularity of golf is of still more recent growth. Golf was an ancient pastime in Scotland long before anybody in England took to it. Now, however, it has spread everywhere, notwithstanding the profanity which seems to come naturally to everybody who wields a driver or a niblick. The game of bowls was, of course, not for boys.

It is what is called an old man's game. But it must have been played in our town from very early days, since a tavern in the suburbs bore the name of the Bowling Green, though no green was attached to it in my time. The historic pastime, however, was still pursued in a neighbouring town—the picturesque old town of Tewkesbury. There, at the rear of a delightful old tavern, was a green overlooking the Severn that commanded beyond as exquisite a prospect of rural peace and beauty as any spot in England. But the laws of the street and the history of bowling are two such different matters that it is time to draw this chapter to a close.

CHAPTER VIII

SCHOOLS AND SCHOOLMASTERS

IT is not very easy for the present generation to realise the state of general education in the first half of the nineteenth century. To be able to read and write was a distinction then. Anybody who could do more was almost accounted a phenomenon. I am speaking, of course, of the poorer classes. All the other orders of society had chances which were denied to the poor. For the masses of the people very few schools were provided, and the instruction imparted in them was of the commonest quality. If a man was lamed or otherwise unfit for manual labour, he was often considered quite good enough for a schoolmaster. One used to hear it seriously argued, too, that people who were not educated had better memories and made better workmen than people who were. The idea was so prevalent even as late as the time of John Stuart Mill that that eminent thinker set himself to confute it. It was, indeed, an era of ignorance, the era in which persons of sixty or seventy passed their earlier years.

My own education, such as it was, was begun in a dame's school somewhere. The fact would have passed out of recollection altogether if it had not happened that the old lady shook and touzled me in such a manner that I was led out into the back yard sick and ill. But the dame's school doesn't count. The Sunday School does, however, though the vague remembrances I retain of it are not pleasant. It was connected with a Wesleyan chapel. The small tradesman who conducted it was severe in his dealings with the children. This is all I recollect about him, except an incident that may convey a moral for persons in similar authority. He promised to call at our house to complain about something or other. He did not call, and I never believed anything that he said after. The only other circumstance in respect to the Sunday School that remains in my memory is the dreary time we children had of it when we were marched off to attend the morning service in the chapel. Our seats were in the gallery, but so placed there that we could not see the preacher without standing up. As we could not understand him either, for of course he was preaching to adults, we were restless and fidgety till the sermon was over. The time of the sermon, indeed, was a time of purgatory. The preacher whom I best remember became afterwards, I think, President of the Conference. It was his practice to read his text, expound it, revert to it over and over again, and keep the Bible open at the verse or chapter till near the end of his discourse. The boys had learned that the closing of the Bible was an infallible sign that the hour of their deliverance was at hand. Boy after boy used, therefore, to stand up in his seat, peep over the gallery front, and steal a glance at the sacred volume. If it was still open, the youthful peepers would sit down, sadder but not wiser boys. When, however, the long-desired sign was seen, an eager whisper ran along the benches, "Book's shut!" The jubilation of the little crowd was now so great that nothing but the knowledge of speedy relief could have kept them in order. Perhaps this little incident also may convey a moral for persons concerned.

There was a national school in our town—only one; also a British school—only one. The latter was held under a chapel belonging to the Countess of Huntingdon's Connexion; the former was, of course, connected with one of the Established Churches. The Church of England, or some of the clergy of the Church of England, must be credited with originating and providing, as far as Cheltenham was concerned, almost the only effective facilities that existed for educating the people in the early years of last century. The national school was founded by the National Society—a society which, supported by the clergy and adherents of the Established Church, rendered unmistakable service to a past generation. Other religious bodies, however, soon followed suit, notably the Wesleyans. But at the time of which I am speaking the only two schools for poor children were situated too far away to be available in my case. So I was sent to one of the few private seminaries that then flourished in the town. It was known as Gardner's Academy.

The proprietor of this establishment was Joseph Aldan Gardner—a fiddler and dancing master as well as a teacher of youth. Mr. Gardner had one distinct qualification for the office he had assumed. He was a clever penman—the cleverest I have ever known. Writing was almost the only accomplishment I acquired under his tuition. But his cleverness with the pen unfitted him for other duties in the school. Most of his time even in teaching hours was employed in producing elaborate specimens of his skill. These specimens, executed with Indian ink on big sheets of cardboard, consisted of the usual flourishes, among which facsimiles of the business cards of the tradesmen of the town, with here and there the visiting cards of the gentry, were more or less artistically dispersed. It was understood that the tradesmen whose names and callings were thus reproduced—the butcher, the baker, the candlestick-maker—paid the penman for the honour he had done them. As for the specimens, they were, when completed, handsomely framed, exhibited in shop windows, and finally sold for a fair price. But the schoolmaster at one time occupied in the estimation of his boys a secondary place in his own academy. The first place was then held by a tame magpie, which performed the twofold duty of diverting the scholars and making an intolerable mess of benches, desks, and copy-books. It need hardly be said that the education imparted in a school which was conducted in the free-and-easy fashion I have described was not of the highest or soundest quality.

Most of the scholars, however, fared much better than I did. The difference arose in this way. My dear old grandmother was too poor to pay even the small fee required—sixpence or eightpence a week. It was therefore agreed that she and her daughters should do an equivalent amount of laundry-work for the schoolmaster and his family. The arrangement was not satisfactory so far as I was concerned. Looked upon as belonging to a lower social grade than the boys who paid for their schooling in cash, I received much less attention than the other scholars. I learnt how to read and write—that was all. Cyphering should have come next, but did not. All I recollect in respect to it is a gross piece of injustice from which I suffered. I was set to do a certain sum without having received the least instruction as to the manner of doing it. And I was told I was to be "kept in" till I had completed the task—manifestly impossible in my case, since I had no intuitive knowledge of arithmetic. Wherefore, being left alone in the school-room, and knowing that I was utterly helpless, I did what any other boy would have done in the circumstances—I decamped without leave. Next day an unmerciful flogging was administered. The physical pain was soon forgotten, but the sense of wrong and outrage remained, and remains to this day. It was probably the special and unfair treatment extended to me by Aldan Gardner that induced the fatal habit of "mooching," as playing the truant was called in our part of the country. That habit once firmly rooted, there was not much chance of further improvement at Gardner's Academy.

One of the locations of the academy was a rather large room that bore the name of Sadler's Wells. It had been a place of entertainment, and it had taken its name from that once famous theatre in London where Mrs. Siddons had impersonated the heroines of Otway and Shakspeare, and where at a much later date, in the year of the Great Exhibition, I had the pleasure of seeing Phelps as the immortal misanthrope, Timon of Athens. It was while the school was held in this old temple of the local drama that an incident occurred which marks the immense difference between that time and this in the matter of sanitary precautions. The daughter of the schoolmaster fell ill of the small-pox. The school was not closed, as it would have been in these days. But, as the little girl wanted a playmate during the period of convalescence, I was selected to join her, because I had already suffered and recovered from the frightful disorder! Whether other scholars were also immune I cannot now recollect. It is probable that some were and some were not; for small-pox, as I shall have to explain later on, was as common then as many more ordinary and far less fatal ailments are now.

These other scholars were for the most part the sons of small tradesmen in the town. Only one of them, as far as I know, rose to any sort of eminence. The exception was a little fellow—George Stevens, the son of a barber—who became known in later years as a steeplechase rider. Poor George met a tragic death while still at the height of his successful career as a jockey, not in the pursuit of his profession, but in the course of a regular ride between the town and his own place among the Cleeve Hills. He was thrown from his horse near a noted hostelry called the Rising Sun, and was found dead by the roadside. I have pleasanter recollections of the jockey than of another of the barber's sons. This youth was the first snob that had come within my ken. Proud of his delicate white hands, he held them out before a party of his school-fellows, and challenged any boy in the company to say what he could: "These hands have never done an hour's work since they were made." I do not know what the rest felt; but I held the little creature in ineffable contempt ever after.

My school days at Gardner's Academy ended at a very early age. A situation as errand boy at a bookseller's was then found for me. A circulating library was attached to the business. My duties were to clean boots and knives and brasses, and then carry books and magazines to the houses of the gentry who were subscribers to the library. The occupation was not uncongenial (except that I used to get awfully tired and thirsty), for I was able to steal a peep at literature which would not otherwise have come within my reach. The book that was then in the greatest demand, as I gathered from so often carrying it from one house to another, was Eliot Warburton's "Crescent and the Cross," and next to it, I think, came Tennyson's poems. Pictorial advertisements of Dickens's "Chimes" were at this time (1844) exhibited at the bookseller's door. The work at the library became at last too heavy for me. And so I was sent for an all too brief season to school again. The Wesleyans had lately built a new chapel—the date on the building is 1839—under which they opened a day school. It was to this new school that I was sent. The schoolmaster knew his business; the lessons were made intelligible; the classes were made interesting; the singing and other exercises were really entertainments. Enormous was the contrast between the old school and the new. There was no more mooching—no more the least desire to absent myself from form or desk. It was a delightful time. I verily believe I derived more advantage from the few months I spent under the Wesleyan master than from all the years I had spent under Aldan Gardner. Alas! I had soon to relinquish the pleasure I derived from the instruction I was receiving. The time had arrived when I must choose a trade, and begin the real business of life. The regret felt at leaving school just when I was beginning to realise the benefit of schooling was speedily submerged by the new delight of mixing with men in a workshop. I was a boy still, but I thought myself a man. No other boy was half my importance; no man, even, strutted the streets with anything like the dignity I assumed during the first few weeks of my apprentice days.

CHAPTER IX

APPRENTICE DAYS

THE choice of a trade was a serious question—perhaps more for my grandmother than for me, since she had to make herself responsible for a burdensome premium. There were family discussions on the subject. I wanted to be an engraver; if not, then a saddler. The reasons were curious. Aldan Gardner had at least taught me to write well, and I was fond of copying printed letters; wherefore it was thought I would make a good engraver. The saddler idea was suggested by the fact that an older boy of my acquaintance, for whom I had conceived considerable admiration, was apprenticed to that trade. Efforts were made to procure a place at an engraver's; but the only firm at that time in the town had then no opening. I was outvoted on the saddler question. But the nearest thing to an engraver was a printer. We compromised on that. I became a printer.

The result of much negotiation with the proprietor of the *Cheltenham Journal*—John Joseph Hadley—was that I was apprenticed to him for the term of seven years. The indentures, drawn up by a lawyer, inscribed on parchment, and duly signed and witnessed, were dated June 6th, 1846. It was rather a one-sided arrangement. The legal expenses were needlessly heavy. There was the lawyer's fee, and there was the cost of the stamp—one pound. Worse than these things was the premium. I was bound to serve John Joseph Hadley for seven years—the first year for nothing, all the other six years for very small wages; but my old grandmother bound herself to pay John Joseph Hadley no less a sum than fifteen pounds. Fancy £15 for a poor old washerwoman! It had to be paid in instalments, of course; but the obligation was discharged to the last penny. Mr. Hadley had a long way the best of the deal. I was to be taught the trade and craft of a printer. As a matter of fact, I was taught little more than what I picked up myself, and that only in one branch of the business. Seven years were no doubt the regulation term for such apprenticeships as mine; but seven years were at least two years longer than were absolutely required. All the same, I had a fairly happy time, except during a period to be mentioned presently. I completed the twenty first year of my age a good while before the expiration of my indentures. I could then have claimed my freedom, as apprentices in like circumstances usually did; but I deemed it more honourable to observe the strict letter of the bargain, and so served my full term of seven years.

The company into which a young lad is introduced when he begins his working career may be the making or the marring of his character. There is something, but not everything, in old Robert Owen's doctrine, that man is the creature of circumstances. It is certain that many men are of the nature of chameleons, taking their colour from their surroundings. Nobody can question the immense advantage to a youth if he should be brought under wholesome influences in a workshop. But there are despicable people who seem to take a delight in corrupting their younger companions. Happily, on the other hand, there are decent people who endeavour to counteract the evil tendencies of the rest. I was neither more fortunate nor more unfortunate than the common run of apprentices. The men in our office were "much of a muchness." One was as gruff as a Griffin—which, indeed, was his name; another was coarse and ugly and vain; a third was equally vain, and as vile in his habits as in his conversation. The remaining three were honest, respectable men. If I suffered no harm, I cannot honestly say that I derived any good, from contact with my fellows in the office.

Of course I had to pay my "footing," and equally of course the proceeds of the exaction were spent on drink. Drunkenness was prevalent then as now, but, I think, more prevalent now than then. Strange are the depths to which even respectable men will descend when the means of indulgence can be had for the asking. It was always the oldest and most respected man in our office who was detailed to lie in wait for the commercial travellers as they came round for orders. It seemed to me even as a boy that the process was not only undignified, but contemptible. It was beggary in its worst form, because hardly distinguishable from extortion. We were printing a mad sort of book on the Prophecies for an eccentric and benevolent old gentleman in the town. And we could always tell when the old gentleman was reading his proofs in the counting-house, from seeing through the office windows tribes of mendicants hiding and peeping round corners. They were waiting to pounce upon their prey. What better were the old and respectable printers who waited to intercept the representatives of the paper and ink firms who did business with the office? But the odious system is still in vogue—indeed, has grown so much worse as to become intolerable. "From the man who buys the ink to the man who minds the printing machine," a leading ink-maker has said, "there is an organized scheme for blackmailing the manufacturer." Notice was therefore given by this gentleman's firm that from and after February 1st, 1900, it would not give itself nor allow any of its servants to give "chapel money," Christmas box, or wayzgoose subscription to anybody employed by its customers. The proceeding may or may not crush out the vicious system; but it is quite certain that working men will never command the respect to which their calling entitles them as long as they descend to the tricks that were practised in my apprentice days.

The gentleman to whom I was bound had many peculiarities—peculiarities of appearance as well as character. He took snuff and wore frills. The two are connected because the frills often bore traces of the snuff. A serious man, too, was John Joseph Hadley. I don't think I ever saw him laugh, except, as in duty bound, when the Rev. Francis Close told him the story of the old Jew clothes-man. The sincerity of his religious convictions was shown in a way that caused infinite discomfort to all in the office. The paper he owned and worked—for he always made up the formes himself—was a Church and King paper. A picture of the Crown and the Bible adorned its title head-line. It was published on Monday morning—an arrangement which would in ordinary cases necessitate Sunday labour. But Mr. Hadley avoided the desecration of the Sabbath by obliging us to work till twelve o'clock on Saturday night and resume operations at twelve o'clock on Sunday night. This preposterous regulation almost completely destroyed three days of the week, so far as any enjoyment or sensible pursuit was concerned. Never shall I forget the misery I felt when I had to be roused at midnight, after having, as the result of three or four hours' tossing about in bed, just fallen asleep. The very remembrance of the time is like a hideous nightmare. Napoleon talked of the two o'clock in the morning kind of courage. For my part, as a growing boy, I used to think that twelve o'clock at night was as good a time to be hung as any.

My first duties as the youngest apprentice were to sweep out the office, ink small bill formes with dabber or roller, and deliver the newspaper to subscribers in the surrounding villages. Blistered hands came from one of these operations, blistered feet from another. When I went my rounds on Monday morning, I was given a few extra copies of the paper in case I should come across a purchaser on the road. This, however, rarely happened; not so much, perhaps, because the paper was dear as because few people could read it. The Taxes on Knowledge were in full operation at that time. No newspaper could be published without the Government stamp, while a heavy duty was imposed on the raw material. And so the public was required to pay fivepence for an article that contained only about an eighth part of the matter to be found in a penny paper of our own day. The office swept, the papers delivered, and other odd jobs performed, I was set to pick up types—what we called "pie" in the first instance. Pie is type put together anyhow for the convenience of distributing the letters into their proper boxes in the cases. [9] But I considered myself a person of no small importance when, standing on a stool, I was put to set up a bit of reprint copy. It was a humorous paragraph from a Gateshead paper—written, I have no doubt, by a gentleman (Mr. James Clephan) whose colleague I became in Newcastle many years later. The very words of that paragraph I could recall long after, so highly did I rate my first achievement at "case."

The machinery and appurtenances of the office were of a very primitive character compared with those of newspaper offices now. Down in the cellar (in one corner of which, by the way, was the only convenience in the establishment) was an old wooden press, and a cylinder machine that was turned by a handle. One man, with another to feed the machine and a boy to take off the printed sheets, could turn out the whole issue of the Journal in an hour. The four pages of the paper were made up by old Mr. Hadley himself, who, when he ran short of matter or desired to curtail expenses, used to fill up a couple of columns of space with a huge standing advertisement of Grimstone's Eye Snuff—a patent commodity that has long since disappeared from the market. The formes were locked up with wooden quoins and sidesticks, and then carried below to the machine. One day a page was wrecked at the foot of the cellar stairs, whereupon a lad in the office pointed to the mass of pie and cried to the man who had been carrying the forme, "There it is, sir!" But I daresay it will require a printer to understand the ludicrous humour of the incident. Another feature of our working-day life that will be better understood by printers than by the public was the difficulty we experienced in working by candle-light. The candles were fixed in little leaden sconces, which were in their turn fixed in the "c" box of the case. When the candles guttered, as they did very often, for they were of the commonest quality, the box was filled with tallow and the air with imprecations. It will be seen from all this that our office was a very old-fashioned affair. We had old-fashioned ways, too, one of which was that of keeping a galley of standing headings for use when required. A revolution broke out in Paris in the second year of my apprenticeship. But there had been a revolution in Paris eighteen years before. And there in 1848, among the standing headings on the galley, was a line in big type that had done duty in 1830—"The French Revolution."

The office in which I served my time is no longer an office; the newspaper we printed has been dead many years; the family to which it belonged is no longer resident in the town. The old gentleman passed away during the time I was an apprentice, while two of his sons, after continuing the paper till a few years before it expired, obtained appointments elsewhere—the elder on the staff of a Birmingham newspaper, the younger (Thomas Russell Hadley, a gentlemanly fellow to whom I was much attached) as chief reporter to an Australian Parliament.

CHAPTER X

HEROES OF THE STAGE

EARLY in my apprentice days I came under the influence of the drama. It was the travelling, not the regular drama. I was entitled to threepence a week pocket-money. All went in a ticket for the back seats. Every Saturday night in the season, as I left work at twelve o'clock, I used to climb up a spout to read by the light of a street lamp the names of the plays that were to be performed the following week. It would, of course, have been intolerably tantalising if, with the playbills about the town, I had had to wait till Sunday to learn the fare for Monday. If I was impatient to see the name of the play, it need not be said that I was still more impatient to see the play itself. Monday was my only night for the drama. Having started work at midnight on the Sunday, I was not required on the Monday to continue at work till eight o'clock, the usual hour of happy release on the other days of the week. So I was always in good time for the rise of the curtain. Luckily for me, with my small allowance of coppers, there were no early doors then.

The drama, as I have said, was not the regular drama. There had been no regular drama since the regular theatre had been burnt down. The ruins of the burnt building, blocked up with boards, were still to be seen in another part of the town. I had promised in my indentures that I would not "haunt taverns or playhouses." But a booth was not a playhouse. As booths were not mentioned in the indentures, I assumed that I was quite at liberty to haunt them. Anyhow, I did haunt them as often as they came round. The best known of these enterprises was Hurd's. [10] It had its regular circuit, and it came round at regular intervals. Hurd's Theatre was as famous in Gloucestershire as Prince Miller's in Scotland or Billy Purvis's in Northumberland. The booth was set up in an inn yard— the Nag's Head or the King's Arms. An outside show always drew a big crowd. It was the custom of the performers—comedians, tragedians, acrobats, and ballet dancers—to parade up and down an open platform, dressed in all their stage finery, with the view of inducing the spectators to walk up and see the wonders to be presented within. The outside show was sometimes supplemented by the offer of prizes for the boys who, stripped to the waist and with hands tied behind their backs, could soonest eat the treacle rolls that were suspended from a rope across the platform. This was before the days of paraffin lamps. The platform was illuminated by great pans of blazing grease, which had now and then to be stirred up with an iron rod, and which, when thus stirred up, threw out almost as much black smoke as it did flame, accompanied by a penetrating and suffocating stench that set the poor actors and actresses a-coughing. The inside arrangements were just as primitive as those outside. A couple of hoops, fitted with sconces for eight or ten tallow candles, and hung from the roof of the booth, afforded all the light that was thrown upon the stage. As the performance proceeded, the light grew more and more dim, till the audience, scarcely able to discern one actor from another, raised loud cries of "Snuff the candles." Then an old super would lower the hoops by means of a piece of twine, doing what was required, sometimes with his fingers and sometimes with a pair of snuffers, and the next act of the drama could be better seen. Of course, if any of the audience stood or sat under the "chandeliers," they ran a pretty good chance of getting their best clothes soiled and spoiled with droppings from the "long sixes" above them.

It was while I was so standing that I was induced, or rather compelled, to make my "first appearance on any stage." Though I was a very small boy at the time, I remember the whole occurrence perfectly. The great attraction of the evening's entertainment, sandwiched between the farce which began and the tragedy which concluded it, was a series of conjuring tricks by Ramo Samee, described on the bills of the play as "the celebrated Indian juggler." After he had executed some astonishing feats, such as swallowing a sword, producing endless articles from an empty hat, and so forth, the magician intimated as usual that he wanted a lad from the audience to assist him in the next item of the programme. Thereupon the tragic actor, who also was standing under the candles, without leave asked or granted, lifted me on to the stage. I was terrified—terrified of the juggler, but perhaps still more terrified by the sight of the sea of faces surrounding me; for, besides the audience in front, the members of the stock company were gathered at the wings. Terrified as I was, however, I seemed to understand what Ramo Samee wanted. And Ramo Samee himself must have known from previous experience exactly how any small boy would act in the circumstances. Well, seating me on the floor beside him, the juggler told me to open my mouth and keep it open. Of course, I was too frightened to disobey orders, not even though I half-suspected that he was going to make me swallow a sword too. But it was an egg, and not a sword, that I was expected to gulp down. The egg was produced, thrown into the air, and caught as it descended. The hand which caught it was suddenly clapped over my wide-open mouth. "Did ye swallow it?" cried the Indian in an Irish accent. Fearing that unutterable things would befall me if I did not give the answer he required, I stuttered out, "Y-e-e-s." The feat was received with thunders of applause. More thunders followed when Ramo, fiddling about his involuntary assistant's ear, feigned to extract from it, not only the egg, but yards and yards of coloured ribbon. It was my first appearance on the stage—and the last.

The actors and actresses who formed the company of that canvas booth in an inn yard were veritable heroes and heroines to the lads and lasses who watched and wondered in the back seats. Tommy Hurd was the leading comedian. Never did he speak without setting the house in a roar. What Tommy had said and what Tommy had done in the farce we had seen on Monday lasted me and my companions for delightful conversation the whole of the week afterwards. But the tragedian and his wife—Mr. and Mrs. Maclean—were held by us in special awe and reverence. If we met them in the street, as we often did, we followed them at a respectful distance, admiring every strut and movement. If they looked at us, we were as proud as Punches; if they had spoken to us, it would have been heaven; if they had shaken us by the hand or patted us on the head, we should have gone clean crazy. These two great actors— for they were the greatest we had seen, or ever expected to see— played the leading parts in a piece which had a strange and alarming effect on the mind of one of their youthful admirers. The story might as well be told.

There is an incident in the second chapter of Hall Caine's "Manxman" so perfectly true to boyish life that one cannot help thinking it is really part of the author's own experience. The incident is an adventure in which two of the chief characters in the novel are concerned—how Philip and Pete, having been fired by reading the story of the Carrasdoo men, set about becoming pirates and wreckers themselves; how they wandered away to a cave on the seashore; how they there kindled a fire with the object of decoying unwary mariners on to the rocks; how, while dozing and blinking by the fire, they heard voices from the sea which they at first mistook for the voices of betrayed and perishing sailors; and how it turned out that the voices were those of relatives in search of the young wreckers themselves, one of whom was coddled and the other welted back to their respective homes. "Aw, yes," as a Manxman would say, "I have gone through the same sort of performance myself, though." The story of the Carrasdoo men had much about the same effect on Pete and Philip as the drama of the "Miller and his Men" had on the writer of this narrative. As the lads in the "Manxman" tried to become pirates and wreckers, so was this other lad inspired with a wish to become the chief of a band of brigands. The drama was a stock piece of the blood-and-thunder sort. It was played as an afterpiece to "Romeo and Juliet" at Covent Garden Theatre on a famous occasion in 1829—the occasion when Fanny Kemble made her *début* as Juliet, and so took the town by storm that she retrieved the fortunes of her father, then the lessee of the theatre. And it was played again at the Haymarket later, when, as Sir F. C. Burnand informs us, it was ever so much more funny than a burlesque of it that was produced at the Strand. It remained popular in the provinces long after it had disappeared from the London boards, and in the canvas booths long after it had ceased to be performed in the regular theatres. Thus the horrible misdeeds of Grindolf, the miller, were represented by Mr. Hurd's dramatic company in the later forties. The chief character was personated by our great tragedian, Mr. Maclean, while his wife, of course, was the miller's companion in desperate adventure. Marvellous was the impression the play produced, notwithstanding the dire climax of the drama, when mill and miller, maid and men, were all blown up together! "Aw, yes, I would become a robber myself, though." A little girl who used to frequent the back seats was to be the "maid of the mill." So earnest and enthusiastic did the young playgoer grow that he bought a pistol in preparation for the enterprise. Moreover, knowing that robbers would need to accustom themselves to work while their victims were asleep, he wandered into the suburbs at night, away from the lamps and the shop-lights, in order to overcome the fears and terrors that were always in his mind associated with darkness. But these expeditions were not very successful; for the embryo chieftain of a robber gang was, as I can testify, always mighty glad to get back to the town again. As for the pistol, which was the only appurtenance of the bandit profession he ever acquired, it was borrowed by another lad, who said he wanted it for an amateur performance, and was never seen afterwards.

That the imaginative youth who longed to set all the world wondering with his fiendish exploits did not develop into a meek and weak sort of Hooligan was probably due to the fact that he took a serious turn before he was two years older. But he did not cease to take interest in the drama, as may be gathered from his recollections of Barry Sullivan and Ira Aldridge, who both appeared at an improvised theatre in the town somewhere about 1853. Barry Sullivan, then a tall, slim young fellow, played Hamlet; Ira Aldridge, being a negro, played Othello without needing to blacken his face. Sullivan became a great favourite in the provinces; Aldridge travelled and performed in almost all parts of the world. Bayard Taylor, the American traveller, records that one of the strangest spectacles he ever saw was a black man playing an English tragedy to a Tartar audience at the great fair of Nijni-Novgorod in the interior of Russia. The black man was Ira Aldridge.

CHAPTER XI

PENNY DREADFULS AND CHEAP LITERATURE

THE popular literature of the first half of the century was as scant in quantity as it was for the most part poor in quality. It is true there was no overpowering demand for literature of any sort, for the reason, as already indicated, that the masses of the people were unable to read. Creditable, but perhaps not altogether successful, efforts were made by the Society for the Diffusion of Useful Knowledge to supply such want as existed. The *Penny Magazine*, which was issued by that society, was full of facts, often very dry facts—interesting, but not enlivening. Charles Knight, William Howitt, and William and Robert Chambers tried to do better, and succeeded in doing better. The publications of the Messrs. Chambers suited the popular taste then, as some of them suit the popular taste now. There was and is so judicious a blending of light and heavy literature in *Chamber's Journal* that that periodical has helped to educate, inform, and entertain many generations of the British public. Whenever it came in my way, as it did sometimes, I revelled in its pages. The *Penny Magazine* also was a great delight on the rare occasions that I saw it. But I remember best the *Family Herald, Reynolds's Miscellany*, and Lloyd's "penny dreadfuls."

Excepting "Pilgrim's Progress," "Gulliver's Travels," and the "Arabian Nights," I saw and read none of the books which entrance young minds. The religious meaning of the first, the satirical meaning of the second, and the doubtful meaning of the third were, of course, not understood. The story was the great thing—the trials of Christian, the troubles of Gulliver, the adventures of Aladdin. "Robinson Crusoe" was never accessible till late in life, when the taste for such productions had departed. So with "Don Quixote," Captain Cook's voyages, and Mungo Park's travels. There are certain books which must be read at the period of life suitable for enjoying them, else they are rarely enjoyed at all—never with the gusto they would have excited at the proper season. Great, therefore, was the disadvantage that poor boys of my age and condition suffered. But great was our delight, too, when chance opportunities came in the way of such of us as could read. An opportunity of this kind arrived when a firm of printers in London, sometime about 1844 or 1845, brought out a penny Shakspeare—a play of Shakspeare's for a penny! Well do I remember this cheap treasure. It was my first introduction to the great bard. Gracious! how I devoured play after play as they came out! I was a poor errand boy at the time. When on my errands I used to steal odd moments to read my penny Shakspeare. A painful incident— inexpressibly painful to me at the time—arose out of this habit. One day another lad—a bit of a rogue I knew—asked to look at the play I was reading. Out of pure devilment (for he couldn't read himself) he refused to return it. I followed him through many streets, thinking he was playing a joke, and imploring him to give me back my precious property. But I never saw the little book again. To this day the remembrance of grief and mortification is as vivid as ever. The scene, the book, the thief—all are clearer now than greater events of yesterday. The popular reading of the time was not all as elevating and as wholesome as Bunyan, or Shakspeare, or even Swift. Much of it, indeed, was the very reverse. At a period when newspapers were five or six times the price they are now, and when village innkeepers found it a payable custom to let them out on hire for a penny an hour, stories of the "penny dreadful " class were issued in weekly parts. The publisher was Edward Lloyd. Mr. Lloyd was the legitimate successor of the old Alnwick printer—Catnach of the Seven Dials. He began business as the printer of sheets that were hawked and sold by the "flying stationers"—records of prize-fights, of murders, of executions, and of what purported to be "last dying speeches and confessions." Then, as time went on, he issued whole libraries of fiction, started many periodicals, and established two important and successful journals. When he died in 1890, he was the proprietor of great paper mills at Sittingbourne, of a great London daily, and of the well-known weekly that bears his name. The latter venture was as successful as any of his enterprises. It was so successful that he was enabled to pay Douglas Jerrold, the most famous wit of his age, a salary of a thousand a year for little more than the mere use of his name as editor. Lloyd's fiction was always of the strongest and most sensational character. The publisher knew how to select stories that would make the blood curdle and the flesh creep—also how to select the authors who could write them. Next to the selection of a strong story was the selection of a strong title. Mr. Lloyd and his writers were equal to this too. The names of a few of the stories, all of which, as will be seen, have subsidiary titles relating to mystery or bloodshed, may give an idea of the intellectual food on which the masses of the people were fed in the old days:—

Ada the Betrayed, or the Murder at the Old Smithy.
Adele, or the Pirates of the Isle.
The Curse, or the Outlaws of the Old Tower.
The Old Monastery, or the Deed of Blood.
Gonzalo the Bandit, or the Bereaved Father.
Olivie, or the Mysteries of Pigani Castle.
The Black Monk, or the Secret of the Grey Turret.
Alice Home, or the Revenge of the Blighted One.
The Black Mantle, or the Murder at the Old Ferry.
The Smuggler King, or the Foundling of the Wreck.
Villeroy, or the Horrors of Zindorf Castle.

Many of those terrifying narratives were published in *Lloyd's Penny Weekly Miscellany of Romance and General Interest*. Others were issued in weekly instalments. The latter were illustrated with rude woodcuts. One of these woodcuts haunted me for years after I had first seen it. A masked robber, holding a dark lantern in one hand and an uplifted dagger in the other, was seen creeping towards a bed on which an old gentleman, with his arms outside the quilt and a tasseled nightcap on his head, lay sleeping. I could see and hear the rest of the tragedy—the stealthy tread of the robber, the sudden plunge of the dagger, the blood-stained bedclothes, the dying groans of the night-capped victim. Another picture also haunted me. It was one of the illustrations to "Villeroy." The vaults of a castle; a trapdoor evidently leading to the dungeons below; the villain of the story, or rather one of the villains of the story, peering into the depth by the light of a mediæval lamp. The very attitude and costume of the villain are before me now. A stage attitude, wide-topped boots, trunk hose, slashed doublet, belt studded with daggers, slouch hat and long feathers—every detail is there. The pictures rivalled each other in horror. I retain a vivid recollection of the "fearful joy" I used to snatch from them every week through the window of a small newsvendor's shop in the town. I was too poor to buy the serials myself; but I borrowed from somebody a bound copy of "Villeroy, or the Horrors of Zindorf Castle." It is of this specimen of penny dreadful literature that the most vivid remembrances remain.

The romance was appropriately named, because it was filled with horrors from the first page to the last. Where Zindorf Castle was supposed to be situated I cannot now recollect; but I do recollect that it was supplied with the usual assortment of secret doors, secret passages, and secret dungeons. The villainous personages that passed through these doors, the crimes that were committed in these passages, and the sufferings that were endured in these dungeons, were depicted and combined in such a manner as to make the young reader, if not the old, dream dreadful dreams when he went to bed. One never-to-be-forgotten evening was spent in the company of the occupants of Zindorf Castle. The elder people were all engaged in an adjoining outhouse, so that I was left alone in the family room— kitchen and sitting-room in one. There, by the light of a tallow candle (for we had neither gas nor oil lamps in those days), the development of the drama was followed with absorbing interest and terror. As crime succeeded crime, as villain followed villain, the nervous and excited reader fancied that one or other of the robbers and murderers who danced through the pages of the romance would suddenly make his appearance in person. So entirely did this idea obtain possession of his morbid and juvenile mind that he took the precaution of placing the carving knife on the table beside him! When he went to bed that night, he buried his head deep under the sheets, dreamt of thieves and cutthroats, and woke next morning to dream again all day of the horrors of Zindorf Castle. Ah! poor lads of sixty years ago—such of them as could read at all had to be satisfied with literary matter of a parlous character. And yet—and yet—I don't know that the lads of the present day, with all their advantages, are really any better than we were.

It may be that stories of the "Villeroy " stamp, like the chap-books of the period, encouraged and developed the taste for reading; and the taste for reading, once acquired, came in due course to need higher pabulum to satisfy it. Before it could be satisfied, a complete revolution in companionship became necessary. Frequent occasions had arisen for feeling dissatisfied with the chums of my boyhood — once particularly when some of them, having taken a bird's nest, tore the little fledglings to pieces. Protests provoked only laughter and scorn. Other incidents occurred to produce estrangement. Some of the lads had already begun to contract bad habits. Was there not a danger that bad habits would be contracted by all the rest? I resolved to sever the connection. One Sunday afternoon the usual call was made for a ramble in the fields. Word was sent to the callers that their old companion was not going to join them. I heard from an upper room, not without a certain amount of tremor, their exclamations of surprise. They wandered off into the fields in one direction; I, with a new companion, wandered off into the fields in another. My new companion was Young's "Night Thoughts." The old companions were never joined again. A new life had begun.

CHAPTER XII

CODDLING AND CULTURE

ALL the old reformers fought hard for education—the education of the people at the expense of the people. The fight was hopeless till the franchise was extended. "Education for all," I wrote myself in a little pamphlet entitled "An Argument for Complete Suffrage," printed at Manchester in 1860, "is an inevitable consequence of the enfranchisement of all." And I was right. The extension of the suffrage was very soon followed by the multiplication of schools. But schools have been multiplied without producing the great and beneficial results that ardent reformers expected from them—hence disappointment. The people are educated—educated at great cost— but they are neither better nor wiser than the people who were left to educate themselves.

There has been coddling as well as culture. But coddling is not necessary—isn't even desirable—nay, is positively pernicious. It corrupts the character, prevents the development of self-reliance, makes no distinction between the fit and the unfit. It will, in the end, if unchecked, prove disastrous to society. Coddling is costly also. The coddling of the London School Board, for example, costs the ratepayers of London a million sterling per annum—an average, it was computed in 1899, of £28 per child, or eleven shillings per week, which is about the wages of an agricultural labourer in many parts of the country! "And yet," said a leading journal, "the parents of one child in five won't have the Board's education even at this price." If the money were well spent, there would not, perhaps, be much objection to the vast outlay. But is it? This is a question for experts. The unfairness, however, would remain. Many a struggling parent who pays for the education of his own children, though he is perhaps less able to do it than many of those whose children are taught at the public expense, can only afford for the purpose £10 a year each. Again, the cost of a thing is not always a criterion of its value. My own education never cost much more than sixpence a week. It was not much of an education, but it sufficed. It supplied me at any rate with the tools of knowledge. And the tools of knowledge are about all that the State ought to be expected to provide gratis, except in the case of promising and deserving scholars. Given these tools, the child can work out its own career. Gilt-edged tools can do no more—not even such gilt-edged tools as dancing and deportment. It is well to educate the people, but the tendency of much of the School Board policy of the day is to pauperise the people. Yet School Boards ought, above all things, to beware of undermining the independence of the individual. That lost, the nation becomes little better than a machine—a mere affair of cogs and wheels.

We managed these things better in the forties. And we had no Hooligans either. I was myself, I daresay, the nearest approach to that undesirable character. We who were poor had few facilities—no free scholarships, no subsidies from Government, no classes supported by public funds; but those among us who had learnt to read and write could employ our advantages to acquire what else we desired. Every avenue of culture was open to us if we had the perseverance and the capacity to penetrate it. We had, as I have said, the tools of knowledge. Having these, it depended entirely upon ourselves what use should be made of them—whether, in fact, they should be used at all, or left to rust and decay. Some of us kept our tools bright and keen with constant friction; others neglected them as they would have neglected the widest education itself. A lad of finer parts would, of course, have turned to better account the small benefits received from school. But I was only a very ordinary lad— gifted with nothing more than a desire to shine and a sort of feverish activity in the way of realising it. An old diary of the period, when I was off with the old companions and had for some time been on with the new, records classes or meetings every night in the week except when work detained me at the office.

If I did not at that time educate myself, I at least did the next best thing—I tried to. English grammar was picked up from Cobbett; the lessons in Cassell's *Popular Educator* afforded some insight into Latin; French was studied from the same pages in conjunction with another youth; and arrangements were made with an enthusiastic disciple of

Isaac Pitman [11] to plunge into the depths of phonography, when a change of circumstances cast these and all other educational projects to the winds. Cobbett's Grammar has long since been superseded by newer treatises; but it is still an intensely interesting work, if only because of the characteristic way in which the author makes political friends and political foes supply examples and illustrations of good and bad English. John Cassell, a vendor of coffee and a lecturer on temperance, had tried several small ventures in periodical literature before he commenced his famous *Educator*. One of these was the *Family Friend*—a pleasant and cheerful publication in which Parson Frank stirred up the ambitious instincts of the young people of the day. But the *Popular Educator* was the great enterprise. It came out in weekly parts. It was badly printed, and was full of blunders and blemishes; but it contained lessons to suit all aspiring tastes, and satisfied the requirements of the young folks in a manner they had never been satisfied before. Most of the self-educated people of my age and of later generations owe a deep debt of gratitude to John Cassell. It was with such aids as have been indicated, together with readings and scribblings at odd moments of the day or night, that the desire for knowledge was in some manner gratified.

There was flourishing in Cheltenham in my young days a rather exclusive society—exclusive, I mean, in being beyond the reach of poor boys—known as the Philosophical Institution. It has gone the way of many similar societies—the way, also, of most of the old mechanics' institutes; but the handsome building in the Promenade, modelled on the outside after a Greek temple, retains a precious place in my memory, from the lectures I heard there on literary and scientific topics. Tickets of admission occasionally came my way. When they did, they were highly appreciated. The lecturers, as the title of one of Browning's poems runs, were "people of some importance in their day." Dr. Wright, a resident physician, and the Rev. T. W. Webb, a Gloucester clergyman, frequently elucidated branches of the sciences on which they were distinguished authorities—geology and astronomy. Charles Cowden Clarke came now and then to lecture on the poets, George Dawson to expose the weaknesses and foibles of mankind, and Clara Lucas Balfour to tickle the cultivated tastes of the members on matters of a light and airy character. George Dawson—George Dawson, M.A., as he was always described in the programmes—was probably the most popular lecturer of the middle years of the century, while Mrs. Balfour, mother of the unhappy and unscrupulous Jabez Balfour, enjoyed the distinction of being about the first lady to make a reputation on the platform. Of the former—his "raucous voice," his sarcastic humour, his conversational style, and his general appearance—I retain the clearest recollection. I do not think any lecturer of my time in the matter of quiet ease and entertaining power ever quite came up to Dawson's standard.

But the institutions of a more modest (and I regret to say more ephemeral) character—more suited to our humble means, I mean— were either started by us, or were warmly supported by us after they had been started. One was held under a Baptist Chapel; another in the vestry of the Unitarian Chapel; a third in a private house that had been purchased for the purpose by the agent of one of the political parties in the town. The Baptist Chapel affair was chiefly memorable to me from the engagement of a strange and eccentric person—a great rogue as it turned out afterwards—who professed to teach us elocution; but the story of his eccentricities and his rogueries must be told in a later chapter. The minister of the Unitarian Chapel had been the Rev. Henry Solly, who devoted many years of his later life to the task of founding Working Men's Clubs in all parts of the country, and who, when he was over eighty years of age, published his memoirs in two interesting volumes. [12] It was, however, under Mr. Solly's successor—the Rev. John Dendy, a son-in-law of the Rev. Dr. Beard of Manchester—that we were granted the use of the vestry for the meetings of the Cheltenham General Literary Union.

Unfortunately, the union was not a success, though many advantages accrued to the members from their evening chats and readings under its auspices. The longest lived of our societies was the People's Institute. The house in which it was held—21, Regent Street—became rather notorious afterwards on account of the use that was alleged to have been made of it in the manufacture of faggot votes. But the place was very popular in my time. The management was sufficiently catholic to allow all sorts of movements to be conducted in its rooms. Even Chartist meetings were held there. I presided over some of these meetings myself, although a mere boy at the time. Books and newspapers could be read in one of the rooms; classes for the study of various subjects were held in other rooms; debates on topics of current interest or speculative value took place once a week; and occasionally essays that had been awarded prizes in competition were read by the ingenious writers. We were fond of controversy in those days, some of us because we wanted to propagate what we thought were new ideas. Many a time and oft, after floundering about in a maze of confusion in the debating class, have we delivered wonderful speeches on the way home, overpowering in argument and eloquence, confounding our opponents, and establishing as on a rock the principles for which we had been contending!

But our thirst for controversy was not satiated by the weekly debate. We had a little magazine of our own—the *British Controversialist*, which ran into several volumes, and to which we contributed papers on the negative or positive side of the questions which the editor selected. My own gratification at the acceptance of a paper on Mahomet was much marred when I came to read the production in print—shamefully and brutally disfigured by the editor's improvements! It did not occur to me then that I should in after-years have to shamefully and brutally maltreat the productions of a younger generation of aspirants. We wrote essays, too. The prizes that were offered for the best were only just sufficient to encourage effort. An amusing entry relating to this matter, dated July 13th, 1850, may be quoted from an old diary:—"Proposed to raise essay fund, and to subscribe one shilling towards it." The entry has no interest except as showing the poverty of our resources and the bent of our inclinations. A very big scheme was initiated, however, when Boswell's "Life of Johnson" and two smaller books were offered as prizes for the three best essays on the "Advantages of Knowledge." The competition in this case was only remarkable because the award was made by a clergyman of the Church of England, the Rev. F. J. Foxton, author of the "Popular Christianity"—a neo-theological work of some repute in its day. [13]

With the desire for culture there had come a passion for politics. This passion was stimulated by the French Revolution of 1848. I was a reader of *Reynolds's Miscellany*. One day, soon after the proclamation of the Republic in France, there appeared in it a picture of the members of the Mountain—Ledru Rollin, Louis Blanc, Pierre Leroux, Victor Schœlcher, and the other ardent Republicans and Socialists who composed the Extreme Left of the National Assembly. The picture was followed by the announcement of a new publication—*Reynolds's Political Instructor*. It supplied what some of us wanted, though not all that the most insurgent among us longed for. But the stirring events in Paris and the newer literature that began to be issued sent the young men of my age wild with excitement and enthusiasm. I had previously read the "Rights of Man" and other political works of Thomas Paine, which had seduced me from bed at five o'clock for many mornings in succession. And now I was fairly in the maelstrom.

CHAPTER XIII

THE DISEASES OF OTHER DAYS

THE diseases of one age may cease to afflict the next. Much depends upon conditions independent of human will or control: much also upon the good sense men and women exercise in applying the results of experience. Leprosy has disappeared—from the British Islands at all events. Why should not other maladies—those, for instance, which are undoubtedly generated by the improper feeding of infants? The ignorance of other days was often the cause of the diseases of other days. Our great-grandfathers cared nothing about ventilation, nor very much about sanitation either, as may be gathered from the horrible arrangement that lasted all through my apprenticeship in the printing office of a Cheltenham newspaper. Every person who could afford it luxuriated in a four-post bedstead. And curtains were drawn closely around the sleeper so as to exclude every breath of fresh air. The consequences to our ancestors of thus inhaling for hours together the atmosphere they had themselves contaminated can readily be understood in these times. Is it any wonder that they suffered from complaints which are hardly known even by name now? As we increase in knowledge and in the wisdom to use it, healthier lives will be lived by the people. But we have not yet discarded the prejudices that fettered our predecessors. Moreover, it may be, we are by new habits and vices planting the seeds of fresh penalties for the races that are to come.

It sometimes happens that old disorders, coming at infrequent intervals, are accounted new. This, I imagine, was the case when an epidemic of influenza reappeared after an interval of many years. People talked of it as if it had never been heard of before. Their elders, however, knew better. But the same fallacies were current in my young days. I remember hearing then of a terrible disorder. It was called influenza; but it was thought and said to be something that had not previously afflicted mankind. Yet visitations of exactly the same mischief seem to have been recorded in the Middle Ages. No such mistake was made with respect to cholera. That terrible affliction paid many visits to England during the last century. It is a singular fact, however, that it always left Cheltenham untouched. The circumstance that it did so, as I have recorded in a previous chapter, was inferentially ascribed by the Rev. Francis Close to the appeals for the intercession of the Almighty that had been offered up in the parish church. But the reverend gentleman was not so emphatic on the subject as was his colleague, the Rev. Archibald Boyd, on the subject of the sudden death of the Czar Nicholas during the Crimean war. Preaching at Christ Church, Mr. Boyd told his congregation that he regarded the event as a distinct answer to prayer. "Only a fortnight ago," he said, "the people had assembled in the house of God, and bowed themselves before Him in humble supplication. But none of us could have dreamt in what way our prayers would be answered. None of us could have imagined that, ere ten days had passed, the Angel of Death would come and lay his icy hand on the proud Nicholas and lay him in the dust." A much more rational explanation of the immunity of Cheltenham was given later by a German medical writer, that the reason it was not visited by cholera in 1832 was in consequence of the abundance of trees in its streets and squares and gardens. But indeed the place has been singularly salubrious at all times; in testimony whereof the local historian records on August 4th, 1860—"Only five persons were buried in Cheltenham this week out of a population of 40,000. The united ages of these five were 399 years, or an average of 80 years each."

But neither trees nor prayers could save the people from visitations of small-pox. That loathsome disease made regular, frequent, almost constant appearances in England in the earlier part of the century. It was reckoned among the inevitable ailments of childhood or maturity—as certain to come as teething itself. Since it was impossible to escape the dreadful affliction, the virus was deliberately implanted in infants. An entry in the Annals of the Northern Counties for October 21st, 1787, reads thus:—"The Duchess of Northumberland arrived in Newcastle, from whence she went to Heaton Hall, one of the seats of Sir Matthew White Ridley, where her children underwent inoculation for the small-pox." The practice that was favoured by the faculty in the eighteenth century continued in favour with the populace down to near the middle of the nineteenth. Old people in my time came to the conclusion that the best thing to do was to meet the disease halfway: so they prepared their children with purgatives—brimstone and treacle chiefly—in order, as they said, to purify the blood, and then got the patients inoculated. The children who were subjected to this treatment were not placed in the hands of doctors or even druggists. A relative of my own, a very worthy woman, who, however, was not acquainted with even the elements of medicine or surgery, performed many of these operations for her neighbours. And she continued to perform them till one of her patients had the narrowest escape from death. Afraid then of the consequences of continuing the service, she inoculated no more. I was myself subjected to the process. And I suffered from so severe an attack of the malady that I bore the traces of it for many years, as did thousands of other people in my younger days. And now the visitations of the foul plague are so rare that the present generation hardly knows what "pockmarked" means.

The immunity enjoyed in our day is attributed to vaccination; but vaccination is so curious and out-of-course a process that large numbers of good folks, not understanding the mystery, have an incurable prejudice against it. Here I may record another fact within my own experience. A baby of a few months old suffered from a horrible eruption. For many months the poor mother could not fondle it—could hardly touch it, in fact, except to wash and poultice it. For weeks and weeks, indeed, the little sufferer had to be carried about on a pillow. "Ah!" said the neighbours, when they saw it, "that comes of vaccination." But the infant had not been vaccinated at all. If it had been, the mother herself, I daresay, would have accepted the same conclusion; for whatever follows vaccination is generally put down as the result of vaccination, whereas, as in the case I have mentioned, there are certain obscure ailments that attack children under all circumstances whatsoever.

The ravages of small-pox were so conspicuous on the faces of the people in the thirties and forties that one could not pass through the streets of our towns without seeing somebody or other who had been disfigured by the disease. A Newcastle magistrate, Mr. John Cameron Swan, when a case of so-called "conscientious objection" (which is often only another name far pure prejudice and ignorance) came before him in 1899, remarked that he remembered the time "when every third or fourth person one met in the street was marked with small-pox." My own recollections coincide, if not exactly, at all events generally, with Mr. Swan's, as must those of all who have reached or passed the age of three score and ten. The late Lloyd Jones, well-known throughout the country as a lecturer on social and political subjects, records that the one thing which struck him, when he revisited his native town of Bandon after many years' absence, was the disappearance of pock-marked people from the streets. Testimony to much the same effect is borne by William Lovett, one of the originators of the Chartist movement. Mr. Lovett, who was born at Newlyn, Cornwall, in 1800, tells us in his autobiography that he caught the foul disorder from a little girl who, her "face and arms still thickly beset with the dark-scabbed pustules," was brought into the school he was attending. "So terrible were the ravages of small-pox at that period," he writes of the first decade of the nineteenth century, "that I can vividly remember the number of seamed and scarred faces among my school-fellows. Vaccination had not been introduced into our town, though inoculation was occasionally resorted to; but it was looked upon as sinful and a doubting of Providence, although about one in every fourteen persons born died from the effects of the disease."

Statistics of mortality are alleged to bear out the impressions of observers and the testimony of medical men. According to a little pamphlet written by Mrs. Ernest Hart in 1896, and published in the same year by the Society for Promoting Christian Knowledge, small-pox was so terrible a plague in the last century that it killed three thousand people every year out of a million of the population. "Out of every hundred children born, ninety caught the small-pox and one-sixth of them died, and scarcely anybody grew up without having had it." Mrs. Hart remarks further that the deaths per million of the population after vaccination had been introduced fell to 600 per annum; that after Parliament had granted funds to make vaccination gratuitous, though not obligatory, the deaths fell to 305;

that after vaccination had been made obligatory, but was not efficiently enforced, the deaths fell to 223; and, finally, that between 1872 and 1891, when the compulsory clauses of the Vaccination Acts were more strictly carried out, the deaths fell to 89. "The population of England and Ireland," says Mrs. Hart, "now numbers thirty million, and there would at the present time be a probable annual death-rate of about ninety thousand from small-pox if it were not for vaccination." Facts and figures to the same purport were quoted by Dr. Henry W. Newton at a Medical Congress in Newcastle. "Wherever vaccination was adopted," he said, "small-pox had been excluded, as was illustrated in the case of Germany and Austria. In Spain there were no vaccination laws in force. During the year 1889, there died from small-pox in the province of Almeria 3,080 per million, in Murcia 2,070, in Cordova 1,400, in Malaga 1,340, in Cadiz 1,330. For the same year the death-rate in protected Germany was four per million." Professor Corfield at the same Congress warned "those who were foolish enough not to accept the advantages offered by vaccination" that they "would gradually perish by one of the most loathsome diseases that had ever afflicted the world."

It was an outbreak of an epidemic of small-pox in the city of Gloucester that elicited the warning of Professor Corfield. That outbreak, it was alleged, was the result of the neglect of vaccination. Here we have a case of a prophet not being honoured in his own country; for Edward Jenner, the discoverer of vaccination, was a member of an old Gloucestershire family. Born at Berkeley, a few miles from the city in one direction, Dr. Jenner practised medicine for many years at Cheltenham, a few miles from the city in another direction. The local connection is further strengthened by the circumstance that another Cheltenham physician, Dr. Barron, was the biographer of Jenner. But the fatal experience of the inhabitants of Gloucester has failed to remove the popular prejudice and ignorance on the subject, since Parliament itself, bowing to popular clamour, has decreed that the laws of vaccination, no matter what the consequences to the public health may be, shall no longer be enforced where the parents of children allege or fancy that they have "conscientious objections to the practice." The folly of placing the welfare of the community at the mercy of individual caprice would perhaps be realised too late if the awful horrors of a loathsome complaint should show themselves at the beginning of the new as they did at the beginning of the old century.

CHAPTER XIV

BALLOONISTS, MESMERISTS, CONJURORS

SMALL events as much as great may indicate the condition of life in the days that are gone. Nor may they be altogether lacking in interest even if they have no bearing on the conditions of life at all. The small events that are now going to be grouped together, without any distinct connection between them, will only serve such a purpose as the indulgent reader may choose for himself.

The coronation of Queen Victoria lives in my memory, from the illuminations which marked the rejoicings in our town. The well-to-do houses, the lights in the windows, the wheelbarrow by which I was standing, are all as fresh as ever. The long line of houses, built of one pattern, were in a fashionable quarter; and the windows, being of the same size, contained of course the same number of panes. Plate glass was at that time either unknown or but little used. It had not at any rate found its way into domestic architecture. Every window, therefore, contained sixteen or twenty squares. And each square was furnished with a candle. The effect of the burning candles, so regularly disposed, so uniformly bright, and so many thousands in number, was almost entrancing. I had never seen anything so beautiful before, and I am not sure that I have ever seen anything in the way of illuminations so really effective since.

An indistinct impression of a dark object floating and flapping in the sky, causing consternation and wonderment, crosses my mental vision. It was an air balloon, cast adrift by an aeronaut who had descended in a parachute. There had happened just before a fatal accident to another aeronaut who had attempted the same feat from Vauxhall Gardens, London. The unfortunate adventurer was named Cocking. Cocking's fate, however, did not deter a rival balloonist named Hampton from desiring to follow his example. Hampton's ascent took place in 1838 from the Montpellier Gardens, Cheltenham. But the local magistrates, while assenting to the ascent in a captive balloon, forbad the descent in the manner projected.

74

Hampton, however, defied the authorities, cut himself loose from the earth, and made, as the local records say, "one of the most successful parachute descents in England." The exploit was deemed a world's wonder in an age that had not seen the far more hazardous and sensational leaps from the clouds of the present day. Not long before Mr. Hampton performed his daring feat, Mr. Green, another famous aeronaut, ascended from the Montpellier Gardens in the "great Nassau balloon." Mr. Green was accompanied by Mr. Rush, the American Minister in London, and the balloon travelled a distance of ninety miles in three hours. There was much rivalry between the two principal spas in the town—the Montpellier and the Pittville, the Old Wells having fallen out of the running. The proprietor of the Pittville establishment announced a balloon ascent too. But as pipes were not laid down to the more distant gardens, it was resolved to inflate the balloon at the gas-works, remove it to the spa grounds, and there tether it till the time for its ascension arrived. Crowds of small boys were early astir to witness the removal. A gang of men held the balloon captive, while the aeronaut directed operations from the car. The work of transporting the ponderous sphere on a windy morning through the narrow streets of the town was exciting and difficult. It furnished, however, as I recollect, immense enjoyment to the small boys. Unfortunately, after escaping many perils, the balloon was wrecked near St. Paul's Church, before it had performed half its journey to Pittville Gardens. Collision with a chimney stack caused a great rent, and the trouble and labour that had been spent were lost. Night-capped heads protruded from every window along the route, as the shouts of the crowd awoke the sleeping inhabitants. When the collapse occurred, loud were the cries of the outsiders to close the windows lest the escaping gas should in some way cause an explosion. There was no further attempt in my time to make a balloon ascent from Pittville.

Churches were plentiful in Cheltenham, and chapels were fairly numerous. Other places of faith, and emotion were also in evidence. There was much talk of Mormonism among the poor in the thirties and forties. Indeed, one heard now and again of bands of converts— Latter-Day Saints was the name they assumed—migrating to the sacred city that had been founded near the Great Salt Lake. But the movement received a considerable check when the leader of the sect was transported for robbing a firm of jewellers. Much commotion was caused about the same time when a young fellow who called himself Shiloh, and proclaimed himself a prophet, appeared in the town. Shiloh's career, however, owing to the disturbances his mad antics provoked, was cut short by the police. [14] Worse disturbances happened when, in 1850, the Pope announced the establishment of a Catholic hierarchy in England. A public meeting was held in the Town Hall to protest against "Papal Aggression." Measures were taken later to burn the Pope and Cardinals in effigy. The effigies were exhibited in a tailor's shop window, and many tons of coal and loads of faggots were purchased for the great bonfire. So intense was the excitement and so great the apprehension of riot there from that the magistrates issued a notice forbidding the proceedings. The mob, however, not to be defrauded of its entertainment, attempted to set fire to the Catholic Chapel, tore down the railings in front of it, and broke open the premises of several Catholic tradesmen. Hundreds of special constables having been sworn in next day, no renewal of the row occurred.

Spiritualism, which has become a sort of religion in these days, was practically unknown in the first half of last century. It began with table-rapping. I was invited to one of the earliest performances—the exponents were strangers to the town—but, unfortunately, the tables wouldn't rap a rap. About the same time clairvoyants could be consulted by fashionable people for a fashionable fee. Hypnotism and thought-reading were not familiar names till long afterwards. But mesmerism, which seemed to be akin to both, was quite a common topic of discussion. It was discussed at our debating class. There I became intimate with a family which had the gift or faculty of mesmerism to a remarkable degree. The father was an ordinary stonemason, while his children were engaged in various occupations of a humble character. I remember one night going to the house of my friends to witness some experiments. It should be said that no member of the family made any public display of the strange powers most of them possessed, though, of course, in private circles it was well known that the father, sons, and daughters were addicted to mesmeric practices. On the occasion to which I allude I was accompanied by a mutual friend of the Winters family. The eldest daughter, a girl of my own age, was mesmerised by the father, much in the same manner as people are now supposed to be hypnotised. When in the mesmeric state, with her eyes completely closed, she went about the house in a methodical way, poking the fire, setting the chairs to rights, and doing such other things as she was accustomed to do in her waking condition. Afterwards I held the girl's eyes, while the other visitor produced from his pocket a book she had never seen—a copy of Collins's poems—which was opened at random, and the verses on the open page of which she read as distinctly as if she could see them, though I am quite sure, from the manner in which I held her eyes, that she could not possibly see anything at all. My companion then held the girl's eyes, while I drew from my pocket some scraps of paper on which I had written a few exercises in French and English, the writing never having been seen by anybody but myself. The English part of these exercises was read without the least difficulty; but when she came to the other she quietly remarked, "Oh, that's French; I can't read French." I offer no explanation of the phenomenon; I merely put it on record.

Mesmerists and spiritualists alike have been denounced as quacks and charlatans. Two names are most prominently associated in England with the supposed exposure of spiritualistic tricks—those of Messrs. Maskelyne and Cooke. Both belonged to Cheltenham. One was an innkeeper's son apprenticed to a watchmaker; the other was as poor a lad as any in the town, with no relative but his mother. Cooke and Maskelyne, brought together as young men, commenced business as conjurors, Mr. Maskelyne being, as he still is, the inventive genius and leading member of the firm. Before establishing themselves in London, where for many unbroken years their entertainments have nightly drawn appreciative audiences to the Egyptian Hall, they amused and bewildered the country folks in the small towns and villages around Cheltenham. And hereby hangs a tale.

A Revising Barrister is holding his court at Cheltenham. The Tory party is represented by its legal agent—Mr. Frederick Stroud, author of the elaborate "Judicial Dictionary" which bears his name, now

Recorder of Tewkesbury, a dear friend of my youth and ever since. A vote is claimed for Mr. Cooke by the Liberals; but objection is taken by the Tories on the ground that the house for which the vote is claimed is rented for the claimant's mother, that the claimant himself does not reside in Cheltenham at all, and that consequently he is disqualified by reason of non-residence. "What is Cooke?" asks the Revising Barrister. "A conjuror," replies Stroud. "Where does he live?" "Well, your Honour, he lives a wandering life—here to-day and gone to-morrow." "Oh! what the law in old times called a vagabond, then." "Precisely, your Honour—a vagabond." The vote is disallowed.

Years elapse. Maskelyne and Cooke are drawing crowded audiences to the Egyptian Hall. The principal attraction is the exposure of what the conjurors call the tricks and frauds of spiritualistic mediums— the Davenport Brothers, the Fays, Dr. Slade, and others. There is a cabinet on the stage. The two performers, securely tied with ropes, take their places inside the cabinet, and a member of the audience is invited to take a seat beside them, so as to make sure that they can obtain no help from any quarter. The moment the door of the cabinet is closed the "manifestations" begin—that is to say, the usual noises are heard within, the ringing of bells, the beating of tambourines, etc. (This is the thing the Davenport Brothers did, as they said, with the aid of spirits from another world.) Mr. Stroud, happening to be in London, sends in his card to the entertainers. They, delighted to see an old acquaintance, assign him one of the best seats in the house. The cabinet performance is about to be given. Maskelyne and Cooke are tightly bound, and an invitation is offered to anybody in the audience to come and see fair play. Mr. Stroud is inquisitive, and volunteers. As he is seen advancing over the stage, Maskelyne whispers to Cooke, "Here's Stroud coming. Let's pay him out for that vagabond business." All forgetful of his delinquency, and ignorant of the sudden conspiracy against him, Mr. Stroud greets his friends and takes his seat in the cabinet beside them. The door is shut; there is total darkness; and then—the band begins to play. Mr. Stroud sees nothing; but he hears and feels a great deal more than he had bargained for. "A vagabond, am I?" he hears Cooke exclaiming as he feels his ribs punched, his back slapped, his head tumbled and touzled by both performers. "For God's sake, Cooke, drop it, or we shall have the show down," he cries as he rolls about on his seat. "I've had my turn now," says Cooke, as he gives his friend a parting tickle. The shouts and shrieks of laughter are heard by the people in front, who wonder what in the world is taking place inside the cabinet. Suddenly the doors are thrown open. Maskelyne and Cooke are seen released from their bonds, while the lawyer wears an amused, but somewhat bewildered smile. The performance brought down the house.

If there be any moral to the story, it is this—that it never pays to play jokes with a conjuror, unless, like the Recorder of Tewkesbury, you are prepared to join in the laugh at the finish,

CHAPTER XV

TRIALS AND TRIBULATIONS

MURDERS and crimes of all sorts, even though the bulk of the people could not read about them themselves, were the subjects of most absorbing interest to young folks and old "in the days when we went gipsying, a long time ago." Terrible was the impression produced by Greenacre's monstrous villainy. Somehow I formed the notion that a working man who used regularly to pass our door bore a resemblance to the murderer. And I never saw this poor man without shuddering, and even sometimes running away to hide myself. The Greenacre sensation was, however, eclipsed by that which the later crimes of the Mannings and of James Bloomfield Rush created—crimes which were, in their turn, eclipsed in tragic interest by the poisonings at Rugeley, the pathetic misdeed of Madeleine Smith, and the mysterious fratricide of Constance Kent.

Homicides were probably fewer, but executions were more common, at the beginning than at the end of the century. Men and women were hung for almost trivial offences—hung in batches, too, after almost every assize. My grandmother used to talk of five or six poachers being hung together in front of Gloucester gaol. Townsend, the noted Bow Street runner, giving evidence before a Committee of the House of Commons in 1816, testified to these grim facts:—"We never had an execution wherein we did not grace that unfortunate gibbet at the Old Bailey with less than ten, twelve, sixteen, or twenty wretches—I may say forty, for in the year 1783, when Serjeant Adair was Recorder, there were forty hanged at two executions." The gaoler of Newgate, being asked by the Recorder a few years later how many could be executed at one time on a new gallows, complacently replied: "Well your worship, we can hang twelve upon a stretch, but we can't hang more than ten comfortably." The hangings in those days, and till long after, were always done in the open, the contention being that the gallows, like the gibbet, was a great "moral teacher." I happened to be passing Newgate Street a few minutes after nine o'clock one morning in

1857. Suddenly the street was filled with the most villainous-looking characters I ever saw in a single crowd. They were laughing and shouting and jostling each other as they hurried along—a great stream of gaol-birds. Whence had they come? Enquiries elicited the information that they had just been enjoying an execution—fresh from the teaching of the gallows. Similar spectacles drew similar crowds to the county gaols all over the country.

We in Cheltenham always knew when Calcraft had been at work from the cries of the dealers in patter literature. Our local Catnach was Thomas Willey, a printer of ballads and broadsheets. Mr. Willey was always ready with a "last dying speech" for every criminal who was executed at Gloucester. It was generally the same speech, altered to suit the name and circumstances of the new culprit; and it was invariably adorned with a ghastly woodcut, showing the figure of a man or a woman, as the case might be, dangling from a gallows. The passage leading to Willey's printing office was crowded on the morning of an execution with an astonishing collection of ragamuffins and tatterdemalions, greasy, grimy, and verminous. Soon they were bawling their doleful wares all over the town. Where they came from was as much a mystery to the inhabitants as whither they disappeared when the last dying speech had been sold. But penny papers and recognised reporters drove the flying stationers from the streets. Marwood by this time had succeeded Calcraft—Marwood, who told a party of pressmen who had met to compliment him that he should die happy when he had hung a reporter! Thomas Willey, by the way, was succeeded by his grandson, Thomas Hailing, and Thomas Hailing in after years made the old office famous for some of the most artistic printing ever done in England.

There were other sensational trials besides those of murderers. One of these occurred at Gloucester Assizes in 1853. But I must go back a few years earlier—to 1847 or 1848. It was the period of the dawn of youthful enthusiasm for all sorts of things—useful or useless knowledge among others. I had joined an elocution class, held under the Baptist Chapel mentioned in a previous chapter. The class was a complete *fiasco*, because the teacher was a charlatan. The man called himself Dr. Smyth, wore a shabby-genteel cloak, and put on pompous airs. It was evident from the first that he knew little or nothing about the art he undertook to teach, and so it came to pass that the committee of the society to which the class was attached gave him his dismissal. Instead of teaching the youngsters who attended his prelections anything about the proper method of reading and reciting, he occupied their attention by telling stories about himself. One of these was intended, he remarked, to illustrate the doctrine he held, that children should be addressed as if they were grownup people, because, if so addressed, they would soon lose their baby ways. The story was precisely similar to one which is, no doubt falsely, ascribed to Dr. Johnson. Dr. Smyth, so he told us, was driving towards Bristol, when a woman with a child asked him for a lift. Consent was given on the understanding that no baby-talk should be used. In the course of the journey, however, the mother forgot this condition, and said something about "Georgy-porgy getting a ridey-pidey." Down, observed the professor of elocution, the mother and her child had to get, making their way to Bristol as best they could without his help. A still more extraordinary doctrine was set forth by the reputed Dr. Smyth—the doctrine that sleep was not only unnecessary, but unnatural. Cattle never slept, he declared, for he had spent night after night in the fields watching them!

The professor of elocution, dismissed at Cheltenham, turned up in a new character at Gloucester Assizes a few years later. Sir Hugh Smyth, of Ashton Court, near Bristol, had died without direct issue, leaving an estate of the annual value of £20,000. A claim to the property was set up by a person who alleged that he was the son of the late baronet, that the secret of his birth had long been kept from him, and that he had commenced proceedings for the purpose of acquiring his real position in life. Mr. Bovill, afterwards Chief Justice of Common Pleas, was counsel for the claimant when the case was entered at Gloucester. The claimant, in the course of his evidence, and in proof of his claim, produced some jewelry which he declared had belonged to old members of the Smyth family. The crisis in the trial came when Sir Frederick Thesiger, who appeared for the defence, asked the witness if he knew the name of a certain jeweller

82

in London. It was the name of a jeweller who had manufactured for the claimant the very articles in question! The witness was confounded, his counsel threw up their briefs, and the Court ordered him to be taken into custody. Tried afterwards for perjury and forgery, the pretended Sir Richard Smyth, who was not a Smyth at all, but a certain Thomas Provis, son of a Somersetshire labourer, was sentenced to twenty years' transportation. I believe he died about twelve months after his conviction. But the Dr. Smyth who professed to teach elocution, and the Tom Provis who tried to filch an estate, were one and the same person. Augustus Hare states in his autobiography that Provis's wife, "a daughter of De Wint the artist, had already ordered a carriage, in which she was to make a triumphal entry into Bristol, when the cause suddenly collapsed."

A more extraordinary case than even that of Tom Provis occupied the attention of the people of Cheltenham for many years. The peace and comfort of a reputable family were utterly wrecked and destroyed by the pertinacity of an unscrupulous barrister. A British admiral, Sir Robert Tristram Ricketts, Bart., died at his residence, The Elms, in 1842. Soon after his death, Mr. Augustus Newton, who had married one of his daughters, commenced proceedings which lasted from that time till 1849, and indeed were not finally concluded till 1861. Mr. Newton began operations in the magistrates' court. There he charged Lady Ricketts, the widow of the admiral, Dr. Thomas Wright, the eminent physician and geologist previously mentioned, who had married another of the admiral's daughters, and Mr. J. C. Straford, the family solicitor, with forging the admiral's will. The prosecutor occupied several days in ventilating insinuations of forgery, fraud, conspiracy, cruelty, and murder against the unfortunate accused. Not a tittle of evidence being produced to support the accusations, the magistrates dismissed the case without calling upon the prisoners (for they had all been apprehended) for their defence. A few days later, the solicitor was presented with an address of respect and sympathy, signed by nearly every professional man in the town. But Mr. Newton was not dismayed. Application was made for a warrant to apprehend the proprietors of a newspaper, the *Cheltenham Examiner*, that had commented on the previous proceedings; but again the magistrates refused to comply.

Next year indictments were preferred at Gloucester Assizes against Lady Ricketts and others for perjury and conspiracy, and against the newspaper proprietors for libel. Both actions failed, the grand jury in the former case unanimously declaring that "there was not the shadow of a shade of evidence in support of the charge." Mr. Newton now transferred his operations to London. Poor Lady Ricketts was arrested and dragged before the magistrates at Guildhall. The case was dismissed here also, the bench expressing "deep regret " that so base and baseless a charge should have been made. We next heard of Mr. Newton being a prisoner himself—a prisoner in Gloucester Gaol under the Insolvent Debtors Act. Other actions were instituted in 1844, the principal being a suit for £10,000 damages before the Court of Common Pleas at Westminster against the proprietors of the *Examiner*.

Many of the most prominent lawyers of the day were engaged in the affair, including Mr. Cockburn, afterwards Lord Chief Justice Cockburn, and Mr. Fitzroy Kelly, afterwards Chief Baron Kelly. Again was the pertinacious prosecutor foiled, though he never paid a single penny of the costs of the defence which he was ordered to defray. Then ensued actions against the High Sheriff of Gloucester, against the Sheriff's officers, and against the solicitor to the newspaper proprietors. Two further actions against the *Examiner* were tried in 1847, making six in all. Mr. Straford in the same year was indicted on the old charge, and with the old result, in the Court of Queen's Bench. Two years later, the judgment of the Prerogative Court, accompanied by indignant animadversions on the conduct of the opposing parties, established the validity of the admiral's will. Although the prosecutor was subsequently disbarred for unprofessional practices, the end of his outrageous proceedings was not reached till the appeal case, "Newton v. Sir Cornwallis Ricketts," was dismissed by the House of Lords in 1861.

The newspaper which had suffered so much from the attentions of Mr. Newton remarked at the close of the case in 1849 that "those who are inexperienced in the harassments of litigation know nothing of the vast amount of wrong and persecution which may be inflicted under colour of the law." For a period of seven years the unhappy family of Sir Robert Ricketts and its legal adviser were "tortured by the most cunning devices, subjected to the most harassing disquiet of mind and body, and mulcted in legal expense which of itself swells into a fortune." It is lamentable that the forms of law should permit the perpetration of so much cruelty and mischief. But Lady Ricketts, who survived her trials and miseries for two years, was fortunate in one respect. The case against her was not taken up by the populace; nor did noblemen and members of Parliament provide her pursuers with vast sums to assist the persecution: otherwise Augustus Newton might have become as great a figure in the annals of chicane as Arthur Orton himself. The butcher of Wapping was so much the hero of the hour that it was almost dangerous to doubt the truth of his story. And this reminds me of an incident which shows how some of the humbler classes looked at the Claimant's claim. The time was in the crisis of the case, when Orton, being under cross-examination by Mr. Coleridge, was wriggling and frizzling on a moral gridiron. I was travelling in a third-class carriage between Cheltenham and Tewkesbury. Enter a labouring man in fustian. "How is Sir Roger gettin' on now?" he asked. "Oh, very badly," I replied, looking up from a newspaper. "Well," continued the labouring man, "it wud be a pity now, wudn't it, if he wus to lose the estate after all the trouble he's bin at to get un?"

CHAPTER XVI

CHARTISM

IT has already been mentioned that I found myself very early in life whirling and swirling round the political maelstrom. I was a very youthful atom indeed when, fired by the enthusiasm that seemed to impregnate the air, I became a member of the National Chartist Association—the association that was formed to demand the immediate adoption of the People's Charter. The Chartist movement was the only movement of the time that seemed calculated to captivate the imagination of young and earnest politicians. I had not then reached the mature age of seventeen. Before I was two years older I was taking the chair at Chartist meetings and corresponding with members of Parliament concerning the treatment of Chartist prisoners. But even at that time I was "a Chartist and something more," for it appeared to me that the Charter fell far short of the ideal that ought to be sought and must be attained before society could be constituted on a proper basis. And so, while still active in Chartist circles, I was at the age of eighteen years and a half elected president of a Republican Association! Of course I had all the confidence of youth. What did statesmen or philosophers know about the way to manage national affairs, or the principles on which governments should be based, compared with what I and my comrades knew? We had generous impulses in those days at all events. We lacked judgment, discretion, every sort of prudent virtue; but we despised all mean and sordid interests. It is perhaps the only excuse that can be offered for the conceit and presumption with which we of the younger race of politicians astounded and affronted our elders.

The Chartist movement was some eight or ten years old when I entered it. The history of the movement—probably the greatest popular movement of the nineteenth century—has yet to be written. Materials for a work worthy of the subject are perhaps not abundant. The "Life of Thomas Cooper," the "Life and Struggles of William Lovett," the sketch published many years ago by R. G. Gammage, will assist the future historian. But the story of that stormy episode in the political life of the working classes could only have been told with effect by a writer who shared in its passions and was a witness of its weaknesses. And one by one all those who possessed the requisite acquaintance with the period have disappeared from the scene. John Arthur Roebuck was (with an exception to be presently named) the last survivor of the politicians who, meeting in conference in 1837, passed the resolutions which afterwards formed the basis of the People's Charter. But as the most interesting period of the Chartist movement did not commence till after the Charter had been formally approved at a great meeting in Birmingham in 1838, there were others besides Roebuck who could have related as it ought to be related the history of the great agitation. These, too, however, have also disappeared. So it is extremely unlikely that any competent or satisfactory narrative of a stupendous national crisis will ever now be given to the world.

The demand for universal suffrage and other changes in the mode of representation grew out of the natural discontent of the masses of the people with the Reform Bill of 1832. That great measure—for, after all, it was a great measure—satisfied the middle classes; but it made no change whatever in the political position of the bulk of working men. There had been a sort of understanding that the power which would be acquired by the passing of the Reform Bill would be used afterwards for securing still further improvements in the distribution of the franchise. But when the expectations thus formed were not realised, the working classes established associations of their own. One of these had been initiated by a Cornish carpenter named William Lovett. The People's Charter, as intimated above, was the outcome of a conference between representatives of Lovett's association and certain members of Parliament who sympathised with the popular demand. The members of Parliament comprised Daniel O'Connell, Charles Hindley, John Temple Leader, [15] William Sharman Crawford, John Fielden, Thomas Wakley, John Bowring, Daniel Whittle Harvey, Thomas Perronet Thompson, and John Arthur Roebuck.

Having agreed to certain propositions, the conference appointed a committee of twelve persons—six members of Parliament and six members of the London Working Men's Association—to draw up a Bill embodying the principles that had been approved. The working men so appointed were Henry Hetherington, John Cleave, James Watson, Richard Moore, William Lovett, and Henry Vincent, while the six members of Parliament were O'Connell, Roebuck, Leader, Hindley, Thompson, and Crawford. The document which was drawn up by the committee, and which came soon to be known as the People's Charter, made formal demands for six points— universal suffrage, vote by ballot, annual parliaments, equal electoral districts, payment of members, and the abolition of the property qualification. The Charter, adopted at a great meeting held in Birmingham on Aug. 6th, 1838, was submitted to a meeting held in Palace Yard, London, in the following month, when one of the resolutions was moved by Ebenezer Elliot, then famous as the "Corn-Law Rhymer."

THE CHARTIST CONVENTION OF 1839.
(From a contemporary print.)

It was resolved at both gatherings to call a Convention of Delegates, and to obtain signatures to a National Petition beseeching Parliament to enact the Charter. The Convention, which consisted of fifty-five delegates, said to have been elected by three millions of persons, met first in London, and subsequently in Birmingham. The meeting in London was held at the British Coffee House, Feb. 4th, 1839. A print of the scene, giving portraits of some of the principal members of the Convention, was published at the time. All the members are now dead, George Julian Harney, who died in 1897, being, I believe, the last survivor. The National Petition, bearing, it was alleged, 1,280,000 signatures, was placed in the hands of Mr. Thomas Attwood, then member for Birmingham, the leading spirit of one of the Political Unions which had been chiefly instrumental in carrying the Reform Bill. There were probably exaggerations as to the numbers which took part in the election of delegates; but the rapidity with which the movement spread to every part of the country, and the enthusiasm with which it was received in all the great centres of population, could not be exaggerated. The portentous agitation was viewed with some alarm by the Government, which set about an attempt to arrest it. Unfortunately, the purposes of the Government were assisted by the Chartists themselves; for they indulged in foolish language, resorted to foolish threats, and commenced preparations for still more foolish proceedings. Arms were bought; bands were drilled; the "sacred month" was suggested. But the Convention dissolved in the autumn of 1839, and the Charter was as far off as ever.

The popular power which the movement had developed, however, did not dissolve with the Convention. Many men of mark and vigour, besides the originators of the Charter, joined the agitation. Not the least eloquent of these was Thomas Cooper, and not the least energetic George Julian Harney. But the most prominent of them all was an Irishman—Feargus O'Connor. Gifted with great talent for winning the favour and applause of the populace, O'Connor was then and for long afterwards the idol of the day. Hundreds of thousands of working men were almost as devoted to him as the better spirits of Italy at a later date were devoted to Joseph Mazzini. When he addressed in the rich brogue of his native country "the blistered hands and unshorn chins of the working classes," he appeared to touch a chord which vibrated from one end of the kingdom to the other. Wherever he went he was sure of a vast and appreciative audience.

The popularity of the *Northern Star*, which O'Connor had established as the organ of the movement, was almost equal to his own. But, powerful as O'Connor was, and vast as was the circulation of the Northern Star, no great progress seemed to be made in influencing either the Ministry or the Parliament. A new Convention was subsequently summoned in London—John Frost having in the meantime made his abortive attempt at Newport—and a new association was projected by Lovett. Bitter feuds, however, broke out between O'Connor and the rest of the Chartist leaders, so that much of the strength of the agitation was wasted in personal squabbles. Moreover, the most absurd schemes were proposed for forcing the Government to yield to the popular demands.

I have alluded to the "sacred month." This was a proposition that the working classes should enter upon a strike for that period throughout the whole country. Thomas Cooper tells us how an old Chartist, who had been a member of the first Convention, proposed at a meeting in the Potteries "that all labour cease till the People's Charter becomes the law of the land." The same wild scheme, not long subsequently, was submitted by Dr. McDouall, who had then become a prominent leader of the movement, to a meeting of the Chartist Executive in Manchester. Another singular device was that the people should abstain from consuming excisable articles, so as to paralyse the financial arrangements of the Government. There were partial strikes in Lancashire; Chartist families here and there (my own included) abstained for a time from using tea, coffee, sugar, spirits, and tobacco; but the attempt to obtain the Charter by these means failed as utterly as the attempt of Frost to promote an insurrection of the labouring classes in Wales.

The aims and claims of the Chartists were, to a certain extent, shared and approved by middle-class Radicals. With the view of separating what was reasonable in the movement from what was ridiculous—the principles of the Charter from the violent means which were advocated to secure them—there had been formed what was called the Complete Suffrage party. Joseph Sturge, an estimable Quaker of Birmingham, was the chief figure in the new party. Associated with Edward Miall, Laurence Heyworth, the Rev. Thomas Spencer, and the Rev. Patrick Brewster, Mr. Sturge had entered into negotiations with Lovett, Collins, Bronterre O'Brien, and other old Chartists who dissented from O'Connor's tactics. The result was another conference—the Birmingham Conference of 1843. Four hundred delegates assembled on the occasion. The Conference was, perhaps, the most important—certainly the most influential—gathering of the kind that had been held since the Charter had been promulgated. Thomas Cooper, who was present, informs the readers of his biography "that the best orator in the Conference was a young friend of Lovett's, then a subordinate in the British Museum, but now known to all England as the highly successful barrister, Serjeant Parry." But neither Parry's eloquence nor Sturge's good intentions could evoke harmony out of the discordant elements that had then met together. If there had been anything like union, the political future of England might have been changed. As it was, the Conference broke up in confusion.

The divisions which were manifested in Sturge's Conference became more marked in the councils of the Chartists themselves. O'Connor added to these divisions by mixing up with the demand for the suffrage his disastrous and preposterous Land Scheme. Nevertheless, he kept his hold of the movement down to the time of the great demonstration on April 10th, 1848. Excited by the events which had just taken place in France, the Chartists thought they saw an opportunity of impressing the Government with the extent of their numbers, if not with the justice of their claims. Unfortunately, they only succeeded in frightening the Government into acts of trepidation and terror. Nor did the new National Petition they promoted produce any effect on the Legislature. The failure of the demonstration on Kennington Common marked a turning-point in the history of Chartism. Down to that time it had at least maintained its position in the country; but after that time it began to decline.

The authority and influence of the great Feargus, weakened by the events of April 10th, weakened still further by the gradual collapse of his land ventures, rapidly faded away. Other men became prominent in what remained of the movement—Ernest Jones, Gerald Massey, and the founder of *Reynolds's Newspaper*. Various attempts were likewise made to resuscitate the agitation—notably by Thornton Hunt and George Jacob Holyoake. But Chartism as a political force was beyond redemption. Julian Harney and Ernest Jones helped to keep it alive by means of publications—*Red Republicans, Friends of the People, Vanguards, Notes to the People, People's Papers*, and other periodicals whose very names are now almost forgotten. But the few that continued the struggle quarrelled among themselves. Harney at last abandoned the now hopeless business. Jones, however, supported by a declining number of adherents, maintained the fight down to 1857, when he too was starved into surrender. Penury was the lot also of one of the best known of the Chartist officials. For many years during the latter period of the agitation the name of John Arnott as general secretary appeared at the foot of all the official notices of the Chartist Association. Some time about 1865 I was standing at the shop door of a Radical bookseller in the Strand. A poor half-starved old man came to the bookseller, according to custom, to beg or borrow a few coppers. It was John Arnott! Chartism was then, as it really had been for a long time before, a matter of history.

CHAPTER XVII

YOUNG CHARTISTS AND OLD

FEW men now living, I fancy, had an earlier introduction to Chartism than I had. My people, though there wasn't a man among them, were all Chartists, or at least all interested in the Chartist movement. If they did not keep the "sacred month," it was because they thought the suspension of labour on the part of a few poor washerwomen would have no effect on the policy of the country. But they did for a time abstain from the use of excisable commodities. There were other indications of their tendencies. We had a dog called Rodney. My grandmother disliked the name because she had a curious sort of notion that Admiral Rodney, having been elevated to the peerage, had been hostile to the people. The old lady, too, was careful to explain to me that Cobbett and Cobden were two different persons—that Cobbett was the hero, and that Cobden was just a middle-class advocate. One of the pictures that I longest remember—it stood alongside samplers and stencilled drawings, and not far from a china statuette of George Washington—was a portrait of John Frost. A line at the top of the picture indicated that it belonged to a series called the Portrait Gallery of People's Friends. Above the head was a laurel wreath, while below was a representation of Mr. Frost appealing to justice on behalf of a group of ragged and wretched outcasts. I have been familiar with the picture since childhood, and cherish it as a memento of stirring times.

Another early recollection is that of a Sunday morning gathering in a humble kitchen. The most constant of our visitors was a crippled shoemaker, whose legs were of little use except to enable him to hop or hobble about on a pair of crutches. Larry—we called him Larry, because his Christian name was Laurence, and we knew no other—made his appearance every Sunday morning, as regular as clockwork, with a copy of the *Northern Star*, damp from the press, for the purpose of hearing some member of our household read out to him and others "Feargus's letter." The paper had first to be dried before the fire, and then carefully and evenly cut, so as not to damage a single line of the almost sacred production. This done, Larry, placidly smoking his cutty pipe, which he occasionally thrust into the grate for a light, settled himself to listen with all the rapture of a devotee in a tabernacle to the message of the great Feargus, watching and now and then turning the little joint as it hung and twirled before the kitchen fire, and interjecting occasional chuckles of approval as some particularly emphatic sentiment was read aloud. But Larry had other gods besides Feargus. One was William Cobbett. Among his cherished possessions were two little volumes of Cobbett's works—the "Legacy to Parsons" and the "Legacy to Labourers." These volumes, I recollect (for Larry, though I was but a lad, loaned them to me as a special and particular favour), were preserved in wash-leather cases, each made to fit so exactly and close so tightly that no spot or stain of any sort should reach the precious pages within. Poor old Larry had a brave and wholesome heart in a most misshapen frame. Dead for fifty years, he yet lives in at least one loving memory.

The humble shoemaker, though he longed for the emancipation of his class, and made what sacrifices he could to achieve it, turned his modest circumstances to the best account. No pot-house politician he. Larry and his wife were as cheerful a couple as could be found in the town. Riches are not necessary to produce the blessings and comforts of home. A bright fireside is not incompatible even with poverty, or at least with the very humblest of means. This was demonstrated in Larry's cottage. It consisted of just two rooms—a kitchen and a loft—though it had what almost unknown advantages in large towns: a plot of ground for flowers in front and a bigger plot for fruits and vegetables at the back. But it is Larry's kitchen—at once his parlour and his workshop—that lives in my recollection. To say that it was as "clean as a new pin" is to give but a faint idea of the spotless brightness of everything in it. The very floor, brick though it was, was better scrubbed than many a dining table I have seen since. The pots and pannikins, the cans and canisters, those simple tin or pewter ornaments of the mantelshelf, shone like silver. All else about the apartment, where there was a place for everything and everything was in its place, was equally conspicuous for the polish that was given to it. Larry's cottage, as the result of the industry of Larry's wife, was a veritable palace for cleanliness and comfort. Even the old cripple's low shoes were a wonder; for they shone so brilliantly that a cat, seeing her reflection in them, as in the pictorial advertisements of Day and Martin's blacking of that time, would have almost arched her back for a conflict with her counterpart. And the venerable couple, in spite of their penury, were probably as happy a couple as any in the kingdom. If all Chartist homes had been as well kept as Larry's, there might have been less discontent in the country, but there would have been more force and vitality in the movement to which the masses of the people gave their sanction. As a striking example of devotion to political ideals among the poor, the lame old shoemaker retains a treasured place in the recollection of the days that are gone.

While I was still a boy, though even then interested in political affairs, our town was visited by two of the Chartist chiefs. One was Feargus O'Connor, the other Henry Vincent. Some excitement was caused by the intimation that the former gentleman was expected to arrive by a certain route at a certain time. I joined a party of elder people to go out and meet him. We went to a neighbouring village, sat on a bridge, and waited. Our visitor did not come—at least, not our route. That night or the next night I have a faint recollection of seeing an orator in his shirtsleeves addressing a crowd in the markets. It was Feargus. He was expected again in the first month of 1848, when a procession of carts and waggons passed through the town on the way to Snig's End, one of the estates which had been purchased under the Land Scheme. This time, however, he did not come at all. Vincent's visit occurred about 1841. It was after the "young Demosthenes," as he was called, had suffered two periods of imprisonment—first in Monmouth Gaol, and afterwards at Millbank and Oakham. The meetings he addressed were held in a stable or coach-house—at any rate the room or building was in a livery stable yard. I recollect the locality well, though not a word that was said there. What I do recollect also is the suspicions that were expressed in our household as to the cause of the change of tone observable in Vincent's utterances before and after imprisonment. The fiery and reckless orator of 1839 had become sober and restrained. The simple people of that day could only account for the change on the ground that the Government had somehow found means to influence or corrupt him. When Vincent next appeared in the town, it was as the spokesman of the Peace Society, not of the Chartist Association.

Chartism had interested me as any other stirring movement with which my friends and relatives were connected would have done. But the time soon arrived when I became interested in it on my own account. The local leader of the party was a blacksmith—J. P. Glenister. Others with whom I became associated—all much older than myself—were shoemakers, tailors, gardeners, stonemasons, cabinetmakers, the members of the first-named craft greatly predominating. There had been an earlier leader of the name of Millsom, a plasterer; but he, I think, was then dead. Next to Glenister's the names I best remember among my old associates—all forgotten now save by a very few—were those of Hemmin, Sharland, [16] Glover, Hiscox, Knight, Ryder, and Winters. They were earnest and reputable people—much above the average in intelligence. Glenister was probably the least educated among them. But he had one qualification which the others had not—he could make a speech. Not much of a speech, perhaps, though the speaker generally contrived to make his audience understand what he wanted to say. The old blacksmith usually, in virtue of his standing among us, presided over our meetings. One night, while he was so presiding, somebody spoke of Tom Paine. Up jumped the chairman. "I will not sit in the chair," he cried in great wrath, "and hear that great man reviled. Bear in mind he was not a prize-fighter. There is no such person as Tom Paine. Mister Thomas Paine, if you please." Glenister soon afterwards emigrated with his family to Australia, and one heard of him occasionally as doing well in his new home—which, being an honest and industrious man, he was every way likely to do.

It came to pass that the insignificant atom who writes this narrative, having all the effrontery of youth, took a somewhat prominent part in the Chartist affairs of the town. The first important business in which he was concerned was the National Petition for the Charter which was set afloat immediately after the French Revolution of 1848. It was alleged to have received 5,700,000 signatures; but the number was subsequently reduced to 2,000,000, which included many fictitious names—the work of knaves and enemies in order to bring discredit on the document. The animated scenes at our meetings where the petition lay for signature are still fresh in the memory. Then came active operations for getting Chartist leaders to the town.

Thomas Cooper was rather a frequent visitor. Two impressions remain—one, that he recited Satan's speech from Milton with magnificent effect; the other, that he had a most irritable temper. I had been concerned with another youth in organizing a lecture at the Montpellier Rotunda. We had occasion to whisper to each other about some matter of business while the lecture was being delivered. Cooper caught sight of us, stopped, and then covered us with confusion as he solemnly assured the company that he would only resume his discourse "when those two young men have finished their conversation." The matter of business, whether it suffered from the delay or not, had to stand over till the close of the meeting.

Cooper's visit happened in March, 1851. Three months later came Ernest Jones. Our gathering, in default of a better place, was held in a market garden. It was not a large gathering—only 150 or 200 present, the result, probably, of showery weather. Jones had been in prison the year before for uttering seditious language. The treatment he had suffered was abominable. Petitions for inquiry were promoted; a select committee of the House Commons was appointed to investigate; a blue book containing the evidence was printed; and there, I think, the matter ended. As chairman of one of the meetings, I had some correspondence with Mr. Grenville Berkeley, then member for Cheltenham. The hon. gentleman was courteous in his replies, sent me a copy of the blue book, but could not, or at any rate did not, do anything else.

Our next Chartist visitor, I recollect, was Mr. R. G. Gammage, the author of a sketch of the history of Chartism, who subsequently studied medicine under great difficulties, and settled down as a practitioner in Sunderland. Gammage's visit coincided with the occurrence of the General Election of 1852. We therefore got him nominated so that he might have an opportunity of making a speech from the hustings. This was all we wanted, for of course it would have been utterly useless to go to the poll in the then state of the franchise. Suffice it to say that Gammage made what we all thought a capital speech for the Charter.

There will be other occasions for describing the old electoral methods. But I may perhaps be excused for referring in this place to an affair preliminary to the contest of 1852 in which I bore a small part. The Chartists, even though they had few votes, were at that time numerous enough to make their favour worth cultivating. The agents of the Whig party therefore organized an open-air meeting of the working classes in the Montpellier Gardens. It was attended by about 2,000 persons. The resolutions were ingeniously framed to propitiate the Chartists and at the same time assist the candidature of the Whig nominee. Having, I suppose, made myself conspicuous at some of our meetings, I was invited to take part with Glenister in this gathering of working men. One of my aunts happened to be passing the Gardens, heard the cheers and saw the crowd, and so went to see what was the matter. Great was her astonishment to observe her precocious nephew on the platform proclaiming at the top of his voice the inalienable right of every man to the suffrage! The agents of Mr. Craven Berkeley, then the Whig candidate for the town, turned the meeting to good account, advertising in all the local papers the resolutions that had been adopted, with the names of the working men and others who had proposed and seconded them. I was told I had done well on the occasion. [17] If so, it was the only time I ever did well in like circumstances. But I had an uneasy consciousness that we had been "used" by the party wire-pullers; as, indeed, we no doubt had been. Used or not, however, we had the satisfaction a few weeks later of hearing our own candidate propound the true doctrine from the hustings.

CHAPTER XVIII

FOOLISH AND FIERY CHARTISTS

CHARTISTS were of many sorts. There were moral-force Chartists and physical-force Chartists; there were Chartists and something more; there were whole-hog Chartists, bristles and all; and there were Chartists who cried aloud, "The Charter to-day, and roast beef the day after!" Indeed, the divisions among them were almost endless—at least as endless as the men who set up as leaders, for every little leader had his little following, while the bigger leaders had bigger followings. It was these divisions that robbed the movement of the power it would otherwise have wielded and of the success it would otherwise have achieved. But the chief cause of dissension was the means that should be pursued to attain the end desired. While the wiser heads were advocates of moral pressure, the more foolish and furious contended that carnal and lethal weapons were the only weapons Governments could be made to fear or understand.

There was, no doubt, some excuse for the wilder spirits of the movement, inasmuch as the middle classes not long before had set the example of truculence. The men of 1832, who demanded "The Bill, the whole Bill, and nothing but the Bill," were just as violent in the language they used as the bitterest of the Chartists. Nor did they scruple to threaten the direst consequences to the aristocracy, and even to royalty itself, if reform should be denied. An instance of the desperate measures to which the middle classes were prepared to resort at that period was disclosed to William Lovett by one of the principals engaged to carry out the scheme. "When," writes Lovett, "the Duke of Wellington was called to the Ministry, with the object, it was believed, of silencing the Political Unions and putting down the Reform agitation, an arrangement was entered into between the leading Reformers of the North and Midland Counties and those of London for seizing the wives and children of the aristocracy and carrying them as hostages into the North until the Reform Bill was passed. My informant, Mr. Francis Place, told me that a thousand pounds were placed in his hands in furtherance of the plan, and for hiring carriages and other conveyances, a sufficient number of volunteers having prepared matters and held themselves in readiness. The run upon the Bank, however, having been effective in driving the Tories from office, this extreme measure was not necessary." Moreover, the surrender of the Duke of Wellington, who confessed that he had to choose between civil war and compliance with the wishes of the people, had gone a long way to warrant the conclusion that Governments were more amenable to force than to reason.

The Chartists had, perhaps, another excuse in the ferocious sentiments which a minister of religion had uttered in the course of the agitation against the New Poor Law. This agitation was in full swing when the Charter was framed. The year which witnessed the inception of that instrument witnessed also the unrestrained eloquence of Joseph Rayner Stephens. This reverend firebrand, whose biography has been written by George Jacob Holyoake, was not a Chartist. As a matter of fact, he seemed to care little for the political rights of the people so long as certain of their social and domestic rights were not infringed. But it was no fault of his that he did not plunge the land into fire and bloodshed. Speaking at Hyde on Nov. 14th, 1838, just after the Charter had been promulgated, he advised his hearers to "get a large carving-knife, which would do very well to cut a rasher of bacon or run the man through who opposed them."

Earlier in the same year (on January 1st) Mr. Stephens was in Newcastle. This is what he is reported to have said there:— "The people are not going to stand this (the New Poor Law), and he would say that, sooner than wife and husband, and father and son should be sundered and dungeoned and fed on 'skillee'—sooner than wife or daughter should wear the prison dress—sooner than that, Newcastle ought to be, and should be, one blaze of fire, with only one way to put it out, and that was with the blood of all who supported this abominable measure."

Mr. Stephens declared in the same speech—"He was a revolutionist by fire; he was a revolutionist by blood, to the knife, to the death. If an unjust, unconstitutional, and illegal parchment was carried in the pockets of the Poor Law Commissioners, and handed over to be slung on a musket or a bayonet, and carried through their bodies by an armed force or by any force whatever (that was a tidy sentence), and if this meeting decided that it was contrary to law and allegiance to the Sovereign—that it was altogether a violation of the Constitution and of common sense—it ought to be resisted in every legal way. It was law to think about it, and to talk about it, and to put their names on paper against it, and after that to go to the Guildhall and to speak against it. And when that would not do, it was law to ask what was to be done next. And then it would be law for every man to have his firelock, his cutlass, his sword, his pair of pistols, or his pike, and for every woman to have her pair of scissors, and for every child to have its paper of pins and its box of needles— (here the orator's voice was drowned in the cheers of the meeting)— and let the men, with a torch in one hand and a dagger in the other, put to death any and all who attempted to sever man and wife."

With such examples before them, it was not surprising that the Chartists also used violent language. Nor was it surprising, perhaps, that they went further, and conceived violent projects.

Violent projects were certainly conceived in many parts of the country. A plot was formed to seize Dumbarton Castle; Frost, Williams, and Jones endeavoured to raise an insurrection in Wales; there was even a scheme to burn down Newcastle. The story of the Tyneside episode is told by Thomas Ainge Devyr. The book in which it is recorded is rightly enough named—"The Odd Book of the Nineteenth Century." It was published by its author in New York in 1882. Patrick Ford had at that time accorded Devyr "the privilege of having letters addressed to him at the office of the *Irish World*." It was in that office in that year that I made his acquaintance. The acquaintance was renewed some years later, when Devyr, then a very old man, revisited the scene of the agitation in which he had taken an active part fifty years before. My old friend had led an adventurous life—in Ireland, in England, in America. He was a Nationalist in Ireland, a Chartist in England, a kind of revolutionist even in America. Anyway, he had only scorn and contempt for the politicians of America. "Democrats?" he said to me: "they call themselves Democrats, but they are all thieves." While in England, he served on the staff of the *Northern Liberator*—a Radical newspaper which had been established in Newcastle by Augustus Beaumont, a member of the Jamaica Legislature, but which was afterwards acquired by Robert Blakey, then a prosperous furrier in Morpeth, later a professor in an Irish College. Devyr, as a writer on the *Liberator* and the corresponding secretary of the revived Northern Political Union, seems to have written most of the turgid manifestoes of the party that appeared during 1838. Many are set out at length in his "Odd Book." It is clear, too, that he was closely associated with the sanguine or sanguinary men of the period—Thomas Horn, Robert Peddle, John Rewcastle, Dr. Hume, William Thompson, John Mason, Thomas Hepburn, James Ayre, Richard Ayre, John Blakey, Edward Charlton, and a blind orator named Cockburn—down to the time when he deemed it prudent to seek safety across the Atlantic. Now to his story.

Disturbances occurred in Birmingham early in August, 1838. "Then," says Devyr, "commenced the work of 'preparation,' and from that time to November we computed that 60,000 pikes were made and shafted on the Tyne and Wear." The number, he admits, would seem to be exaggerated. But—"I was present in some part of nearly every Saturday at the pike market, to take sharp note of the sales. The market was held in a long garret room, over John Blakey's clog shop in the Side. In rows were benches or boards on tressels, among which the Winlaton and Swalwell chain-makers and nail-makers brought in their interregnum of pikes, each a dozen or two, rolled up in the smith's apron. The price for a finished and polished article was two and sixpence. For the article in a rougher shape, but equally serviceable, the price was eighteenpence." Besides pikes and pike-shafts, caltrops, intended to be strewn over the roads for the purpose of laming the horses of the cavalry, were manufactured at Winlaton. On one occasion, as Devyr tells us, a case of fifty muskets and bayonets was imported from Birmingham. And shells and hand-grenades were manufactured to scatter destruction all around.

The conspirators meant business, or at any rate mischief. One of the orators had declared—"If the magistrates Peterloo us, we will

Moscow England." The secret organization, according to Devyr, took the form of classes of twelve, each with a captain, and all sworn to obey orders, maintain secrecy, and execute death upon traitors. "It was strongly urged that on the night of the 'rising' all the Corporation police should be slain on their beats." The outbreak was to begin on a Saturday night. But only seventy men out of ten times that number who had enrolled themselves gathered on the night preceding it. "Finding they were not in a condition for a stand-up fight, it was strongly urged that the torch should be resorted to." Newcastle was to be reduced to a heap of blackened and smoking ruins.

Meantime, news had arrived of the failure in Wales. It was resolved to await events. But the old desire for burning and bloodshed came back again. "We have resolved to do it," cried John Mason: "we must rouse the people by some desperate action, and the torch is to be the action." Devyr protested; but the conspirators informed him that "flame and combat would have full possession of Newcastle before midnight." All the same, the day dawned without disturbance, and soon afterwards the conspirators were either in flight or in hiding.

Such is the story of my Irish friend, Thomas Ainge Devyr. It is a story I have heard old Chartists dispute, and other old Chartists say they believe. Devyr concludes his narrative with the mention of two humorous incidents. One was that James Ayre, a builder to trade, declared when he was arrested that he would agitate no more in the old way, but for the time to come would "agitate the bricks and mortar." The other incident was that Robert Peddle, "a man of all work or any work," threatened Devyr and Rewcastle with the scaffold, because they would not furnish him with a horse and carriage to capture Alnwick Castle! The castle, Peddle averred, contained arms and treasure, while "its pastures were filled with just such rations as the revolutionary forces required." "A young butcher followed in his train for several days to take charge of this department!"

The spirit of violence, or rather to threaten violence, animated some of the physical-force Chartists long after the Newcastle conspirators had fled or been imprisoned. When George Julian Harney was nominated on the hustings at Wakefield against Lord Morpeth, an old friend of mine who was present describes the striking effect produced as a forest of oak saplings rose in the air in answer to the call for a show of hands for the Chartist candidate. Nor was it the Government alone that was apprehensive of disorder on the day of the memorable demonstration on Kennington Common. The fear was general that the great gathering would end in a deluge of blood. I remember reading in the newspapers of the time (and not without a glow of satisfaction on my own part) how an Irish orator had exclaimed that London would be in the hands of the Chartists on April 10th, and that that would be the signal for insurrection in all parts of the kingdom. A later friend of my own, I know, went armed to the gathering. Happily, neither he nor others had occasion to use their weapons. An echo of the trepidation among simple folks was heard as late as 1854. When a deaf old lady in Gateshead was alarmed by the great explosion of that year, she hurried away to her friends in Sunderland. Asked what was the matter, she replied: "Aa's afeared the Chartist bodies hev brokken lowse!"

CHAPTER XIX

THE FATHERS OF THE CHARTER

THE usual notion of an agitator is that he is a man with the "gift of the gab"—what the Americans call a spellbinder. But five of the six representatives of the Working Men's Association who assisted in framing the People's Charter were not platform people at all. None of the five—John Cleave, Henry Hetherington, William Lovett, James Watson, Richard Moore—made any pretence to oratory, and seldom appeared before the public in person. But every one of them was as thoroughly honest and single-minded as any similar number that ever entered a public movement. Moreover, they had all been concerned more or less intimately in the great struggle for a free press. Lovett, a born organizer, organized many political and social associations of an advanced character—advanced, I mean, for that time. Cleave and Hetherington were printers—Hetherington the printer of that *Poor Man's Guardian* which helped so much to establish the liberty of unlicensed printing. I had the honour of the acquaintance of Moore and Watson. Moore, married to a niece of Watson's, lived a life of industry and great domestic happiness in Bloomsbury, took an active part in the Radical affairs of the Borough of Finsbury, and served his day and generation effectually as the chairman of the committee of the Society for the Repeal of the Taxes on Knowledge. But of Watson, whom I knew intimately for twenty years, I must write at greater length.

James Watson was a native of Malton, where he was born in 1799. His mother, who was left a widow soon after he was born, obtained a situation at the parsonage, where she read Cobbett's Register and "saw nothing bad in it." James himself was apprenticed to the clergyman to learn field labour; but his indentures, owing to the reverend gentleman leaving Yorkshire for another part of the country, were cancelled before he had finished his time. Thereupon the youth set out for Leeds in search of friends and employment. While working in a warehouse, he too began to read Cobbett's Register and "saw nothing bad in it." Besides Cobbett's writings, he early made the acquaintance of other Radical literature of the day—Wooler's Black Dwarf and Carlile's Republican. He made the acquaintance also of some of the Radical politicians of Leeds. Richard Carlile was at that time fighting the Government for the right of free discussion. When the intrepid bookseller, his wife and sister, were thrown into prison, he appealed to his political friends in the country to come up and help him. Watson was the second volunteer who went from Leeds. For the heinous offence of selling publications of which the authorities did not approve, he was, as I shall have occasion to show, thrice condemned to imprisonment.

It was while assisting in the agitation for a free press that Watson learned the art of a compositor, in the office in which the *Republican* was printed. There was then in London, associated with all the fearless movements of that exciting time, a young man of rare talent and large fortune—Julian Hibbert. When Watson was attacked with cholera in 1825, Hibbert took him to his house, nursed him, and saved his life. After his recovery, Hibbert, who had set up a press of his own, employed him to print some works in Greek. Watson's friend and saviour, around whom there hangs a haze of mystery and romance that can never be penetrated, died early, leaving Watson his press and printing materials. With the help of Hibbert's legacy, after an interval of propagandism on behalf of the views of Robert Owen, the Yorkshire Radical commenced business as a printer and publisher on his own account. For something like a quarter of a century, assisted by his estimable wife, who was as devoted as himself to the propagation of Radical ideas, he sent forth a flood of the most advanced literature of the day. The works he issued were the classics of the working classes—such as Paine's "Rights of Man," Godwin's "Political Justice," Lamennais' "Modern Slavery," Volney's "Ruins of Empires," and Owen's "Essays on the Formation of Character." His little shop, too, was the rendezvous of Radical writers and thinkers. We shall see presently that he did not neglect other duties while attending to his own business. Watson contrived, by printing and folding as well as selling his publications, to make Radicalism pay its way. So that when he retired from the publishing trade in 1854 he had realised a small but sufficient competence.

Thereafter, with one or two exceptions, as when he assisted in 1858 to form a committee of defence for Edward Truelove, then being prosecuted by the Government for publishing an alleged libel on Louis Napoleon, he lived a life of quiet enjoyment and well-earned ease. Dying in 1874, he left behind him a name and fame that ought not, even by Radicals of a later era, to be allowed to perish or sink into oblivion. If I devote a little further space to recollections of James Watson, it is because the exposition will serve to elucidate the dejected condition of the press when he and other daring men of the period undertook its emancipation. Radicals of our day have had no experience, and can form but a poor conception, of the trials, difficulties, and privations to which the Radicals of a former generation were exposed. The struggle for an unstamped press was maintained with a courage and enthusiasm which almost excite one's wonder—which certainly arouse one's admiration—as its incidents are recalled to mind. It was the policy of the Government of that date to repress alike liberty of thought and liberty of speech. The former of these objects was sought by prosecutions for what were then called blasphemous and seditious publications; to attain the latter, no newspaper was allowed to be issued without a fourpenny stamp. Carlile, Hetherington, Cleave, and Watson, aided by a host of Radicals in the provinces—notably Abel Heywood in Manchester—fought the Government on its own ground. We have seen how Carlile, his wife and sister, were all in prison at one time. Carlile himself spent nearly ten years of his life in prison altogether. The number of his shopmen and assistants, men and women, who shared his fate, could be counted by the score. Hetherington, publishing his *Poor Man's Guardian* in defiance of the stamp law, brought another contingent for the Government to prosecute and imprison. No fewer than five hundred persons were sent to gaol in the course of three years and a half for selling the unstamped *Guardian* alone! Mr. Spring Rice, at that time Chancellor of the Exchequer, informed the House of Commons in 1836, that three hundred persons had been imprisoned in the course of a few weeks for selling unstamped papers in the streets, and that, too, without in the slightest degree decreasing the sale! Indeed, the gaols of the country were almost choked with political prisoners, when the Government, assigning as a reason the impossibility of enforcing the law, surrendered to the champions of a free press.

It was during this magnificent agitation that James Watson underwent his three imprisonments—twelve months in 1823 for selling Palmer's "Principles of Nature," six months in 1833 for selling the *Poor Man's Guardian*, and six months again in the following year for selling the *Conservative*, another of Hetherington's papers. What he suffered in these repeated incarcerations is told in the memoir which Mr. W. J. Linton wrote and published in 1880. Suffice it to say that he was "subjected to the same treatment as pick-pockets, swindlers, passers of bad money, committers of rape and other criminal acts of a like kind." It will perhaps surprise many who read what I am now writing that it was through such tortures as these, inflicted on hundreds of the best people in the country, that we eventually came into possession of an untaxed and unfettered press. Owing to the exertions of Watson and his comrades, the stamp duty was reduced from fourpence to a penny. But the agitation did not stop here, though it afterwards took another form. As everybody knows, or ought to know, the efforts of the Society for the Repeal of the Taxes on Knowledge resulted on the total abolition, not only of the stamp duty, but of the paper duty as well.

And now I may be pardoned a few words on the personal qualities of the man. James Watson had the purity of a saint, the spirit of a hero, the courage of a martyr. He was not only free from reproach— he was, like Cæsar's wife, above suspicion. The trying period during which he was most prominent was fatal to many reputations. It was an age of imputation. But nobody, from first to last, ever questioned Watson's sincerity. While lying in prison, he wrote to his wife that "the study of the cause and remedy for human woe engrossed all his thoughts." The man who thus wrote while surrounded by some of the lowest criminals of a metropolitan city had literally no ambition—none, at least, of a vulgar or even a personal sort. He neither cared for the platform nor sought reputation as a writer. It was his business and his pride to give currency to thoughts and opinions which were calculated, he believed, to improve and elevate mankind. From his shop, almost always in an obscure thoroughfare in the centre of the publishing trade, most of the Radical literature of the last generation was distributed over the country. But the work for which he will be best held in remembrance is the service he rendered to the cause of the freedom of the press.

The sixth member of the Working Men's Association which originated the People's Charter was Henry Vincent. And he differed from his five colleagues in that he was an orator, or at any rate a speaker who could, as it were, carry his audiences off their feet. Mr. Vincent, also a printer to trade, very early in life threw himself into the political agitation which then prevailed in the country. An earnest and impassioned advocate of the extension of the franchise, he was only about twenty-four years of age when he joined the committee which formulated the Charter. Of the movement which followed the promulgation of the demand for the famous six points, he was, as already mentioned, designated the Demosthenes. It was in that character that he denounced the Government of the day as a set of knaves. Using still stronger language at Newport, Monmouthshire, he was prosecuted and imprisoned in 1839. The riots in that town, for which Frost, Williams, and Jones were condemned to death, were alleged at the trial of the three prisoners to have had for their object, not an armed insurrection of the people, but the rescue of the Demosthenes of Chartism.

Reference has been made in a previous chapter to the suspicions that were entertained to account for the marked moderation in the tone of Vincent's speeches after he came out of Monmouth Gaol. So far as the change was ascribed to the effect of improper influences, I have not the least doubt that the imputation was absolutely unwarranted. Mr. Vincent had grown wiser in prison—that was all. It was no long time subsequent to his release that he turned his great talents as a speaker into other channels, though, I believe, he never altered his opinions as to the justice of the principles he had formerly done so much to spread abroad. Within a month of his restoration to liberty, he married a daughter of his old colleague, John Cleave. A man of fine presence, of powerful voice, of impressive delivery, Henry Vincent became one of the most popular lecturers of the day. Towards the end of the sixties he was lecturing in the Music Hall, Newcastle. I went to hear him. It was a fine performance—splendid as a piece of declamation, but neither pregnant with thought nor of much value as a literary effort. But the torrent of words, poured forth with the skill of a master, brought down thunders of applause. Henry Vincent died in 1879, save John Temple Leader the last survivor of the Chartist Fathers.

CHAPTER XX

JOHN FROST AND THE NEWPORT RIOT

JOHN FROST.
(From a contemporary engraving)

ONE of the most stirring events in the history of Chartism occurred at a very early stage of the struggle. I allude to the riot at Newport. The People's Charter was adopted at Newhall Hill, Birmingham, on August 6th, 1838. Within twelve months of that date Henry Vincent had been arrested in London, brought to Newport, tried at Monmouth, and sentenced to a year's imprisonment in Monmouth Gaol. Great was the excitement thoughout Wales, for the prisoner was a prime favourite in that quarter of the country. There were disturbances in Newport when he was brought there in custody, and there were disturbances again when he was brought before the magistrates. The popular excitement increased from the time of Vincent's conviction on August 2nd, till it culminated in an armed attack on Newport on November 4th. It is probable that the explosive character of the people of the Principality lent itself then, as it has lent itself frequently since, to turbulent proceedings. Be this as it may, Wales became for the time being the cockpit of the kingdom. And the name of the chief actor in the turbulent proceedings which marked the close of 1839 was for many years honoured and revered by the working people as no other name in England was.

John Frost, a prosperous linen-draper in the town, had been Mayor of Newport in 1836. Three years later he had so completely identified himself with the popular movement that he was one of the leading figures in the first Chartist Convention. Furthermore, he exercised great influence over the working people in the Welsh mountains. Associated with Williams and Jones, he put himself at the head of an operation which was presumed to have had for its object the overthrow of the constituted authorities, but which the legal defenders of the prisoners at the subsequent trial at Monmouth contended had no more serious design than the rescue of Vincent from prison. Miners and others, armed with muskets and pitchforks, descended from the mountains many thousands strong. The seizure of Newport by the Welsh Chartists, so the agents of the Government alleged, was to have been taken as a signal for the Chartists of the Midlands to rise in insurrection also. Whatever the intention, the attempt at Newport was an entire failure. A great storm in the hills delayed the march of the reputed insurgents, frustrated the intended surprise, and enabled the authorities to prepare for the defence of the town. But much blood was shed, and some dozen lives were lost, during the attack on the Westgate Hotel. Occupied by the mayor and magistrates, and defended by constables and soldiers, the hotel was never captured. Marks of the conflict, however, remained for years afterwards in the wooden pillars which supported the porch. When the hotel was rebuilt some years ago, the old pillars, pierced with bullet-holes, were considered of sufficient historic interest to be preserved in the hall of the new building. There they will probably remain for many generations to testify to the tragic scenes that were witnessed around them in 1839.

The leaders of the movement—Frost, Williams, and Jones—were arrested, tried for high treason, and sentenced to be executed. I remember my elders telling me as a boy the horrifying detail, that the condemned men could hear in their cells the noise of the carpenters erecting the gallows. The extreme sentence, however, was commuted to transportation for life. As a consequence of these occurrences, John Frost was regarded as a hero and a martyr throughout the Southern and Midland Counties. The three companions in adversity were despatched in a convict hulk with a cargo of other prisoners to a penal colony at the Antipodes. Fifteen years were spent by them among those unhappy culprits who in due course helped to found some of the settlements that have now become flourishing communities of free and honoured citizens.

First a conditional and then a free pardon having been granted to him and his companions, Frost returned to this country in 1856. It was a period of public apathy. An attempt was made to give him a popular reception. But by that time the Chartist movement had practically died out, Ernest Jones, with scarcely a shirt to his back, vainly striving to keep the cause alive. The exile had come back to a country that had almost forgotten him. Still there was a procession in London. I remember seeing it pass through Fleet Street. It was a sorry affair. What was worse, it excited the derision of the shopkeepers who bestowed any notice on it at all. Two or three hundred people at the most constituted what was intended for a great democratic demonstration. Poor Frost retired to Stapleton, near Bristol, whence he contributed to the *Newcastle Weekly Chronicle* fragmentary accounts of his experiences and sufferings, and there, nearly twenty years later, he died at a very advanced age.

But Frost's name and memory are still respected in Newport. Only a few years ago a later Mayor of Newport was presented with a watch that had been presented to Mr. Frost at the time he occupied the same position. And the new owner of the watch, as he informed the dinner-party at which it was handed to him, was present when the old Chartist was arrested. "John Frost," he added, "was a very clever fellow; but unfortunately he got carried away by his feelings until he lost himself." Though nobody doubts now, even if anybody ever doubted, that the project of the Welsh Chartists was utterly lacking in prudence and foresight, the man who led them and shared in their dangers must at least be credited with generous impulses.

The condition of our penal settlements was at that date indescribably horrible. Humane ideas in regard to the treatment of offenders had then hardly even begun to enter the minds of people in authority. After his return home, Mr. Frost endeavoured to arouse the attention of the public to the gravity of the ulcerous iniquities we had established in the southern hemisphere. For this purpose he published a pamphlet on the subject. Therein he described, as far it was permissible for any decent person to describe, the infinite horrors of convict life. I must have written to him about the publication, for I find a reply in a letter dated December 4th, 1873. "You tell me, my dear sir," he says, "that you have read my pamphlet with great interest. I cannot explain to you my feelings when I found the utter indifference to the state of society among the convicts and the cause which produced it. I sent this pamphlet to members of both Houses of Parliament, and the only notice taken was by a member of the House of Commons, who sent me the pamphlet back again." But the old Chartist's exposures may have had an effect of which the author was unaware. Certain it is, at any rate, that the system of transportation has long since been abolished, and with it have disappeared the penal settlements themselves. No more will any political or any other offender suffer tortures such as must have driven to distraction all but the coarsest and most degraded of the prisoners subjected to it.

I have said that some fragmentary papers of Mr. Frost's were published in the *Newcastle Weekly Chronicle*. They were the outcome of a suggestion that the venerable gentleman should write out his recollections of the exciting events in which he had taken part. "I have received your letter," he replied on December 4th, 1873, "and shall feel pleasure in complying with your request." The fragments already mentioned were the result. Then came the following letter, the handwriting of which betrayed no sign of age or weakness : —

STAPLETON, *Dec.* 15, 1873.

MY DEAR SIR, —I have received your letter and the *Chronicle* which accompanied it. I have seen no newspaper so full of useful and interesting matter. I shall be happy if I can to extend the circulation. I have for years been thinking on the subject of my long and suffering life, and I feel anxious that the circumstances should be placed before the public in a way likely to be interesting to the rising generation.

The plan I propose is this: —In the letter which I sent you I describe my situation after the escape from Newport, my return to the town, my apprehension, and my being placed in Monmouth Gaol. The next letter should contain an account of the trial, the verdict of the jury, the committal of myself and my companions to the condemned cell, what took place during our confinement there, our removal to Chepstow and passage to the *York* hulk at Portsmouth, our passage to Van Dieman's Land on the *Mandason* convict ship, our passage to the penal settlement at Port Arthur, my residence there as clerk to the magistrates, my transfer without any offence to one of the gangs, and other interesting matter connected with the treatment of the convicts and the terrible effects resulting from it. Then should follow an account of the various situations I filled in the colony for fifteen years, my conditional pardon, the voyage from Hobart Town to Callao, the voyage from Callao to America, my residence there for twelve months, my free pardon, and the events from 1856 to 1873.

I will endeavour to render the narrative instructive and amusing. However, one thing must not be forgotten. I am in my eighty-ninth year: therefore it can hardly be expected that the narrative will be such as a younger man would produce. A few weeks ago I had a terrible fall, which has shaken my mind and body terribly, and from the effects of which I shall not recover. My memory has suffered, but not as to past events: these are almost as fresh as ever. I am also much troubled about my eyes. I am apprehensive that I shall become a poor blind old man. May God avert it!

I am, dear sir, respectfully your obedient servant,

JOHN FROST.

The fears which crossed Mr. Frost's mind when he penned this letter were unhappily realised. I heard from him no more. Nor did any further instalment of the narrative he sketched for himself ever reach the *Chronicle* office. Mr. Frost died a few weeks later. It is much to be regretted that he did not live to complete the task he had planned. Had he so lived, many inaccurate statements that were made at his trial would have received authoritative correction, while much interesting light would have been thrown on a somewhat obscure phase of Chartist history.

CHAPTER XXI

FEARGUS O'CONNOR

FEARGUS O'CONNOR.
(From a contemporary engraving.)

SIR GEORGE CORNEWALL LEWIS once wittily said something to this effect, that life would be tolerable but for its amusements. Much in the same way, it might have been said that the Chartist movement would have been tolerably successful but for its leaders—some of them. There were many able men in the ranks—earnest and eloquent men. Some of them were earnest without being eloquent; a few, perhaps, were eloquent without being earnest. The great fault of all, more or less, was impatience—a desire to reap the harvest before they had sown the seed. Next to this fault was the disposition to quarrel. But quarrelling was almost inevitable when not one man, but many men, desired to become dictator's. It was almost equally inevitable when such a man as Feargus O'Connor, who had few of the qualities of a powerful leader save extraordinary force of character, had acquired absolute dominion over the cause. O'Connor quarrelled with all in turn—McDouall, O'Brien, Cooper, Harney. There were minor quarrels too—between Bronterre O'Brien and Ernest Jones, between Ernest Jones and Julian Harney, besides other rivalries among smaller men in the movement. And we of the rank and file took sides with one or the other—with fatal consequences, of course, to the movement itself.

The ascendency of Feargus O'Connor would have been unaccountable but for the fact that he owned the *Northern Star*. That paper, besides being the source of his power, was a sort of small gold mine to the proprietor. It was almost the only paper that the Chartists read, and it had in consequence a very extended circulation. Through it Feargus every week addressed a letter to his followers—"The blistered hands and unshorn chins of the working classes." The letter was generally as full of claptrap as it was bestrewn with words and sentences in capital type. But the turgid claptrap took. The people of that period seemed to relish denunciation, and O'Connor gave them plenty of it. Blatant in print, he was equally blatant on the platform. More of a demagogue than a democrat, he was fond of posing as the descendant of Irish kings. "Never a man of my order," he was in the habit of declaring, "has devoted himself as I have done to the working classes." It was his delight, too, to boast that he had "never travelled a mile or eaten a meal at the people's expinse." He even claimed in 1851 that he had spent £130,000 in the cause of the Charter. It pleased the working people to hear themselves addressed as "Fustian Jackets," "Old Guards," and "Imperial Chartists." Nor did it displease them when their leader assumed a royal title and called himself "Feargus Rex."

The reports of some of his speeches indicate the kind of fustian in which he now and then indulged. Here is part of what he is recorded to have said at a meeting in Palace Yard, Westminster, on September 17th, 1838:—

The people were called pickpockets. Now, he would ask, what difference was there between a rich pickpocket and a poor pickpocket? Why, there was this difference—the poor man picked the rich man's pocket to fill his belly, and the rich man picked the poor man's belly to fill his pocket. The people had borne oppression too long and too tamely. He had never counselled the people to physical force, because he felt that those who did so were fools to their own cause; but at the same time those who decried it preserved their authority by physical force alone. What was the position in which the working classes stood? Why, they were Nature's children, and all they wanted was Nature's produce. They had been told to stand by the old constitution. Why, that was the constitution of tallow and wind. The people wanted the railroad constitution, the gas constitution, but they did not want Lord Melbourne and his tallow constitution; neither did they want Lord Melbourne and his fusty laws. What they wanted was a constitution and laws of a railroad genius, propelled by a steam power, and enlightened by the rays of gas. They wanted a Legislature who had the power as well as the inclination to advance after the manner he had just pointed out. They wanted that the science of legislation should not stand still. The people had only to show the present House of Commons that they were determined, and its reform must take place. But still, such men as Sir Robert Peel and little Johnny Russell would try and get into it, even though they got through the keyhole. But it was said the working classes were dirty fellows, and that among them they could not get six hundred and fifty-eight who were fit to sit in the House of Commons. Indeed! He would soon alter that. He would pick out that number from the present meeting, and the first he chose he would take down to Mr. Hawes's soap factory; then he would take them where they should reform their tailors' bills; he would next take them to the hairdresser and perfumer, where they should be anointed with the fashionable stink; and having done that by way of preparation, he would quickly take them into the House of Commons, when they would be the best six hundred and fifty-eight that ever sat within its walls. He counselled them against all rioting, all civil war; but still, in the hearing of the House of Commons, he would say that, rather than see the people oppressed, rather than see the constitution violated, while the people were in daily want, if no man would do so, if the constitution were violated, he would himself lead the people to death or glory.

This was a specimen of Feargus's early style. Mr. Gammage has preserved a specimen of his later. Describing a speech delivered at the Hall of Science, Manchester, in August 1846, when he was fighting with other Chartists about his Land Scheme, Gammage says:—

While addressing the meeting, O'Connor hit upon every sentence calculated to rouse the hostility of his audience against his detractors, and to elevate himself. He told them he had the evidence of a respectable gentleman (whom he did not say), and also that of a boy, that at the *Examiner* office they were in league with navvies to assassinate him, which led to groans and cries of "Oh! the villains!" Again he said, "Villains who quaff your sweat, gnaw your flesh, and drink the blood of infants, suppose that I too would crush their little bones, lap up their young blood, luxuriate on woman's misery, and grow fat upon the labourer's toil." (Shouts of "No, never!" and waving of hats and hand kerchiefs.) "No, I could go to bed supperless, but such a meal would give me the nightmare; nay, an apoplexy." (Loud cheers, and "God Almighty bless thee!") "I have now brought money with me to repay every shareholder in Manchester." (Shouts of "Nay, but we won't have it!") "Well, then, I'll spend it all." (Laughter and cries of "Do, and welcome!") Again, he said, as an instance of his condescension, "It was related of the Queen, that when she visited the Duke of Argyle's, she took up the young Marquis of Lorne, and actually gave him a kiss, and this was mentioned as a fine trait in her character. Why, he (O'Connor) took up forty or fifty children a day and wiped their noses, and hugged them. (Cheers, and expressions of sympathy from the females in the gallery.) Did they think he was the man to wring a single morsel from their board, or to prevent their parents from educating and bringing them up properly? No, he was not: he loved the children, and their mothers also, too much for that." (A female in the gallery: "Lawk bless the man!") For more than three hours did O'Connor address the crowded and excited meeting, which was so densely packed before he commenced that the reporters had to be pushed through the windows into the hall.

It was considered curious that Feargus's visits to towns in the provinces generally synchronised with the appearance in the same towns of a lady who was then a star in the theatrical world. This lady was Mrs. Nisbett. There was as much gossip in Chartist circles about the two as there was in Irish circles forty or fifty years later about Mr. Parnell and Mrs. O'Shea. O'Connor himself does not seem to have made much secrecy of the relations between himself and the actress; for in a letter to a person who had helped him at the Oldham election, dated August 28th, 1835, he sent his best regards to the man and his wife, "in which Mrs. Nisbett begs to join." The alliance, such as it was, was probably consecrated by some measure of affection, since it was stated that the lady, when O'Connor had to be removed to a lunatic asylum, left the stage, and nursed and tended him as long as he lived.

The common notion of O'Connor outside the ranks of his personal followers was that he was a charlatan and a humbug—an adventurer who traded on the passions of the people for his own profit and advantage. A correcter notion would have been that he was a victim of his own delusions. It is certain that he did more than any other man in the movement—more probably than all the other men in the movement put together—to ruin the Chartist cause. But this is not to say that he was dishonest. The Land Scheme which he grafted on to the demand for political reform was one of the wildest and maddest schemes that ever entered into the mind of a rational being. It was doomed to disaster from the very beginning, and it brought loss and disappointment upon all who touched it. The originator of the scheme, however, was the greatest sufferer, for he lost his reason. The fact that the failure had this terrific effect may perhaps be regarded as at least some evidence of the man's sincerity.

The melancholy fate of Feargus O'Connor was, I think, hardly more melancholy than that of another Irishman who figured prominently in the Chartist agitation. James Bronterre O'Brien was "a Chartist and something more." It seemed to him that political reform was less important than agrarian reform and currency reform. The doctrines he taught on these latter subjects made him an authority among a small school of Chartists. But poor Bronterre ended his days as a loafer in Fleet Street. It was there that I used to see him towards the close of his career—shabby, snuffy, beery. A good speaker even to the last, he was in demand at the Cogers and other debating halls of the Metropolis. For opening a discussion in a pothouse, he was rewarded with five shillings and his night's liquor. Another O'Brien shone or flickered in the same arenas. And of him or of Bronterre—I am not sure which—a wit of the period parodied Tennyson:

And I saw the great O'Brien sloping slowly to the West.

CHAPTER XXII

TWO DOCTORS AND A SCHOOLMASTER

THE more conspicuous of the early leaders of the Chartists (next to those already mentioned) were John Taylor, Peter Murray McDouall, Thomas Cooper, and George Julian Harney. The two first were Scotchmen, both members of the medical profession, and both advocates of what were called "ulterior measures."

Dr. Taylor, a native of Ayr, was arrested in Birmingham, during the sitting of the first Convention in that town, for alleged participation in the Bull Ring Riots of 1839. Harney describes him as looking like "a cross between Byron's Corsair and a gipsy king," with "a lava-like eloquence that set on fire all combustible matter in its path." It was said that he had inherited a fortune of £30,000, the greater part of which he spent on revolutionary enterprises. Insurrections in Greece and conspiracies in France were alike in his line. A picturesque figure was Dr. Taylor. Hardly less picturesque was Dr. McDouall, whose long cloak and general style helped to give him the appearance of a hero of melodrama. McDouall also was often in trouble with the authorities. Subsequent to 1848, he settled down to the practice of his profession in Ashton-under-Lyne. But not for long. Agitation had unfitted him for a regular life. Friends subscribed funds to enable him to emigrate to Australia, where, according to a sworn statement of his widow, he died "about May, 1854." That Dr. McDouall was a man of some taste and culture may perhaps be gathered from the following lines, written to the air of the "Flowers of the Forest" while he was a prisoner in Chester Castle, previous to 1840:—

> Now Winter is banished, his dark clouds have vanished,
>   And sweet Spring has come with her treasures so rare;
> The young flowers are springing—the wee birds are singing,
>   And soothing the breast that is laden wi' care.
>
> But loved ones are weeping—their long vigils keeping—
>   The dark prison cell is the place of their doom;

The sun has nae shining to soothe their repining—
　　To gild or to gladden their dwellings of gloom.

To them is ne'er given the loved light of heaven,
　　Though sair they are sighing to view it again;
Though fair flowers are blowing, in full beauty glowing,
　　They flourish or fade for the captives in vain.

And thus are they lying—in lone dungeons dying—
　　The sworn friends of freedom—the tried and the true;
By slow famine wasted—life's bright vision blasted—
　　'Tis Summer's prime shaded by Winter's dark hue.

In vain are they wailing—nae tears are availing,
　　But tyrants exult o'er their victims laid low,
Or look on unheeding, though life's race is speeding;
　　Their fears will depart with the death of their foe.

But I look not so proudly, and laugh not so loudly,
　　Nor dream that the struggle of freedom is o'er;
Your prisons may martyr the chiefs of our Charter,
　　But the bright spark it kindled shall burn as before.

And Winter is coming, wi' wild terrors glooming,
　　To weaken the sunbeam and wither the tree;
The loud thunder crashing—the red lightning flashing,
　　Are the might of a people resolved to be free.

No more remarkable testimony to the exciting character of the decade from 1839 to 1849 can be adduced than the fact that almost every man who rose to prominence in the Chartist ranks during that period came under the lash of authority. Thomas Cooper was no exception to the rule. Either the Chartists were too much given to violent language and threats, or the magistrates and judges were too much given to a stringent interpretation of the law. We owe to Cooper's incarceration, however, that remarkable prison poem, the "Purgatory of Suicides." First a shoemaker, then a schoolmaster, afterwards a newspaper reporter, the author of the "Purgatory" had reached what might well be called the years of discretion before he plunged into the stormy waters of Chartism. While serving as reporter on a Leicester journal, he came to learn the miseries of the Leicester stockingers. Also, in his official capacity, he came to attend Chartist meetings. The two experiences combined to drive him into the Chartist whirlpool. From reporting Chartist lectures he came to deliver Chartist lectures himself. Before long he was the acknowledged leader of the Leicester Chartists. Somehow, he associated Shakspeare with Chartism, and gave to his particular society the name of the bard. Other eccentricities could probably at this time have been laid to his charge. But the charge which caused him to be prosecuted in the first instance was that of having preached arson at Hanley. Acquitted on this count, he was afterwards prosecuted for sedition and conspiracy, receiving sentence of two years' imprisonment. When he had served his time and written his poem, he varied his speeches for the Charter with lectures on literary, critical, and historical subjects. Among his lectures was a series on Strauss's "Leben Jesu," then just translated by Marianne Evans, better known later as George Eliot. I remember to this day the strange effect which the reading of the summary of these discourses produced on a youthful and unsettled mind. The summary appeared in *Cooper's Journal*, a weekly periodical of much greater value than the common run of Chartist publications. But the lecturer did not himself long remain steadfast to the views he expounded. As he had changed from piety to rationalism, so he changed from rationalism to piety again. And the rest of his long and active life was spent in preaching the Gospel to all the earth that he could reach.

Thomas Cooper had the "defect of his qualities." I have given one example of his irritability. Many others were known to his friends. Indeed, he was quite unfit for controversy. This he came to acknowledge himself: so that all through his later career as a lecturer and preacher he systematically declined discussion. Warm in his friendships, he was bitter in his animosities. An old comrade has recorded how, while he was still on good terms with O'Connor, he broke off in a speech he was delivering in Paradise Square, Sheffield, to lead the crowd in singing the Chartist song:

The Lion of Freedom has come from his den;
We'll rally around him again and again!

When he quarrelled with the Lion of Freedom, as he did soon afterwards, he was as impassioned in denunciation as he had before been in praise.

But Thomas Cooper had other qualities that redeemed his defects. Innumerable instances of his kindness and generosity are recorded. It is a loving trait in his character that he never forgot or neglected any old friend whom he knew to be living in any of the towns he visited during his later peregrinations. These peregrinations continued till he was near or past eighty years of age. When his work was done, and just before he died at the venerable age of eighty-eight, he received a grant of £200 from the public funds. The grant was made on the application of Mr. A. J. Mundella, then member for Sheffield, one of his earliest political converts at the time he was leading the Leicester Chartists. Close upon a quarter of a century before his demise in 1892 (that is to say, in 1868) he corrected an erroneous report respecting himself in an amusing letter to the *Lincoln Gazette*:—"The Nottingham papers say I am dead. I don't think it is true. I don't remember dying any day last week, though they say I died at Lincoln on Tuesday. 'Lord, Lord,' as Falstaff said, I how the world is given to lying!"'

Thomas Cooper, besides being a preacher and lecturer of no mean ability, was a man of marked literary eminence. Poet, essayist, novelist, he was also the author of a model biography. "The Life of Thomas Cooper, Written by Himself," published twenty years before he died, is so admirable a piece of work that it will keep alive his fame for years and years to come. But it contains one passage which does not, perhaps, do justice to his reasoning powers. It is a passage in which he claims that his life was once saved by what seemed like a special intervention of Providence. When on his way from London to fulfil an engagement in the provinces, and about to enter a railway carriage at Euston Station, he was induced by a porter to take a seat in another part of the train. The carriage which he did not enter was smashed to atoms in a collision, the people in it being killed or maimed, while the carriage which he did enter was in no way injured! Thomas Cooper left it to be inferred from his narrative that Providence had interposed to save his life.

The story is as little credible as another story of a similar kind about Bishop Wilberforce—Wilberforce of Oxford and Winchester. One night, so this latter story runs, the Bishop was returning home from his club. A man's figure passed him in the street, ran up the steps to his front door, and then suddenly turned round and faced him. The man's figure was his own. Back went the Bishop to his club instead of entering his house. Next morning he heard that a chimney-stack had fallen through the roof on to his bed!

CHAPTER XXIII

GEORGE JULIAN HARNEY

NO leader of the Chartist movement left behind him a fairer record than George Julian Harney. He was the last survivor of the National Convention of 1839. John Frost lived to a greater age than Harney; but he was an older man when he associated himself with the agitation. Frost died at eighty-nine, Harney at eighty-one. Frost had reached years of maturity at the time of the Convention; Harney was only twenty-two. It is likely that he was the youngest member of that notable assembly. When he died in 1897, there died with him a fund of information about the exciting political events in which he had taken part that can now never be supplied.

GEORGE JULIAN HARNEY.
(From a photo taken in 1886.)

It was the eventful struggle against the Newspaper Stamp Act—a struggle which filled the common gaols of the country with earnest men and women—that first drew Harney into politics. He was then sixteen years of age. For three years afterwards he was in the very thick of the Unstamped fight. The battle raged most fiercely around the *Poor Man's Guardian*, which, as Henry Hetherington announced on the title-page, was "published in defiance of law, to try the power of Right against Might." Harney was twice thrown into prison for short terms in London. His offence was that of selling the *Poor Man's Guardian*. Then he went to Derby to commit the same "crime." "One Saturday evening," he wrote, "at a court hastily, unusually, and for all practical purposes privately held, I was sentenced to pay a fine of £20 and costs, or go to prison for six months." He underwent the imprisonment; but the pains of it, as he gratefully recorded, "were somewhat mitigated by the humane intervention of the late Mr. Joseph Strutt—an honoured name—then Mayor." The revolt of the people—for it was a revolt—was, as already narrated, completely successful.

Three years after the imprisonment at Derby the agitation for the People's Charter was in full swing. Notwithstanding his youth, Harney was sufficiently well known throughout the country to be elected one of the delegates for Newcastle to the Convention of 1839. The proper title of that body—for it is as well to be particular in historic matters—was the General Convention of the Industrial Classes. The delegates for Newcastle—Robert Lowery and Dr. Taylor were Harney's colleagues—were "elected at a large open-air meeting in the Forth on Christmas Day, 1838, which meeting was attended by deputations, in some instances processions, from the district on both sides of the Tyne." Among other extravagant things that Harney seems to have favoured was the "sacred month." It was one of the "ulterior measures" the Convention discussed when the House of Commons had rejected the National Petition for the Charter. All the delegates from Newcastle supported it. But the scheme was foolish, and, being foolish, failed—though it is fair to point out that the old Chartists differed from all later strikers in this, that they sought nothing for themselves alone, and that the sacrifices they proposed to make were intended to achieve objects that would, as they believed, benefit the nation at large.

Harney had the reputation of being a fiery orator. He was certainly consumed with enthusiasm. It was almost impossible for such a man at such a time to avoid coming into collision with the authorities. Two such collisions occurred—first in 1839, for a speech at Birmingham; the second in 1842, for taking part with fifty or sixty others in a convention at Manchester. For the Birmingham speech Harney was arrested in Northumberland, handcuffed to a constable, and taken back to Warwickshire. The arrest took place at two o'clock in the morning. There were fewer railway facilities in those days than there are now, accounting for the circuitous route the captors pursued with their prisoner. First a hackney coach from Bedlington to Newcastle; then the ferry across the Tyne to Gateshead; then the rail from Gateshead to Carlisle; then the stage coach over Shap Fell to Preston, at that time the terminus of the North-Western Railway; and finally the train from Preston to Birmingham. But the police in the end had all their trouble for nothing, since the grand jury at Warwick declined to find a true bill against their prisoner. Harney was next arrested at Sheffield for the Manchester business. The trial of the fifty or sixty Chartists was held at Lancaster in March, 1843. Harney was appointed by his comrades to lead the defence. This he did with so much energy and eloquence that O'Connor, in the published report of the trial, bore the following testimony:—"It would perhaps be invidious to point particular attention to the address of any individual where all acquitted themselves so well; but the speech of Harney will be read with peculiar interest, and fully justifies the position which he occupied as first speaker." But this trial was abortive, too; for, though the prisoners, or some of them, were found guilty, the Court of Queen's Bench afterwards pronounced the indictment bad.

Meantime, Harney had gone through his first Parliamentary contest—if such a term can be given to encounters in which never a vote was given to the Chartist candidate. Lord Morpeth, afterwards Earl of Carlisle, was in 1841 seeking the suffrages of the electors of the West Riding of Yorkshire. Harney was nominated in opposition. The nomination took place at Wakefield. It has already been mentioned that an extraordinary effect was produced when, in response to the call for a show of hands for the Chartist, a forest of oak saplings rose in the air. But Harney's great feat in the candidate line was in opposing Lord Palmerston at Tiverton in 1847. Nominated by a Chartist butcher named Rowcliffe, he delivered a vigorous criticism of Lord Palmerston's foreign policy in a speech two hours long. The "judicious bottle-holder," as the noble lord was called, is said to have confessed that his policy had never before been subjected to so searching an examination. Nor did he forget his old opponent. Years afterwards, when somebody was soliciting subscriptions in the lobby of the House of Commons for Chartists in distress, Palmerston asked about his "old acquaintance, one Julian Harney." Being told that Harney was in America, he replied: "I hope he is well; he gave me a dressing at Tiverton, I remember." The contest at Tiverton was remarkable, inasmuch as the opposition candidate, though he went to the poll, did not receive a single vote. The borough returned two members, and the result of the election is thus recorded in the Parliamentary Poll Book:—

John Heathcote (Liberal)	148
Viscount Palmerston (Liberal)	127
George Julian Harney (Chartist)	0

Besides lecturing and agitating in all parts of the country, Harney was busy with journalism. He was first sub-editor and then editor of O'Connor's paper, the famous *Northern Star*. When, owing to a disagreement with O'Connor, he severed his connection with the *Star*, he started periodicals of his own—first the *Democratic Review*, then the *Red Republican*, and then the *Friend of the People*. I was a subscriber to them all. Also he founded in 1849 a society called the Fraternal Democrats. I had always voted for Harney as a member of the Chartist Executive, and now I joined the Fraternal Democrats. A letter to him on the subject brought about an acquaintance which, becoming more and more intimate as the years advanced, lasted till his death—a period of nearly half a century. The collapse of the Chartist movement drove Harney to other ventures. From 1855 to 1862 he was editing the *Jersey Independent*. Then he betook himself to America, where he remained till, broken in health, he settled down at Richmond-on-Thames to struggle and die. It was under his cheerful and untiring guidance that I saw the sights of Boston in 1882. He was then living at Cambridge, not far from the "spreading chestnut tree" under which the "village smithy" stood, nor far from the house of Longfellow himself. The old Chartist had adorned his home in Massachusetts, as he did afterwards his apartments at Richmond, with portraits and relics of the poets he loved, of the patriots he admired, and of the friends and colleagues with whom he had worked—Shakspeare, Byron, Shelley, Burns; Kosciusko, Kossuth, Mazzini, Hugo; Cobbett, Oastler, Frost, O'Connor; Linton, Cowen, Engels, Marx. Some of the portraits are now mine. Among the relics was a handful of red earth from the memorial mound of Kosciusko at Cracow.

It was Harney's opinion that the art of letter-writing was dying out. He himself, however, did his utmost to keep it alive. Hundreds of his letters, now lying in lavender, testify to his epistolary industry — all characteristic and all long, some long enough to fill a newspaper column. In his letters as in his private intercourse, he was an incorrigible joker. He joked even about his ailments and his agonies. For years he was a martyr to rheumatism. As far back as January, 1884, he wrote me from Cambridge, U.S. :—"I am 'all in the Downs.' The rheumatism in the shoulder less painful (of late), but always there. But my understandings wuss and wuss—especially my feet. By Heaven! the man with the peas in his shoes hardly had a worse time of it. That ass might have boiled his peas; but there is no such resource for me. Aching, burning, shooting, and other varieties of pain; and no sham pain either—as West [18] would say, 'not a blessed dhrop.' " Closing a longer account of his increased infirmities ten years later, he sardonically exclaimed: "Oh! what a piece of work is man!" While residing at Richmond as the guest of a daughter of another old Chartist agitator, though he was wracked and twisted and helpless, he amused everybody with his jests. Mrs. Harney, who had a profitable connection as a teacher of languages in Boston, had to let him come to England alone. Once, when she had crossed the Atlantic to stay with him, she took him out in a Bath chair. Loud were his jokes with the chairman. "Oh, Julian!" cried Mrs. Harney. "Ah!" said the servant-maid to the hostess, "Mrs. Harney doesn't know Mr. Harney as well as we do!"

All his sufferings notwithstanding, he was able to the very last to write or dictate admirable contributions to the *Newcastle Weekly*

Chronicle. These contributions were generally on books—not formal reviews, but discursive comments on authors and their works, interspersed with delightful touches of personal experience. It is not a matter of feeling, but of fact, that one of the most effective pieces written in 1896 on the centenary of Burns's death came from Harney's pen. Occasionally he diverged into politics. Here he aroused both anger and enthusiasm—anger in one party, enthusiasm in another. The Editor had as much as he could do to keep the peace among his readers when Harney had his fling at Mr. Gladstone. The old Chartists hated the Whigs more than they hated the Tories. Much in the same way, Harney disliked the Liberals more than he disliked the Conservatives. It was not quite easy to account for his intense rancour against Mr. Gladstone, whom he called, not the Grand Old Man, but the Grand Old Mountebank. The mention of Mr. Gladstone, even after he was dead, seemed to have the same effect as a red rag is supposed to have on a mad bull. Yet the veteran was judicious and impressive when he discussed political principles instead of political parties. A testimonial was presented to him shortly before he died. Replying to the deputation which presented it, he thoughtfully said: "We have not now so much to seek freedom as to conserve it, to make good use of it, to guard against faddists who would bring us under new restrictions as bad or perhaps worse than the old." For the rest, he expressed his philosophy of government in the pregnant lines of Byron :

I wish men to be free,
As much from mobs as kings, from you as me.

The last days of the old Chartist were rendered as happy and as comfortable as his pains and his helplessness would allow by the devoted attentions of his wife. That lady, sacrificing her professional business in America, came over to nurse him to the end. When that end came, there passed away from earth no worthier citizen or braver spirit than George Julian Harney.

CHAPTER XXIV

THE LATER CHIEFS OF CHARTISM

THE history of the-Chartist movement is divisible into two periods—the period before and the period after 1848. During the former period, the movement was, speaking generally, gaining strength; during the latter, it was unmistakably losing it. Some of the leaders whose names are familiar to the student of politics were connected only with the earlier phase of the agitation; others were connected with both its earlier and its later phases; others, again, came into it only when the popular fervour for the Charter was transparently declining.

The most noted of the later leaders was undoubtedly Ernest Jones. Like Thomas Cooper, Ernest Jones plunged into the agitation, not as a youth, but as a man of mature years. Feargus O'Connor claimed descent from an Irish King; Ernest Jones was the godson of a German King. The royal favour was bestowed upon the younger chief of Chartism while his father was serving as equerry at the Court of Hanover. The family did not return to England till Ernest had already given indications of those poetic and literary talents which he afterwards so abundantly displayed. The fiery and sympathetic spirit of the youth had also been shown in an attempt to assist the insurgent Poles. Although he was educated for the law and was admitted to the Bar, he had no need to pursue the profession till late in life. Certain land speculations of his, however, cost him his fortune. It was then that he joined the Chartists. Mr. George Howell has told the story of these transactions in a series of articles that were published in the *Newcastle Weekly Chronicle*. The narrative, based for the most part on a singularly bald diary kept by Ernest Jones, leaves the impression, whether well or ill founded, that Chartism would not have gained its conspicuous recruit if his speculations in land had not terminated disastrously.

But Ernest Jones made up for his late entrance into the movement by the enthusiasm and even violence of his advocacy. It came about that he shared the fate of all the other leading spirits of Chartism: he was prosecuted and imprisoned. No consideration was at that time shown to political prisoners, and less than usual was shown to Ernest Jones. The indignities he suffered, however, neither damped his ardour nor curbed his tongue. But he could not keep alive a dying cause. A last flicker of the candle occurred when it was proposed to establish a *People's Paper* under the joint editorship and control of Harney and Jones. The proposed editors quarrelled; the scheme came to naught; Harney quitted the field; and his rival was left with a feeble and squalid following to carry on what remained of the agitation. Ernest Jones kept the old flag flying till he was almost starved into surrender. When near its last gasp, he was in the habit of addressing open-air assemblages on Sunday mornings in Copenhagen Fields, now the site of Smithfield Cattle Market. I walked from a distant part of London, through miles of streets, to hear him. It was during the Indian Mutiny. The old fervour and the old eloquence were still to be noted. But the pinched face and the threadbare garments told of trial and suffering. A shabby coat buttoned close up round the throat seemed to conceal the poverty to which a too faithful adherence to a lost cause had reduced him. A year or two later even Ernest Jones had to confess that Chartism was dead. He turned his attention again to the law, settled in Manchester, and was soon on the road to acquiring a lucrative practice.

Then came his great discussion on Democracy with John Stuart Blackie, the famous professor of Edinburgh. It was about this time that I saw and heard him at Newcastle Assizes. Josiah Thomas, a botanical practitioner who was highly respected in the town, was charged with some technical error. Ernest Jones was retained for the defence. The defence was so well managed that the accused, much to the gratification of the general public, was honourably acquitted. Not long afterwards, just when he was on the point of being chosen one of the members for Manchester, Ernest Jones died. Before this sad and sudden event occurred, it is satisfactory to know that Harney and Jones, comrades in a great fight, had become reconciled.

Ernest Jones was a poet: so was Gerald Massey, the Felix Holt of George Eliot's novel. But Gerald Massey was more fortunate that

Ernest Jones in the attentions he received from authority; for while Jones was prosecuted by one Government, Massey was favoured with a pension from another. There was nothing dishonourable in either transaction, so far as the recipients of punishment or pension were concerned. It was Massey's poetry that won the kindly notice of the advisers of the Crown. The poet was very young when he caught the fever of revolutionary politics. Poor as he was, he yet found means to start a revolutionary paper—the *Uxbridge Spirit of Freedom*. If it did not live long, that was not because it had not merit enough to entitle it to live. Unfortunately, the Chartist movement, when Gerald Massey joined it, was in a moribund condition. But he made his mark in it before it died. Harney was publishing his *Red Republican*, one of the best of his literary ventures. There appeared in it some verses in praise of Marat that seemed to ring like a trumpet. They were written by the Hon. George Sydney Smythe, afterwards Lord Strangford. Harney had copied them from a work entitled "Historic Fancies." No young Revolutionist could have read them without a thrill. Far greater was the thrilling sensation when the verses were dramatically recited. Gerald Massey used to recite them at Chartist meetings. A friend of mine who had heard him described the effect as magical. But the poet not only declaimed the inspiring poems of others: he wrote inspiring poems of his own. One of these, appearing in Harney's publication, led on to fortune. It is Harney who tells the story. I had a long letter from him in 1884—as long as this chapter—written from Cambridge, Boston, Massachusetts, where I had enjoyed his hospitality two years before. The letter is full of characteristic humour—as, indeed, all his letters were. The humour is notable even in the way he relates how Gerald Massey came to attract the notice of the authorities:—"Hepworth Dixon had no umbrella. Taking refuge from the rain in a news-shop doorway, he saw the *Red Republican*. He bought a copy, and read Gerald Massey's 'Song of the Red Republican.' That introduced Massey to the *Athenæum*. The *Athenæum* introduced Massey to good society. Lord Alfred and Lady Beatrice were struck by the beauty of the poetry and the face of the young R.R.; and so, and so, at last a pension." The poet has enjoyed the pension for many years, has devoted much of his time since to inquiries into mystic subjects, but did not forget his old comrade when a testimonial, mainly promoted by the Editor of the *Newcastle Weekly Chronicle*, was presented to George Julian Harney on the anniversary of his eightieth birthday.

The founder of *Reynolds's Newspaper* was better known to the public of his day as a writer of romances than as a political leader. Yet he came to the front as a Chartist chief subsequent to the ferment which the Revolution of 1848 caused all over the Continent. George W. M. Reynolds occupied about the same position in English literature as Eugene Sue occupied in French literature. The stories he published dealt mainly with mysteries and scandals, especially mysteries and scandals of courts and society. To a certain extent he was before his time. The reading public in the middle years of the century thought his romances coarse and vulgar, and left them to the appreciation of the patrons of penny numbers. With the taste for sensation and salacious details which the modern novelist and the modern dramatist have cultivated, it is not at all unlikely that he would, if he had flourished at the end of the century, have been admitted to the hierarchy of fiction. It was understood that he was the son of an admiral, and that he had wasted a fortune of ten thousand pounds in the attempt to establish a daily newspaper before he found his vocation as the author of highly-flavoured tales. *Reynolds's Miscellany* was a popular periodical when the excitement produced by the French Revolution encouraged its proprietor to undertake another adventure. This was *Reynolds's Political Instructor*, to which Bronterre O'Brien and other Chartists and Democrats contributed, and in which the portraits and biographies of prominent Chartists and Democrats were printed every week. *Reynolds's Political Instructor* was the forerunner of *Reynolds's Weekly Newspaper*. Reynolds himself came then before the public in person, made speeches on Chartist platforms, and was elected a member of the Chartist Executive. I do not think, however, that any large number of Chartists accepted him seriously. O'Connor and O'Brien, Jones and Harney, all had their followers; but Reynolds had no such distinction. Indeed, it was rather as a charlatan and a trader than as a genuine politician that G. W. M. was generally regarded by the rank and file of Chartism.

The movement was already fast declining when Thornton Hunt, George Jacob Holyoake, and William James Linton began to take an active interest in its fortunes. Hunt was less of a Chartist than a

Littérateur, Holyoake less of a Chartist than a Socialist, Linton less of a Chartist than a Republican. The election of all to the Chartist Executive failed to save the cause. R. G. Gammage and James Finlen were still lecturing in the provinces; but George White, John West, and James Leech seemed to have dropped out of the running. The Executive consisted of nine members. Of these nine members on January 1st, 1850, only two or three are remembered even by name now:—Thomas Brown, James Grassby, Thomas Miles, Edmund Stallwood, William Davies, G. J. Harney, John Milne, G. W. M. Reynolds, and John Arnott. An election later in the same year gave the following result:—Reynolds, 1,805; Harney, 1,774; Jones, 1,757; Arnott, 1,505; O'Connor, 1,314; Holyoake, 1,021; Davies, 858; Grassby, 811; Milne, 709. Not elected:—Hunt, 707 ; Stallwood, 636; Fussell, 611; Miles, 515; Le Blond, 456; Linton, 402; Wheeler, 350; Shaw, 326; Leno, 94; Delaforce, 89; Ferdinando, 59; Finlen, 44. Thornton Hunt was elected subsequently, but Bronterre O'Brien, Gerald Massey, and Thomas Cooper had declined to stand. It will be noted that the highest vote in 1850 was 1,805, indicating that the number of active members of the National Chartist Association was probably not more than two or three thousand. In 1852, however, even this small membership must have fallen off one half, for the highest vote recorded then was only 900. Four new names appear in the list of the Executive for that year—those of W. J. Linton, John Shaw, J. J. Beezer, and Thomas Martin Wheeler. Anthony came to bury Cæsar, not to praise him. The new members must have come to bury Chartism, not to praise it. Funds were falling short, too. The subscriptions for the first quarter of 1852 amounted to no more than £27—hardly sufficient to pay the secretary's salary, not to speak of office expenses, with never a penny for printing or propagandism. The Chartist movement was indeed dead, though neither then nor later was there any formal burial.

But the movement could not in one sense be considered to have failed. The principles embodied in the Charter have been at least partially recognised. The suffrage has been extended; the property qualification has been abolished; vote by ballot has been enacted; and the anomalies connected with electoral divisions have been rectified. Payment of members and annual Parliaments are really the only two of the six points of the Charter that yet remain untouched. The changes effected in the law, however, are less remarkable than the changes effected in public sentiment. People who have not shared in the hopes of the Chartists, who have no personal knowledge of the deep and intense feelings which animated them, can have little conception of the difference between our own times and those of fifty or sixty years ago. The whole governing classes — Whigs even more than Tories — were not only disliked, they were positively hated by the working population. Nor was this hostility to their own countrymen less manifest on the side of the "better orders." More or less of the antagonism here indicated continued down to the death of Lord Palmerston. Then a transformation was worked in the sentiments of the great body of the people. Thanks to the political earnestness, but still more to the political intrepidity, of later statesmen, working men, enfranchised by household suffrage, commenced for the first time to associate themselves closely and actively with the orthodox parties in the State. We still have our disputes; we still differ materially in opinion on questions of the day; we still prefer Mr. Balfour to Sir Campbell-Bannerman or Sir Campbell-Bannerman to Mr. Balfour; but we are no longer, in the sense we once were, two nations.

CHAPTER XXV

A ROMANCE OF THE PEERAGE

DURING the whole period of the Chartist agitation, and indeed for years before and after it, the representation of Cheltenham was controlled and practically owned by the Berkeleys. But who were the Berkeleys? The answer to that question is a romance of the peerage that has frequently been recounted before the law courts.

The romance begins towards the end of the eighteenth century. Berkeley Castle, the Berkeley estates, and the Berkeley earldom were held in 1784 by Frederick Augustus, the fifth Earl of Berkeley. Frederick Augustus seems to have been a rake of the first water. The evidence adduced at the several trials to establish the claim to the earldom leaves no doubt on that point. Nor does the lady whom he married after many years of illicit connection appear to have been a model of virtue. The lady was Mary Cole—called by the common folk Moll Cole—the daughter of a Gloucester butcher. Mary, as well as at least one of her sisters, fell an easy prey to the blandishments of rank and wealth. Both were no doubt attractive in person, and both became the mistresses of men of fashion. Susan figures only in the chronicles of scandal; but Mary, owing to the attempts that were made to prove that she was married to the Earl of Berkeley eleven years before she actually was married, figured also in the chronicles of the law. None of these discreditable facts would perhaps have become public property if the illegitimate products of Mary's misalliance had shown the same respect for the honour of their mother as the eldest of her legitimate sons did.

Mary Cole gave birth to several sons before she became Countess of Berkeley. William Fitzhardinge Berkeley, afterwards Earl Fitzhardinge, was the eldest of these sons. Among the others were Henry Fitzhardinge Berkeley, member for Bristol, the mover of an annual resolution in favour of the Ballot; Craven Fitzhardinge Berkeley, member for Cheltenham, but not otherwise notable; and Maurice Fitzhardinge Berkeley, an Admiral of the Fleet and member for Gloucester, who, on the death of his elder brother, was elevated to the peerage as Baron Fitzhardinge. There were also legitimate sons of the connection between Mary Cole and the fifth Earl of Berkeley, for the couple were married at St. Mary's, Lambeth, in 1796. The eldest of these legitimate sons was Thomas Moreton Fitzhardinge Berkeley, while another was Grantley Fitzhardinge Berkeley, who made some little noise as a novelist and a writer of books on sporting matters. When the fifth Earl of Berkeley died in 1810, William, the eldest son, who had sat in the House of Commons as Viscount Dursley, claimed the earldom, but, as the result of a great trial in 1811, failed to sustain the claim. Some years later, probably for political reasons, Colonel Berkeley, as William came to be called, was created first Baron Segrave and then Earl Fitzhardinge. The eldest of the legitimate sons of the Earl of Berkeley, Thomas Moreton Fitzhardinge Berkeley, chivalrously declined to claim the peerage and property because it would have been necessary, in order to establish his title, to asperse the character of his mother. The earldom at his death went, therefore, to a distant kinsman, a descendant of the fourth Earl of Berkeley. The ruling of the House of Lords in 1811 was confirmed, after another and last trial, by the House of Lords in 1891. Many extraordinary facts adduced in the case were recited by the Lord Chancellor in delivering the final judgment of the law.

A desire seems to have entered the minds of the Earl and Countess of Berkeley, somewhat late in life, to make out that they had been secretly married in Gloucestershire in 1785, eleven years before they were admitted to have been married in Lambeth. To bolster up this claim there were believed to have been tamperings with the parish register of Berkeley, the earl himself, it was alleged, having had a hand in the forgeries. But Mary Cole, according to her own testimony, was at the very time when the banns of marriage were said to have been published at Berkeley (published, by the way, in an inaudible voice by the officiating clergyman) living in Kent in the service of a Mrs. Foote. Other evidence of the butcher's daughter, contravening the pretensions she subsequently set up, was given at second hand by the Rev. John Chapeau. Mary Cole at the period of the conversation to which the reverend gentleman testified was known as Miss Tudor, the mistress of Lord Berkeley. Mr. Chapeau, taking shelter from the rain in Miss Tudor's house in London, found her discharging a servant who had come from the country, and trying to persuade her to return to her friends. The girl refusing, "saying she liked to stay in London better," Miss Tudor remarked to Mr. Chapeau that "a girl with a good countenance, and dismissed from service without money, would be sure to fall a prey to some man or other." And then she added that she had once been in a similar situation herself.

The story Miss Tudor thereupon related to Mr. Chapeau, as given in Mr. Chapeau's evidence, is one of the most extraordinary, that was ever told, even at second hand, in a court of law. Being discharged and destitute, so she is said to have said, she at first found refuge in the house of a friend of her mother's. The kindness she received there, however, was not long continued; for the gentleman, fearing scandal, informed her that she must go down to her friends in Gloucester. So she was turned adrift with a present. Mary had two sisters in London, one of whom, Ann Farren, was living in dirt and penury. The other sister, Susan, she had been enjoined by her mother never to speak to again. But she was so distressed at the miserable circumstances in which she found Ann Farren, and so reluctant to remain in her house, that she resolved to disobey her mother. And now comes the most wonderful part of the narrative she is alleged to have imparted to Mr. Chapeau:—

I went to my sister Susan's, took up the knocker, and gave a loud rap. Who should come to the door but (as if it had been on purpose) my sister Susan herself, dressed out in all the paraphernalia of a fine lady going to the opera? She took me into her arms, carried me into the parlour, and gave me refreshment; began to tear a great many valuable laces of 16s. a yard to equip me for the opera, and when I was so dressed I looked like a devil. I went to the opera, and was entertained with it, and at night returned again to my sister's; and there I found a table well spread, not knowing that my sister ever had any fortune. At that table were Lord Berkeley, Sir Thomas Kipworth, I think a Mr. Marriott, and a Mr. Howarth. The evening went off very dull, and they soon left the place. The next night we went to the play in the same manner and returned in the same manner, and with no other difference than a young barrister, whom I thought agreeable, and if I had been frequently with him should have liked him very much. When they went away, I requested my sister to give me a cheerful evening that we might recount over our youthful stories. The day was fixed, and our supper consisted of a roast fowl, sausages, and a bowl of punch. In the midst of our mirth a violent noise was heard in the passage, and in rushed two ruffians, one seizing my sister by the right hand and the other by the left, trying to drag her out of the house in order to carry her to a sponging-house.

The rest of this amazing story is given in Mr. Chapeau's own words:—

She told me the men declared they would not quit Susan, her sister, unless they received a hundred guineas. She fainted away; then, when she came to herself, she found Lord Berkeley standing by her sister Susan who was not there before. Miss Tudor fell upon her knees, and desired my Lord Berkeley to liberate her sister; that she had no money to do it herself, and, if he would do it, he might do whatever he would with her own person. He paid down a hundred guineas; the ruffians quitted their hold; and my lord carried off the lady. "Mr. Chapeau," she concluded, "I have been as much sold as any lamb that goes to the shambles."

Strange and almost incredible as this narrative is, it was accepted by Lord Eldon in 1811, and was not questioned by his successor eighty years later. Further, as the Lord Chancellor of 1891 remarked, not only was Lady Berkeley not called to contradict it, but evidence was given by the Marquis of Buckingham that corroborated it. Lord Berkeley told him, the marquis deposed, that "he had got hold of Mary Cole in London, and that he had paid a large sum of money for her." The Marquis of Buckingham's story was in other particulars hardly less astounding than that of Mary Cole. The Earl of Berkeley, he said, was afraid, from the circumstances of his family, that the castle and honour of Berkeley would be severed from the title. To avert this catastrophe, as he thought it, he entertained the idea that his brother's son, who would probably inherit the title, should marry his (Lord Berkeley's) illegitimate daughter. The child who was thus to be bartered was at the time only three years old. But the device, as the Lord Chancellor explained, was not pursued, not because of the infancy of the girl, but because she died before it could be accomplished.

Gossip was making free with Lord Berkeley's affairs even before Lord Berkeley died. Thus Lady Jerningham, whose correspondence was published in 1896, wrote from Brighton in 1806: —

Lady Berkeley was a Housemaid, but always a Virtuous Woman. Lord Berkeley's Fancy for Her was so Imperious that he resolved upon regular matrimony. After a time, Repenting of this measure, he prevailed on the Clergyman to tear the Leaf out of the Register that witnessed his being a married man. But then again Regret Came, as a Child had arrived every year, so He married the same Maid again; and the fourth Son was Supposed to be the inheritor of his title. But soon after, the Clergyman who had first tied Him in Wedlock dyeing, He then declared the date of his previous marriage and proclaimed that his first Born Son was Lord Dursley. He Could not Say this during the Clergyman's Life, as the tearing the Register is Felony. So all this made a sad work, but Lord Thurlow declared there is not a doubt but that the first marriage was Legal, and the Eldest Son is accordingly Stiled Lord Dursley.

The sons of the fifth Earl of Berkeley, legitimate and illegitimate, washed a lot of their dirty linen in public. William, the eldest son, was, like his father, a desperate rake, and made his house at Cheltenham—where he lived at one time with the wife of Alfred Bunn, the "poet Bunn" of Drury Lane—the centre of many scandals. [19] A fascinating Don Juan he must have been too; for it was said that prudent mammas made it a point of sending their daughters away when his lordship came to town. Nevertheless, it was the custom to ring the bells of the parish church when Lothario paid his periodical visits to German Cottage. Moreover, he propitiated the fashionable classes by providing stags for them to hunt and hounds with which to hunt them. But it came to pass one day that the parish bells were silent when Earl Fitzhardinge honoured the place with his presence. Loud was the clamour which arose, especially as about the same time the nominee of Berkeley Castle was rejected by the electors. The august patron of the borough, we were told, would withdraw his patronage; his house and furniture would be put up to auction; the glory of German Cottage would be no more. As a matter of fact, he did for a season refuse to supply the stags for the hunt, and imperiously demanded that the hounds should be at once returned to Berkeley Castle. A furious quarrel broke out among the brothers also. Grantley, who figured conspicuously in the quarrel, was member for one of the divisions of Gloucestershire. As I remember him, he was a tremendous dandy. It was during the general election of 1847, when Grantley Berkeley had revolted against his brother, and when Grenville Berkeley, a cousin of his, was set up in opposition, that the family's dirty linen was washed in public. Grantley, in spite of his dandified appearance, or perhaps because of it, was the more popular candidate ; anyway, he carried the election against Grenville. [20] The political literature of the time, however, throughout the whole constituency of West Gloucestershire was besmirched with personal scandals.

The story of the Berkeley family, interesting as a romance of the peerage, is not without interest also as exemplifying the enormous political influence which territorial nobles, notwithstanding the scandal of their private lives, exercised in England even after the Reform Bill of 1832.

CHAPTER XXVI

OLD ELECTION PRACTICES

THE Ballot is said to have robbed the general election of all its colour and picturesqueness. It is true. An election now is a humdrum affair—tame, featureless, devoid of bustle and animation. Of course I am speaking comparatively. Very different were political contests when every man knew how every other man voted, when candidates had to stand the ordeal of the hustings, when the state of the poll was declared every hour of the day, and when the victor was carried in triumph round the constituency that had chosen him. But these were the days, too, when all manner of evils were rampant—bribery, treating, intimidation, and violence. After all, the old contests are pleasanter to remember than they were to witness.

Preparations for a contest were commenced, as a rule, long before the contest itself would occur. Party paraphernalia, indeed, were generally ready to be produced the moment they were wanted. This especially was the case when aristocratic families supplied hereditary candidates, as the Berkeleys did in Cheltenham. The Berkeleys were Whigs, and the Whig colours were orange and green. Flags and banners of these tints, and bearing the old Whig mottoes and devices, were brought forth to do duty at every election, and stowed away at the end of it in readiness for the next occasion. They made a brave show, these flags and banners, as they were borne aloft through streets and squares. Bands of music and processions of partisans accompanied them in their peregrinations. Night after night for weeks before the nomination the town was kept alive with party clamour. Blue was the Tory colour; but as the Tories were not so well organized as the Whigs, and, moreover, had no hereditary candidates, we usually saw fewer of their banners and heard fewer of their bands. Party tunes were not numerous, but they were sufficiently distinct and lively to set the rival partisans at loggerheads. "Bonnets of Blue" was the favourite tune of the Tories, "Old Dan Tucker" that of the Whigs. Fights were frequent, while dissipation was general. Black eyes and broken heads were more numerous at election times than at peace meetings in war times. Terrible were the ructions when two processions met, particularly in a narrow street, and when neither would give way to the other. On these occasions, banners and trumpets, with the heads of the men who carried or blew them, came to general grief. They were stirring times, I tell you, the election times of other days.

The first formal business of the election took place in the open— before all the people. This was the nomination at the hustings. The hustings in our case were erected in Sandford Fields—a half-private, half-common piece of property on the outskirts of the borough. There a great structure of wood, divided into compartments for the opposing candidates and their friends, with a compartment for the returning officer and his assistants between them, was set up ready for the interesting function. The supporters of the Whig candidate, all with favours and many with banners, bands of music accompanying them, assembled opposite the Whig compartment. The supporters of the Tory candidate, distinguished in a similar way and cheered by similar devices and strains, arranged themselves opposite the Tory compartment, so that a sharp line divided the two forces. When the candidates appeared, wild shouts of approval or hostility greeted them from the crowd beneath. Nor these only; for rotten oranges and rotten eggs, and occasionally harder but less unsavoury missiles, shot across the neutral zone to discompose one or other of the parties on the hustings. The returning officer having opened the proceedings, the proposers and seconders of the candidates stepped forward, each being applauded by his own side, but howled at by the other. This formality performed, often in dumb show, the candidates themselves essayed to address the free and independent electors. Meantime, there were free fights where the frontiers of the two crowds joined. But the speaking was at length ended, though hardly a word had been heard. And then the returning officer took a show of hands. A mere formality this, also, for the proposer of the candidate who lost it generally demanded a poll. All was over for the day, except shouting and fighting, band-playing and processioning with banners. Chartist candidates were often nominated, not with the idea of going to the poll, which would have been useless in the then state of the franchise, but for the purpose of making a speech, which pleased the populace at all times. Mr. R. G. Gammage was so nominated at Cheltenham in 1852. But as no compartment was provided for the Chartists on the hustings, he and his proposer and seconder were invited to speak from the place reserved for the returning officer. Gammage's speech was good—we sent a deputation to thank him for it afterwards—but the show of hands was not on this occasion in favour of the Chartist, as it usually was on the like occasions in other boroughs, but in favour of the Tory candidate.

It should have been said that the sharp electioneerer had done a good stroke of business for his candidate before the rival parties had been gathered round the hustings. Canvassers, messengers, watchers, and so-called workers of all sorts had been engaged at high rates to assist in the election. The number of persons—all voters—appointed to these posts far exceeded the requirements of the candidate. But there was method in the extravagance. It was simply an effective form of bribery. The canvassers and messengers and watchers who were of real service in the contest were early astir on the morning of the poll. Indeed, the confidential men of the party had been at work all night—securing their own voters or spiriting away the voters of the opposite side. For, be it known, there was a great art in corruption. It was not enough to buy a vote : the main thing was to see that the vote was recorded for the right man. The cleverest electioneerer was the electioneerer who could bribe or bottle up the biggest number of the enemy's supporters. And it was in nefarious practices such as this that much of the night preceding the poll was spent. Free breakfasts and free beer were the order of the polling day. The candidate who was niggardly in providing these comforts for the electors was voted shabby, and was generally defeated. Yes, a contested election was a royal time for the mercenary, the corrupt, the creatures without conscience. Even hired bravoes were sometimes paid to keep the rival intimidators in check—loafers, pugilists, ruffians of every degree. A noted prize-fighter was engaged to supply a band of men of the same stamp as himself for one of the candidates at a Sunderland election, because there was a rumour that the like thing was being done on the part of the other candidate. When the fight was over and the noted prize-fighter was being paid for his services, he quietly informed the election agent that it was he who had set the rumour afloat!

But the poll has been opened. Exciting scenes took place round the polling booths. Voters were brought up—sometimes in batches, sometimes in single file. There was no doubt as to how they voted, for their names and the disposition of their suffrages were inscribed in the poll books. If popular feeling, stimulated by popular treating and popular largesses, happened to run high, the free and independent elector had to run the gauntlet of a turbulent mob. Whether the voter had been bribed or not, he had still before him the risk of intimidation, especially if he should have had the courage to wear the unpopular colours. Fights of course were frequent in the neighbourhood of the polling booths. Nor were they less frequent, perhaps, around the centres at which the hourly returns of the state of the poll were exposed. These hourly returns were the cause of great excitement and speculation—never allayed all day till the last vote had been recorded and the last return had been issued. Then came the declaration of the poll—another lively performance, though the partisans of the losing candidate generally left the field to the partisans of the victor. Next day the successful candidate was chaired—that is to say, carted in triumph round the constituency. The most animated and picturesque chairing I recollect occurred in 1847. The Tories that year made a tremendous effort to win the seat. Sir Willoughby Jones was brought from Norfolk to perform the trick. Money was spent as it had been spent in no previous election. Every man who had a vote and was willing to sell it was passing rich for many days after, not to say gloriously drunk also. As, in addition, the Norfolk baronet was a presentable candidate— handsome, gracious, and a fair speaker—he succeeded in ousting the sitting member, the Hon. Craven F. Berkeley, who had sat for the borough ever since its enfranchisement in 1832. The jubilation of the Tories found expression in the ceremony of chairing. A brewer's dray, covered with blue cloth, surmounted by a throne upholstered in blue silk, was drawn by a team of brewers' horses caparisoned in blue trappings. Aloft was seated in imperial pomp and isolation the victorious favourite, also arrayed in all the glory of the party colour, smiling and bowing in acknowledgment of the loud hozannas of the crowd below and around. The march through the town, with bands blaring and banners waving, was a memorable spectacle. The Tories that day painted the town blue. But the triumph, as we shall see, was but short-lived.

The election usually ended with the chairing of of the candidate, unless, as happened in 1847, there was a petition against his return, in which case the venal voter got a chance of a free trip to London, and free entertainment while there, with of course a handsome *douceur* besides, in order to testify before a committee of the House of Commons to the scandalous conduct of the agent who had corrupted him. If the petition was dismissed, all was over save paying the piper. But if the candidate was unseated, and the constituency was not disfranchised, another election took place, though on this occasion, should the agents have become more cautious, there was less treating and less bribery, and consequently less violence and debauchery. The triumph of the Tories in 1847 was, as I have said, short-lived. Their candidate was unseated in the following year, when a new election was held. This time it was the turn of the Whigs to crow, and the turn of the Tories to petition. A local brewer, Mr. James Agg-Gardner, who had been nominated by the Tories in 1841, was selected once more to contest the seat against Mr. Craven Berkeley. The decision of the previous year was reversed in 1848. Again there was a petition, and again the petition was successful. Mr. Craven Berkeley was unseated. Another election was held—the third within two years. Mr. Grenville Charles Lennox Berkeley, nominated in the place of his cousin Craven, won the seat and held it for four years. Then the old rivals confronted each other again, with the result that Berkeley Castle resumed its dominion. Thereafter a Berkeley succeeded a Berkeley for many years—almost down to the time when Whig and Tory both changed sides.

Sir Willoughby Jones died at his seat, Cranmer Hall, Norfolk, in 1884. Mr. Ruskin was writing his autobiography, "Præterita," in 1885. Some of his school-fellows came up for mention and judgment, among them "A fine, lively boy, Willoughby Jones, afterwards Sir W., and only lately, to my sorrow, dead." It was announced at his death that the old Cheltenham candidate had long ago joined the Liberal party, "with which he remained identified to the close of his career." Two years later another conversion was announced. The newspapers of August, 1886, proclaimed it thus: "The Berkeley family, whose residence is the historic castle of that name in Gloucestershire, has for generations been noted for its strong support of the Liberal cause. This state of things has now been altered, Lord Fitzhardinge, the head of the Berkeleys, having accepted the post of president of the Tewkesbury Conservative Association." These were not the only transformations that have been witnessed since the forties and fifties. Whigs have become Liberals; Tories have become Conservatives; Liberals and Conservatives have become Unionists. The hustings have disappeared; successful candidates are no longer chaired; constituencies are not now debauched; voters are seldom either bribed or brow-beaten. Here, again, the old order hath yielded place to the new. The political conditions described in this veracious chapter are matters—of ancient and almost forgotten history.

CHAPTER XXVII

IDEAL REPUBLICANISM

CHARTISM was not satisfying. We were Chartists and something more—we young men of Cheltenham. What that something more was we probably could not at first, if we had been asked, have clearly defined. The Charter, as a declaration of rights, was excellent. It covered the whole ground of political demand. But popular power proclaimed—what then? Even if roast beef came the day after, it would be but a sorry triumph. A pitiful life, indeed, is that which is content with beer and skittles. Higher aspirations entered our heads, suffused our thoughts, coloured our dreams. "Happiness," we had been told, "is a poor word: find a better." We were trying to find a better. Some of us were Democrats, pledged to afford material help and sympathy to the struggling peoples of the Continent. George Julian Harney had founded the movement, which had for its organ a monthly publication, edited by himself, called the *Democratic Review*. This was better. But we longed for something better still. We had found a programme, but we wanted a religion. It came to us from Italy.

Another of Harney's publications bore a fierce and defiant title—the *Red Republican*. We did not like the title. It savoured of blood. Also it seemed to suggest a return of the Reign of Terror, with new Marats and Couthons to horrify the world. We were Republicans, but not Red Republicans. The title was altered to the Friend of the People. The paper was the same, though the name was changed. No paper then published so satisfied our longings for an ideal. Presently there appeared in it a series of articles in exposition of the principles of Republicanism. The writer was W. J. Linton, poet, artist, propagandist. The scheme Mr. Linton put before his readers was based on a proclamation which the Central Democratic Committee had issued to the peoples on the organization of Democracy. The proclamation, dated London, July 22nd, 1850, was signed by Joseph Mazzini, as representing Italy; Ledru Rollin, as representing France; Albert Darasz, delegate of the Polish Democratic Centralization; and

Arnold Ruge, member of the National Assembly at Frankfort. It was the work of Mazzini, the greatest teacher since Christ. As a declaration of principles, I do not hesitate to say that it is loftier, broader, and more enduring than even the Declaration of Independence. The Declaration of Independence was meant for a nation: the Proclamation to the People was meant for mankind. Let me quote a few of its inspiring passages:—

We believe in the progressive development of human faculties and forces in the direction of the moral law which has been imposed upon us.

We believe in association as the only regular means which can attain this end.

We believe that the interpretation of the moral law and rule of progress cannot be confided to a caste or to an individual, but ought to be confided to the people enlightened by national education, directed by those among them whom virtue and genius point out to them as their best.

We believe in the sacredness of both individuality and society, which ought not to be effaced, nor to combat, but to harmonise together for the amelioration of all by all.

We believe in Liberty, without which all human responsibility vanishes:

In Equality, without which Liberty is only a deception:

In Fraternity, without which Liberty and Equality would be only means without end:

In Association, without which Fraternity would be an unrealisable programme;

In Family, City, and Country, as so many progressive spheres in which man ought to grow in the knowledge and practice of Liberty, Equality, Fraternity, and Association.

We believe in the holiness of work, in its inviolability, in the property which proceeds from it as its sign and its fruit:

In the duty of society to furnish the element of material work by credit, of intellectual and moral work by education:

In the duty of the individual to make use of it with the utmost concurrence of his faculties for the common amelioration.

We believe, to resume, in a social state, having God and His law at the summit—the People, the universality of the citizens, free and equal, at its base—progress for rule, association as means, devotion for baptism, genius and virtue for lights upon the way.

And that which we believe to be true for a single people we believe to be true for all. There is but one sun in heaven for the whole earth : there is but one law of truth and justice for all who people it.

The authors of the proclamation proceeded in the same document to apply to nations the principles they had laid down for individuals:—

We believe, in a word, in a general organization, having God and His law at the summit—Humanity, the universality of nations, free and equal, at its base -common progress for end, alliance for means, the example of those peoples most loving and most devoted for encouragement on the way.

The French Revolution had deified Right, which, in a narrow and restricted sense, meant selfishness, indulgence, mere material comfort. It was reserved for Mazzini to preach the higher doctrine, Duty, which meant sacrifice, service, endeavour, the devotion of all the faculties possessed and all the powers acquired to the welfare and improvement of humanity. The Duties of Man, in the great Italian's conception of the revolutionary programme, were the necessary accompaniment of the Rights of Man. Rights, indeed, took a secondary place, being only, as the proclamation set forth, "the results of accomplished duties"—of value only as enabling nations as well as individuals to fulfil their obligations to each other.

153

Decorations are worthless shams that are not the symbols of honours bravely won. So are rights the reward of enterprise and valour: nor reward only, but the means and opportunity of doing our special work in the world, helping the weak, consoling the afflicted, encouraging the reliant, paying tribute to virtue and genius. This exalted idea runs all through Mazzini's teachings; but it is perhaps best expounded in his masterly treatise on the "Duties of Man." It found expression in his private letters as well as in his public writings: it was part of himself; and it is the legacy he left to mankind. "Life," he wrote to Henry Vincent, "life is a mission, not a seeking for happiness." And the humble followers of Mazzini adopted his motto of "God and the People," and drew solace from the old Puritan consolation—"Let it not grieve you that you have been the instruments to break the ice for others: the honour shall be yours to the world's end."

The exposition of the greatest democratic document of the century fell upon the minds of some of the young men of the period like fertilising rain upon a parching soil. Here was the "something more" for which they had been yearning. Here, indeed, was a doctrine that deserved their devotion. Here, in a word, was the religion for which they were longing and pining and praying. Yes, they were Republicans—these ardent youths—with a more definite notion of what the word implied than the mere rejection of monarchy. The Republic, as they understood it, was not so much a form of government as a system of morals, a law of life, a creed, a faith, a new and benign gospel. Uneffaced—perhaps ineffaceable too—is the recollection of the thrill of delight that the revelation caused. And when the author, at the close of his papers, asked all who approved of the principles he had expounded to communicate with him at Miteside, Ravenglass, Cumberland, the young enthusiasts rejoiced to believe that a chance might be given them to participate in a propaganda that would and must end in the redemption of the world.

The scheme put before them was that they should in their different localities form associations for the "teaching of republican principles." It was an educational, not a revolutionary work, to which they were summoned. Along with a small band of ardent youths in the town, I entered eagerly into the scheme—how eagerly, and with what temerity and conceit, may be surmised from the fact that I accepted the post of president of the local society months before I was out of my teens. Part of our method of procedure was to hold family meetings, after the manner of the old Methodists. These meetings, held weekly in the homes of the members, were intended for instruction as well as propagandism. The works of the revolutionary leaders were read and discussed; candidates for membership were examined; the prospects of the cause abroad and at home were pondered; plans were devised for making our ideas known by personal canvassing and the circulation of tracts; and occasionally essays by the members themselves on some point of doctrine or practice were produced for consideration and debate. Old Chartists looked askance at our proceedings, called us foolish striplings, and would have nothing to do with us. When Ernest Jones, on a visit to the town, was asked what he thought of the movement, he replied that it was just another division in the ranks, and as such calculated to impede the general advance of the popular cause. But we were never strong enough to impede anything; for our rules were so strict and our demands on the understanding of our associates were so exigent that our total strength at the best of times could not have exceeded a score. I have indicated that candidates for admission to our society had to undergo an examination. It was no formal examination either. We insisted that they should thoroughly comprehend the principles that they were going to teach. It was not enough that they should call themselves Republicans: we demanded that they should give good reasons for the faith that was in them. There was therefore a catechism which all candidates were required to master. So our comrades were few. I find in an old diary for May, 1851, the following statement on the subject:—"Our numbers have augmented considerably, amounting to twelve or thirteen members, with great hopes of getting more." But we were not only few in numbers—we were miserably poor in purse. A report of a family meeting held in April of the same year records that "sixpence by voluntary contribution was gathered." As a matter of fact, we were as poor as the Apostles, and not much more numerous. Still, small as was the contingent we could muster, we were young, earnest, and enthusiastic, and, what was more, we knew we had got an idea which would regenerate mankind if mankind would only accept it. One does not need to say that the time for that acceptance seems as far off as ever.

CHAPTER XXVIII

THOUGHT AND ACTION

MAZZINI had taught us that "every divorce between thought and action is fatal." Wherefore to the best of our modest means we acted upon our thoughts. The idea of Fraternity was as sacred to us as any other of the ideas expressed in our republican formula. And Fraternity, if it meant anything, meant the offer of such help as we could give to the struggling peoples of the Continent. Help, however, by the time of which I am writing, could only take the form of comfort and protection for the exile.

The Revolution, of February had been followed by insurrections in almost all the countries of Europe—in Venice and Vienna, in Rome and Berlin, in Pesth and Dresden. But all had failed, so that the last state of the peoples was worse than the first. The struggle in Hungary was longest sustained. We, who had followed with absorbing interest the varying fortunes of the Magyars, and had read with unbounded delight of the valiant feats of Bem and Dembinski, were cast into the depths of dismay when we heard of the surrender of Georgey and the flight of Kossuth. All was over. Despotism had once more triumphed. Even France had chosen an adventurer who was afterwards to seize her by the throat. It was no longer possible to encourage insurgents in the field. The duty that now devolved upon us was to clothe and feed the refugees who had sought our shores. They came in great numbers—Poles and Hungarians chiefly. Every man of them was a hero, and every one of them was destitute. If ever sympathy was demanded, it was for these victims of fate and tyranny.

My first contribution to the press was written at this time—May, 1851. It was an appeal on behalf of the fugitives who had been landed in Liverpool. The printing of that letter produced an exaltation that no similar honour has ever produced since. An American authoress (Louisa M. Alcott) has described her own feelings when she read that a little tale of hers was going to appear in a Boston paper—one of the "memorable moments " of her life. She was on her way to school. "It was late; it was bitter cold; people jostled me; I was mortally afraid I should be recognised; but there I stood, feasting my eyes on the fascinating poster, and saying proudly to myself, in the words of the great Vincent Crummles, 'This, this is fame!' That day my pupils had an indulgent teacher; for while they struggled with their pothooks, I was writing immortal works." My own "memorable moment" is still fresh in recollection. It seemed to me that everybody must have read that letter, that everybody must be talking about it, that everybody must be looking at the author as he passed down the street. Nor could there be any doubt that ample provision would now be made for the destitute refugees. What else, I asked myself, could be the result of that eloquent supplication of mine? Alas! we were too poor in Cheltenham to do more than supplicate. All the same, we gave much anxious thought and deliberation to the project of taking charge of at least one of the exiles.

Friends of freedom were active in the same cause in other parts of the country. Committees were formed in many of the large towns to raise funds and locate the soldiers who had fought and failed on the plains of Hungary. There was a public meeting in Newcastle, with Sir John Fife in the chair, and Mr. Joseph Cowen as the chief speaker. But the principal committee was established in Liverpool, with James Spurr as secretary. A small publication, called the *Refugee Circular*, issued from time to time between April 16th and August 19th, 1851, gave particulars of the disposal of the unfortunates. From a complete collection of these circulars, still preserved, I gather that the North of England provided for no fewer than fifteen, some of whom became afterwards well known in Newcastle and Gateshead. One of them, Constantine Lekawski, was for years connected with the Tyne Ferry Company, but returned to Poland in 1870 and died there; another, Marian Plotnicki, rose to a good position in the firm of Hawks, Crawshay, and Co. Away in Gloucestershire we could render no such help; but we did the next best thing—we subscribed to the utmost of our small means to save the exiles from want and beggary.

Other foreigners came in later years to need our assistance—notably men who had fought with Garibaldi in Rome. Red Shirts, indeed, were at one time as numerous as Poles in England. Italy had claims on our sympathy as strong as Poland. And these claims were kept constantly before the people by the publications of the Society of the Friends of Italy. There was a Society of Friends of Poland, too, with Lord Dudley Stuart at its head; but it, unfortunately, laboured under the imputation of favouring only the exiled aristocracy of that country. No such disability affected the Italian association. Mazzini had won the admiration and the confidence, not only of his own compatriots, but of many hundreds of conspicuous Englishmen. There were, in fact, countrymen of ours who were as devoted to him as any native of Italian soil. Mr. Sidney Milnes Hawkes, relating how he once undertook a dangerous mission to Paris, assured me that he and others had at that period so little doubt of Mazzini's absolute wisdom and judgment that they would almost have slain their own kindred if he had told them to do it. The Friends of Italy comprised many persons eminent in learning and literature who did not ordinarily concern themselves with the politics of the day. Douglas Jerrold, David Masson, George Dawson, Walter Savage Landor, Francis William Newman—these are some of the names I can recall. And then there were life-long associates with the work which Mazzini was prosecuting—Joseph Cowen, James Stansfeld, and Peter Alfred Taylor. We in Cheltenham were members of the society also. Then and often afterwards we sent our small contributions to Mazzini's special funds—the Shilling Subscription for European Freedom, the loan to the Universal Republican Alliance, and so forth. But the influence of the Friends of Italy far exceeded the value of the funds they could collect; for there came a time when the very policy of England seemed to be affected by it. When, for instance, Garibaldi made his descent upon Sicily, it was the fortuitous interposition of a British squadron between the Austrian fleet and the Thousand of Marsala that saved the expedition, and so permitted the liberation of Southern Italy.

There were occasions, especially during the reign of Louis Napoleon in France, when the claim of England to offer an asylum to the fugitives from oppression appeared to be in danger. On all such occasions we were instant in protest or denunciation. Out of our scanty means we contrived to print little tracts or leaflets, which we distributed wherever and whenever we had opportunity. One of these tracts or leaflets, written by the present writer, was entitled the "Right of Refuge." It was a vigorous attempt to warn the public of the possible demand that would be made upon the British Cabinet for the expulsion of foreign exiles. Turgid as was the style, and defective as was the composition of the piece, it yet expressed the popular feeling of the day. For once at all events the populace and the propagandists occupied the same ground and entertained the same ideas. Not long afterwards one of the most powerful Governments of the century fell to pieces in a week over a dastardly attempt to truckle to imperial intimidation on this very subject. England was the sanctuary of nations. No political offender ever sought her protection in vain. It was to maintain this sacred character and to preserve this sacred trust that we poor propagandists spent our substance and exhausted our feeble energies. Even to this day we may claim that herein we did the State some service.

Ten or a dozen years before our small operations were performed great disgrace had been brought upon our country by the subservience of British Ministers to a foreign despotism. The letters of Mazzini had been opened by their order in the Post Office, and the contents had been communicated to the Austrian Government. It was Lord Aberdeen and Sir James Graham who had authorised this infamy. The information thus obtained was supposed to have been used by the Austrians in procuring the capture and execution of the martyrs of Cosenza—Attilio and Emilio Bandiera, together with seven of their comrades. The indignation aroused against the Ministers was intense, particularly against Sir James Graham, who was then Home Secretary. Popular resentment found vent in various ways. Among others in inscriptions on the envelopes of letters: "Not to be Grahamised." Here was an earlier evidence of that reverence for the right and duty of sheltering the exile which has always been a marked feature of the English character. But it might not be improper in this place to record the fact that certain investigations of Madame Jesse White Mario in Italy has relieved the English Government of part of the odium it brought upon itself. It is true that Mazzini's letters were opened; it is true also that the information they contained was communicated to the Austrian authorities; but it is not true that this information led to the tragedy at Cosenza. Madame Mario, writing from Italy on July 14th, 1895, showed that the Bandieras and their companions were the victims of an Austrian plot. The intentions of the patriots had been made known by a man who lived and moved among the Italian exiles in Paris, but who was proved, when his papers came to be examined after his sudden death, to have been a spy in the service of Prince Metternich and the Austrian police in Milan. More than this, Metternich and the Austrian Government were shown to have actually incited the patriots to land in Calabria, providing them with money and a ship for the voyage, knowing beforehand that the Neapolitan Government would be ready to capture and execute them! Such is Madame Mario's revelation. It does not relieve Aberdeen and Graham from the odium of having done a shameful thing; but it at least discharges them of the crime of having been instrumental in procuring the slaughter of a band of noble youths.

CHAPTER XXIX

BRANTWOOD

FOLLOWING hard upon the close of Mr. Linton's exposition of republican principles came Mr. Linton's announcement of the *English Republic*. The new publication took the form of a monthly magazine. The editor was its chief contributor. Almost all the original matter that appeared in it was written by him. With the exception of the proclamations and other documents of the Democratic Committee, a series of articles on Russia by Alexander Herzen, a series of extracts from Theodore Parker's sermons, and a paper on Mary Wollstonecraft by an anonymous writer, it may be said that the whole of the contents of the four yearly volumes of the *English Republic*, prose and poetry alike, was the result of one man's effort.

For the first year (1851) the *Republic* appeared in monthly parts at sixpence. Now and then, but not often, there was given a portrait or other engraving by the editor. But the first year's venture was not a success, so a change was made in the second. Retaining the same shape and size of page, the *Republic* was issued during 1852 and 1853 in the form of a weekly tract. A further change was made in 1854. The *Republic* reverted to the monthly issue, with more portraits and engravings. And thus it continued during that year and for two or three months in 1855, when it finally ceased. The three volumes of the publication are now literary curiosities. But they bear traces on every page of a political earnestness and elevation that contrasts strangely with the frivolous products of a later period. We were dreamers, enthusiasts, fanatics, what you will—we Republicans of the middle of the century; and yet, when one comes to consider the matter, it will be admitted that we set before ourselves a nobler ideal than that which was expressed in the clamour of the Roman populace for bread and the circus—nobler even than the demand of the present day for less work and more football.

The later issues of the *English Republic* (1854-55) were printed at Brantwood—a mansion and small estate on Coniston Water which the help of financial and political friends had enabled the editor to acquire. The mansion was not large, ten or twelve rooms perhaps, and the estate was not productive, being mostly fell; but the situation, facing the lake and Coniston Old Man, and commanding views of other great mountains, was delightful. There was at one time, I believe, a bench in the gardens which was given the name of Wordsworth's Seat, because the poet of Rydal had said that one of the loveliest prospects in the Lake District could be obtained from the spot. Here a printing establishment was set up for the purpose of producing the *English Republic*. Types and presses had of course to be imported: so had persons to use and work them. I was one of the imported persons. Two other young men—Thomas Hailing and James Glover—were also imported from Cheltenham. We were all members of the Republican Association, and all ardent disciples of Mazzini. Our duties were evenly distributed. I was the compositor of the small establishment, Hailing the pressman, Glover (being a gardener) a sort of man-of-all-work. Between us, labouring earnestly and harmoniously together, we produced the *English Republic*, the *Northern Tribune* (the Newcastle magazine of that name), and such other printed matter as was needed.

Press and cases were at first fixed in one of the bedrooms of the mansion. This, however, was only a temporary arrangement, pending the erection of a special building—rough, but suitable and commodious—at the rear. Apart from its rude character (funds were not available for architectural adornment), there was only one thing peculiar to the Brantwood Printing House: it bore on its front, scratched in the plaster-work, two inscriptions that must have puzzled the passing country folks—"God and the People" and "Laborare est Orare." Years afterwards, when I walked over to Brantwood, during a short holiday in the Lake District, I noticed that the building had been pulled down. This was not surprising, for the only excuse for its existence was its usefulness, and Mr. Ruskin, who then owned the property, had all his printing done in the South of England.

The sort of work we were doing in the printing office, as I knew from my intercourse with the villagers in Coniston, caused us to be eyed with suspicion. But it is perhaps a mistake to speak of intercourse with the villagers. As a matter of fact, we succeeded in establishing very little intercourse with them at all. Sometimes they were hardly civil to us; at other times they were decidedly rude. Once, during the severe winter of 1854-55, the winter of the Crimean War, when the upper part of the lake was frozen over, and I ventured on to the ice with the rest, there was a deliberate and apparently combined attempt to trip me up. We were on intimate terms with nobody; on friendly terms with the schoolmaster and schoolmistress only; on speaking terms with scarcely a dozen people besides. The suspicions of the small tradesmen of Coniston took the unpleasant form of hesitating to measure us for clothes or boots before we could show the money to pay for the goods. [21] But, as neither tailor nor shoemaker was a penny the worse for our transactions with them, it must be presumed that the veiled dislike of the neighbours arose from resentment at the seclusion we deemed it proper to maintain in our printing operations.

Our life at Brantwood was of the most unconventional order. We had no watches, knew no time, ate when we were hungry, and went home when we were tired. It was a long way home, too. Two of us lived at Yewdale Bridge, three or four miles from Brantwood, while the third lived at Torver, two or three miles further still. Now and then we had to work late into the night, and sometimes all night, to get our publications into the market. On these occasions the journey home seemed dreadfully long and wearisome. As part of our road lay through woods and plantations, the intense darkness of the winter nights made locomotion difficult. The hooting of the owls and the soughing of the wind through the trees did not improve the walk, especially when, as sometimes happened, one or other of us had to perform the journey alone. Once I got a pretty fright myself. It was late at night and pitch dark, the trees overhead hiding even the faint light from the stars. Suddenly there was heard a tremendous clatter some distance behind. Nothing but a herd of wild horses, I thought, could make such a row. I got into a ditch out of the way of the phantom hoofs. The terror was short-lived, for the alarming noise was caused by a collection of dried leaves careering along the hard and frosty road driven before a high wind!

The two of us who lived at Yewdale Bridge, being bachelors, became tenants of a pretty cottage there. It was unfurnished. Nor had we much furniture of our own besides books and boxes. The window-sill was my desk and a wooden chest my only seat. There was absolutely nothing else in the room except a heap of books and manuscripts scattered over the floor. Our domestic arrangements were on a par with these sumptuous surroundings. A row of bricks did duty for a fender, a stick for a poker, and a sheet of brown paper for a tablecloth. But we were young and hardy then, and our wants were few. The duties of the household were divided between us. While one made the humble beds, the other made the coffee and the porridge. I have no doubt we performed our respective offices with satisfaction. At any rate we found no fault with each other, nor threatened each other with a month's notice. Having no artificial tastes in those days, whatever we may have since acquired, we needed neither beer nor spirits, nor even tobacco; and, being full of life and vigour and enthusiasm, we were healthy and contented to boot.

For a short period at the commencement of our enterprise we had the assistance in the printing-room of a staymaker—George Robert Vine, a disciple like ourselves. Vine was vain—vainer even than the rest of us. But vanity was not an undesirable quality in his case; it gave him confidence. And confidence was essential for the mission he was going to undertake. That mission was nothing less than the conversion of England to Republican ideas. Vine thought himself sufficiently equipped for the venture with a hand-cart and a load of democratic publications, mostly copies of the *English Republic*. The cart was decorated with a flag and a motto. The flag was blue, white, and green, supposed to be the Republican colours; the motto was "God and the People." We never saw the missionary again. Where he got stranded, or how, I never knew, or at all events have forgotten. I know he passed through Preston, because he wrote from that town about a great strike of cotton-spinners that was then in progress. Thereafter, so far as my recollection goes, silence. Vine started on his mission in 1854. Nearly thirty years later the following curious communication was received from him:—

To LINTON, NEW HAVEN.
HILL TOP, SHEFFIELD,
May 20th, 1883.

I will just give you a few words about myself. I am still working at my trade (stay business), and if not enjoying riches, I am enjoying calm. I have been in my leisure hours building up a fame in the scientific world, being recognised by men of science as one of the chief authorities on the class of studies to which I have given particular attention (palaeontology); and by my writings I am pretty well known in scientific circles in America.

GEORGE ROBERT VINE.

Vine's failure simply preceded our own. It could not be said that the scheme of establishing a printing-office in a remote corner of the country, seven or eight miles from the nearest railway station, was a very prudent scheme. As all our materials had to be carted over the mountains from Windermere to Brantwood, and all these same materials, after we had converted them into magazines and pamphlets, had to be carted over the mountains from Brantwood to Windermere back again, the whole concern was burdened with unnecessary cost. So, in a little more than a year, there came an end to our hopes and our enterprise together.

Brantwood for a time was rented by Gerald Massey, and at last sold to Mr. Ruskin. But Mr. Ruskin had his doubts about the purchase at one stage of the negotiations. The extension of the railway to Coniston, with a distant view of the obnoxious train service from Brantwood, caused him to hesitate. Ultimately, however, he overcame his scruples, made the home of our experiment his home, and gave to the old mansion on Coniston Water a unique place in the political and literary history of England.

CHAPTER XXX

ON TRAMP

OUR little company at Brantwood was dispersed in the spring of 1855. We had been working together for little more than a year. But the public not wanting our wares or our politics, the *English Republic* expired. This, however, did not mean that we had lost faith in our principles or intended to cease propagating them. Linton went to London to try his fortune with *Pen and Pencil*, an ephemeral competitor of the *Illustrated London News*. I, being the youngest of the party and then unmarried, left first, Hailing and Glover remaining behind to "sweep up." Glover eventually resumed his old occupation of gardener in the neighbourhood of London, while Hailing, before returning to establish the reputation of the Oxford Press in Cheltenham, obtained employment at Windermere. Mr. Garnett, stationer and stationmaster there, had also a small printing-office. A rather large order had come to him from Harriet Martineau, then residing at Ambleside. Mrs. Martineau—as she preferred to be called, though she was never married—had received what she thought was a warning to prepare for eventualities. Wishing that the public should receive from herself after her death an account of the transactions in which she had been concerned, rather than learn of them from anybody else less qualified to tell the story, she set about writing her autobiography. And to guard against any tampering with the manuscript when she could no longer prevent it, she wanted the work printed off at once—ready for issue, precisely in the form she desired, as soon as she had departed hence. Hailing was engaged for the job, worked at it for some months, printed one volume and part of another, but, running aground for want of copy, had to leave it for other hands to finish. This was in 1855; but the careful authoress lived for two-and-twenty years after she had brought her book to a conclusion! Creaking doors do sometimes hang long on their hinges.

As for myself, I had a journey of two hundred and seventy-four miles before me, with only seventeen shillings in hand for the undertaking—obviously too small a sum even for a railway ticket. How came this lack of funds? Well, wages were of no consequence to us, so long as we had enough to pay our way. We hadn't come to Brantwood to make money, but to serve a cause. Besides, we had been preaching the virtue of sacrifice, and now we were practising it. So it never entered our heads to murmur, except, perhaps, when the villagers seemed to doubt our honesty. If subscriptions for the magazine were paid, we had our share of them. But if subscribers failed to subscribe, we were at least testifying to the faith that was in us. Of course we did not live like princes. But what did it matter? We gratefully ate our porridge, and devoutly believed that we were beginning a great work.

When the dream was over—at all events for the present—the prospect of having to take to the road did not alarm me. The loneliness would be tiresome; nor was I without apprehension that I might fall among thieves—as, indeed, I did. But the tramp was nothing, since I had money enough for a bed and a crust on the way. During my apprentice days, I used to envy the ragged and dusty wanderers who were to be seen passing through the town all summer-time. The fields and the woods, the hills and the hedgerows, the rills and the rivers, the songs of the birds and the odours of the flowers—these things, I thought, to say nothing of the chances of communing with Nature, lent fascination to the life of a tramp. Yes, I hoped to be a tramp myself some day. And now had come the opportunity. So I set off from Coniston with a light heart and a bundle of tracts; for I reckoned that our mission, though we had failed at Brantwood, was by no means ended. The tracts were of course explanatory of republican principles. Some I gave to school children to give to their teachers; some I hung on bushes by the highway; others I distributed among the inmates of the common lodging-houses at which I slept. I talked, too, with the tramps whom I overtook or who overtook me on the road; and I even entered in my diary—now a stained and almost obliterated record—that I thought I had converted a militiaman! Also I called on Republicans whom I knew by name or repute in the towns that lay on my route. There had been an association at Macclesfield. This I endeavoured to resuscitate, but in vain. The efforts that were thus made to spread the true political gospel, feeble and fruitless as they were, helped to relieve the tedium of the long journey. Only once, I fancy, did I feel particularly sad and forlorn. It was on a fine Sunday evening in April, when, at the end of a dreary tramp, I entered Lancaster tired and footsore. The good folks of that town were enjoying their Sabbath strolls. Then I thought that my own people were at that very hour sauntering through pleasant lanes and pastures at home, while I, a solitary wanderer on the face of the earth, knew not a soul that I met. For a time I felt melancholy and depressed, and wished the long tramp was over.

Besides the bundle of tracts, I was not burdened with much baggage. A small parcel contained everything. Printers need to carry few tools. A composing stick and an apron were all I required to begin work anywhere, and even these were not indispensable. I called at all the newspaper offices on the route, begging some brother man to give me leave to toil. Not an odd job anywhere, nor any relief either except a shilling at Birmingham when I showed my indentures, for I was not a member of the union, there being then no branch at Cheltenham or Coniston. The times were out of joint. It was the winter of the Crimean War—the severest as regards weather, the dreariest as regards depression, the direst as regards distress, that we had had for years. I find in my old diary a note on the state of the country:—"Everywhere the cry is want of work. In Macclesfield especially, steady men, industrious men, have great difficulty in obtaining bread. The militia, some of whom may not perhaps be so steady, recently disbanded at Stockport, went home to Macclesfield, failed to get work, and returned to re-enlist. The weavers 'play' nearly as often as they work, some of them oftener. 'I have never known such a winter,' has been the expression of all with whom I talked at Macclesfield. One young man in Newcastle-under-Lyme, now compelled to seek bread by 'busking' (singing in public-houses), a thrower by trade, said he had been offered 6s. 6d. a week at a factory in that town. Another man—a plasterer by trade, who had been out of work for weeks—was offered 25s. to do a job for which he would have had to pay 15s. to his labourer. The number of tramps I meet on the road—some limping with sore feet, others bending beneath their burdens of care—is positively alarming.

Every other man one meets is almost sure to be in search of employment. But notwithstanding all this distress, the beer shops are not without customers. Men come and spend their last penny— in one particular case I saw at Preston leaving wife and family at home to starve. In the midst of poverty there is still a deeper degradation—the degradation of drunkenness." When this was the general condition of things, it was not wonderful that the letters of introduction with which I had been furnished availed nothing. Three of these letters were to gentlemen of the press or having influence with the press—Joseph Livesey, proprietor of the *Preston Guardian*, Edward Peacock, a director of the *Manchester Examiner*, and George Dawson, lecturer and preacher at Birmingham. Mr. Livesey and Mr. Peacock received me courteously; but work there was none. Mr. Dawson was away from home; but Mrs. Dawson saw me instead. She wanted to know what we had been doing at Brantwood. I told her. "You are a pretty lot," she said, laughing, "and we are not much better."

My first night on the road was not comforting. It was spent at Kendal. I knew nobody there: so I asked for accommodation at the sign of the Black Bull. The house seemed small and humble enough to suit my circumstances. I slept with a double-thumbed musician— a drunken performer on the key-bugle who shoved me out of bed. The company at the Black Bull was not much to my liking. It was rowdier than any company I had ever been thrown into before. Early in the evening every man in the tap-room (the only common room in the inn) was maudlin drunk. And the language! Our army in Flanders couldn't have sworn more horribly, not even if there had been a competition in blasphemy. Tired of the men and their conversation, I went out and bought materials for next morning's breakfast—coffee, sugar, bread, etc.—and then to rest. I was awoke at midnight. The roisterers were coming to roost, bringing bottles of beer with them. The key-bugler, helplessly drunk by this time, was, much to my horror and disgust, put in beside me. He stank like a fitchet, and snored like a saw-mill; but fortunately his back was towards me, as of course mine was towards him. Soon he was fast asleep. And then the trouble began. The strange bedfellow with whom poverty had thus made me acquainted commenced to back himself like a stubborn horse. I shouted to him to desist; but the more I shouted the more he backed—the further I got away from him the nearer he came to me. I was on the edge of the bed by this time. To avert the prospect of a violent ejectment, I reversed the order of things—got out on my side of the bed and got into his. "Now, my friend," I thought, "if you go on backing, it is yourself, and not me, that you'll back on to the floor." My scheme was successful. The musician bothered me no more. I was glad, however, to take an early departure from the Black Bull. Perhaps it should be added that the lodgings there, if nasty, were at all events cheap; for I find a note in my diary, written at noon next day, some miles from Kendal, that my total expenses thus far had been one and threepence halfpenny.

The second night was connected in a rather curious way with the first. I was overtaken on the road to Lancaster by another musician—a fiddler this time. It turned out that the fiddler had been travelling with the bugler—that they had quarrelled and dissolved partnership. I was in luck's way now; for my new acquaintance, who had been a sailor on board the Imperatrice, and intended to go back to the sea, would take me with him to a house where he was known. The house, kept by one Bartholomew Kelly, was clean and orderly. The company also was an improvement on that of the Black Bull, though most of the component parts of it were beggars and thieves. One of the men was chaffingly asked about his friend Captain Blank. "Oh yes," said he, "I left him yesterday morning." Captain Blank was the governor of Lancaster Gaol! I was seen to be writing—much to the wonderment of the company. "Ah!" said a man who was looking over my shoulder, "I'll put ye on to a splendid lay." It was to start business as a writer of begging letters! Beggars and thieves as they were, the men and women in Bartholomew Kelly's lodging-house treated me as kindly as I had ever been treated anywhere. This, perhaps, was not an uncommon experience, since the very poorest of the people are frequently the most generous. My friend the fiddler arranged for everything and paid for everything. We were going together to Preston next day—I bound for Manchester, he for Blackburn. For some modest refreshment at Garstang on the road he insisted on paying also. Nor did his consideration end there; for he took me to all the places I wanted to find in Preston—the printing-offices, the lodging-houses, etc. Here the lodging-houses were so filthy that I preferred taking my chance at a tavern; but I had to sleep in the same room with two drunken market men. The following day I met my friend again. Again I begged him to let me pay my share of our joint expenses. "No," said he, "I am among friends; you are not." And we shook hands and parted. We shall never meet more; but I should deem myself guilty of gross and contemptible ingratitude if I did not retain in my memory to the last day a warm place for John Connolly—sailor, fiddler, tramp.

But I had other experiences of life on the road—curious if not edifying—that must be told in a new chapter.

CHAPTER XXXI

TRAMP LIFE

THE lodging-houses of Preston were too filthy to be trusted; but they could scarcely have been filthier than that which I had the misfortune to sample at Chorley. This place–described in my diary as "a small neat town, supported by its manufactories"–was only nine miles from Preston. I was, however, weary and footsore when I reached it at six o'clock in the evening, for I had been walking about Preston for many hours before resuming my tramp at three o'clock in the afternoon. "When in doubt, ask a policeman." Could he tell me where I could get a bed for the night? My appearance, I dare say, didn't suggest that I wanted one of the best hotels in the town. Anyhow, he directed me to a lodging-house. The Chorley constable was more helpful than a member of the same order whom I encountered when in much the same difficulty some years later on a tour through the Scottish Highlands. The encounter took place in Callander. Would the policeman be kind enough to give me the name of a good hotel in the place? The reply was not a bad example of Scottish discretion. He didna ken, he said, as it behoved people in autho-rity to be cotious! But the Chorley policeman could hardly be suspected of recommending one fourpenny lodging-house more than another. All the same, I ungratefully wished afterwards that he had sent me somewhere else.

The common room of the common lodging-house at Chorley–a dingy, dirty, squalid apartment–was full of people when I entered it. Most of them were of the tramp type; but one or two girls–probably daughters of the proprietor–were apparently factory operatives. I had not been much edified by the conversation I had heard in similar places. Even that in the thieves' kitchen at Lancaster, though the place was clean and its occupants considerate, was of a coarse and vulgar character. Here, however, I could not qualify the conversation, for the reason that I had not then made the acquaintance of the Lancashire dialect, which, as I listened to it at Chorley, was as much like a foreign language to me as anything I had heard before. Only a word dropped here and there, such as "bobbin" and "mill," led me to infer that the people, for part of the time, were talking about work at the factories. It was my practice while on tramp to go to bed early–always, however, in fear and trembling least I should have to put up with a bedfellow. I had a couch to myself at Chorley, but I had more bedfellows than I quite knew about at the time. The other three beds in the apartment were occupied by a weaver, a tailor, two labourers, and a bookbinder turned labourer. These five gentlemen combined to produce such a concert in their sleep that night was made hideous. If by accident the performers in the three beds took a short rest, my own bedfellows made the most of the interval. Real repose was quite out of the question, so that I fled from the abode of horrors as soon as daylight enabled me to see that I was putting on my own clothes, and not somebody else's. But my torments were not over when I had escaped from that registered inferno; for, after all, though I was careful as to the garments I donned, I carried off more than belonged to me. That day was the most miserable I passed in the whole of my tramp. My ankles ached; my feet were blistered; all the other unexposed parts of my unfortunate anatomy were in a state of intolerable irritation. Overtaking a waggon, I gave the waggoner twopence to let me ride into Bolton. There the newspaper offices were visited, with of course the usual result. Then I limped away to Manchester, calling as I passed through Salford at Peel Park, with its Museum and Free Library, at that time an almost isolated example of municipal enlightenment.

The freemasonry of the road is one of the charms of tramping. Every tramp chums with every other tramp, just as if he had known him from boyhood. What is more, almost every tramp thinks it his bounden duty to do his best for his comrade of the hour. It is only the curmudgeons of the profession who behave differently. I fell in with the custom, and could therefore learn nearly all I wanted to know about a place before I reached it. One result of the chumming process was that I did not stop in Manchester, except to call at the newspaper offices. A young fellow who overtook me drew so dismal a picture of the lodging-houses there that I resolved to hurry on to Stockport. But I was too tired and too miserable to walk the five miles further. Consequently, I committed the extravagance of travelling by rail. But I paid dearly for it; for, having to make the journey in an open truck, which at the period did duty for a third-class carriage, I got "a perishment of cold." Then followed a further extravagance. I put up at a coffee-house. Here the bill for tea, bed, and breakfast amounted to 1s. 8d. Fancy a tramp indulging in such luxuries! However, I did not lament an expenditure that was so much out of keeping with my financial resources. The comfort, the cleanliness, the quietude of the coffeehouse made me a new man next day. All the same, I felt like a criminal, because I feared that I must have left behind many of the undesirable acquaintances I had made at Chorley.

Another adventure befell me at Newcastle-under-Lyme. On the way thither I conferred with the brethren at Macclesfield. There, being among friends, I fared very well. Arrived in Newcastle, I inquired for accommodation at a small inn–the Antelope–but neglected to stipulate for a single bed. That, however, did not matter, I thought, since nobody else was in the house, except drinking people. Even the appearance at a later hour in the evening of an old man and his wife was not disconcerting, because of course the venerable tramps would sleep together. Wherefore I retired to rest in an easy frame of mind. Still I thought it desirable to prepare for the worst. Instead of getting in between the sheets, I got in between in the sheet and the blanket. "Now," I said to myself, "if, contrary to present probabilities, anybody should share the bed with me, there will at least be a sheet between us." Complacent and satisfied, I went speedily to sleep. An hour or two afterwards I was aroused by the rest of the inmates fumbling up the stairs. The bed was on a landing, with a room beyond it. I listened. Yes, there were three voices–the landlady's, the old man's, and the old woman's. Gracious! they were not going to sleep together, were they? I pretended to be oblivious; but I was wide enough awake when I heard the landlady solving the riddle. "You get in there," she said to the old man; "and you," meaning the old woman, "come in along of me." Sold! Still the sheet would be a protection. I chuckled at my own cleverness and forethought. What it was to anticipate things! The old man got into bed and blew out the candle. Then–oh! horror!–I heard him mutter:

"D! I'm in the wrong place." And he got out of bed and got in again–this time beside me. Sold again, and after all my precautions too! But I fared better than I expected. My new bedfellow behaved better than the drunken bugler at Kendal–better even than the weaver and tailor and labourers at Chorley. I was neither kept awake nor kicked on to the floor.

It was my last unpleasant adventure on the road. My final night as a tramp was spent at Stratford-on-Avon, which was out of my way, but I wanted to see Shakspeare's birthplace. Here the woman at the inn, when I asked for a drink of water, was amazed. "What!" said she, "can't ye afford a drink of beer?" Well, she would take pity on my poverty. And she gave me a glass of fourpenny. It was vile stuff; but I was thirsty, and the gift was kindly meant. Another day's tramp–thirty two miles–and I was among friends again. These thirty-two miles seemed shorter than any twenty I had previously walked. Such is the happy effect of the prospect of once more mingling with dear old folks at home.

Mark Twain knew something of the tramp in America–especially the travelling "comp.," who "flitted by in the summer and tarried a day, with his wallet stuffed with one shirt and a hatful of handbills; for if he couldn't get any type to set, he would do a temperance lecture." I also knew the character, long before I became a tramp myself. Some of the fraternity came once and were seen no more; others came round as often as the regulations of the trade society enabled them to draw relief. A man belonging to the former class–this was in 1848– persuaded me to give him a shilling for writing an acrostic, and next night was seen gesticulating on a Chartist platform, partly for my edification. Two members of the latter class were rather famous in their day. One was the Bonny Light Horseman; another the Prince of Munster.

I had a pretty long acquaintance with the Prince of Munster. Dominic Macarthy had worked for a few months on *Galignani's Messenger* in Paris, and on the strength of this circumstance was considered a person of some note in the trade. He was a good workman; he possessed considerable intelligence; but he was afflicted with an incurable desire for roaming about the country whenever the proper season came round. Every year, or at least as often as relief could be obtained at the societies in the various towns through which he passed, the Prince was accustomed to make his appearance. It frequently happened that a job was to be had in the office in which I was apprenticed, and Dominic in this way became a familiar character in our establishment. As a lad, I liked nothing better than a crack with the royal "comp." Not that I think now that his habits or his influence were altogether wholesome for a youth of an impressionable temperament; for I recollect that he used, when he had the means, to bring into the office a supply of spirits to serve him till he could visit the public-house again. Now and then his royal highness would disappear beneath his "frame," and emerge from his seclusion wiping his mouth with the back of his hand, and discharging through the office an odour of Old Tom.

During the few days he remained at a time–and he never remained much longer than a week together–he had frequent "bouts." I remember that he defended these weaknesses of his on the ground that Buchan or some writer on hygienic matters contended that occasional excesses in intoxicating drinks had a healthy effect on the person who gave way to them. Dominic, as I have said, was never able to stay long in one place. When he got his wages, or as much of them as he had not anticipated, on a Saturday night, we could never be sure that he would turn in again on the Monday morning. Indeed, if he had nothing to draw, he was liable to disappear any day. When this happened, we would see nothing more of him till he came his rounds again a year later. The passion for roving was too strong to be resisted for many days together. The Prince could no more settle in one town in summer-time than a swallow can resist the impulse to seek another clime.

Later on in life I made Dominic's acquaintance in London. There he invariably spent the winter months hanging about the office of the society in Racquet Court, and getting an occasional job as a "grass hand," until the return of spring enabled him to resume his vagabond life.

Some years passed. I was then in Newcastle. One night, when leaving the office, I heard my name pronounced as I passed a ragged figure standing near the door. Turning round, I discovered that I had been accosted by my old friend the Prince of Munster. His highness was raggeder, haggarder, and dirtier than I had ever seen him before. A quarter of a century of wandering hither and thither, together with the unknown quantity of spirits he must have consumed in that time, had told heavily on the Prince. I took him home with me; I gave him a good supper; I supplied him with a suit of old clothes; and I set him on his way rejoicing with a few shillings in his pocket. I never saw him again. The probability is that he died in some workhouse hospital or other.

Dominic Macarthy always seemed to me a type of the vagabond class. And I never think of him, and of my own feelings when I first made his acquaintance, without believing that I had a narrow escape of becoming a vagabond too.

VOLUME II

CHAPTER XXXII

LONDON IN THE FIFTIES

AS nobody seemed to want my services in the provinces, I set out for London. There I had friends, introductions, the promise of work. It was not my first visit to the great city. Four years before—to use a form of words which passed for wit in Gloucestershire—I had "shown London a fool." It was the year of the Great Exhibition. The memory of that marvellous creation—surpassed in size, but not eclipsed in grace or interest, by any effort that has succeeded it— remains as a dream of fairyland. Nothing I have ever seen has impressed me as it did. If I did not see all the wonders it contained, it was not so much my fault as my misfortune; for I spent the greater part of three days within its crystal walls—one day from ten in the morning till six at night. The Exhibition of 1851 was the first of its kind, and the most enchanting.

The London of 1855 differed vastly from the London of to-day. It had no Thames Embankment, no underground railways, no street trams, no magnificent avenues, no suburban theatres. Hornsey was a rural village, so was Streatham, so were dozens of other pretty places now absorbed in what Cobbett called the Great Wen. Kennington Park was a common; Smithfield Market was held in the City; and the Percy lion with its poker tail came down from Northumberland House every day it heard the clock strike twelve! The first-class playhouses could almost be counted on a single hand, and music halls were few and far between. I can remember only four halls of any note—the Canterbury, the Oxford, the Holborn, and the Eagle. The Brill, the New Cut, and Petticoat Lane were favourite places for Sunday morning marketings. The Polytechnic was in its prime; the Coliseum was still patronised; and Vauxhall and Cremorne Gardens were bringing together nightly strange mixtures of the decent and the dissolute. J. M. Bellew, Thomas Binney, and Robert Montgomery were notable among preachers, while a young man of the name of Spurgeon was beginning to draw audience and attention.

Gye and Mapleson were rival caterers at Her Majesty's and Covent Garden. Grisi and Mario, Alboni and Lablache, were still stars, albeit falling stars, of the operatic stage. The three former appeared together in "Lucretia Borgia," during a series of popular representations at Drury Lane, when the house was full of fog as well as people, and we on the Olympian heights could only see the performers flitting like shadows across the stage. English opera, with the help of Balfe and Wallace, and of Pyne and Harrison, was holding up its head too: the song of the Muleteer, as I heard Harrison render it, was, I thought, as fine as the song of the Toreador in "Carmen." Webster reigned and played at the Adelphi, Buckstone at the Haymarket, Phelps at Sadler's Wells, Charles Kean at the Princess's. It was in 1851 that I saw Phelps in "Timon of Athens," but it was not till years later that I saw what I thought was the greatest performance to be seen on any stage—Phelps's rendering of Sir Pertinax MacSycophant. Charles Mathews retained his place for years as the prince of light comedy. Wright and Paul Bedford were leading low comedians, so were Mr. and Mrs. Keeley, while people were beginning to talk about a clever little fellow at the Grecian—Frederick Robson, who, ascending to the major stage, made the burlesque of "Medea " as fearsome as a tragedy. And then a few years later there came a sort of race for the first prize in the dramatic world between Henry Neville and Henry Irving.

Temple Bar was a picturesque obstruction; the Adelphi Arches gave shelter to homeless hundreds; and the River Thames was an open sewer. Long stretches of filthy slime, the playground of mud-larks, were exposed at every falling tide, and gave off such evil odours in hot weather that people had to hold their noses when they crossed the bridges. There was a threat of pestilence as a consequence. And then the authorities, seeing that something must be done, conceived a great sewerage scheme, and replaced the foul shores with that pride and glory of London—the Thames Embankment. Other improvements—the construction of Holborn Viaduct, the widening of many thoroughfares, but, above all, the sweeping away of pestilential rookeries, such as the Seven Dials—have made the metropolis a far sweeter and handsomer city in the twentieth century than it was in the middle of the nineteenth.

The order observed in the streets, the unwritten law of the people, was even then remarkable. I may give an example. The *Morning Star* was at that time the leading Radical daily in London—almost the only Radical daily, indeed. It was my custom every morning (Sundays excepted, of course) to buy a copy at a news stall near the Horns Tavern at Kennington. My business was in Fleet Street. The route thither from the Horns was along Kennington Road, through Newington Butts, past the Elephant and Castle, along London Road, then along Blackfriars Road, and then over Blackfriars Bridge. So orderly was the traffic throughout that route that I could, by keeping to the right, read my paper the whole way. And I had nothing left to read in it—at least, nothing that I wanted to read—when I reached Fleet Street, nearly an hour's walk from Kennington. The feat—if it was a feat—was only possible when people kept in line. All I found it necessary to do, where the traffic was thickest, was to walk immediately behind somebody else. Pedestrians at that period who did not observe the rule of the pavement had as bad a time of it as a dog in a fair. Indeed, they were so buffeted about that they very soon discovered that it was really compulsory to "keep to the right."

A well-known rendezvous for Reformers in the middle years of the century was the John Street Institution, situated near Tottenham Court Road. It had been a chapel, I think, but was then leased by the followers of Robert Owen. Lectures were given there; meetings were held there; classes were conducted there. A more useful centre of social and political activity did not exist in all London. The platform was perfectly free. Chartism, Republicanism, Freethought, Socialism—all sorts and conditions of thought could be expounded in John Street if capable exponents desired to expound them. I had heard Mrs. C. H. Dexter lecture there in 1851 on the Bloomer costume, and in the Bloomer costume. There also, five years later, I heard the venerable Robert Owen, then a patriarch of eighty-four. The subjects discussed were of the widest and most varied character—social, political, religious, literary, scientific, economical, historical. And the lecturers who discussed them were as varied as the subjects—Thomas Cooper, Robert Cooper, Samuel Kydd, Dr. Mill, Dr. Sexton, Iconoclast, Henry Tyrrell, Richard Hart, Joseph Barker, Brewin Grant, George Jacob Holyoake, and many another whose very name is now forgotten. Of all the able men who endeavoured to enlighten the public from the John Street platform not one survives save George Jacob Holyoake. When the lease of the institution expired, a source of real light and ventilation expired also.

There were other institutions which Reformers used to frequent when they saw a chance of expounding their ideas. These were the debating rooms that were attached to certain taverns. The leading three in my day were the Cogers, near St. Bride's Church; the Discussion Hall, in Shoe Lane; and the Temple Forum, in Fleet Street. The Cogers was an ancient institution, dating from 1755, but was then fast dying, though it survived in a way till 1886, when its hall and all that belonged to it were put to the hammer. Many who afterwards played a prominent part in the politics of the country, or attained high distinction at the bar or on the bench, had learnt to know the rules of debate and acquired an aptitude for public speaking at Cogers Hall. Curran and Daniel O'Connell were both members, as also were John Wilkes, Orator Hunt, and many of the early English Radicals. Among the legal Cogers who attained eminence were Lord Chief Justice Cockburn, Mr. Baron Maule, Mr. Justice Hannen, Serjeant Parry, Serjeant Ballantine, and Sir Edward Clarke. Dickens, too, belonged to the ancient and honourable Society of Cogers; and George Augustus Sala has told how he made, or rather tried to make, his first speech to the Grand Coger in the chair. The Temple Forum, I think, had no history. It was held in a back room of the Green Dragon, small and ill-ventilated. The only time I visited the place, the debaters, whom I could scarcely see for smoke, were discussing a celebrated case of the day—I think that of Constance Kent. But the Discussion Hall had better quarters and a better set of speakers.

The landlord of the tavern in Shoe Lane was named Walters, and the hall in which the meetings were held was a really presentable apartment—long and lofty, comfortably furnished with seats and tables, with a canopied chair for the president, who generally smoked a long pipe, and drank brandy and water. As the rest of the company smoked and drank too, the scene had a free and easy air about it. Oil paintings of some of the celebrities who had shared in the debates decorated the walls of the room, including those of Thomas Hardy, Alderman Waithman, and William Carpenter, all famous Radicals in their day. The subject for discussion, together with the name of the gentleman who was to open it, was announced beforehand in the window of the tavern. It was a point of some importance to get a good opener. And as a fee of five shillings, with free drinks for the evening, was attached to the performance, there was no difficulty in getting clever, broken-down men from Fleet Street to accept the engagement. Poor old Bronterre O'Brien, a tribune of the people in the palmy period of Chartism, but then a social and almost intellectual wreck, was often in demand for this purpose. The permanent chairman for some years was Andrew Middlemass, who was supposed to be a journalist, who had formerly been an accountant in Newcastle, and whose death was recorded in 1889. After each speech, the chairman used to make an important announcement—"The waiter's in the room; give your orders, gentlemen." Many admirable speeches were delivered in Discussion Hall, although, as the night wore on, the applause, which was accompanied by the jingling of glasses, became rather boisterous. The speakers *could* speak too. One talked so well about finance and taxation that he went by the name of the Chancellor of the Exchequer. Others were great on questions of foreign policy; others, again, on legal and social subjects. They were not all beery people either, for among the frequenters was Mr. Fleming, then a member of the staff of the *Morning Advertiser*, but better known for his connection with Robert Owen's movement, having been, like Lloyd Jones and George Jacob Holyoake, a social missionary appointed by the great philanthropist to expound his theories and doctrines to the people. The discussions which took place in my hearing rose far above the curious surroundings—so much so that I brought away from Discussion Hall a much more favourable opinion of the intelligence than of the habits of the debaters.

The last visit I paid to the place was late at night. It was in the company of Austin Holyoake, younger brother of George Jacob, and of John Watts, elder brother of Charles Watts. We had been engaged in producing Mr. Bradlaugh's paper, the *National Reformer*. When we had completed our work, it was proposed that we should go and see how the debaters finished up their proceedings. Discussion by that time had degenerated into a noisy and general hubbub, in which everybody seemed to be talking at once. All manner of strange characters, most of them more or less muzzy and muddled, were holding forth to each other. Political orators, writers for the *Standard*, sub-editors of the *Family Herald* and the *London Journal*, contributors to other popular periodicals, waiters on Providence, hirelings of the press and of the platform, were among the men of light and leading who were enjoying a midnight revel in Shoe Lane. Instead of reeling home when the tavern closed its doors, most of them adjourned to a "night house" in Farringdon Street, where, being joined by other sweepings from the streets and the newspaper offices, they continued their noisy drinkings and disputations till far into the morning. One of the new revellers was notable at the time for his appearance on Chartist and Radical platforms. John Henriette was a sort of Silas Wegg, a democratic orator with a wooden leg. I was amazed, though the rest of the company seemed rather amused than amazed, when he openly boasted of having been employed by Lord Palmerston to assist in creating political diversions at electoral contests in the provinces. It was the only time I ever had an opportunity of seeing how the lesser literary men of the day comported themselves at the close of the week's work, and I neither desired nor sought another. The spectacle, so far from being impressive or elevating, was calculated to take the heart out of a young and ardent propagandist.

CHAPTER XXXIII

A PROPAGANDA OF IDEAS

WE did not forget our obligations—we poor propagandists. Bear in mind that we were Republicans, not Revolutionists. It was no part of our business to disturb, or attempt to disturb, the established order of things. We wanted to make Republicans, not a Republic. When we had done that, we felt and knew that the change would come as naturally and with as little disturbance as the fruit succeeds the flower. The explanation, though it may not save the propaganda from ridicule, may at least help to save it from opprobrium. Another thing—we were not the friends of every country but our own. We were friends of the peoples, it is true, but we were friends of our own people first of all. Patriots and propagandists, we had, we thought, an even higher idea of national honour than some of those who ruled the destinies of England. Anyway, whether Monarchy or Republic, England was our home, our country, our beloved mother. It was her heroes we revered; it was her people we wished to elevate; it was her renown we longed to increase. The design was perhaps sufficiently dignified to redeem the small efforts we made from contempt or derision. There was already a Republican association in London when two of us, after the break-up of the Brantwood experiment, found ourselves in the great city. The brethren received us warmly. Nor was it long before we had commenced such active operations as the nature of the movement sanctioned. The very first distinct step we took was, I think, the distribution of tracts among the crowds that assembled in Hyde Park to celebrate the conclusion of peace after the Crimean War. That insignificant effort was followed by the preparation of special leaflets that were scattered about with great care and discrimination. It was intimated at the foot of the leaflets that copies of others could be had gratis at four addresses in different parts of London; but I do not recollect that a single application was ever received in consequence. As, however, we were all young then, and had been told by Mazzini to "revere the enthusiasm of youth," the disappointment did not disconcert us.

Our numbers never at any time, I think, exceeded twenty. Yet we regularly held our family meetings—sometimes in Holborn, sometimes in Bethnal Green, sometimes in the City Road, at other times in the neighbourhood of the Regent's Park. There we discussed schemes for the regeneration of mankind, subscribed our pence for propagandist efforts, and solemnly devised means and measures for converting the rest of the world to our views! The minute book of the association, which is still preserved, clearly indicates that something much higher than material welfare entered into the ideas and the aims of the members. There was nothing selfish or sordid in our methods or objects. It was not to benefit ourselves, to increase our own leisure, advance our own interests, or promote our own enjoyment, that we combined. Rather did we find satisfaction in sacrifice—the sacrifice of time, energy, and such poor resources as we possessed. The members of our little society were so restricted in this world's goods that the audit of the first year's accounts showed an income from subscriptions of one pound six shillings and fourpence halfpenny, an expenditure of one pound six shillings, and a balance of fourpence halfpenny! Nevertheless, impoverished as we were, we managed every now and then to contribute to the funds of the Continental Revolutionists of that day, thus helping to the utmost of our means in the liberation of oppressed nationalities. Besides these small endeavours, we occasionally commissioned one or more of our members to attend meetings in the Caledonia Fields and elsewhere to advocate our doctrines or defend from aspersion the leaders of patriotic and revolutionary movements abroad.

A pathetic interest attaches to some entries in the minutes relating to one of these leaders. Stanislas Worcell, a venerable Polish nobleman, known to us all and beloved by us all, was then living in an obscure corner of London—a grave and dignified victim of Russian tyranny. The minutes referring to Worcell begin in December, 1856, with a request to the members for information as to the price of a copy of a certain edition of Hutton's "Course of Mathematics." The society resolved to purchase and make him a present of the book, the members subscribing five shillings and sixpence for that purpose. A month later it was reported that efforts to obtain the book had failed, when the secretary was instructed to write to Mr. Worcell asking him whether any other edition would suit his requirements. Then came the meeting for February, 1857. "The secretary," so runs the report, "said that he had written to Mr. Worcell respecting the book which he required, but was sorry to inform the brethren that since doing so the brave-hearted old man had died—another victim to the inflexible tyranny of Russian misrule." And then occurs this entry:— "As the only tribute of respect they could pay to his worth, and to show their abhorrence of the system which had made him an exile and a martyr, it was agreed that as many of the brethren as possible should follow his remains to Highgate Cemetery."

The funeral of Worcell was a remarkable event. It was attended by natives of almost all the countries of Europe—Poles, Hungarians, Italians, Russians, Frenchmen, nearly every man of them an exile, and nearly every man of them with a price upon his head. There was, first and foremost, Joseph Mazzini, for whom the Austrians, after a rising in Milan, had searched the very coffins as they were being carried to the graveyard—slight of stature, sorrowful of countenance, intellect and power in every flash of his eye, in every line of his face, in every hair of his beard. Then there was Alexander Herzen, who, flying from Russia, had managed to save his property from confiscation—the only man among the exiles who was not almost penniless. And then there was Ledru Rollin, a leading member of the Provisional Government of February, who had fled from France in consequence of a violent protest in which he had shared on behalf of Poland. The procession from Hunter Street to Highgate was preceded by a band of music playing the "Dead March." Speeches, of course, as happened on all such occasions, were made over the grave—in English, in French, in Polish. The speech in English was delivered by Peter Alfred Taylor, the friend of suffering peoples, afterwards and for many years member of Parliament for Leicester. Ledru Rollin, who had great fame as an orator in France, looked the character (being handsome, tall, and portly) as he poured forth a flood of mellifluous language in denunciation of a despotism that had driven such men as Worcell to perish in a foreign land. The Poles who spoke registered a vow of undying hatred of the Russian Government. The company which thus bore testimony to deep affection for the exile was small; but most of the men composing it had been, and continued to be till they died, a terror to the despots of the Continent.

Another political funeral occurred a year or two later. It was that of Simon Bernard. The mourners on this occasion were much more numerous than those who had followed the remains of Worcell. One reason was that Dr. Bernard had not long before been charged with complicity in the attempt of Orsini against Louis Napoleon. The acquittal which followed the trial was regarded as a popular triumph. The death of the accused so soon after the verdict of the jury had set him at liberty naturally attracted a good deal of attention. Hence the large crowd which, also accompanied by a band of music playing solemn airs, marched in procession to the Kensal Green Cemetery. But, though the crowd was larger, it did not seem to me to be composed of the same elements or distinguished for the same dignity as that which had assembled at Highgate. Perhaps the explanation was to be found in the character of the two exiles. While Worcell was a man of saintly life and aspirations, Bernard was a bit of a madman—moreover, a furious Socialist, which at that time was much the same thing. I shall give an example of his mad humour presently. The main body of the mourners seemed to be made up of that type of revolutionist that is never happy except in revolt—the type that would destroy for the mere sake of destruction—the type that in later years produced a Ravachol and a Vaillant. But I remember three notable men among them. One was Felix Pyat, who was subsequently associated with the lurid affairs of the Paris Commune. Another was the Russian exile Bakunin, a man of gigantic stature, who had lately performed the unparalleled feat of escaping from Siberia down the Amoor, and who afterwards became the chief of the Nihilists. The third was Thomas Allsop, the friend of Lamb and Coleridge and Hazlitt, who also had been suspected of participation in revolutionary plots. It was Allsop who told me, as we walked in the procession to Kensal Green, how Bernard had ventilated the theory that reverence for sacerdotalism would never be uprooted till a Pope in full canonicals was slain at the very altar! Orations were delivered over the grave, but I have forgotten all about the people who delivered them.

Hyde Park, the scene of the Peace Commemorations in 1856, was the scene a few months later of much more exciting occurrences. We young men of the Republican Association were interested spectators of the occurrences—nothing more. It was a paltry question to us— the question of the observance of the Sabbath. As to beer, with which the question was then mixed up, we knew it to be the ruin of political effort. Still we had interest in all popular excitements. The rumpus arose from an attempt of Lord Robert Grosvenor to close the public-houses on Sundays. A bill for the purpose had been introduced into Parliament. Then the mischief began—rowdy on the part of the mob, violent on the part of the police. Strange means were adopted to excite the passions of the populace. I remember seeing outside the premises of *Reynolds's Newspaper*, then a purely demagogic organ, a large placard bearing these coarse lines:

D—their eyes
If ever they tries
To rob a poor man of his beer!

Other imprecations of like character had been preceded by invitations to the mob to "go and see how the aristocracy kept the Sabbath in Hyde Park." Fashionable people were in the habit of enjoying Sunday rides or drives in Rotten Row. The first Sunday after the incitement crowds lined both sides of the roadway, hooting and jeering the horsemen and carriage folk. It was the prelude to disgraceful riots. Next Sunday the ladies and gentlemen who ventured into the Row had to run the gauntlet of showers of turf and stones. The angry mob had become brutal, as all angry mobs are apt to. Another Sunday came round. I went to see what was going to happen. Very few riders presented themselves; but those who did were so pelted with stones that they had to gallop for their lives. The scene was shameful. Now came the turn of the police. Orders were given to clear the park. But the park was thronged by people who had no hand in the riots. The majority of those I saw seemed to be well-dressed, well-behaved persons, belonging to the working and middle classes. Most of them, like myself, were spectators of the demonstration rather than participators in it. But the police, when charging the multitude in obedience to orders, necessarily came into collision with people who were not offenders at all. Such certainly was the case in that part of the field which came under my notice. I was sauntering among the crowd, when down came a long row of constables, raining blows on the heads of such as could not get out of reach of their *bâtons*. It was necessary no doubt to suppress disorders; but I thought at the time, since I was very nearly a victim myself, that it might have been done with much less violence than was used. The mob, driven out of the park, took its revenge on the houses in Mayfair. Lord Robert Grosvenor thought it prudent to retire into the country; his proposed legislation was abandoned; and the Sunday riots in Hyde Park became a matter of history.

Our little band of propagandists kept the flag flying till the end of the fifties. Then, as the more active among them left London for the provinces, the Colonies, or the United States, the movement quietly died out. There were republican agitations afterwards; but we had little or no sympathy with them, because they were based on no principle and informed by no elevated ideas. What would be the value of a revolution which had for its root the accidental unpopularity of a prince of the blood? What, again, was the worth of that paltry cry about the Cost of the Crown, raised by Sir Charles Dilke before his own tremendous lapse? It was not because a prince was temporarily unpopular, nor because the Monarchy was supposed to be expensive, that the young men of the fifties gave themselves to a republican propaganda. It was because, high above all accidents, high above all sordid interests, there shone and flamed before them the ideal of an exalted and duteous people.

CHAPTER XXXIV

THE "ILLUSTRATED TIMES"

THE Crimean War afforded a splendid opportunity for journalistic enterprise. Few newspapers, however, on account of the Taxes on Knowledge, were able to take much advantage of it. The *Times*, of course, did wonders with the letters of the first war correspondent, William Howard Russell. Rather late in the day Henry Vizetelly, who had had a hand in initiating the *Illustrated London News*, projected a cheaper rival, the *Illustrated Times*, with a special artist at the front, Julian Portch, who unfortunately died at his post. This new paper was an immediate success; for the Crimean War was followed by exciting criminal trials—for example, the trial of William Palmer for the Rugeley poisonings, and that of Madeleine Smith for the murder of her sweetheart in Glasgow. Mr. Vizetelly, a brother of Frank Vizetelly, who was slain or lost with Hicks Pasha in the disastrous expedition to the Soudan in 1884, was the director of the paper—though it was understood that David Bogue, the Fleet Street publisher, provided most of the capital. As I recollect him at the time, Vizetelly was an active, excitable, wayward sort of man— whimsical and changeable, too, which led to extravagance in management, and eventually to failure. But he had, as we shall see, the faculty of finding able assistants.

The brothers Vizetelly—Henry being then the sole member of the firm—had a printing and engraving business in Gough Square, next corner to Dr. Johnson's old residence. It was there that the *Illustrated Times* was produced. I was lucky enough to present a letter of introduction, just at the time when Vizetelly was making his preparations for the new venture. My work at an office in Fetter Lane had been precarious. Here I was for a while in clover. I was assigned a frame with a good light. Permanently employed, and earning what the pitmen call "good money," I was happy and contented, and to a certain extent prosperous. The change which came later will furnish materials for a sad and bitter paragraph. My highest ambition then and long afterwards was for a settled situation at "case" on a well-established newspaper. Such a situation enabled the fortunate compositor not only to live comfortably, but to pass his leisure hours in the pursuits and activities that pleased him. If happiness and comfort be the things to be desired, I, who have tried other avocations, know of no condition of life to be preferred to that of the workman who has constant and regular employment at the trade that he likes, provided he is fairly paid for the best he is capable of producing. Many printers in London were thus pleasantly circumstanced. But there were others—the waifs and strays of the trade—whose state was miserable enough. These were known as "grass hands." Too dissolute, many of them, to hold a permanent appointment when chance placed a permanent appointment in their way, they lived from hand to mouth—hanging round the offices of the society till a call came from this or that newspaper for temporary help on the day or night (usually the night) preceding publication. I was a "grass hand" myself for a time, and suffered accordingly.

The work on the *Illustrated Times* was at the beginning agreeable and profitable. But the companionship—the general body of compositors—was of a mixed order. Some of my comrades were sots; the conversation of some others was of the vilest character; but the majority were respectable and intelligent men. One was an authority on music, another had a good knowledge of art, a third was well versed in literature. We could talk at our work, and the talk was often about books and pictures and operas. We even formed a magazine club—purchasing periodicals, reading them in turn, and then distributing them among the members. Thackeray's "Virginians" and Dickens's "Little Dorrit" were, I recollect, among the serials for which we subscribed. But we had our little troubles. There was an irrepressible disposition among us to chaff each other. My Gloucestershire dialect was still so pronounced that I could at first never utter a word aloud without hearing an aggravating echo all along the room. I did not like it, but I had to put up with it. One day, however, I noticed that my chief tormentor—a Scotchman—had also peculiarities of speech. These I imitated as he had imitated mine. The effect was instantaneous. I had turned the tables. No longer the butt of the room, I chaffed the rest as much as the rest chaffed me. The incident conveys a moral. Other young workmen may learn from it that the best way to relieve themselves of disagreeable attentions is to bestow similar attentions on the men who annoy them. There will then be equality of—treatment at all events—which, after all, is the best that need be desired. I have said that some of my comrades were sots. There were two in particular. One young fellow, when I had chaffingly alluded to his then unhappy condition, informed the whole room that I wasn't man enough to get drunk! Of the other it was said that he had made various attempts to visit the Great Exhibition, but had found so many public-houses on the road that he never got there at all!

The indifference of people to famous things or places in their own neighbourhood has been the subject of comment and surprise from ancient times downwards. It was Pliny, I think, who told of a fountain in Italy that was visited by travellers from far distances which was yet scarcely known to the people who lived near it. The same curious aptitude is observable everywhere, especially in London. Among the compositors in Vizetelly's office was an intelligent man who had passed St. Paul's Cathedral twice a day for many years, and yet had never once had the curiosity or the inclination to look inside the memorable fane. And another member of the companionship, whose work was chiefly with engravings, and who was not without some feeling for art himself, was born and still lived almost within a stone's throw of the National Gallery, but had never taken the trouble to inspect the treasures on its walls. It is the country cousins who pay flying visits in great shoals to the Metropolis that see most of the sights. But country cousins, as a rule, make short work of the business. I recollect being in the National Gallery when a party of provincial visitors, hot and perspiring, passed me. One of the ladies, while mopping her face with a handkerchief, exclaimed: "There now, we've done this place; let's be off to the Museum." If ever Londoners do visit Westminster Abbey or the Tower, it is in the company of friends from the country.

The *Illustrated Times* was one of the brightest productions of the fifties. All manner of clever young writers, as well as some older writers, were connected with it. Macrae Moir was the editor; James

Hannay, author of "Singleton Fontenoy," wrote the leading articles; Edmund Yates began with the "Lounger at the Clubs" that system of personal journalism which has since been widely imitated; William White, a doorkeeper of the House of Commons, described the inner life of Parliament, anticipating the want which is now satisfied by Parliamentary letters in the daily press; Edward Draper contributed an informing weekly paper on Law and Crime; Sutherland Edwards supplied musical criticisms, the Brothers Brough dramatic criticisms, Noel Humphreys antiquarian notes; Augustus Mayhew did such pictorial work as painting in prose the scenes of the Rugeley poisonings; and George Augustus Sala wrote—when he could be got to write—reviews of books, descriptions of engravings, and in one case a serial novel. All these gentlemen were much about the office.

One night Sala came in a white waistcoat and a red face, looking so comically like a peony set on a tablecloth, that the compositors at the cases had to bury their noses in the space boxes. Vizetelly had more trouble with George Augustus than with any other of his team. When copy was wanted from him, he had to be hunted from one haunt to another. He said himself that he always found a printer's devil alongside his boots in the morning. It happened on one occasion that he was locked in a room at the office with a pot of porter and a packet of cigars till he had finished an article that was required at once. But a more serious difficulty arose later. Sala was writing his story, "The Baddington Peerage." Nothing could induce him to keep up to time with the instalments. At last Vizetelly hit upon an effective device. An announcement was put in type that the editor would no longer apologise for the failure of the author to supply the continuation of the story, that he was tired of chasing him through all the taverns of Fleet Street and the Strand, and that he was now resolved to let the reader know with whom the responsibility for the lapse really lay. A proof of this announcement was sent to Sala, with an intimation that it would appear in the ensuing issue of the paper unless the copy of the next instalment of the novel was in the hands of the printer by a certain hour. Not only was the copy in hand at the time specified, but I believe there was no further trouble with the eccentric author till the story was finished. It is not a little curious that no fewer than four of the gentlemen associated with the *Illustrated Times*—Vizetelly, Sala, Yates, and Edwards, all dead but Edwards—have published volumes of reminiscences.

The companionship of the *Illustrated Times* had a pretty happy time till Mr. Macrae Moir was succeeded by Mr. Frederick Greenwood. Mr. Greenwood, a brother of James Greenwood, the "Amateur Casual," had been a printer's reader in a well-known book office. I remember him as a spruce young fellow with a rather supercilious air and a black lace necktie. Long afterwards he was credited with suggesting to Mr. Disraeli that the Government should buy the Suez Canal shares; and only lately he has been described in a book about J. M. Barrie as "the good fairy of Barrie's literary life." A disastrous change in the circumstances of the poor compositors come about when Mr. Greenwood took control of the copy. It may not have been his fault, but we did not know whose else it could be. The change had come with the change of editors. Moreover, had not a heartless reply been returned to a piteous appeal we had made to the new man? It is certain that our lives were made miserable. We had to be at our cases every morning and all day afterwards lest work should come and others be put in our places. But day after day it happened that work did not come till it was just upon time to go home; and then we had to stand at our cases till every scrap of copy was set— always till midnight, often till four or five o'clock in the morning— with the result that next day we had nothing to do again till the editor condescended to send round a great batch of copy in the evening, when of course the same dreary process had to be repeated. The only consolation that the unhappy compositors had as they crawled homewards was in "nailing" (which does not mean blessing) the author or authors of their misery.

It was an awful time for us all. Part of my way had to be traversed alone, and then I must often have slept as I walked, for I now and then seemed to wake up with a start. To add to our troubles we had to run the risk of being garrotted. London was then in a state of alarm. Almost every morning we read on the newspaper placards— "Another Garrotte Robbery," with sometimes the addition: "Death of the Victim." Policemen, I remember, paced the streets in couples or in parties. Luckily I was never molested, though I had to go home at the loneliest hours of the night and morning—probably because I took the precaution, when by myself, of walking in the middle of the road. The Society of Compositors, I hope, has so reformed the laws and regulations of newspaper work in London that no poor devils have now to endure the horrors that fell to our lot in the fifties.

Mr. Greenwood, I have said, was a printer's reader—printer's reader at the office where Carlyle's books were printed. It was said that he had preserved and bound several volumes of the great man's proofs and manuscripts. Carlyle was a terror to the printers—not so much on account of his handwriting as on account of his fearful tampering with the proofs. Harriet Martineau, in that book of autobiography which my friend Hailing set up at Windermere in 1855, tells an amusing story on the subject. One of Carlyle's works was going through the press in London. A man from Edinburgh, where his earlier productions had been printed, was given some of his copy. The man dropped it as if it had burnt his fingers. "Lord have mercy!" he cried, "have you got that man to work for? Lord knows when we shall get done with all his corrections!" I was myself for a short time employed in the same office. The "Life of Frederick the Great " was being set up there. I saw some of the proofs. It was the third that lay on the stone. The matter was still in columns, not in pages, for paging was out of the question till the author had exhausted even his almost illimitable power of changing his modes of expression. This third proof was so covered with corrections of all kinds that it would have taken little more trouble and time to reset the whole than to make the alterations. Scarcely a sentence remained unchanged, while flags and circles enclosing new forms and phrases were scattered all over the sheet. I have seen many "dirty proofs," but I never saw anything dirtier than Carlyle's—and that the third too!

CHAPTER XXXV

THE COUP D'ETAT

THE year 1851 was memorable for two things—the Great Exhibition in London and the Coup d'Etat in Paris. The one was a triumph of enlightenment, the other the most appalling crime of the century. The Coup d'Etat, indeed, surpassed in wickedness and horror, in treachery and remorselessness, anything that has ever been recorded, or is ever likely to be recorded, in Western history. The East alone can furnish parallels to the infamy, and even these sink almost into insignificance alongside the supreme and monumental infamy of the Second of December.

The vast majority of the people now living are not old enough to remember the events of 1851. It may be that they have heard of them or read of them. But they have no knowledge from personal experience of the thrill of horror that ran through the country when the news reached it of a diabolical outrage that had placed France at the mercy of "five base galley slaves." We stood aghast—every one of us, from the highest to the lowest. Every newspaper in the land proclaimed its abhorrence of the iniquity, its loathing of the adventurers who had perpetrated it. What had happened in Paris was such a crime as could not have been conceived possible by the most lurid and diseased imagination. It was, in fact, more than a crime: it was combination of all crimes—perjury, treason, treachery, the subornation of the soldiery, the overthrow of law, the wholesale arrest of all the leading citizens of France, the calm, deliberate slaughter of thousands of innocent people. No civilized city in the whole world was ever the scene of so foul a saturnalia as Paris on that darkest day and night in all the annals of villainy.

The chief criminal was a man whom the French people had chosen as President of the Republic. He was supposed to be a Bonaparte, though there was some doubt as to his actual parentage. He called himself Prince Louis Napoleon, and he claimed to be the inheritor of the Napoleonic legend. Twice he had made theatrical attempts against the French Government—once with a tame eagle at Boulogne, which had been taught to fly to the top of a column, but which failed to carry out its instructions. But the name he bore, or pretended to bear, helped him with the ignorant peasantry when, after the proclamation of the Republic of 1848, they were required to elect a President. The election to the Presidency was the first step to absolute dominion. But it was necessary that he should take an oath to preserve the Republic. This he did on Dec. 20th, 1848, in the following terms: "Before God and the French people represented by the National Assembly, I swear to be faithful to the Republic, and to fulfil the duties imposed on me by the Constitution." And then, as if to throw the representatives of the people off their guard, he added a declaration of his own. But what is an oath more or less to the felon who means to break them all?

The President lost no time in preparing his plans; but it took him nearly three years to find the suitable instruments for putting them into execution. These instruments were all men of blemished reputations. One had been in trouble in Algiers: he was made Minister of War. Another had been dismissed from a prefecture in the provinces: he was made Prefect of Police. Three or four of the conspirators were, as Kinglake says, known by names that were not bestowed upon them at baptism. It was St. Arnaud who was given the Ministry of War; it was Maupas who was placed in the Prefecture of Police. Among the rest were Morny, Magnan, and Persigny. Magnan was Governor of Paris. But the chief parts in the villainous drama were played by Maupas, Morny, Persigny, and St. Arnaud, with Louis Napoleon of course at the head of them—Victor Hugo's "five base galley slaves." If the reader desires to know more about the scoundrels, as well as about the atrocious things they did, he is advised to consult the first volume of Kinglake's "History of the Crimean War."

The night came. It was the night preceding Dec. 2nd. What happened was told by Maupas himself in a book of confessions published in 1884. To allay suspicion the President gave a party at the Palace of the Elysee. To further disarm suspicion, Maupas and St. Arnaud left the drawing-rooms of the Elysee by the principal door. A few minutes after ten o'clock the conspirators had all assembled in the Prince's study. "General St. Arnaud and myself," says Maupas, "again enumerated the measures we had prepared. We both reasserted our confidence in the execution of our orders, and then we parted. The Prince shook hands, as he would have done on any ordinary occasion, calm and confident, like all great men who require no effort to raise themselves to the level of the situation." Bear in mind that the level of the situation to which the Prince raised himself was that of throttling the nation he had sworn to serve. The soldiery had already been corrupted by a feast of sausages and champagne at the camp of Satory. For the officers there was gold. Before the conspirators dispersed, the Prince divided with St. Arnaud the contents of his cash box. "Officers were presently seen breaking rouleaux of gold like sticks of chocolate, and thrusting the pieces into their pockets." At six o'clock in the morning, Morny, or De Morny, took possession of the Home Office with two troops of Lancers. "A quarter of an hour later—and most punctually, for all the agents in this dark night's work had been made to set their watches by that of De Maupas—seventy detachments of detectives and gendarmes, penetrating into seventy different houses, arrested three score and ten of the most popular men in France, and drove them off to prison." Mazas was crowded with victims—statesmen, generals, journalists, members of Parliament, the two quæstors of the National Assembly. Among them, dragged out of their beds in the early hours of a December morning, were M. Thiers, General Changarnier, General Cavaignac, Colonel Charras, General Lamoricière. Not a man of any mark in Paris was left at large. France, held by the throat, was at the mercy of conspirators and ruffians.

The Coup d'Etat was consummated. But the bloodiest part had yet to be done. It was necessary to strike terror into the heart of the people. St. Arnaud and Magnan had filled the Boulevards with troops, "bribed, excited, intoxicated, pitiless." The citizens, curious and wondering, were looking from their windows or strolling along the sidewalks, not understanding what it all meant. Women and children were mingled in the crowd. There was resistance elsewhere. Here there was none. Not a man in the throng bore a weapon of any sort. All at once the order was given to fire. From end to end of the occupied Boulevards the rifles rang out. Men fell, women fell, children fell. Never a soul within sight was spared. It was a battue—with peaceful, unarmed people for game, and a drunken soldiery for sportsmen. The soldiers even entered some of the houses, slaughtering everybody they could find in them. "The troops," said the *Times* of Dec. 12th, "were ordered to select by preference as their victims persons of the class least akin to Socialist insurgents." The gutters of the Boulevards ran with blood; the trees of the Boulevards were watered with blood; a disreputable adventurer was wading through blood to a throne. The Coup d'Etat at the beginning looked too grotesque to be serious. After the massacre of the Boulevards, it assumed another shape—ghastly, horrible, fiendish. The mountebanks had become demons. The slaughtered, according to a list at the Prefecture of the Seine, numbered two thousand six hundred and fiftytwo—all ages, all ranks, both sexes. Then came the proscriptions. Eighty-eight representatives of the people were proscribed; tens of thousands of citizens were imprisoned, transported, interned; the pestilential colonies of Cayenne and Lambessa were choked with patriots who had been sent thither without even the semblance of a trial.

The criminals had overthrown the Republic. They were next to overthrow the Law. Article 68 of the Constitution which the chief criminal had sworn to maintain declared—"Any measure by which the President of the Republic dissolves the National Assembly is a crime of high treason." In the midst of the confusion and bloodshed of Dec. 2nd, two hundred and twenty members of the Assembly signed this decree:—

The National Assembly, extraordinarily assembled at the Mairie of the Tenth Arrondisement,

Considering the 68th Article of the Constitution,

Considering that the Assembly is prevented by violence from discharging its functions,

Decrees:

Louis Napoleon Bonaparte is stripped of his functions of President of the Republic.

Citizens are bound to refuse him obedience.

The Judges of the High Court of justice are summoned immediately to pronounce judgment on the President and his accomplices.

The High Court of Justice met immediately, and decreed as follows:—

In virtue of the Article 68 of the Constitution, the High Court of justice declares,

Louis Napoleon Bonaparte committed for the crime of high treason.

The High National jury is summoned to deliver judgment without delay.

The declaration was signed by Hardouin, President, and Delapalme, Pataille, Moreau, Cauchy, Judges. But the conspirators who had crushed the Republic now crushed the High Court of Justice. There was from that time no law in France but the will of perjurers, traitors, assassins.

Complete as was his triumph over France, the Republic, and the Law, Louis Napoleon, smeared and reeking with gore, was long uneasy on his blood-stained throne. Even the despots of Europe held aloof from a "cutpurse of the Empire"— cutpurse and cutthroat too. He wanted an alliance—matrimonial and political. Austria declined the one. England, to her shame and sorrow, yielded the other. A weak and vacillating Ministry misled her into the trap. It was Louis Napoleon's business to make war somewhere upon somebody. He chose for quarrel the question of the Holy Places— the paltry question whether the Greek or Latin Churches should control the Sepulchre of the Saviour. England was invited to join him against Russia. The Emperor Nicholas had unfortunately aroused suspicion by proposing that the nations of Europe should prepare to divide the effects of the Sick Man. We drifted into war. It cost us thousands of lives; but it made the Conspirator of December respectable. English people were not averse to the war, because they hoped that the independence of Poland would be revived as one of the consequences. But there was really no intention of doing much harm to Russia—certainly none of liberating Poland. As Kossuth said at the time, the attack on the Crimea was like striking at Russia in the heel of her boot. The war was a dismal failure. Only one thing was gained—the recognition and establishment of the Second Empire.

Other humiliations followed for this country. It had to receive the usurper as an ally. Worse—it had to witness the scandal of his foul lips kissing both cheeks of the Queen of England. When we read of this last indignity at Cherbourg, there was not an honest woman's face in Britain that did not burn with shame. Four years—four sad and disgraceful years—had sufficed to blind the Press and the Government, and to some extent the people also, to the iniquities of M. Bonaparte. But Victor Hugo would not let us forget them. A translation of the poet's scathing philippic was published by Edward Truelove, then a bookseller at Temple Bar. So subservient, however, had even our authorities become to successful villainy that the police tore down the placard announcing it. Yet at that very moment thousands of French citizens, for no other crime than that of faithfulness to their country, were languishing and perishing in the swamps of Cayenne. Others, more fortunate, had found refuge in the Channel Islands. When, later, these exiles ventured to protest against the contamination involved in the visit of Royalty to the scene of the massacres of December, we had to submit to the ignominy of seeing them expelled without warrant and without trial. It is worth while recalling the shame of that lamentable time if only as a warning against ever again paying homage to triumphant wrong. The events recalled, too, are necessary to explain what were for us the still more exciting incidents of 1858.

CHAPTER XXXVI

'TYRANNICIDE'

THE burden of the crimes of the Second Empire did not fall on France alone. Italy also shared that burden. It was, however, before he had waded through blood to a throne that Louis Napoleon had begun the treason against Rome. When the Republic was proclaimed in the Eternal City, he despatched General Oudinot with a fratricidal expedition to Civita Vecchia, solemnly declaring it was not his object to "force upon the State a government contrary to the will of the people." This was in April, 1849. "Three months after," says Mazzini, "Rome, her Government, the will of her people, were inexorably crushed." The heroic defence of Garibaldi failed; the bombarded city surrendered; the Triumvirs, Mazzini the chief, wandered about the streets dazed till friendly advisers found them shelter and safety; Garibaldi himself, after incredible hardships, during which he lost his beloved Anita, escaped to the coast and thence into exile. From that time for many years forward the throne of the Holy Father was poised on the points of French bayonets. Hope there was none for Italy as long as France, misled by the man who had mastered her, remained at the head of the coalition of enemies. Every Italian knew this—nobody better than a Roman citizen who had valiantly fought against fearful odds in the defence of his home, Felice Orsini.

The patriotic spirit of Italy, during all the dreadful, dreary years that followed the occupation of Rome, was kept alive by fervent appeals from Mazzini, by schemes which he organized, by revolts and risings which he inspired and in which he shared. But Orsini was impatient of Mazzini's policy. He had taken part in many of the daring adventures and struggles of his time. He had made a marvellous escape from the fortress of Mantua. The story of that escape, told by himself in a little volume, was as widely read in England as the earlier story of Silvio Pellico's imprisonment in the fortress of Spielburg. Coming to this country, he had lectured here and there on the cause of Italy and his own sufferings in connection therewith. Also he had written and published a book of Memoirs. His earnest faith, his intense patriotism, his absorbing passion—all centred in his beloved Italy—made for him friends and admirers in England. But he longed for some speedier and more certain results than any that had yet followed the efforts of the revolutionary party. Writing in 1855 from his dungeon in Mantua, he declared his distrust of the old methods—conspiracies, outbreaks, insurrections. Again, in his Memoirs, published in 1857, he wrote:—"Italy finds herself at the present moment in the most deplorable condition that can be imagined. This state of things, however, will not last long, because all depends upon Napoleon, and this man will not be tolerated long, with his government based on despotism and treason." It would seem that Orsini was even then contemplating the movement which a year later startled all Europe—a movement which was to employ for the salvation of Italy the very methods which had been employed in 1851, but with infinitely more awful accompaniments, for the subjugation of France.

Felice Orsini
(1819-58)

It came to pass on the night of Jan. 14th, 1858, that Louis Napoleon was returning from the opera. Bombs burst under his carriage, spread terror and destruction all around, but failed to do more than affright the intended victim. The explosions—clumsy, ineffective, fatal to many innocent people—were the work of Orsini and his accomplices. It was thus that he hoped to rid Italy of the one man who made her redemption impossible. The attempt failed in everything except in arousing the conventional indignation of Europe. Orsini, who had staked his life on the hazard of a desperate venture, resigned himself to his fate. He died, as Mazzini a few months later counselled Louis Napoleon to die, "collected and resigned."

Louis Napoleon
(1808-73)

Throughout England there was one long howl of execration. The newspapers forgot the provocation—forgot the bombardment of

Rome, the maintenance of the subjugation of Italy—forgot the crime of Dec. 2nd, which had begot the crime of Jan. 14th—forgot their own bitter imprecations of the author of the parent crime. [22] Orsini, from one end of the land to the other, was denounced as a vulgar assassin. Every epithet of abhorrence was heaped upon his name. It seemed to be thought that there was absolutely no difference between him and the vilest ruffian that had ended his days in Newgate.

But surely there was another side to the picture. Would not somebody take cognisance of the cause of the attempt, of the motive that impelled it, of those not very distant events which had generated in an otherwise high-souled man a fierce and implacable passion? The question presented itself to some of us. It presented itself to me. I prepared a paper which was in some measure a protest against the universal chorus of condemnation, and at the same time an attempt to explain some of the ethical points involved in the catastrophe. The production was juvenile enough; but it did at any rate show that the event which had so excited and enraged the Press had really another aspect than that alone which the exponents of public opinion were content to recognise.

The manuscript was offered in the first place to George Jacob Holyoake, then a publisher in Fleet Street. Mr. Holyoake declined the offer, for one reason, I understood him to say, because he was already in treaty with Mazzini for a pamphlet on that very subject. "Very well," I said, "if Mazzini or anybody else will raise a voice against the pitiful clamour of the day, especially the beatification of Orsini's intended victim, I will pitch my own little screeching behind the fire." The pamphlet which Mr. Holyoake had in his mind was probably that terrific indictment of Louis Napoleon, one of the classics of the Revolution, which was published a few months later by Effingham Wilson. If Mazzini's letter, which must have made even imperial villainy squirm, had appeared earlier, this chapter would not have been written. But, like Orsini, I was impatient: so the manuscript was offered to Edward Truelove at Temple Bar. It was the beginning of a life-long friendship. Mr. Truelove was pleased with the piece that was submitted to him—almost as pleased, I think, as the young author himself. Yes, he would get it printed at once. But he had two suggestions to make. One was that the title of the pamphlet should read—"Tyrannicide: Is it justifiable?" The other related to a name or *nom de-plume* for the title-page. The manuscript was anonymous: it was intended to be anonymous. "The name," I said, "is nothing, the argument everything. The argument can stand by itself: the authority for it will add nothing to its weight, particularly an unknown authority." Mr. Truelove then suggested a *nom-de-plume*. "Well," I said, "if there is to be a name, it shall be my own." So the thing went forth. But nobody believed the name to be other than fictitious. The pamphlet was said to be the work of a French exile. I was told myself that Louis Blanc was the author. Even workmen in the office who knew me and knew my name, when discussing the pamphlet and the prosecution, did not associate me with the authorship. It remained an open mystery to the end. [23]

Edward Truelove
(1809-99)

The police of the Metropolis were vigilant in those days. It is likely that they acted under orders; for despatches had already been received from the French Government. Anyway, the pamphlet had not been on sale for more than a few hours before an inspector of police invited Mr. Truelove to accompany him to Bow Street. The invitation was so imperative that he was not allowed to do more than change one coat for another. That day I was taking my usual walk with a fellow compositor during the dinner hour towards the Strand. We had passed the book-shop at Temple Bar. Suddenly I was clutched by the arm. "Come, I want you: Truelove has been arrested." The person who spoke was urgent and excited. It was the wife of the publisher—a refined and accomplished lady, herself devoted to advanced ideas. I was enjoying a smoke at the time, but my pipe was effectually put out for the rest of the day. I went into the book-shop. There I learnt what had happened. I, the cause of the trouble, the real offender in the case, was ready to become a substitute for the publisher. What else could a poor compositor do? But this, I was told, would make two victims instead of one. Besides, the police, believing that I was a myth, had no warrant against me. Mr. Truelove remained in durance—only a few hours—till sufficiently substantial friends could be found to go bail for his appearance before the magistrate next morning.

The result of the proceedings at Bow Street was a foregone conclusion. Mr. Truelove was committed for trial. The charge against him was that of having "unlawfully written and published a false, malicious, scandalous, and seditious libel of and concerning his Majesty the Emperor of the French, with the view to incite divers persons to assassinate his said Majesty." The charge itself was a false and scandalous libel. First of all, there was not the smallest intention on the part of author or publisher to incite anybody to do any thing. Nor was there any incitement either, except such as may arise from indignation at the recital of past crimes. As for libel, the pamphlet could have been voted libellous only on the old doctrine "the greater the truth, the greater the libel." The pamphlet, it is true, pointed out that the outrages of tyrants and usurpers are apt to inspire desperate men, and even sensitive and judicious men, to attempt the vindication of their country's rights and honour. If an adventurer violated his oath, dragged the foremost men of the country from their beds, cast the representatives of the people into dungeons, suppressed and dispersed the courts of justice, slaughtered thousands of unarmed people in the streets, shipped without charge and without trial tens of thousands of innocent citizens to a penal and pestiferous colony, made himself by these and other foul and infamous means the master and oppressor of the people—was he therefore to be absolved from the consequences of his villainies? This was the question that was asked. A writer in the *Times*—the author of the "Letters of an Englishman," understood at the time to be Mrs. Grote, the wife of the historian of Greece—had declared that "a man who sets himself above the law invites a punishment beyond the law." The doctrine proclaimed by Mrs. Grote after the Coup d'Etat was merely reasserted after the attempt of Orsini. But no name was mentioned in the pamphlet. All the same, said Mr. Bodkin, who prosecuted for the Crown, there could be no doubt as to the person meant. The description could apply only to his Majesty the Emperor of the French. The cap fitted him exactly. Where, then, was the falsehood? Mr. Truelove, however, was committed to take his trial before the Queen's Bench.

CHAPTER XXXVII

"A LAME AND IMPOTENT CONCLUSION"

THE prosecution of Edward Truelove was seen at once to be an attack on the liberty of public discussion. As such it was resented by most of the leading Radicals of the day. The prosecution was all the more resented because it had clearly been commenced at the instigation of a foreign Government and to appease a foreign despot. A Committee of Defence was formed; a fund was opened for defraying the expenses of the trial; and local committees in the provinces busied themselves in collecting subscriptions. John Stuart Mill contributed £20 to the Defence Fund. Among the other contributors were Harriet Martineau, Professor F. W. Newman, W. J. Fox, Joseph Cowen, James Stansfeld, P. A. Taylor, Dr. Epps, Abel Heywood, Edmond Beales, besides many more whose names, though forgotten now, were well known and even famous at the time. Charles Bradlaugh was appointed secretary to the committee, and James Watson accepted the office of treasurer. The duties of the committee were afterwards increased by a second press prosecution—the prosecution of a Polish bookseller in Rupert Street for publishing a pamphlet by three French exiles, Felix Pyat, Besson, and Alfred Talandier. It may be mentioned, as indicating the bitter spirit of the day, that the *Times*, which had seven years before printed diatribes as fierce as any in the two pamphlets, refused to advertise the appeal of the committee for subscriptions. Though the press was hostile, however, the public was not unfriendly; for the announcement that Henry J. Slack, eminent in later years as a microscopist, was going to deliver a lecture on the subject of the prosecutions, drew together a crowded and enthusiastic audience at St. Martin's Hall. Professor Newman saw more clearly than most people, not only the real character of the English pamphlet, but the consequences that would follow the success of the Government attempt to punish its publisher. "The question," he wrote, "is not whether Mr. Adams's doctrine is right or wrong, but whether, as an Englishman addressing Englishmen, he has a right to advocate it. Substantially he protests against the confused application of the word 'assassination,' similar to the confused application of the word 'murder' to all deeds of battle. It is permissible for a free citizen to argue even against the law under which a felon has been condemned. If Mr. Adams may not endeavour to convince us that Orsini's deed, though punishable and punished at law, is not morally wrong, I do not see how Englishmen can retain the right of censuring the law at all. Free moral criticism is effectually stopped." As for the doctrine of tyrannicide, the sentiment embodied in that doctrine, said Professor Newman, "is that which for ages predominated among Hebrews, Greeks, and Romans, the three nations which have been the chief feeders of our moral and intellectual life." "If," he added, "we have now outgrown certain sentiments and judgments of those three nations, it is rather too much to prosecute, or rather persecute, those who hold to the old opinion that lynch law against a treasonable usurper is better than no law at all."

The classical and scriptural doctrine against which so great a hubbub was raised in 1858 had not, however, lost favour even among modern statesmen and poets. Many examples were cited when the subject was of public interest. Two or three may be cited here. Walter Savage Landor was almost fanatical in his pronouncements. "I have," he wrote to the Marquis d'Azeglio, "never dissembled my opinion that tyrannicide is the highest of virtues, assassination the basest of crimes." Mr. Disraeli had published in 1834. his "Revolutionary Epic," wherein occurred the well-known lines:—

> And blessed be the hand that dares to wave
> The regicidal steel that shall redeem
> A nation's sorrow with a tyrant's blood.

But only fourteen days before Orsini's attempt a poem of Matthew Arnold's on an incident in Greek history had appeared. And this is what the poet wrote:—

> Murder! but what is murder? When a wretch
> For private gain or hatred takes a life,
> We call it murder, crush him, brand his name.

211

But when, for some great public cause, an arm
Is, without love or hate, austerely raised
Against a Power exempt from common checks,
Dangerous to all and in no way but this
To be annulled—ranks any man an act
Like this with murder?

Quite as truly could the charge of incitement have been preferred against Matthew Arnold as against the author of the "Tyrannicide " pamphlet.

The prosecution—hateful to the people because it had been instituted at the instance of a Government whose origin and practices were alike odious—was fatal to the Ministry which undertook it. Lord Palmerston, only a few months before the Orsini affair, had swept the constituencies. Bright, Cobden, and Milner Gibson all lost their seats. Ministers had a stronger majority than any previous Ministry for many years. But they truckled to a foreign Power, and they went speedily to pieces. The fate of Lord Palmerston's Government is an object lesson in English politics. Although the Prime Minister had as Foreign Secretary exhibited indecent haste in recognising the Government of Dec. 2nd, the favour he had shown it was not reciprocated seven years later. Following the Orsini attempt there came despatches from Count Walewski, Minister of Foreign Affairs to Louis Napoleon, that were almost insolent in tone. England was charged with harbouring murderers, and was practically commanded to restrict her own liberties for the protection of the French Emperor. And swashbucklers of the French army demanded to be led against what they called a "den of assassins." It was under the pressure of these insults and menaces that the Government of Lord Palmerston ordered the prosecution of Dr. Bernard, commenced proceedings against the publishers, and even had the supreme folly to attempt a revision of English laws. So much subserviency could not be tolerated. When the Conspiracy Bill—otherwise popularly known as the French Colonels' Bill—came up for consideration, an amendment proposed by Mr. Milner Gibson, who had returned to Parliament for a new constituency, shattered to pieces one of the most powerful

Ministries of the century. Lord Palmerston, as a consequence, surrendered the seals of office to Lord Derby.

The new Government did not abandon the prosecutions; but it showed an evident reluctance to press them; and it eventually succeeded, with the aid of an unprincipled counsel, in finding a way out of the difficulty. The prosecution of Mr. Truelove commenced in February; but the lame and impotent conclusion of the affair was not reached till the end of July. Meantime, there had been informal negotiations between the Committee of Defence and the Law Officers of the Crown. It was intimated to the Government at the outset that the author was ready to surrender himself, provided the proceedings against the publisher were withdrawn. But the offer was declined. This was in February. Three months later the author committed a grave indiscretion: he got married. It was one of the best day's work he ever did, though he saw afterwards that it would have been more prudent to wait till the so-called libel business was settled. During the time he was taking a brief holiday in the Isle of Wight, wandering from Ryde to Brading, from Brading to Ventnor, from Ventnor to Newport, from Newport to Ryde again, with no postal address anywhere, an important change occurred in the legal situation. The Crown authorities, who had refused the proposal of the Defence Committee, now offered to accept it. The very night the author returned from his short honeymoon he attended a meeting which was called to decide whether he or his friend Truelove should run the risk of a trial that might or might not end in a residence of six or twelve months in one of her Majesty's gaols. Of course he placed himself unreservedly in the hands of the committee. That body, however, seeing in the overtures of the Government clear evidence of weakness in the prosecution, declined to help the legal advisers of the Crown out of the quagmire. Preparations were therefore made for the coming trial.

It was the desire of the defence that a question which involved a distinct violation of the liberty of the Press should be fought out before a British jury. Eminent counsel were retained. Mr. Edwin James had at that time achieved considerable popularity by an impassioned address he had delivered at the Old Bailey on behalf of

Dr. Bernard. It was supposed, too, that he had every prospect of rising from office to office till he finally reached the Woolsack. But he must even then have begun to disclose to keen observers those faults of character which wrecked his career. Dickens, after a single sitting, as Edmund Yates records, drew his portrait as Mr. Stryver in "A Tale of Two Cities." Soon after the inglorious conclusion of the Truelove trial, he found it necessary to take flight to New York, where he made a further mess of his life. But these things had not happened when Edwin James was thought to be the best man at the Bar to conduct a great trial. The selection turned out to be a blunder. We were all expecting a new vindication of the right of public discussion. What we did not know was that intrigues were in progress to defeat the desired object; that the man who had been chosen to lead the defence was going to betray it.

The trial was finally fixed for June 22, 1858. It was to take place in Westminster Hall before Lord Chief Justice Campbell and a special jury. The prosecution was to be conducted by the Attorney-General (Sir Fitzroy Kelly), Mr. Macauley, Mr. Bodkin, and Mr. Clarke, while associated with Mr. James for the defence were Mr. Hawkins, Mr. Simon, and Mr. Sleigh. I was working late, as usual, the night before. Mr. Truelove came to me in a state of great indignation and excitement. He had just been informed that the case was to be compromised. Edwin James, without consulting the defendant or the defendant's friends, had settled the matter with the Law Officers of the Crown. It was never known what was the consideration. All that was known was that cause and client had both been sold. But, I said, could not new counsel be retained? No, it was too late. Well, then, could not one of the juniors act for us? No, it was contrary to the etiquette of the Bar. So a pregnant opportunity was lost. The rights of a British subject, the rights of the public itself, had been sacrificed to satisfy the conveniences of the Government. Then came the farce at Westminster Hall. Sir Fitzroy Kelly solemnly informed the court that the indictment would not be tried; that he understood his learned friend was prepared on behalf of his client, who was "a respectable tradesman, and the father of a large family," etc., etc. And then Mr. James solemnly disavowed that either the writer or the publisher of the pamphlet had any intention to incite, etc.; that Mr.

Truelove, believing, etc., had agreed to discontinue the sale of the pamphlet; and that he trusted, etc. And then Lord Campbell solemnly told the jury that it was satisfactory to know, etc.; that the pamphlet was such, etc., that he should have said if the trial had proceeded, etc.; that the defendant had acted with the utmost propriety in the course he had taken, etc. And then the jury solemnly returned a verdict of not guilty. And so the solemn farce ended.

The prosecution was begun by Sir Richard Bethell under the Government of Lord Palmerston, and was abandoned by Sir Fitzroy Kelly under the Government of Lord Derby. It would probably not have been begun at all if a less subservient Minister had been in office. As it was, Lord Derby and his colleagues were no doubt greatly relieved when they found that they had to deal with so obliging a gentleman as Edwin James. But the mischief did not end there; for the very changes in the law which were defeated in 1858 were effected at a later date without anybody seeming to know much about it. Thus was the liberty of discussion restricted. And thus did it become perilous to show that the slaughter of Garibaldians at Mentana was simply another challenge to tyrannicides. It was on this occasion that Du Faillu, reporting to the French Government how Italian patriots had been mown down in swathes, exultantly exclaimed: "The Chassepot has done wonders!" An indignant protest, warning the perpetrator of the outrage of the consequence of his misdeeds, though printed and prepared for publication, had to be suppressed. So were despots and usurpers protected from fitting condemnation, while the very danger which Professor Newman had anticipated befell the country. But an inexorable fate asserted itself at last. Twelve years later the despot and usurper who had triumphed on the Boulevards disappeared in shame and ignominy amidst the blood and smoke of Sedan.

CHAPTER XXXVIII

THE WORKING MEN'S COLLEGE

FACILITIES for the higher education of the people were far from abundant in the middle of the last century. Even mechanics' institutes were few and far between. But scant as were these facilities, it almost seemed that the supply was equal to the demand. The masses of the community, indeed, were so ignorant that they placed little or no value on education of any sort. Nor had they grown much more enlightened towards the end of the century; for many were the parents—mothers especially—who, when Mr. Forster's Education Bill had become law, resented the intrusion of the School Board officer. A few years after that event, I remember accompanying an antiquarian friend on a visit to some historic buildings in the neighbourhood of Tuthill Stairs, Newcastle. We were surprised to notice the effect of our appearance—women hurrying their children into the houses, or hiding them in other ways. When we came to inquire the cause of the commotion, we were told that we were thought to be officers of the School Board! It was really among the educated classes that the necessity for educating the people was first recognised. Mechanics' institutes and other similar enterprises were thus promoted, formed, and supported by persons who had no need for the establishments themselves. Precisely in the same way was that best of all institutions of the kind—the Working Men's College in London—set on foot.

The Rev. Frederic Denison Maurice, the founder of the College, was a distinguished scholar and divine. More than that, he was a distinguished friend of the people. He had been associated with Thomas Hughes and Charles Kingsley in what was known as the Christian Socialist Movement. And he was so much respected and beloved that I found myself, when any point or problem in the doctrine or practices of the Church of England struck me as absurd, asking the question: "How, then, can such things obtain the assent or approval of Mr. Maurice?" The question settled one difficulty at any rate: that there could be nothing inherently absurd in the matter, else so good and so able a man would not preach or conform to it. Yet I knew Mr. Maurice only from seeing and hearing him occasionally at our college meetings. It was out of affection for the people, and especially the working people, that he conceived the idea of placing in the hands of as many as could reach or appreciate them the priceless advantages of a collegiate training. The venture was commenced in 1854 at a house in Red Lion Square, Holborn. After two years' successful operations there, the council announced in its second report that a freehold house, No. 45, Great Ormond Street, Bloomsbury, had been purchased for the further work of the college. The price of the house was £1,500; of this £500 was contributed by Mr. Maurice, and the rest raised on mortgage. So was permanency given to an institution which has conferred infinite benefit on many a struggling student.

The staff of the college—whose services were all voluntary of course—was probably as brilliant as that attached to any other college in the kingdom. Mr. Maurice was the principal. Associated with him were fifty gentlemen, every one of them eminent in art, science, or scholarship. The scholars were distinguished in the list of teachers by the degrees they had acquired at the Universities; the others were described as artists, sculptors, or members of the learned professions. Here are a few of the names:—John Ruskin, Thomas Hughes, F. J. Furnivall, Llewellyn Davies, Lowes Dickinson, R. B. Litchfield, J. M. Ludlow, Godfrey Lushington, Vernon Lushington, Alexander Munro, Dante G. Rossetti, Thomas Woolner, Ford Madox Brown, Frederic Harrison, Edward Burne Jones. Mr. Ruskin taught a drawing class; Mr. Furnivall taught classes in grammar and in the structure and derivation of English words; and the author of "Tom Brown's School Days," still the best book for boys ever written, besides other work in the college conducted, or wanted to conduct, so that the physical as well as the intellectual culture of the student should not be neglected, a boxing class! Teachers and students—at least one-third of the latter belonged to the artizan class—constituted a happy family both at Red Lion Square and at Great Ormond Street; for perfect equality prevailed among all. The only paid officer connected with the college in my time was, I think, the secretary; and this office was held by an old Chartist, Thomas Shorter, whose name I recollected to have seen attached to contributions in *Thomas Cooper's Journal.*

My circumstances when I joined the Working Men's College in the autumn of 1855 were not particularly conducive to study. Being, however, in some sort of settled employment now, the old longing for better education asserted itself. Wherefore I entered three of the classes in the college—Latin, English Grammar, and the Structure and Derivation of Words. But the pursuit of knowledge in my case was necessarily attended by many difficulties. I find in my old diary statements of the conditions under which compositors had to earn their daily bread in the office of a weekly newspaper. An entry for July 12th, 1855, reads thus :—"Worked without intermission for forty hours; slept for twelve, with many intermissions." Other entries show that long hours in the middle of the week were the invariable rule. Monday was our only regular day, and then we worked, or waited for work, from nine o'clock in the morning till eight o'clock at night. "On Tuesday," the old record runs, "we begin at eight, nine, or ten o'clock. From that time till the paper goes to press we work without intermission. Not without interruption, though, especially on Wednesday morning. Always midnight on Wednesday, frequently early hours of Thursday morning, before the last pages are ready for stereotypers. Thus nearly forty hours of continuous work—standing nearly all the time, for to sit is to fall asleep, and run the risk of pieing all the matter we may have in our sticks, as has really happened several times in my own case." The rest of the week we had little to do, except distributing our type ready for the next. But the leisure we got in that way was poor compensation for the excessive toil that preceded it. That excessive toil, moreover, was an indifferent preparation for the study of languages. All the same, the classes were delightful, though I had to give up the Latin from sheer inability to rivet the attention.

The English classes were conducted by Mr. Furnivall. Our tutor was a remarkable man at that date, but he has become a much more remarkable man since. A quarter of a century later he was considered to have done so much excellent work in connection with the study of English philology that he was awarded a pension of £150 a year. It was said at the time that he was the founder of more literary societies than any man living. The Early English Text Society, the Chaucer Society, the New Shakspeare Society, the Society for the Publication of old English Ballads—these are among the learned bodies which owe their existence to his untiring efforts. And the list of books he has edited for the various societies forms a most interesting catalogue of early English literature. Dr. Furnivall's seventy-sixth birthday fell on Feb. 4th, 1901. The occasion was celebrated in a unique and appropriate fashion. A year or more previous fifty of the foremost students and professors of English in different parts of the world—Germans, Americans, Frenchmen among them—combined together to do him honour. They presented him with an old boat—he declined to accept a new one; they persuaded him to sit for his portrait; and they each contributed to a collection of essays and papers which, along with a bibliography of Dr. Furnivall's own productions, was published in a handsome volume by the Clarendon Press on his next birthday. Dr. Furnivall is not only a scholar, but a good deal of an athlete—at least he was even after he had entered his sixties. Like his friend, Tom Hughes— Tom was a term of endearment in this case—he did not, while cultivating the intellectual, neglect the physical element of man. When he had reached the age of sixty-one, and was president of the Maurice Rowing Club, he is recorded to have won in a single season no fewer than three prizes for his skill as a sculler. From what has just been said it will be gathered that he retained at seventy-six his old affection for boating on the river.

But we must hark back to 1855. Our class evenings were exquisite. Part of the time Mr. Furnivall took the words as they followed in the dictionary—dissecting them, showing their origin, and tracing their transformation in sound, meaning, and spelling. Afterwards we read Chaucer and Shakspeare, getting to the root and pursuing the history of every word the poets used. Mr. Furnivall was at that time pale, handsome, and less than thirty. The members of his class were mostly working men. But our tutor put on no airs, as indeed none of the other tutors did. He was a friend and companion even more than a teacher—absolutely one of ourselves. It was his delight to take his class on walking or boating excursions on the Sunday. I remember one glorious afternoon at Kew, for I could not often join the party. Another summer afternoon I remember being at Hampstead, when teacher and class came pelting along the road with coats over their arms. Mr. Furnivall on other occasions invited the students to his chambers after lessons. I joined them one winter's night. The chambers were in Ely Place, Holborn. Every nook and corner was filled with books—all treasures of literature. Here we sat over biscuits and coffee till an advanced hour of the morning, talking or listening to talk about poets and poetry, and languages and literature, and having such a feast of reason and flow of soul as almost never was since Shakspeare had his bout with Ben Jonson at the Mermaid. Ely Place, closed to all intruders by an iron gate in Holborn, was perhaps then the only locality where an ancient custom of the Charlies was still observed. Anyway, we heard the watchman crying in the street below—"Past two o'clock, and a frosty morning." But Dr. Furnivall in those days burnt much midnight oil in his studies, rarely retiring to bed, he told us himself, till five hours "ayont the twal."

Three of the students of the college acquitted themselves so well that they were elected to the Council of Teachers—Rossiter, Roebuck, and Tansley. Rossiter was held in high favour and esteem both by professors and students. And he eminently deserved the position he held, on account alike of his genial qualities, his capacity for acquiring knowledge, and his readiness at all times to impart what he knew to others. Influenced probably by the commanding and attractive character of Maurice, Mr. Rossiter became a clergyman himself. Some ten years after the period I have been writing about, he was instrumental in founding another college in the metropolis— the South London Working Men's College, of which Professor Huxley was for a long time the principal. Ten years later again this institution was removed to Kennington Lane, Lambeth, where Mr. Rossiter, placing his own books at the disposal of the poorer classes of the neighbourhood, opened the first Free Library in South London. Subsequently, a few pictures being added to the library, this small exhibition became the germ of the South London Fine Art Gallery, which, in 1897, having been acquired by the Camberwell

Vestry, was converted into the permanent establishment that is now known as the Passmore Edwards Art Gallery and Technical Institute. I was brought into contact with Mr. Rossiter again some time in the early nineties—how I can't recollect. But at that time he was a regular contributor of dramatic and other notes to the *Newcastle Weekly Chronicle*. When he died in 1897, the event was sympathetically noticed by all the London and many of the provincial newspapers; for he was, as the *Times* said of him, and as I can testify from personal knowledge, "much beloved by all whose privilege it was to share his friendship."

I cannot close this chapter without confessing that large numbers of working people owe a deep debt of gratitude to the eminent and enthusiastic gentlemen who, placing their scholarship at the service of the artizans of London, helped to establish a real bond of union between the richer and poorer classes of the country.

CHAPTER XXXIX

MANCHESTER

THE irritating nature of my employment in London, coupled with the miserable wages I was able to earn, owing to the many hours of weary idleness we had to pass in waiting for "copy," induced me to accept the offer of a situation in Manchester. I had suffered so much, mentally and bodily, from the treatment I had received in common with the rest of our little companionship, that it was no longer a mystery to me why working men hated their employers. If others endured what I had endured, the animosity was not only excusable, but justified. The root of the mischief was want of thought or consideration for people whose lot it was to toil in shop or factory. Indifference to wrongs and evils that can often be easily removed — how can it help but breed bitterness and wrath? Had the captains of every industry behaved to the rank and file as men ought always to behave to men, they would not have planted those seeds of strife which have brought in recent years so plentiful a crop of strikes and disasters. Bad masters sowed the wind, and good masters are now reaping the whirlwind. But I am digressing.

Manchester at the end of the fifties had stoned its prophets. But it was still the seat and centre of the political school to which it had given its name. Mr. Bright, handsome and portly, was often seen in its streets, often heard on its platforms. The Free Trade Hall was filled to overflowing whenever any great question was to be discussed. It was there that I heard Kossuth; it was there that I heard Mason Jones; it was there that I heard Washington Wilks. Kossuth we know; but who were Jones and Wilks? Jones was an eloquent lecturer, Wilks an eloquent politician of the day. The Hungarian exile met with a magnificent reception. The audience seemed to cheer itself hoarse. A few years later I heard Kossuth again. It was somewhere in Clerkenwell. But the audience then was miserably scanty. Between it and the applauding thousands in Manchester the contrast was terrible. The fickle populace had forgotten or forsaken its idol. No wonder that the poor exile, cast down and almost broken-hearted, soon afterwards retired to another clime. The great hall in which so many stirring scenes were enacted was one of the products of the corn-law agitation. Mr. George Wilson, the chairman of the association that conducted the movement, was yet an active force in the town. But when he and other colleagues of his in the old organization ventured to suggest an advance in the direction of Parliamentary reform, they were described and assailed, I recollect, as the "rump of the League." There came a time, however, as we may see later, when Manchester again led the van.

Amusing to me, when I became a resident in the town, was the evil reputation I had heard given to it by the chance acquaintance I had met on the road only four or five years before. The people, I found, were up to the average in behaviour and kindliness—above the average in intelligence and cleanliness. There was not, I thought, a more neighbourly woman in the world than the Manchester woman. As for cleanliness, she took as much pride in the front of her house as she did in her own kitchen, whereas women in other parts I have known never think of even sweeping their pavements, no matter what the filth or foulness accumulated around. But there were black spots about. Part of Deansgate was a nest of thieves. The Irk was a foul and inky ditch, and the Irwell and the Medlock were scarcely less loathsome. The Town Hall was in King Street, and the site of the present municipal palace was a camping-ground for Corporation dust carts.

Of course there was a better side to the town. The first Free Library was established in a building that had been erected by the followers of Robert Owen, and branch libraries were being opened in different districts. The Athenæum was a flourishing institution, as was the Mechanics' Institute, and a Working Men's College was offering immense advantages to poor students. Pomona Gardens in one direction and Bellevue Gardens in another were favourite resorts of the people. Charles Calvert was manager of the principal theatre, and Charles Hallé was giving periodical concerts of the highest quality. Chetham Library was a restful resort, where the quaintest of quaint volumes could be consulted by everybody. Charming places surrounded the town. Whalley Range was a residential suburb of exquisite beauty; Brooks's Bar was away in the country; Greenheys Fields were charged with rural walks; beyond Moss Lane the Moss-side Fields afforded opportunity for a lovely ramble to Northenden. Chorlton-cum-Hardy was a delightful little village within reach of Hulme on a Sunday morning in summer. For Saturday afternoon excursions—factories and workshops and warehouses were all closed at mid-day or soon after—there were Bowden and Alderley Edge and many another point of attraction. So Manchester was not such a bad place after all.

The situation I accepted was that of reader and compositor in a small jobbing office. Our principal business was the production of the *Alliance News*, the organ of the United Kingdom Alliance. Mr. Thomas H. Barker was then the secretary of the society, and Mr. Henry Septimus Sutton the editor of the paper. Mr. Barker was a man of great energy, absolutely absorbed in his work; Mr. Sutton was a bit of a poet ("Emerson thought some of his pieces were worthy of George Herbert ") who ingeniously turned almost every event of the day into an argument for the prohibition of the liquor traffic. What I chiefly recollect about the Alliance at that time was the long, elaborate, and masterly reports which Mr. Samuel Pope, the hon. secretary, used to produce for the annual meetings of the society. [24] Yes, I recollect another thing. A question had been submitted by the Alliance to the clergy and ministers of religion throughout the country, and hundreds of letters had been received in reply. These replies were printed in the *News*, and passed through my hands as reader. I was astonished at the loose, slovenly, and ungrammatical way in which educated men—all of whom had been trained in colleges and some of whom had won degrees in universities—expressed themselves. It occurred to me that these gentlemen had spent so much time in the study of Latin and Greek and Hebrew that they had forgotten to learn English.

The change I had made was, as Mr. Epps said of his cocoa, grateful and comforting. I had regular work, regular hours, regular wages—always my evenings at home or to myself, except once a week. I had now several hours of a night which I could spend in my own pleasures or my own pursuits—in reading, writing, taking a stroll, or attending a class. Life was no longer a weariness: it was a real enjoyment. I was happy and contented: so was my dear companion. There wasn't a happier or more contented couple in all Manchester. The men with whom I worked, too, were generally of a higher order than those I had encountered in London. While there was less dissipation among them, there was also, as may be supposed, a more refined taste. Every man in the establishment, and indeed every boy, took an intelligent interest in public affairs. The talk was of politics, of literature, of cheering events of the day. Men and boys read the newspapers, the magazines, books; and they had views of their own about all they read. The Free Libraries were a boon and a blessing to many of them. Besides borrowing books from the libraries, we had a book club of our own. Thus we kept ourselves abreast of the culture of the time. Better than all, I found lifelong friends in Manchester, one in the office, others elsewhere. The friend I made in the office was one of the gentlest, best read, and most refined gentlemen I have ever met. [25] It was in such sweet companionship at home or on pedestrian excursions among the picturesque dales and peaks of Derbyshire that my four years in Manchester passed like a summer holiday.

There was a Working Men's College in Manchester too. I made other friends at the college. The classes I attended were conducted, the one by a Unitarian minister, the other by a curate of the Church of England. The Unitarian minister was the Rev. William Gaskell, husband of the famous novelist; the curate of the Church of England was the Rev. William Thackeray Marriott, who, leaving the Church, became first a barrister, then a member of Parliament, and finally the Right Honourable Sir W. T. Marriott. Mr. Gaskell was a master of literature. I thought at the time that he was the most beautiful reader I had ever heard. Prose or poetry seemed to acquire new lustre and elegance when he read it. Our literary evenings under Mr. Gaskell were ambrosial evenings indeed. [26] Mr. Marriott's class was devoted to the History of England. The reverend gentleman was as little like a clergyman as he was like a costermonger. There was nothing clerical—nothing even conventional—about him. Free and easy in his manners, he was as familiar with the members of his class as they were with each other. Even his lectures, if they could be called lectures, were notable for their freedom from the least sign of pedantry. It was really a conversation on historic subjects that he carried on with the working men who sat before him. Mr. Marriott's views, moreover, especially on the controversy between the Parliament and Charles the First, were of a very advanced character. Our old tutor has figured in many prominent transactions since 1859, but in none which was more calculated to win the esteem and regard of his old scholars. Besides literature and history, I tried my hand at logic, under Professor Newth of the Lancashire Independent College. But logic, literature, and history, so far as classes were concerned, had to be abandoned when the Working Men's College, greatly to the disappointment of the students, was merged into Owens College, then situated in an old mansion in Deansgate, but now located in a palatial home of its own.

While gratifying my taste for such studies as I had time or capacity for pursuing, I did not forget the republican idea. Whenever chances presented themselves, the editors of the local papers—the *Examiner,* the *Guardian,* and the *Courier*—were pestered with letters in defence of Mazzini or in explanation of revolutionary enterprises. With the view of reviving interest in the Reform question, I wrote, printed, and published at my own expense a rather heavy "Argument for Complete Suffrage." But nobody wanted the pamphlet, and I was burdened with a debt which took me a long time to pay off. Also I wrote, and here and there delivered, a lecture on a still heavier subject—"The Province of Authority in Matters of Opinion." This was printed too, but nobody wanted it either. However, a peculiar opportunity for getting said what I wanted said occurred in the summer of 1859. Somebody speculated on the publication of a weekly paper called the *Buxton Visitor.* It was printed in our office. The speculators had no notion of what was wanted for even an ephemeral journal. All they supplied was a list of the visitors to the Derbyshire town, with of course the advertisements. The rest of the matter had to be found by the printer. I was asked to write the leading articles—gratuitously of course. Yes, I said, if I was allowed to choose my own subjects and treat them in my own way. It was the time when Louis Napoleon went to war for what he called an idea—the idea subsequently taking the substantial form of a couple of Italian provinces. Well, I pegged away at the war and other questions all through the season. The summer butterflies who fluttered about Buxton must have been much surprised when they read, if they did read, the fiery lucubrations that occupied the leading columns of the *Visitor*. At that time I was rejoiced when I could get my opinions before the public, anyhow or anywhere. I would write anything for nothing if I approved of it—nothing for anything if I did not. A quack doctor wanted his wretched treatise revised, and an invitingly handsome sum was offered me to do the work. I refused. Great was the astonishment of the smug printer, who went regularly to church with silk hat and prayer-book of a Sunday morning, when I politely declined a proposition which he thought any poor devil in my situation would jump at. "Old Jacky," as we called him, did not understand how anybody could be fool enough to make a conscience of writing.

Mr. Ruskin, during my time, came to Manchester to lecture on some art subject. The chair, I remember, was taken by the Mayor—then Mr. Ivie Mackie. His worship was a spirit merchant—a man of liberal sentiments, but not, I thought, very intellectual. Stout and stolid, he sat in the chair without moving a muscle of his face or betraying the least interest in the subject. Presently, however, Mr. Ruskin quoted Goldsmith's epistle to Lord Clare for the gift of a haunch of venison:—

> Thanks, my lord, for your venison, for finer or fatter
> Ne'er ranged in a forest or smoked on a platter;
> The haunch was a picture for painters to study,
> The fat was so rich, and the lean was so ruddy.

Here was something the Mayor could understand. It probably revived recollections of feasts he had enjoyed. Anyhow, he laughed consumedly. I think it was the only time he smiled or showed any intelligence throughout the discourse. As for Mr. Ruskin—I had not then read any of his books, and knew little or nothing of his style as a writer of pure and beautiful English—I am afraid I was not very much impressed with either his appearance or his performance. Admiration for the man and the author came later.

CHAPTER XL

"THE NATIONAL REFORMER"

ONE Sunday, in the winter of 1859-60, Charles Bradlaugh, who still called himself "Iconoclast," was announced to lecture in Manchester. I had not seen him since the ignominious collapse of the "Tyrannicide" trial. But we were good friends then, and always afterwards. I had pleasant recollections, too, of an afternoon and evening which my wife and I, fresh from our honeymoon, had spent at his home in Hackney. Of course I went to hear him in Manchester. The expedition had a comical consequence. A baby had come to us by that time, and our little household in Hulme was further augmented by a visit from my wife's sister. Nothing had been said when I left home about company to dinner. After his morning's lecture, however, I asked the lecturer to come and take "pot luck" with me. The invitation was readily accepted—all the more readily because, he said, he had something to say to me. There was consternation in Cuba Street when I landed with a visitor—not because the visitor was not welcome, but because nothing had been provided for his entertainment. The feast (suitable to our means and circumstances) consisted of a small steak, a few potatoes, and an apple pudding—the first article on the menu barely enough for three, certainly not for four. But the ladies were equal to the occasion. Bradlaugh and his host dined on steak and potatoes in a parlour not much bigger than a cupboard, while the hostess and her sister did the best they could with potatoes and pudding in the kitchen! It was rather a memorable event, that Sunday dinner, for it resulted in the end in a complete diversion of the current of my career.

Down to that moment I had had no notion of ever rising to any higher position than that of printer's reader. I had absolutely no ambition beyond that. Work of any honest sort I was willing to do for a living; but literature, so far as I had any capacity for pursuing it, was, I thought, a thing too sacred to be associated with pelf. The hands were for wages; but the brain was for nobler uses. It was a degradation of intellect to accept payment for its products. The idea was romantic. Nevertheless, I have never been able to get thoroughly rid of it. When I heard that men like Thornton Hunt or George Augustus Sala wrote, not what they approved or believed, but what they thought would please their patrons or the public, I could feel nothing but contempt for them. Such doings were dishonest, and worse—they were a prostitution of the intellect. Nor have I to this day been able to get over a feeling of utter disgust when I hear of political journalists transferring their services as readily as they change their garments from one party paper to another. It has luckily been my good fortune to fall in with directors of the press who have respected at all times the conscientious convictions of their subordinates. And these subordinates of the press, I am satisfied, would have done better work and earned a wider respect if, having convictions, they had always insisted on keeping them in mind. But I am digressing again.

Mr. Bradlaugh, after that comical little dinner in Manchester, unfolded a scheme which some of his friends in Sheffield were promoting for the establishment of a weekly paper. It was to be Radical in politics, and Freethought in theology. Would I become one of the political contributors? The proposition took me aback. It had never entered my head that I could be a contributor to anything. The *Buxton Visitor* had not at that time cast its effulgent light over the world. Even if it had, it would have counted for nothing. It was true that I had written a few letters to the papers; but these also counted for nothing. Mr. Bradlaugh reminded me that I had written an essay on Sir John Eliot for one of his earlier periodicals. Still I hesitated. The more I hesitated the more my friend pressed his point. Well, I would try. The result was that the contributions of Caractacus appeared every week in the *National Reformer* for many years—until, in fact, other duties prevented the writer from continuing them. Mr. Bradlaugh was an indulgent editor, for never was a single article rejected or a single sentence altered. Caractacus's effusion was generally the chief political item in the *National Reformer*. But Mr. Bradlaugh accompanied his proposition with a promise—the promise to pay a modest price for each contribution. Though the promise had no weight with me, and I did not hold it binding, it was not altogether vetoed, for my small family would likely become larger and my small income more inadequate. As everybody knows, Bradlaugh's financial circumstances were never very prosperous; but I owed infinitely more to him for comfort and help in adversity than the insignificant score I wiped off the slate when I obtained permanent employment in Newcastle-on-Tyne.

About the time the *National Reformer* was projected, a notable Yorkshireman was returning to England after a few years' residence in America. This was Joseph Barker. Mr. Barker was a man of great natural ability. Whether in writing or in speaking, he had an incisive power which few other men of his time had. But he was plausible rather than convincing. Nor was he much abashed, as we shall see, when his own arguments were brought in evidence against him. If Mr. Barker had been less given to change, less saturated with egotism and pomposity, he would have been a considerable power in the State. But he never seemed to know his mind for longer than a month or two together. Thus it happened that he boxed both the political and the theological compass. He began as a Methodist in Hanley; then he was a Unitarian in Lancashire; then a Barkerite in Newcastle; then a Freethinker in America; and then—well, he was still a Freethinker when he returned to the old country. Later he went back to some form of orthodoxy, and died in it. Barker's speeches and writings were spotted and dotted with epigrams and dogmas. Indeed, as I knew the man, he was nothing if not dogmatic. And he was as cocksure after every turnabout as if he had always crowed from the same dunghill. Emerson's doctrine suited him exactly: "Consistency is the hobgoblin of little minds." No such hobgoblin troubled Joseph Barker. Whatever the particular housetop on which he happened to be strutting or swaggering, he spoke his mind "as hard as cannon balls," utterly regardless of the fact that he had not long before been hurling cannon balls from altogether different elevations. It is true, too, that he had audacity against the world. There occurred an instance that would have been sublime if it had not been so supremely ludicrous. When Barker was in America, he had written a letter against slavery which was perhaps the finest piece of vituperation he had ever penned. But when the Civil War broke out, he took to delivering lectures in favour of the Southern slave-owners. One night somebody produced and read the letter he had written a few years before. Was he the Joseph Barker who had written it? "No," was the astounding reply. "It is, as everybody knows, a physiological fact that the particles of the human frame are all changed in the course of every seven years. More than seven years have elapsed since that letter was written; therefore I am not the Joseph Barker who wrote it!"

But Joseph Barker at the end of 1859 was coming back to England with a great reputation as a Radical and a Freethinker. He had owned and edited periodicals before he had crossed and re-crossed the Atlantic. His admirers also, I think, had presented him with a printing-press. Such of his old friends as still remained faithful to the wanderer proposed to repeat the gift, and set him up again with the means of reaching and preaching to the multitude. And then another idea was suggested. Instead of starting two papers to cover the same ground—one for Bradlaugh and the other for Barker—why not join forces, and make Barker and Bradlaugh joint editors of a single venture? The proposal was accepted. It was seen from the outset, however, that a joint editorship, which would work very well with two ordinary propagandists, would not work at all with two such masterful men as Bradlaugh and Barker. So a peculiar arrangement was adopted. When the *National Reformer* appeared on April 14th, 1860, it was found that the first half of it was under the exclusive direction of Joseph Barker, while the rest was under the exclusive direction of Charles Bradlaugh. Very soon Mr. Barker began to criticise, and then to denounce, the articles that appeared in Mr. Bradlaugh's half of the paper. These criticisms and denunciations took the insidious form of answers to imaginary correspondents. It was the contributions of Caractacus that seemed to inspire the greatest dislike, especially when the subject under discussion was Garibaldi, or Louis Napoleon, or the American War; for Mr. Barker, in respect to the rights of revolutionists and of negroes, was already beginning to turn his back upon himself once more. Of course there were rejoinders now and then, and once Caractacus threw down a challenge for a set discussion on some doctrine that had been asserted and disputed. But the whole thing became so ludicrous at length that the dual arrangement had to be abandoned. There was a sharp struggle for supremacy; Mr. Bradlaugh became sole editor and eventually sole proprietor of the paper; and the *National Reformer*, with the exception of a short interval during a serious illness, continued to be issued under his control and direction till the day he died.

Mr. Bradlaugh had other colleagues who proved in the end hardly more satisfactory than Joseph Barker. One of these was Edward Aveling; another was Annie Besant.

Aveling was a young man of immense promise when he first connected himself with the *National Reformer*. The variety of his gifts, as then and later shown, was astonishing. A doctor of science of the University of London, he was also an actor, a dramatist, and a general compiler of scientific works. He translated Ibsen, and he dramatised "Judith Shakspeare." For a year or two Aveling was a devoted adherent of Bradlaugh's and a regular contributor to the *National Reformer*. And then he went off into Socialism, played at man and wife with the daughter of Karl Marx, led what appears to have been a dissolute and abandoned life, and perished miserably in 1898. Eleanor Marx died by her own hand—driven to that act of desperation, as certain piteous letters of hers published afterwards indicate, by Aveling's unpardonable misbehaviour. The author of the mischief did not long survive the distracted Eleanor. When he in turn was carried to the grave, it was remarked that "not one of his brethren of the cause was present at Woking to bid farewell to his ashes." The reason of the neglect is to be found in an article in Justice for July 30th, 1898, explaining "what drove Eleanor Marx to suicide." It was not likely that "brethren of the cause" would have much respect for a man who had behaved so ill as Aveling had to the daughter of a high priest of Socialism.

Mrs. Besant became a recruit of Mr. Bradlaugh's about the same time as Dr. Aveling. But she remained longer in the ranks. And while she remained it must be admitted that she fought as valiantly as any. Mr. Bradlaugh was not so much her friend as her idol. Able as she was, and strong-minded as she appeared to be, she was yet the very creature of circumstances. Mrs. Besant made the acquaintance of Thomas Scott, and became a Rationalist; made the acquaintance of Charles Bradlaugh, and became a Freethinker; made the acquaintance of Madame Blavatzky, and became a Theosophist. While she was associated with Bradlaugh, she was so influenced by the vigorous intellect of her idol that she imitated his manners in private, his gestures and methods of argument on the platform. And not very long afterwards she was worshipping a stout old lady who smoked cigarettes. It was simply amazing that she who could not accept the miracles of the Bible should find comfort in the miracles of the Mahatmas. Mrs. Besant had strained at a gnat, but had somehow managed to swallow a camel! The whirligig of her strange career, however, did not stop even at Theosophy. It was announced in 1894 that she had become a Buddhist. Seven years elapsed, and then we heard that she was touring the North of India in a Buddhist dress, proclaiming her belief that she was a Hindoo in a former birth! My acquaintance with the lady was but slight. Once she came to dinner with us. It was a modest little repast enough; but she need not have distressed the poor hostess by speaking of it, as she did more than once, as a luncheon. Worse was to come. The hostess was also a mother. And the great lady—for she had lost none of her fine-lady airs by associating with the common people—completed her own discomfiture by the manner in which she pretended to kiss the children. "She need not have kissed them at all," said the mother; "but if she did, she might have put some heart and feeling into the process, instead of touching them as though they were toffy, and would soil her gloves." From all which it may be concluded that Mrs. Besant, her remarkable abilities notwithstanding, did not make a very favourable impression in our household.

CHAPTER XLI

CHARLES BRADLAUGH UGH

MR. BRADLAUGH filled so large a space in the public life of England at the close of the nineteenth century that it may not be uninteresting if I here tell a little of what I knew about him. It has already been mentioned that he came to be known to me, or I came to be known to him, in 1858. Thenceforward no opportunity of renewing the acquaintance was ever lost. From time to time he was in the habit of stopping at my house when he came round on his lecturing tours. Also at another period I accepted an invitation to breakfast with him every morning till he could tell me of something to my advantage. So in one way and another I knew him perhaps as intimately as most of his friends.

That Mr. Bradlaugh had his weaknesses goes without saying. Who is without these little disorders? There was, indeed, much egotism in the man, but it was a splendid egotism—at all events an egotism that may have surprised, but did not offend other people. Nor was it concealed from his associates. I have heard him myself jocularly proclaim and confess the impeachment. And it had its origin in the knowledge he possessed of his own power. Mr. Bradlaugh—it was amusing at times to hear him talk of The Bradlaugh—would never have won the position he held in the country if he had not, like Lord Beaconsfield, thoroughly believed in himself. It was this belief in himself that lay at the root of the vanity which was the one conspicuous defect of his character. There are some, I dare say, who would hold that he was on occasion a trifle arrogant too. This trait, however, was so much more seeming than real that only persons who may have smarted from an angry lash of his tongue on a platform would magnify a small infirmity of temper.

People who saw nothing but the public side of Bradlaugh, which was probably, after all, his worst side, had little or no idea of his personal or social attractions. When enjoying the company of his friends, he was the most courteous and entertaining of men. It was delightful, for instance, to listen to his account of his adventures in the army. An officious clergyman, when as a mere youth he had begun to take part in public discussions, got him discharged from his employment. Rendered desperate by this scandalous intervention, he entered Her Majesty's service. The regiment in which he had enlisted was a regiment of foot; but the sergeant of the foot regiment, owing a shilling to the sergeant of a dragoon regiment, paid him with a recruit! The young soldier was thus, without being consulted, transferred to the cavalry service. It was all one to Bradlaugh, however. Being sent to a barracks in Ireland, he speedily became popular with his comrades, who called him "Leaves," first because he used to talk to them about teetotalism, and next because he was fond of books. The tales he told of the tricks and escapades that marked his career in the Irish barracks "kept the table in a roar." But it was probably not often that he had leisure for these pleasant indulgences. That he had few amusements may be inferred from the intense and busy life that he led; yet the few he favoured were not clumsily pursued. Thus he was an accomplished hand at chess and billiards, while his feats as an angler, I understood, have seldom been surpassed.

Charles Bradlaugh
(1833-61)

Not the least striking nor the least admired of Bradlaugh's characteristics were his industry and his energy. Whatever his hand found to do he did it with all his might. His motto was "Thorough." And he lived up to it. I am satisfied that his days would have been longer in the land if, heeding the frequent warnings he received, he had presumed less on the magnificent strength he had once enjoyed. But he could no more restrain himself than sparks can refrain from flying upwards. It was his custom at one period, while immersed all the week in commercial transactions (I think they had to do with a scheme for converting Italian sand into steel), to travel through the Saturday night away into the distant provinces, to deliver three lectures on the Sunday, and then on Sunday night to travel back again, so as to be ready for business on Monday morning. If he happened to stay all night at a friend's house (as he did often in mine), the fire-grate of his room would be found when he quitted it filled with fragments of the letters he had answered or of the documents he no longer needed.

Never a moment idle, he lived the lives of half a dozen ordinary men. No wonder that he collapsed at a comparatively early age. Bear in mind also that his lectures involved no slight amount of physical as well as intellectual strain. It is true that the preparations he made were not of an elaborate character when he had once mastered his theme. And, besides, he sometimes lectured on one subject many times over. But, however often he may have treated the theme, he always made it a point, he told me, of drawing up a fresh outline— usually on a single sheet of note-paper—before going down to the lecture hall. Now and then he would seem to allow himself to be carried away in his discourse by his own passions and emotions. A very cataract of words, uttered with all the power and vehemence of a Stentor, would, on these occasions, sweep his audiences before him as in a torrent or a whirlwind. And then at the end of the final outburst he would sink to his seat on the platform—panting, perspiring, exhausted. The result of these efforts, as I often sorrowfully witnessed on the ride home, was such a waste of tissue as no living man, though he were as strong as a Samson, could long withstand.

Here I am tempted to tell a tale out of school. It would not have been told (or rather retold) if I did not know that the humour of the incident was as highly enjoyed by the gentleman chiefly concerned in it as by those who witnessed it. A party of friends from Newcastle were on their way to spend a brief holiday in Ireland. Among them was Thomas Burt, then newly-elected member of Parliament for Morpeth. They were seated in a train at Carlisle ready to start for Dumfries en route to Stranraer. Suddenly there was a commotion on the platform. A working man had been deprived of his seat, and was swearing and gesticulating at large. The Newcastle travellers invited him to take a vacant seat among them. The man was still in a rage. "Joe Cowen shall hear of this," he muttered. The travellers pricked up their ears. "Joe Cowen?" said one of them: "who is he?" "Wat! nivvor hard of Joe Cowen? He's wor member, and winnot see a warking man wranged." "Oh, then, you come from Newcastle?" "No, aa divvent; aa belang Dor'm, and wark at Medomsley." "You will know Mr. Crawford, then?" (William Crawford was then the agent of the Durham miners.) "Aa shud think se—hard him at aall wor demonstrations." "Do you know Mr. Burt too? " "Wat! Tommy Bort? Aa ken him as weel as aa ken ma ain brither." Further leading questions and much silent chuckling. "Hard him at wor last demonstration. Tommy's varry good—varry good for a skuyl-room. But Charlie Bradlaugh's the man for the oppen air." Then followed great praise of Bradlaugh's oratory. And then the train stopped at a wayside station, and the man from Medomsley, bidding his acquaintances good-bye, staggered across the platform to the exit. "Good for a school-room," while it added to the mirth of the party, was accepted as a testimony that the intellectual predominated over the physical powers of the member for Morpeth.

The incident showed the estimation in which Mr. Bradlaugh was held by admirers all over the country. But some who listened to his stormy outbursts were at times inclined to say that the orator was a windbag. A different estimate would have been formed if they had heard him lecturing on what he called the "God Idea." No heat, no passion, never a superfluous word throughout that masterpiece of exposition and reasoning, as I once heard it in Newcastle. Equally effective, and for the same reason, was his speech at the Bar of the House of Commons, as well as other speeches of his in defence of the rights of his constituents. The sustained power and the dignified restraint of these deliverances must have struck everybody who read the reports of them. No statesman in Lords or Commons could have done better—perhaps so well.

When I knew Mr. Bradlaugh first, he was regarded by all the so-called respectable classes of the community as a dangerous, desperate, not to say disreputable character. Iconoclast, as he then called himself, found few friends save among pitmen, factory hands, and other sections of the working classes. If Mr. Bradlaugh had taken to breaking windows, or even breaking heads, instead of breaking images, he could not have been held in greater disfavour. Why, I remember on one occasion, when he lectured at Wigan, the popular resentment against him was so strong that the hotel in which he took refuge was surrounded and invaded by a raging mob. Nor did public opinion change towards him during the whole period of his many years' struggle to obtain a seat in Parliament. Even after he had been duly elected, the House of Commons itself adopted the unconstitutional procedure of refusing to acknowledge his return. Nay, the officials of the House, acting on orders from above, expelled him from the precincts of St. Stephen's by physical force. And yet not many years after these unwarranted and outrageous transactions, prayers and supplications were offered up in churches and chapels for his recovery from a serious illness!

The conduct of the House of Commons in the matter of the election for Northampton was as foolish as it was mean. The House allowed itself to be led into a quagmire by Lord Randolph Churchill and Sir Stafford Northcote, though the way to it seems to have been prepared by Mr. Speaker Brand. Blinded by prejudice and malice, the House committed the extraordinary folly of resolving that Mr. Bradlaugh, holding an unimpeached return for the borough of Northampton, should not be permitted to take the oath prescribed by law. I remember writing of this piece of stupidity at the time:—
"The resolution adopted on March 6th, 1882, has prolonged the Bradlaugh trouble. As a plaster may conceal a wound without healing it, so a resolution may obscure a difficulty without getting rid of it. John Wilkes was expelled from the House because he was detested by the Tories of his day. Subsequently, however, the House

had to submit to the humiliation of expunging from its records the resolutions it had passed in reference to him. The opponents of the admission of Mr. Bradlaugh are preparing the way for a similar humiliation."

Here was a safe prophecy. Before nine years were passed the prophecy was fulfilled. The wrongful orders of 1882 were erased in 1891. But Mr. Bradlaugh was then lying on his death-bed. Nor did he live long enough to learn that the House of Commons had at last done him justice. Public feeling in respect to him, however, had by that time undergone a complete revulsion. He had won by his wise and urbane conduct in Parliament the good will of all classes and parties in the country. The Leader of the House, Mr. W. H. Smith, the successor of Sir Stafford Northcote, paid a respectful visit to the dying man's residence; and, when he was no more, speeches in lamentation of the loss the country had sustained were made from both sides of the House—that very House from which only nine years before he had been forcibly, ignominiously, and in violation of law, expelled.

No public man within my recollection was the mark and object of more calumnies and falsehoods than Charles Bradlaugh. Repeated from mouth to mouth, from platform to platform, from pulpit to pulpit, these stories and inventions were often of the most puerile and paltry complexion. Almost every week the *National Reformer* denied this or that lie. But sometimes, when the offender was particularly offensive, he was compelled to apologise and send a handsome subscription to a charity fund in order to avoid a prosecution for libel. The most cruel falsehood of all, however, was circulated when Mr. Bradlaugh had been six years in his grave. It was contained in a book of reminiscences which Mr. C. A. Cooper, the editor of the *Scotsman*, published in 1897. Mr. Cooper therein asserted, on the alleged authority of a member of the House of Commons, that the Reform League at the period of the great Reform agitation had organized a riot in London, to be followed or accompanied by a series of fires, and that Mr. Bradlaugh, false and treacherous to his own colleagues, disclosed the plot to the Home Secretary, with the result that there was no outbreak and no incendiarism. Mr. Bradlaugh may have been many things which people like Mr. Cooper's informant reprobate; but he was certainly neither a fool nor a scoundrel. I took the trouble to refer the matter to Mr. George Howell, who, as secretary of the Reform League from its commencement to its dissolution, was privy to all its proceedings. "The whole story," he wrote to me, "is a pure invention, a fabrication from beginning to end." And I suggested to Mrs. Bradlaugh-Bonner that she should, in vindication of her father's memory, so wantonly aspersed, demand from Mr. Cooper an explanation or an apology. The demand was made; but Mrs. Bonner was not favoured with an answer to her letters.

Meeting Mr. Cooper in Madeira in the spring of 1901, I called his attention to the injustice he had done to Mr. Bradlaugh. The statement he had published, he said, was made to him by an Irish member of Parliament, whose name he privately mentioned. If a new edition of his book should be issued, he would, he added, after what I had told him, certainly modify or withdraw the statement. As to not answering Mrs. Bonner's letters, he said that he abstained because he did not want to be drawn into a controversy.

CHAPTER XLII

THE SLAVEOWNERS' WAR

IT was while I was residing at Manchester, the seat and centre of the suffering which followed, that the civil war between North and South broke out in the United States. So I saw the beginning of that appalling period known as the Cotton Famine. The exigencies of the conflict compelled the Northern or Federal Government to blockade the Southern ports. Hence no produce from the Cotton States could reach the mills in Lancashire. Though the manufacturers made almost frantic efforts to obtain supplies elsewhere, the factories had gradually to close from one end of the county to the other. The state of the people was terrible; but the privations they endured, mitigated rather than removed by the organization of relief works, were borne with heroic fortitude—all the more heroic because, knowing the cause of the trouble in America, they refused to be misled into supporting a policy which, while it would have terminated their own miseries, would have riveted afresh, and perhaps for centuries, the shackles of the slave.

The public mind of England was in a condition of strange ignorance respecting American affairs at the time the great struggle commenced. Some of us—friends of freedom everywhere—were familiar with the great Anti-Slavery Movement. William Lloyd Garrison, Wendell Phillips, and Theodore Parker were names that ranked in our calendar of braves alongside those of Joseph Mazzini, Louis Kossuth, and Victor Hugo. But the great bulk of the English people knew nothing of the struggle across the Atlantic—of the "irrepressible conflict" impending there, of the Underground Railway, of the Fugitive Slave Law, of the fight for Kansas and Missouri, of John Brown's heroic descent on Harper's Ferry. Even the party names—Re-publicans, Democrats, Free-Soilers—had little or no meaning for people here. Indeed, speaking generally, we were about as ignorant of American politics as we were of politics in Morocco or Bokhara. When, therefore, the war began with the bombardment of Fort Sumter, and the torch was set to a conflagration which veritable seas of blood failed for nearly four years to extinguish, the world at large was in a state of wonderment as to the cause and merits of the quarrel. It was while the public mind was in a state of vacuity that an astute gentleman of Southern proclivities obtained possession of the public ear. This was Mr. James Spence, of Liverpool. Mr. Spence, writing long letters to the *Times*, set up the theory that the tariff, and not the negro, was the cause of the war. And as the Southern States were for Free Trade and the Northern States were for Protection, it was the Southern States, he contended, that were entitled to British sympathies. So was public opinion warped and misled at the outset.

The first clear note on the right side was sounded by John Stuart Mill in the *Westminster Review*. But before this note was struck, large numbers of our people and nearly all our newspapers had already taken sides. Mr. Mill's article, however, helped to arrest the spread of the heresy. We were paying the penalty, he said, of our neglect of contemporary events abroad. If we had kept ourselves informed of American affairs, we should never have fallen into the error of misunderstanding them. Then followed an exposition which made the whole quarrel as transparent as a point in our own polity. The Northern States, it was true, were not for uprooting slavery in the way that Garrison was. But they had adopted a policy which would inevitably extinguish that hateful institution in the end. That policy was that slavery should not be permitted to extend beyond its present borders. But to limit slavery, as the slaveowners knew, was to throttle it. Slave labour could be profitably applied only to the simplest form of cultivation—the cultivation of cotton, for instance. Cotton, however, exhausted the soil in a moderate number of years. Maryland and Virginia, exhausted already, had become mere slave-breeding States. Other States were following in the same downward groove. If, therefore, the "peculiar institution" was to be preserved, fresh slave territories must be opened. But the Northern States had set their faces against any such procedure. Moreover, the election of Abraham Lincoln to the Presidency of the Republic had emphasised the determination of all the free parts of the country. What, then, was to be done? Slavery was threatened with ruin. There was only one way to save it. The Slave States must secede from the Union, get rid of the hampering restrictions of Abolitionists, and proclaim a great Slave Empire. The war which followed this attitude and action was thus to all intents and purposes a war for slavery. The working people of England soon saw to the root of the issue, though other classes did not.

The question that was going to be fought out in America, that was going to cost hundreds of thousands of lives, that was going to lay waste tracts of territory almost as large as Europe itself, was the greatest question of the centuries. It was greater than the Great Rebellion, greater than the French Revolution, greater than the War of Independence; for it involved the slavery or freedom of the worker all over the world. The leaders of the Southern Confederacy were the evangelists and apostles of a new dispensation. Slavery in their eyes was a divine institution. It was not only to be the corner-stone of a new edifice; it was to be spread as a blessing from heaven to the uttermost parts of the earth. Nor were the black races alone to be blessed with the beneficent rule of subordination. All who laboured were to be subjected to the same wise restraints and restrictions. Slavery, said Howell Cobb, was the only method of reconciling the conflicting interests of labour and capital. "By making the labourer himself capital the conflict ceased and the rival interests became harmonized." Such were the brazen arguments of the slaveowners. And the triumph of their arms would have meant the re-establishment for years to come of a base and brutal barbarism—nay, the extension of that barbarism to corners of the globe yet unaffected by its blighting and degrading influence. So I say the question involved in the struggle between North and South was as vital as any that has been fought out since history began.

Doubts on the subject never entered some of our minds—mine among the number. Having written much in defence of the North and against the South in the *National Reformer*, I was invited by a Huddersfield printer to compile a rather elaborate pamphlet on what was then the burning question of the hour. This pamphlet—"The Slaveholders' War: an Argument for the North and the Negro"— proved one thing clearly, that the right to maintain and extend slavery lay at the root of the great conflict. The declarations of

Southern leaders and the resolutions of Southern conventions were cited in great numbers to sustain a thesis that nobody disputes now. Two honours befell the production. One was that the author was appointed a vice-president of the Union and Emancipation Society— a society that did more, under the guidance of Thomas Bailey Potter (long the moving spirit of the Cobden Club), than any other organization in the United Kingdom to keep the country from falling into a terrible blunder. The other honour was a translation of the pamphlet into Gujratee, one of the languages of India. So translated by Jaboolie Roostum at the instance of a Parsee gentleman, the work comprised about fifty pages of curious-looking matter, bearing the imprint of the Duftur Ashkara Press, Bombay. "The publication," the translator wrote to me, "will convince you that India, though distanced from Europe by thousands of miles, is not backward in showing humanity towards a certain race of beings who suffer under the bonds of slavery." And a generous commentator, apropos of the compliment, cited the stanza which a friendly poet had written to the author of "Lalla Rookh":—

> I'm told, dear Moore, your lays are sung
> (Can it be true, you lucky man?)
> By moonlight in the Persian tongue
> Along the streets of Ispahan.

No crisis in which we ourselves were not directly concerned ever excited, I think, the interest in England that the American War did. It entered into all our thoughts, seasoned all our conversation, formed the one topic of discussion at thousands of public meetings. It even invaded our social and scientific congresses. The British Association met in Newcastle in 1863, when the fate of a race, the fate also of the working classes themselves, was still hanging in the balance. Partisans of the South were for the most part partisans of slavery, for the cause of the South could not be dissociated from the cause of slavery; and partisans of slavery were invariably embittered against the negro. The fact was demonstrated in the course of some exciting discussions that took place among the members of the Association in the rooms devoted to Ethnology. The leading advocates against the negro were Dr. Hunt and Mr. Carter Blake, both gentlemen of some scientific attainments. It was their contention that the negro was hardly entitled to be called a man at all. Dr. Hunt, I recollect, laid down this astounding proposition—"If you teach the negro to read, he will open his master's letters; if you teach him to write, he will forge his master's signature." But there was present at the meeting a black gentleman who defended his unfortunate race with singular ability and vigour. This was William Craft, whose escape from bondage with his wife some years before was one of the most romantic adventures in the history of American slavery. Mr. Craft was tall, upright, handsome, full of intelligence, an able speaker, without a trace of those lingual peculiarities which are associated with the Christy Minstrel type of negro. A squabble occurred when Mr. Craft, who delivered a highly interesting address on a visit to the King of Dahomey, was described in the programme as "an African gentleman." Dr. Hunt and Mr. Carter Blake maintained that he was not a genuine negro, for the reason that one of his ancestors was supposed to have been a white man. The difficulty was surmounted, I believe, by describing Mr. Craft as "an American gentleman," though he himself contended in one of the discussions that he was black enough for anything—black enough for slavery at all events! Those who were present are not likely to have forgotten the impression he produced when, replying to the hostile descriptions that had been given of the negro, he recited the fable of the lion and the traveller: how a traveller and a lion had fallen into a dispute as to which was the stronger of the two—how they came to an inn on the sign of which was a picture of a man slaying a lion—how the traveller pointed to the sign as a proof that he was right—how, finally, the lion exclaimed, "Ah, yes, but who painted the picture?" Mr. Craft's manly eloquence produced so excellent an effect that the defenders of slavery were thoroughly worsted in the encounter.

It was my good fortune to see something of Mr. Craft in private life. A finer gentleman in every respect I think I never met. There was then living in Newcastle a venerable Quaker lady, the wife of Henry Richardson. Mrs. Richardson, who died in 1892 at the advanced age of eighty-six, was one of two Newcastle Quakeresses who years before had raised the money to purchase the freedom of Frederick

Douglass. It was at her house that I became acquainted with William Craft. Among the other guests on the occasion was Elihu Burritt, "the learned blacksmith," then engaged in another walking tour from Land's End to John o' Groat's—a tour, however, which he did not live long enough to put on record in a new volume. Mr. Craft's mission to Dahomey had been, so far as he was himself concerned, a financial failure. To recoup the losses he had sustained in the expedition a committee was formed in Newcastle to assist in raising funds. Of the members of that committee (which included Joseph Cowen, John Mawson, Joseph Clephan, Henry Brady, Joseph Watson, and Thomas Sharp), Dr. Thomas Hodgkin and the writer are the only survivors. Soon after this, I understood, Mr. Craft had undertaken a mission to the Republic of Liberia. And then I lost sight of him. When, in 1900, I made inquiries of the British and Foreign Anti-Slavery Society, Mr. Travers Buxton, the secretary, informed me that the latest fact he could find about my African friend was that he was present at a public breakfast which was given to William Lloyd Garrison at St. James's Hall, London, in June, 1867.

CHAPTER XLIII

ENGLAND AND AMERICA

THE attitude of the British nation during the Civil War is persistently (and I sometimes think purposely) misunderstood in the United States. For reasons of their own—often to gain some paltry advantage for their party—politicians endeavour to make out that our people desired and designed the rending of the Republic in twain. Such an interpretation of the state of public feeling in the United Kingdom from 1861 to 1865 is an absolutely false interpretation. Nevertheless, it is probably at the bottom of much of that pernicious folly which is known as "twisting the lion's tail." Some useful purpose may perhaps be served, therefore, if the real condition of affairs be explained here.

This misunderstanding is not altogether unnatural, since the English newspapers, with very few honourable exceptions, preached and pleaded for the Southern rebels. The *Daily News* and the *Morning Star* were, I think, the only journals in London that had a good word for the Federal cause till the assassination of President Lincoln showed the venom of the beaten slaveowners. It was much the same in the provinces. Half a dozen of the most prominent among the provincial journals alone took the Northern side. Indeed, I can recall no more than three—the *Newcastle Chronicle*, the *Leeds Mercury*, and the *Manchester Examiner*. All the others appeared to have taken their cue from the *limes*, which in its turn appeared to have taken its cue from Mr. Spence. Seeing that the English newspapers generally were not friendly to the Federal cause, the Northern people not unnaturally thought that the masses of our population entertained the same views. But they were wrong in so thinking.

Nor were the newspapers alone in upbraiding the North and applauding the South. The governing classes, the influential classes, the aristocratic and fashionable classes—in the eyes of all these the Southern chivalry (fancy the chivalry of a race that begot its own slaves!) found favour. There wasn't much to choose between

Liberals and Tories at that time and on that question. Save Mr. Disraeli, who spoke kindly of the "territorial democracy" of America, there was hardly a Tory statesman who did not sneer at the efforts the *Northern States* were making to subdue their neighbours. Their feelings were perhaps best voiced in the triumphant exclamation of Bulwer Lytton—"The republican bubble has burst!" On the other hand, Mr. Gladstone showed too clearly his mistaken views when he declared in Newcastle that Jefferson Davis had made a nation of the South. The Marquis of Hartington (now the Duke of Devonshire) was young and foolish then, and so brought upon himself one of the most delicate and yet most cutting rebukes on record. When he was introduced to President Lincoln at Washington, he was said to be wearing some kind of Southern favour. The great rail-splitter, taking no notice of the affront, quietly revenged his country: he persistently addressed his visitor as "Mr. Partington."

It is fair to say that Mr. Gladstone, Lord John Russell, and many other Liberals made graceful apologies afterwards for the false positions they had assumed while the conflict was still undecided. Even the *Times* broke its own spears when it came to write of Lincoln's exquisite address at Antietam. Nor did *Punch* at any time acquit itself with better grace or more touching pathos than when it recanted over "murdered Lincoln's bier" all that it once had foully said. To Tom Taylor, playwright and humorist, was ascribed the credit of the verses which made historic amends:—

> *You* lay a wreath on murdered Lincoln's bier,
>   *You* who with mocking pencil wont to trace,
> Broad for the self-complacent British sneer,
>   His length of shambling limb, his furrowed face,
>
> His gaunt gnarled hands, his unkempt, bristling hair,
>   His garb uncouth, his bearing ill at ease,
> His lack of all we prize as debonnair,
>   Of power or will to shine, of art to please!
>
> *You*, whose smart pen backed up the pencil's laugh,
>   Judging each step as though the way were plain;

Reckless, so it could point its paragraph,
  Of chiefs perplexity or people's pain!

Beside this corpse, that bears for winding sheet
  The Stars and Stripes he lived to rear anew,
Between the mourners at his head and feet,
  Say, scurril-jester, is there room for *you?*

Yes, he had lived to shame me from my sneer,
  To lame my pencil and confute my pen—
To make me own this hind of princes peer,
  This rail-splitter a true-born king of men.

But there were those who did not need to apologise—who never doubted as to the cause of the war and never wavered as to its ultimate result. Foremost among our leading public men to sustain the faith of the one side and enlighten the ignorance of the other were John Bright and William Edward Forster. Mr. Bright never in all his great career better served his country or his kind than he did then. The speech he made at St. James's Hall, London, where a magnificent meeting was held to express sympathy with the Northern people, remains in my memory as one of the most powerful I had ever heard. Had Mr. Bright been able to visit America at the close of the war, he would have received such a welcome as no native of another country had ever received there.

The churches as well as political parties were found wanting in the crisis—some of the churches. Moses D. Hoge, a doctor of divinity in the Southern States, was sent over to England to preach the new gospel. And this apostle of slavery was actually permitted to expound his diabolical doctrines in English pulpits. Perhaps worse than this happened. *Good Words* was supposed to be a magazine with a conscience. Yet one month it amazed and outraged its readers by sending out, bound up with some of the best literature of the day, the address of the Southern Churches in praise and exaltation of negro bondage. From defending slaveowners, men in politics and men in the Church, driven from point to point, came to defend slavery. Thus were the minds of shallow partisans—shallow in spite of their learning and their prominence—degraded and demoralised by association with an evil cause.

How, then, can it be said, when statesmen and divines, politicians and journalists, friends of privilege and enemies of social and political progress, were aiding and abetting the Southern Confederacy—how can it be said that England stood for freedom and the slave? Yet so it was. The common people, the people who live in cottages, the people who toil in factories and mines, the real people of this great England, were never for a moment beguiled. If others were blinded by passion or prejudice, they at least saw clearly the meaning of the conflict. The national sentiment was declared in the hundreds of public meetings that were held in all parts of the country. Of all these meetings, only one, I think, passed resolutions of sympathy with the South. And this solitary meeting, held in Sheffield, was perverted by the influence which was there and then wielded by a Radical who had recanted his old faith—John Arthur Roebuck. But the exception proved the rule. The genuine mind of England was declared, not in the newspapers or the pulpits, but in the popular gatherings that assembled in every populous district of Britain.

When Henry Ward Beecher came over to enlighten us, he spoke to great audiences in Liverpool, Manchester, Birmingham, Glasgow, Edinburgh. And it was only in Liverpool that he met with a mixed reception. I heard him in Edinburgh. It was at the time of the Social Science Congress in 1863. Lord Brougham, like other bewildered politicians, had espoused the cause of the South, and had even insulted the Northern people at the Congress. The meeting which Mr. Beecher addressed was the effective reply. So enormous was the crowd that the orator of the evening had some difficulty in gaining admission. The peculiarities of his pronunciation would on other occasions have made the unthinking laugh; but the audience was too earnest for hilarity and too united for opposition. So was public opinion manifested in Edinburgh, as it was nearly everywhere else, for the North.

More impressive even than the evidence of great meetings was the spirit of the starving people of Lancashire. Subtle and crafty appeals were made to their feelings. "Break the blockade," they were told, "and cotton will be abundant again. Then will the mills reopen, and your terrible privations cease." The insidious advice fell on deaf ears. The factory workers, to their everlasting honour, declined to terminate their own sufferings at the cost of the slavery of another race. Rather than help the slaveowners to rivet anew the gyves of the negro, they would perish of starvation. It was this heroic attitude, better than the diatribes of journalists or the plausible pronunciations of statesmen, that indicated the real sentiment of the nation. When somebody at Sheffield ventured to advise that the Government should break the blockade, a voice came from the crowd, "There will be civil war in England first." That voice spoke for the masses. I say again, then, that the heart of the country, the heart of the common people of the country, was as sound for right and freedom as that of New England itself. Emerson's "Boston Hymn" found a response in every workman's breast—

Pay ransom to the owner,
  And fill the bag to the brim!
But who is owner? The slave is owner,
  And ever was. *Pay him!*

Ireland, however, stood on neutral ground. There were patriot sons of hers on both sides, as there generally are when a fight is to the fore. An amusing instance of Irish impartiality occurred in the very middle of the conflict. Terence Bellew McManus, a rebel of '48, having died in America, his body was brought home for interment. One of the orators over the grave told how Irishmen were comporting themselves across the Atlantic. They were, he said, gallantly upholding the reputation of the "ould counthrie." (Cheers.) Thomas Francis Meagher, "Meagher of the Sword," was bravely fighting for the North. (More cheers.) And the sons of John Mitchel were, with equal valour, fighting for the South. (Renewed cheers.) So did the Irish people, both at home and in America, manifest their neutrality. The help they gave to the Federals was counterbalanced by the help they gave to the Confederates. Meagher, however, rose to the rank of Brigadier-General in the service of the Republic.

Wrong as to the cause of the war, partisans of the South got wrong also as to the progress of the war. It was not, indeed, till Richmond fell that many of them could be persuaded that the end was approaching. No maps were published in the newspapers then; nor did we get news from the seat of war till the Atlantic liners brought it. The consequence was that the public mind in this country was often mystified, especially as a battle was rarely announced without a claim being set up for a Confederate victory. Not being able to trace the positions of the rival armies in the different engagements, people here failed to see that the Northern commanders were steadily driving the Southerners backward—closing in upon them in every direction. And so it happened that the final catastrophe came as a great surprise to our countrymen. If others had followed the plan I adopted, they would have understood better the progress of military operations. My plan, commonly pursued since, was simplicity itself. I pasted a good map of the United States on a drawing board; I provided myself with two packets of pins—black pins for the Confederates, and white pins for the Federals; and after the arrival of every fresh mail I altered the positions of the armies (or rather the pins representing the armies) according to the news received. Thus it could be seen that the unhappy South was being gradually strangled by the stronger North. And hereby hangs another tale. One morning, after reading the despatches in the newspapers, I went to my map to make the necessary alterations. Jupiter! what had happened? I was amazed to find both armies scattered in all directions—Federals in Canada and Mexico, Confederates floundering in the Atlantic and Pacific Oceans! It was the industrious maid-servant of the establishment who had swept with her duster all the belligerents off the field, replacing them later in the locations she thought they ought to occupy. The incident, vexatious at first, was intensely amusing afterwards; but it took me a long time, with much consultation of back despatches, to put Grant and Sherman, Lee and Bragg, in their proper encampments again.

The war was bloody and frightful. At no less cost and in no other way, however, could the curse of slavery have been wiped out. The American people never rose higher than they did during those terrible four years. And their armies, like the armies of Cromwell, dispersed without danger to the country. It is no small honour to England that her working people, faithful to the cause of freedom, helped by their efforts and their sufferings to emancipate four million of slaves.

CHAPTER XLIV

THE LAST INSURRECTION IN POLAND

NOBODY knows what real misery is who has not been out of work in London—out of work and out of resources too. The most depressing and forlorn period of my life was passed under these circumstances. It extended from the spring of 1862 to the spring of 1863. The transfer of the *Alliance News* to another office threw me out of employment. Other work not being obtainable in Manchester, we broke up our home, sold or gave away most of our belongings, and returned to unfurnished apartments in Kennington. Our family was small at the time; still it was large enough to cause great anxiety. Work was almost as scarce in London as it was in Manchester. At any rate I could get nothing regular—only a day or two here and there. A god-send was the commission (never wholly paid, though) for compiling the American pamphlet. Soon our little savings began to dwindle, and bread had to be bought and rent had to be paid. I can tell you that the honest man without work and without means in London must be light of heart indeed if he can resist thoughts that need not be named. It was when I was thus suffering that I learnt how good and genuine a friend I had in Charles Bradlaugh.

As it seemed to me to be increasingly difficult to obtain steady employment in the printing trade, I came to consider that I was, perhaps, not destitute of some of the qualifications of a journalist. Indeed, people who had to do with newspapers had made inquiries of Mr. Bradlaugh about the writer of the articles signed Caractacus. Also Mr. Bradlaugh himself had made inquiries of newspaper people on behalf of the said writer. So that I might take instant advantage of anything that should turn up, I accepted, as before stated, an invitation to breakfast with him every morning. This I did for many weeks. One of the gentlemen who had made inquiries about Caractacus was Mr. Joseph Cowen of Newcastle—then Mr. Joseph Cowen, Jun.—well known to all Radicals in England and all Revolutionists on the Continent. Mr. Cowen had lately acquired the

Newcastle Chronicle, and was contemplating certain developments of the property. Would Caractacus be disposed to accept an engagement in Newcastle when the time came? Of course he would. Meantime, would Caractacus write a political article once a week for the *Newcastle Chronicle* similar to that which he had contributed for a few years past to the *National Reformer?* Again of course he would. The articles appeared over the signature of Ironside—the beginning of a series which at a later date ran into hundreds in the *Weekly Chronicle.* Henry Dunckley's "Letters of Verax" had a great vogue in the *Manchester Examiner* at the time, and a Lancashire member of Parliament had the goodness to say that the "Letters of Ironside " were at least equally valuable. For the pride and vanity involved in the mention of so uninteresting a statement I hope (though I may not deserve) to be forgiven.

But before the earlier of these transactions had come to pass a much more interesting event had occurred. The last insurrection—the insurrection of Maryon Langiewicz—broke out in Poland. That unhappy nation, whose history is the saddest in the world, had been crushed, trodden under foot, and divided as spoils among three of the leading vultures of Europe—Russia, Prussia, and Austria. Posen had been harshly treated by Prussia; Galicia, after a time of brutal treatment by Metternich, Szela, and Radetzki, had been utterly subdued by Austria; but Lithuania, which had fallen to the share of Russia, was now and again goaded into desperation by the odious policy and despotism of the Muscovites. Poor Poland! It may be that she owed her downfall to her own internal dissensions—mainly, perhaps, to that fatal "liberum veto" which made an absolutely unanimous vote of the nobles necessary to the authorisation of any change in the law. But, these dissensions notwithstanding, she had once, under the walls of Vienna, saved Europe from a flood of Saracen barbarism. But no service in the past, and no prospects of service in the future, availed against the avarice of her neighbours. Poland was divided and conquered. The patriotic life, however, was not even yet extinct. There were periodical risings in Warsaw, in Wilna, in the provinces—risings in which the peasants, armed with scythes and reaping hooks, fought with desperate valour against disciplined hordes of Tartars and Cossacks. The last of these risings occurred in 1862. Hope was renewed by the daring exploits of Langiewicz and his heroic followers.

Friends of Poland, who were friends also of freedom everywhere else in the world, organized a movement to aid the insurgents. A committee was formed in London, with smaller committees in provincial towns, to raise funds for the Poles, and afford such other aid as could be rendered them. The committee consisted for the most part of men who were always foremost to help any enterprise that promised liberation for the oppressed. Thus Peter Alfred Taylor was treasurer, while other members included Joseph Cowen, William Shaen, Arthur Trevelyan, R. B. Litchfield, J. Sale Barker, Dr. Epps, Serjeant Parry, and Professor F. W. Newman. Among the rest were Lord Teynham, Sir John Bowring, John Stuart Mill, George Moore, J. J. Colman, the Rev. Goodwyn Barmby, and William Charles Macready, the famous tragedian. The Central Committee of the Friends of Poland, which acted "with the authority of the Delegate from the Polish National Government," was in want of a secretary to keep its records and conduct its correspondence. I was appointed to the office. It did not seem to me that I was an ideal or even an efficient secretary, though I suppose I did all that was necessary. But there was at least one qualification that I did not lack—zeal for the cause. The duties of the office were discharged with what ability I could command till in the early part of 1863 I received an urgent summons to Newcastle.

The offices of the committee were situated in Southampton Street, Strand. There I attended every day to answer letters, issue appeals, receive subscriptions, give information to visitors, and arrange such other matters of business as required attention. The work was not arduous, but it was eminently congenial. Our visitors, though not numerous, were many of them interesting. One was a gentleman, Mr. Bullock Hall, who wanted an introduction to the Polish leaders to serve as war correspondent for an English newspaper. Another was commissioned by Mr. James Anthony Froude, the editor of *Fraser's Magazine*, to seek information for an article on Poland. Mr. Grant Duff, not then honoured with a title, but of much repute as a politician on account of the elaborate addresses he used to deliver to his constituents at Elgin, had been invited to join the committee. There was much that was fastidious about the hon. gentleman. And so he came to give a good many excellent reasons why he could not comply with the request. But one morning there arrived a visitor who struck me as being more earnest than any of the rest. I knew him by sight and name, for I had seen and heard him in the Free Trade Hall, Manchester, pleading eloquently for the slaves in America. Did we want a speech for Poland? If so, he was ready to comply. Slightly deformed—almost like a hunchback, in fact—he was a striking figure as he planted himself before the fire and carelessly put the question and made the offer. It was Washington Wilks, author of a "History of the Last Half-Century," who had not long before been summoned to the Bar of the House of Commons for some breach of privilege committed in a Carlisle journal. Opportunity for the speech was soon afterwards afforded by a great meeting in St. James's Hall, which Mr. George Potter, the editor of the *Beehive*, acting on behalf of the committee, organized for the purpose of expressing and eliciting sympathy with Poland.

The funds raised by the committee were handed over to Mr. Joseph Cwierczakiewicz, the Delegate of the National Government. One evening I went with the Delegate to his lodgings near the Haymarket. The room was full of Polish ladies, wives and daughters of exiles, who were busily making flags for the insurgents. How many of these flags reached Poland I know not; but such as did became the spoils of the barbarian hordes of Russia. The unequal struggle continued all through 1863. The insurrection, which had broken out in January, was not finally crushed till February of the following year, and not then till it was computed that 40,000 of the flower of the Polish population had perished on the battlefield. The threat of Gortschakoff had been accomplished—Poland had been converted into "a wilderness of ashes and corpses," and Mouravieff held a feast of horrors at Wilna, slaying men, scourging women, sparing neither age nor sex in his ruthless wrath. Langiewicz escaped into Galicia, was there imprisoned by the Austrians, and two years later joined the great army of refugees in London, dying in Turkey in 1887. As for Poland, "every handful of her soil a relic of martyrs," she remains (and, alas! seems likely to remain) the very Niobe of Nations.

The fatal struggle over, the English people were asked to assist in binding up the wounds. Dr. Barraniecki, who had organized the National Government, succeeded subsequently in collecting and bringing to England a great quantity of jewellery and objects of art—here to be sold for the benefit of sick and wounded Poles. The rich lady sent her necklet of brilliants, the poor widow her wedding ring, the young girl her love token, and the nun her coral beads. These pathetic contributions in relief of national suffering, disposed of at bazaars in London and Newcastle, realised a handsome sum. The sale was principally managed in Newcastle by two ladies—Mrs. Biggar, wife of the Mayor of Gateshead, and Mrs. George William Hodge, wife of the Sheriff of Newcastle. It was the last service English people were asked to render to Poland.

An echo of the insurrection of 1863 came to Newcastle fifteen years later. General Langiewicz, as was said at the time of the struggle, was "accompanied and assisted by a Polish heroine of equal beauty and courage." This lady was the subject of a lying paragraph that appeared in a German newspaper in 1878. "Mademoiselle Pustawaitow, who had served as aide-de-camp to the Polish general, and was by his side on the retreat from his latest field, has," the German scribe declared, "fallen considerably in the world since that time, and has been an inmate of various prisons in Silesia. Truly a melancholy ending to a career that began with so much romance about it." This paragraph somehow found its way into the columns of the *Newcastle Weekly Chronicle*. Then came an indignant protest from France. Writing from Dijon on Dec. 10th, 1878, R. J. Jaworowski, evidently a compatriot of the lady's, informed the editor that Mademoiselle Pustawaitow had ever since the revolution of 1863 been residing in Paris, happily married to a medical gentleman, Dr. Loewenhard, of the Rue Mont Parnasse. The heroine of the last insurrection in Poland was thereafter left in peace to perform her duties as wife and mother.

CHAPTER XLV

"THE CITY OF DREADFUL NIGHT"

WHEN the secretaryship of the Polish Committee became vacant, Mr. Bradlaugh, who was cognisant of my removal to Newcastle, suggested that I should recommend as my successor a young friend of his who lived in his house, and whom I used a few months before to meet every morning at his breakfast table. The recommendation was effective. Mr. Bradlaugh's friend was appointed to the office. I informed him of the duties, handed over all the books and correspondence (including many interesting letters from famous people of the day), and took my leave of London, calling on the way to the North at Manchester and other places for the purpose of consulting with supporters of the Polish cause. A few weeks later I received a letter from Mr. P. A. Taylor, the treasurer of the committee. Could I tell him where my successor was to be found? The new secretary had not been to the office for several days, had left everything in confusion, and had given no indication of his whereabouts. I could only refer Mr. Taylor to Mr. Bradlaugh. It transpired afterwards that the neglect of duty was due to a fatal and incurable weakness. The young man who had so failed in the work he had undertaken to do was the author of "The City of Dreadful Night."

James Thomson, then and for long afterwards a member of Mr. Bradlaugh's family, was a man of gloomy aspect, manners, and ideas. Even his smile was sad. It seemed as if he was suffering from an irrepressible sorrow. Life to him was not a mission, but a mistake. Pessimism, a dismal hopelessness, was written on his countenance, which did not otherwise bear evidence of special aptitude or ability. We were of course on friendly terms, and talked cordially and pleasantly together when we happened to meet. Beyond this there was no intimacy. It is possible I should not have understood him if there had been. I rather fancy that his cynicism was not to my liking, as I know it was not to the liking of some other of his acquaintances. But I had not at this time any knowledge of that dreadful failing which was eventually the cause of his death. Once only can I recall a lively passage in his mood and conduct. A social gathering was being held at the Hall of Science, then one of the centres of the Freethought movement. It was followed by a dance. Thomson, I remember, entered with what seemed to me quite unusual spirit into the amusement. There may have been other occasions when he showed equal sprightliness, but I never saw them. Mr. Bradlaugh not only found him a home, but, when opportunity offered, employment also. Paid contributions of his over the initials of B. V., most of them of a more or less pessimistic character, appeared in the *National Reformer*. And when at a later period Mr. Bradlaugh had embarked in the commercial business connected with Italian sand, I found the poet installed as chief clerk in his London office.

Thomson's intimacy with Bradlaugh was begun in Ireland. Bradlaugh was then a recruit in a regiment of dragoons, and Thomson was a teacher in the garrison school. Of this early connection particulars were given in the *National Reformer* at the time that one of the poet's biographies was published:—"We first knew James Thomson in Ballincollig Barracks, Ireland, in 1851, and for many years we were very intimate. He was a pupil teacher in the garrison school, when we, in the night from nine to eleven or eleven to one, walked 'sentry go' together, he leaving his bed, in defiance of regulations, to make our walk less lonely. When he left Ballincollig for Chelsea, and then for Jersey, we wrote old-fashioned letters, six, eight, and ten pages, to each other. His were charming letters. When, after some ten years, trouble came to him, the writer's home was his, and, with a few severe strainings, the result of one inherited weakness, a close friendship lasted until 1870, and was finally severed in 1874."

While in Jersey, Thomson became acquainted with another old friend, George Julian Harney. Thomson was the garrison schoolmaster, and Harney was editing the *Jersey Independent*. "The garrison schoolmaster," wrote Harney in 1892, "was a quiet, amiable, somewhat melancholy gentleman. I had the pleasure of lending him Carlyle's 'Sartor Resartus' and a few other books. Presently he much more than repaid my small courtesies by sending a few translations of Heine's shorter poems to the *Independent*." The incident was only brought to mind many years later when Harney, then in America, read the translations from Heine in a volume of the poet's verses he had received from England.

Thomson's genius came to be generally recognised only after his melancholy death in 1882, at the age of forty-seven, eight years after the final severance of the Bradlaugh ties. These years must have been years of misery, for Thomson had then lost the restraining influence of the one great friendship of his life. It is a question for psychologists how far the earlier recognition of his genius would have saved him from the wreck he made of himself. The chances are that nothing could have saved him. One of the first to pay tribute to his poetic merit—the first in literary circles, says the Athenæum— was William Michael Rossetti, who for more than a year (from Feb. 1872, to Nov. 1873) was in correspondence with Thomson on the subject of Shelley and other matters. Mr. Rossetti's appreciation, however, could not help the poet to a publisher. And so it happened that the "City of Dreadful Night," the most famous of Thomson's poems, appeared first in instalments in the *National Reformer*, where I recollect many readers thought that it seemed considerably out of place. "Though we do not vaunt our judgment of poetry," wrote Mr. Bradlaugh in 1884, "we gave the best evidence of our personal estimate of Thomson's muse by finding place for its insertion here at a date when no other source of publicity availed, save once in *Fraser's Magazine*, which, however, did not pay its poet." The poem appeared in the early part of 1874, though it was not till years afterwards that it attracted any sort of general attention. George Eliot, however, praised it, as did Dante Rossetti and Algernon Swinburne. But when the author died many biographies were written of him; every scrap that he had ever composed, whether of prose or poetry, was gathered up and printed; and critics and admirers declared that no living poet, except Browning, could be considered his superior. Poor Thomson was not the only bard who was neglected when he lived and adored when he was dead. No fate is more pitiable than that of the victim of incurable intemperance. Thomson's sufferings during his alternate fits of abandonment and remorse must have been terrible. "The demon of hypochondriasis and all kindred and attendant demons," it was said, "seized him and tore and crushed him in the darkness of his insane phantasy."

It was almost natural that a love legend should be invented to account for the poet's pessimism and frequent lapses. One of his biographers expressly states, indeed, that he "lost in his youth the beautiful girl to whom he was engaged." This, however, was pure fiction. Mr. Bradlaugh, who knew the facts, explained them thus:— "The armourer-sergeant's daughter (of the 7th Dragoon Guards), who died in Ireland in 1852, was only a little child; and it was not till long after her death, and in his morbid times, that Thomson, little by little, built the poetical romance about her memory." The "one inherited weakness" about which Mr. Bradlaugh wrote in the same article was the cause of his undoing. Mr. Bertram Dobell, who issued Thomson's works in four volumes, speaks of the poet's father as having "fallen in the social scale, owing to habits of intemperance"—which habits, according to vague report, brought on imbecility. And Thomson himself told another of his biographers that "intemperance ran in his family," and that "nearly all the members of it who 'had brains,' especially a gifted aunt of his, fell victims to its power." It was disease, then, and not love, that led to the poet's downfall.

The manner of Thomson's death was awful. Mr. William Sharp tells the sad story in his account of Philip Bourke Marston, prefixed to a collection of Marston's poems in Walter Scott's "Canterbury Poets." The catastrophe came nearly twenty years after Thomson had misbehaved himself in connection with the Polish Committee. Marston, who also had had a melancholy career, was one of his friends at that period. Thomson, who had now included among his excesses the frequent use of opium, had returned from a prolonged visit to the country, "where all had been well with him." Then for a few weeks his record was almost a blank. Where he had hidden himself, and under what conditions, we can only imagine. Afterwards he so far conquered his control as to be able to visit his friend. Thomson found Marston alone. "I arrived," writes Mr.

Sharp, "late in the afternoon, and found Marston in a state of nervous perturbation. Thomson was lying down on the bed in the adjoining room. Stooping, I caught his whispered words to the effect that he was dying: upon which I lit a match, and in the sudden glare beheld his white face on a blood-stained pillow. He had burst one or more blood-vessels, and the hæmorrhage was dreadful. Some time had to elapse before anything could be done; but ultimately, with the help of a friend who came in opportunely, poor Thomson was carried downstairs, placed in a cab, and driven to the University Hospital." He died the next day, a few hours after Sharp and Marston had called to see him in the hospital ward. It was a tragic ending to a most unhappy life.

CHAPTER XLVI

NEWCASTLE IN THE SIXTIES

NEWCASTLE is an ancient town—"aalwis wes an ancient toon, my lord," as one of her old worthies is credited with having said. But she was more ancient in the sixties than she is now. The paradox is capable of explanation. Many of her ancient edifices have since been swept away by the tide of improvement. The Side and the Sandhill were pictures then. To-day they are only half-pictures. Grand old houses, every line and curve a line and curve of beauty, that dated back almost to the "specious times of great Elizabeth," have been replaced by modern buildings—more commodious and durable, no doubt, but infinitely less picturesque and interesting. This is why I say Newcastle is less ancient now (of course I mean in appearance) than she was when I first had the pleasure of admiring her stately streets.

Grainger and Dobson had completed their grand work of constructing the new town of Newcastle some time before 1863. The tide of population, however, had not yet risen to the height the great builder had anticipated. Clayton Street for the most part was a line of empty shops, showing that the town for the moment had been overbuilt. The Central Exchange, again, had failed to lure the merchants from the Quayside. On the other hand, the severe harmony of the architecture of Grey Street—one of the finest streets in the world—had not been broken by tawdry and incongruous defacements. Nor had Market Street or Shakspeare Street suffered similar mutilations. But Grainger Street, which then ended at the Bigg Market, had been disfigured by painted images and ugly wooden balconies, followed in later years by gigantic and grotesque letters of vulgar gilt. The new Town Hall—so called then, though it is a dreadfully disreputable old Town Hall now—had just been built, while some of the houses of Union Street, now covered by the northern end of the municipal abortion, still stood between Pudding Chare and the High Bridge. There was no Swing Bridge across the Tyne, nor yet any Redheugh Bridge; neither was there any Byker

Bridge over the Ouseburn, or any Armstrong Bridge over Jesmond Dene. The place of the Swing Bridge was occupied by a stone structure of many arches. And near at hand stood the old Mansion House in the Close, dignified even in decay. The river front of the Moot Hall had not been spoiled to make a more convenient assize court; but under the very roof of the older Guild Hall fishwives chattered and chaffered and swore. Two of the ancient towers that once helped to guard the lives and property of the lieges still stood in the sixties—Gunner Tower opposite the Central Station, and the Weaver's Tower on the site of the Public Library.

Changes in the centre of Newcastle have been considerable, but not nearly so considerable as those in the outskirts, during the period that I have been acquainted with the district. Forty years ago Maple Street was the limit of the town in one direction, Victoria Square in another, Graingerville in a third, the Ouseburn in a fourth. Beyond Maple Street there were few houses except along Scotswood Road, where the great Elswick Works were just beginning to be famous. Away up the hill were open fields to Elswick Hall. Elswick Lane, bordered by lovely trees which any decent Town Council would have fought tooth and nail to preserve, provided a delightful walk to Benwell, with exquisite views over the Tyne up the Valley of the Derwent. From Benwell itself there was so sweet a prospect that John Martin is said to have got his idea of the Plains of Heaven from it. Further up the hill other glorious views were at everybody's command from the West Turnpike, for bright and cheerful hedgerows had not then been supplanted by ugly and repellent brick walls. Between Gloucester House (otherwise Cabbage Hall) and the Benwell Reservoir there was nothing but the Workhouse and one or two mansions. Alongside the workhouse grounds a pretty lane gave access to the Nun's Moor. Beyond Jesmond Church, then called St. Spite's, there were pretty pathways to the Apple Tree Gardens, while beyond Brandling Village there were private roads and lanes through the Friday Fields to Matthew Bank. Portland Park was a cabbage garden; but the two cemeteries already faced each other, and Martha Major still flourished at the Minories. Lambert's Leap was much as it was when the incident which gave it its name occurred. Past the bridge the Tippytoe Bank led down a beautiful

ravine to the Washing Tubs and the Ouseburn. Pandon Dene still
retained traces of the loveliness that had inspired a previous
generation of local poets. Over the Ouseburn, Heaton was all fields
and farmsteads, while Byker was little more than a row of old-
fashioned cottages on each side of Shields Road. From this brief
survey anybody may see how rapidly the "canny toon" has grown
since the year 1863.

Thomas Hedley was then Mayor of Newcastle; John Clayton was
Town Clerk; James Hodgson was chairman of the Finance
Committee; Thomas Bryson (who was killed with John Mawson and
a number of policemen and others in the Town Moor explosion) was
Town Surveyor; John Sabbage was Chief Constable; Ralph Dodds,
Ralph Park Philipson, Isaac Lowthian Bell, William Lockey Harle,
Charles Frederick Hamond, Dr. William Newton, Joseph Cowen,
and Joseph Cowen, Jun., were members of the Town Council. All
the members of the Council and all the officials of the Corporation at
the period named are now dead, save only Sir Isaac Lowthian Bell
and Sir Charles Frederick Hamond. The former long ago severed his
connection with the town, but the latter still takes an active interest
in municipal proceedings. Among the other notable natives and
residents at the time were Sir John Fife, Dr. Headlam, Thomas
Doubleday, and William Bell Scott. Fife was a distinguished surgeon
and Headlam a distinguished physician, while Doubleday had
distinguished himself in literature, and Scott, then master of the
School of Design, afterwards won repute in art and poetry.

Newcastle could not boast of a single public park in 1863. Jesmond
Dene, then recently acquired by Sir William George Armstrong
(afterwards famous as Lord Armstrong), was a private pleasaunce,
looking from the outside, with its red walks and comparatively bare
banks, new and raw and barren. Mr. Hamond (now Sir Charles
Frederick Hamond) must, I think, be credited with the first attempt
at park-making. Part of the Leazes was enclosed; but the difficulty
experienced in retaining the water for the lake (there was an old
spring well in the enclosure) gave rise for a long time to much satiric
banter about Charlie's Hole. When Christian Allhusen proposed to
sell the grounds of Elswick Hall for building sites, an agitation arose

for the purchase of the property as a public park. The scheme was at first defeated in the Town Council, owing to the absurd jealousy of the East End members; building operations were actually begun; but a committee of half a dozen enlightened gentlemen—Joseph Cowen, Thomas Gray, Thomas Forster, William Smith, Thomas Hodgkin, and William Haswell Stephenson—acquired the estate for the purpose of holding it till the Council could be persuaded to change its mind, which it ultimately did. The circumstance that led to this happy conclusion was the chance of acquiring, through the generosity of Sir William Armstrong, part of the Heaton Hall estate as a park for the East End. To Heaton Park the same generous donor afterwards added the Armstrong section, and ultimately Jesmond Dene itself. While these facilities for the public pleasure and enjoyment were being provided, measures were taken to do something of a like kind for the northern end of the town. The strip of the Town Moor that lay between Brandling Village and the North Road was a sort of Tom Tiddler's ground in the sixties—partly swamp and wholly neglected. Enclosed and planted, it is now the Brandling Park. On the other side of the North Road was the old Bull Park. The Bull Park and a few acres of the Town Moor adjoining, including the reservoir that once supplied the inhabitants with water, were utilised in 1887 for an exhibition to commemorate the Jubilee of Queen Victoria's reign. When the exhibition was dispersed, the site was converted into a recreation ground. Some time later another recreation ground was constructed out of a section of the Nun's Moor. And so it has come to pass that the citizens of Newcastle in the course of thirty or forty years have acquired no fewer than eight capacious parks and pleasure places. Further, as the indirect outcome of a movement in favour of tree-planting suggested by Robin Goodfellow in the *Newcastle Weekly Chronicle*, the Town Moor itself has been completely surrounded by belts of thriving plantations.

Forty years ago Newcastle as regards many things might have been described as a one-horse town. The Post Office was located in incommodious premises in the Arcade, with no telegraphs, no telephones, and no parcels delivery as parts of its appurtenances and functions. The public conveyances were of the most primitive character. A couple of ramshackle omnibuses ran from Bentinck across the High Level Bridge to Bensham; and a ponderous vehicle plied between the town and Gosforth (then called Bulman Village). Bicycles were unknown: so were electric lights, electric cars, and electric motors. Even tramways did not come till many years later. A few chop-houses and eating-houses supplied the wants of the people who needed substantial refreshments. A noted black man had established a chop-house in Grey Street; the brothers McCree (another brother, the Rev. George W. McCree, was an active missionary and social reformer in London) announced that their customers "fared sumptuously every day" in the Arcade; and a few humble caterers in the Market and the Bigg Market offered roast and boiled to carriers and country traders. This was about all there was then in the way of public accommodation for the hungry. The grills and restaurants and dining-rooms that now flourish in the town are every one of modern growth.

Board schools there were none; but their places were partially supplied by private adventure academies, while the splendid schools which were afterwards established by Dr. Rutherford in Bath Lane served to educate almost half Newcastle. Rutherford College, the Medical College, the College of Science, High Schools for Boys and Girls—these came along subsequent to the sixties. The Grammar School, under Dr. Snape, was situated in Charlotte Square, pending the completion of the new building in Rye Hill. Bruce's School had not begun to decay, and Erlich's School was almost in its infancy. And then there were such other educational establishments as the jubilee Schools, the Clergy Jubilee Schools, St. Andrew's Schools, the Orphan House Schools, and Dame Allan's Schools. Many of these institutions were supported or controlled by the Church or the Denominations. The Church in the sixties was under the jurisdiction of the Bishop of Durham, the Bishopric of Newcastle not being formed till some years later. Clement Moody was vicar of Newcastle, Rowland East vicar of St. Andrew's, Berkeley Addison vicar of Jesmond, Walter Irvine vicar of All Saints, H. W. Wright vicar of St. John's, George Heriot vicar of St. Ann's, Charles Raines vicar of St. Peter's, and Robt. Anchor Thompson master of St. Mary's, Rye Hill. Mr. Thompson had come with a great reputation, but never did anything particular except quarrel with his bell-ringer and the brethren of the hospital. Mr. Wright was known as Fanny, and Mr. Irvine as Mary Ann, while Mr. Heriot was the father of two or three handsome daughters, one of whom made an unhappy marriage with Lord Wentworth, son of Byron's Ada. Many queer or amusing stories were told of Mr. Raines. One was that he was in the habit of prowling around the stable yards of the neighbourhood in search of rats for his terrier to worry. But the best was about a game of pool that he was playing with some friends. As he put down the threepenny pieces when his ball was pocketed, one of the players asked if he was using the collections. ("Ah," replied the reverend gentleman, "I perceive that you recognise your paltry contributions!" The Dissenting ministers of the day, at least some of them, were more earnest than the clergy. The most prominent was Dr. Rutherford, and next to him in prominence and popularity were J. C. Street, H. T. Robjohns, George Stewart, Richard Leitch, J. G. Potter, and Alexander Reid (father of Sir T. Wemyss Reid). Dr. Hogarth was the Catholic Bishop of Hexham and Newcastle; Monsignor Eyre (afterwards Archbishop of Glasgow) was rector of St. Mary's Cathedral; and Father Aylward was the principal priest at St. Andrew's Chapel, which was down a court off Pilgrim Street, and stood on the site of what is now Worswick Street.

The fame of no town in England for political alertness and advancement was spread further abroad in the sixties than that of Newcastle. It had been the home of the Northern Political Union, when Charles Attwood, Charles Larkin, Thomas Doubleday, and John Fife thundered against the Tories; and it was then the home of another movement, the Northern Reform League, the leading spirit and spokesmen of which were Joseph Cowen, Jun., R. B. Reed, William Cook, Thomas Gregson, and J. T. Gilmour. The town at that time was almost invariably the first to make its voice heard when any question of moment, especially any foreign question, demanded the public attention. The members of Parliament were Thomas Emerson Headlam and Somerset Archibald Beaumont. Dissatisfaction arose with Mr. Beaumont in 1865 by reason of his attitude towards Parliamentary Reform. The consequence was an immense requisition to Mr. Joseph Cowen (afterwards Sir Joseph

Cowen) to contest the constituency in the Radical interest. Mr. Cowen was returned at the head of the poll, and Mr. Beaumont, who was defeated, quitted politics and the country. Newcastle remained Radical or Whig and Radical till the Radicals became intolerant, imperious, arrogant. Mr. Cowen, Jun., as the result of much pressure, had succeeded his father. The new member, as he told his constituents on one memorable occasion, was willing to wear the party uniform, but declined to wear the party plush. And so the Radicals, failing to understand the independence or appreciate the services of Mr. Cowen, prepared themselves the way for the triumphs of a Tory candidate. Since that time Newcastle has fallen from her high estate in the world of politics.

CHAPTER XLVII

PASTIMES IN THE SIXTIES

IF one were in want of a phrase to qualify the beginning of this century, I do not know that a better could be invented than the "age of amusement." The contrast in this respect between the present time and the period of the sixties is immense. Most of the pastimes that are now held in greatest favour were absolutely unknown to the general populace forty years ago. Fancy a world in which there was no football, no tennis, no hockey, no golf, no croquet, no cycling! Yet such was the benighted condition of England at the time of my first acquaintance with Newcastle. Winter especially was a sombre season, for then there was really no outdoor pastime for poor people at all except in frosty weather. All the amusements and recreations just enumerated are the growth and invention of less than half a century. It is still true that life is not all beer and skittles; but it is much more beer and skittles now than it was when our old men were in their prime. Yet pastimes, though less varied than those of the present day, were not uncommon in the sixties.

One of the best, which still holds its own as a summer exercise, was cricket. The old cricket field at the end of what was then called Bath Road, now covered with churches, colleges, and drill halls, was both spacious in extent and convenient of access. Many a brilliant match, in which Northumbrians did not fail to distinguish themselves, was played and witnessed in the old enclosure. Unfortunately, interest in what is yet one of the finest of British pastimes went largely out when facilities for pursuing it were lost. For elderly people, fathers of the city many of them, suitable exercise and recreation were provided at the old Bowling Green in Bath Lane. The game of bowls, one of the most ancient of English pastimes, had been played in Newcastle from time immemorial. According to tradition, Charles the First, when a prisoner in Anderson Place, played at bowls with his courtiers and attendants in the Shieldfield, though recent investigations have shown that the game at which he played there was golf. More authentic is the statement that bowls were a

271

favourite pastime on the Forth, the old playground of the people that was swept away to make room for the Central Station. Then came new greens—first behind Northumberland Street, and then behind the old walls of the town in Bath Lane. Before the latter was compelled to give place to Rutherford College, other bowling greens had been made—in Portland Park, in West Parade, in the public pleasure grounds. A game with a similar name, but totally different in character, was much in vogue among pitmen in the sixties. It was called bowling, but it should more properly have been-called throwing or pitching, for the balls of earthenware were thrown or pitched, and not bowled at all. The Town Moor was the chief scene of this recreation. People who wanted to hear blasphemy in the richest burr of Northumberland had only to attend a bowling match. If, besides, they wanted to incur the risk of annihilation, they had nothing better to do during a champion match than to touch a ball or allow a ball to touch them in its flight. When complaints were made of the danger to the ordinary frequenters of the Moor, a special bowling track was laid out for the purposes of the pastime. Trippet and quoit, elsewhere called knurr and spell, which has since gone entirely out of fashion, was also practised on the Town Moor at the period in question.

Wrestling was much in favour, too, in the sixties. The wrestlers had a ground of their own near the Shot Tower. There two or three days' sport was provided every Easter, when the prizes were sufficiently numerous and valuable to induce athletes from Cumberland and Westmorland to join in the competition. Sleet and snow, however, were so often the accompaniments of Easter weather that the tournament was postponed to Whitsuntide. When bad weather pursued the pastime even to Whitsuntide, its patrons and supporters deemed it desirable, not to say necessary, to abandon the tournament altogether. But the sport that commanded the greatest amount of attention on Tyneside forty years ago was boat-rowing. Harry Clasper was still to the fore, and Robert Chambers was then in his prime. Chambers was a man who was sometimes incapable of winning a race, but always incapable of selling one. For this reason the people never lost faith in the simple, honest oarsman. There were others, however, in whom the same confidence was not felt.

When a great race was to be rowed, the banks of the Tyne from the High Level to Scotswood Suspension Bridge were crowded with spectators. Indeed, the factories along the route were all laid idle till the contest was over. The popularity of the sport continued till the district ceased to produce great rowers. I think the age of sterility in this respect set in after Renforth's tragic death in Canada.

As long as Newcastle Races were held on the Town Moor, they constituted a great popular festival. Many thousands of people went to them, not for the purpose of speculating on the winners, but for the purpose of seeing the spectacle and sharing in the excitement of the crowd. But when the races were removed to Gosforth, and became part and parcel of a business transaction, this class of patrons ceased to attend them. My own earliest visits to the races were made when Caller-Ou and Brown Bread were reckoned among the favourites, together with a horse with a Crimean name, Bakhtchisarai, which the populace converted into Back-stitch Sarah or Back-kitchen Sarah. The sideshows and the drinking tents were at least as attractive as the races themselves. A pitman from Durham was asked about the events he had seen run. "Wey," said he, "aa got inte Jerry Jordan's booth, and seed nowt mair." Among the living curiosities exhibited in those days was a fat woman. The lady's husband stood at the door of the tent and bawled invitations to the crowd to "come and see the famous Nanny Clark frae Hooden." This husband himself was the son of a notorious character—"Jack the Deevil"—so called because, when he acquired a small public-house, he astonished and horrified the folks o' Shields by exhibiting his own coffin in the bar.

And then there was Micky Bent with his sparring booth, the "Pavilion of the Fancy." It was a treat to listen to Micky, as, standing on a platform at the door, he introduced his pupils and comrades to the public, detailing the victories which each had won in the ring. Part of the play was, when business was slack, to excite the curiosity of the outsiders. A friend and myself were two of the outsiders on one occasion. Micky was expatiating on the exploits of Young Baldwin, the famous Little Bantam from Lancashire (the bull-necked youth, in fighting trim, stood with folded arms beside him), when a challenge rang out from the crowd. Who was the daring individual? The answer came that it was Jack Covington. "Nonsense," cried Micky, as he shaded his eyes to get a better view. "Divil take me, but it is, though. Make way there for Jack Covington, the champion of the feather-weights." Much handshaking on the platform ensued. And then of course there was an adjournment to the tent, where the Bantam and the champion were to have a pretty "set-to." And equally of course the party from the platform was followed inside by large numbers of the admiring and now excited crowd. After each round with the gloves, the proprietor of the booth would be heard crying: "Give 'em a clap, gentlemen, if you think they are deserving of it," he himself setting the example. So did Micky Bent turn an honest penny, while the hat went round to buy the Bantam a new pair of braces!

Places of amusement were not very numerous in 1863, though they were no doubt sufficient to satisfy the wants of the population. There was only one theatre — the Theatre Royal; but there were four or five concert halls. A photographer named Smith ran the Victoria Hall at the top of Grey Street, and Bagnall and Blakey were the proprietors of the Oxford Hall in the Cloth Market, previously known as "Balmbra's Grand Saloon." The Grainger Hotel, known as "Donald's," at the corner of Market Street and Grainger Street, was also open as a place of entertainment, and an old circus, standing on the site of the Audit Office of the North-Eastern Railway, had been converted by George Stanley into the Tyne Concert Hall. One visit to each was sufficient for the Victoria and the Oxford; Donald's I never entered. Almost all I recollect of either is that Billy Thompson, a fat man with a fund of coarse humour, performed the functions of chairman at the Oxford. The Tyne Concert Hall, which was the forerunner of the Tyne Theatre, was a long way the best of the variety shows. Favourites of the period thereat were Ned Corvan, a local songster who is not yet forgotten; Tom Handforth, a negro minstrel who called himself the Black Diamond; and Joe Wilson, the dialect poet who sang many of his own songs — "Geordy, Had the Bairn," the "Row on the Stairs;" and so forth. The Tyne Theatre, erected at great cost in Westgate, was opened in 1867 under the management of Mr. Stanley. Its first pantomime, "Ye Lambton

Worme," in which Mr. Fred W. Irish played the principal part, was a great success, and for years afterwards all the chief stars in the theatrical firmament flickered and shone in succession on its boards.

The Theatre Royal, long before and long after 1863, was managed by Mr. E. D. Davis. Stock companies were the order of the day then. Among the ladies who were members of these companies the most notable were Emily Cross, Ada Dyas, and Amy Fawsitt. The latter, after achieving great success as Lady Teazle in London, died miserably in America, betrayed and deserted by the villain she had trusted. Another favourite season actress was Fanny Addison. Once she played Juliet with a company of amateurs. Both Juliet and the audience, I recollect, nearly went into hysterics when Romeo tumbled over the balcony! No season company was complete during the greater part of Mr. Davis's management without J. Roberts. "Good old Roberts!" a brother mime wrote of him, "he would play a dozen characters a night, and with the strictest impartiality—making them all alike." Of course he had a part in every play—now a messenger, anon a first robber, at other times the leader of a mob. It happened sometimes that he gave a strange turn to the few words he had to utter. Thus on one occasion, when he had to answer a question by Macbeth, he exclaimed, "'Tis the cry of wimming, good my lord!" On another occasion, when, as leader of the mob of citizens who thronged the Forum to hear Brutus speak on the murder of Caesar, he had to express the contentment of his comrades, he and the rest of the six supers comprising the "multitude" were heard shouting, "We will be satisfized! let us be satisfized!" Alas! poor Roberts! one heard of the death of many greater men with more composure than one heard of his.

The touring system, which came into fashion about the end of the sixties, extinguished the stock company system. Stars, however, preceded touring companies. And so one saw at the Royal and the Tyne many of the leading performers of the day—Helen Fawcit, Lydia Thompson, and Mrs. Scott Siddons, Charles Mathews, Joseph Jefferson, and Samuel Phelps. Lydia Thompson was one of the most popular actresses that ever appeared at the Royal in my time. Very old playgoers will recollect the enthusiasm which this clever and vivacious lady aroused in 1867. As a matter of fact, Lydia took the town by storm; almost everybody was talking and some were even raving about her; and the little house in Grey Street was crammed to overflowing every night of her engagement. It was as a burlesque actress that she was best known—though, for my part, I thought she shone still better in comedy. The part she played in a charming little piece called "Meg's Diversion" remains in my memory as one of the prettiest triumphs I ever saw on the stage. Years afterwards Miss Thompson appeared on the same boards in a clever burlesque with Lionel Brough. The roars of laughter these two produced will not be forgotten by anybody who witnessed their vocal and other antics. It was a wonderful display, devoid from beginning to end of the smallest suggestion of vulgarity. Other performances left vivid impressions too. For example, there was Shiel Barry, whose laugh as the miser Gaspard was as terrific in its way as the wild-cat shrieks of little Robson as Medea. Then there was Jefferson as Rip Van Winkle—a part he had played so often, I heard him say, that he now and then went through some of the scenes as in a dream, wondering, when he recollected himself, whether he had made any mistakes during the period of forgetfulness. But the greatest performance of all, to my mind, was Phelps's Sir Pertinax MacSycophant. It was not acting—it seemed like real life. It was not Phelps one saw on the stage—it was the vile old hypocrite himself. If ever a finer thing was done on the boards, I never saw it.

Critics and admirers of the drama were perhaps more serious in the sixties than they are now. Three gentlemen—known as the "three K's"—brought exceptional knowledge and intelligence to bear on the tragedies they witnessed. One was John Kane, then secretary of the Ironworkers' Union; another was John Kirton, a friend of Anderson's and Macready's; and the third was William Kelly, a minor poet of considerable excellence. Detractors of the drama there might have been then; but none of them could have been as foolish as a relative of Mr. E. D. Davis's, who, when the old manager died in 1887, desired the newspapers to suppress all mention of the fact that he had for twenty or thirty years been the most prominent theatrical personage in Newcastle!

CHAPTER XLVIII

NEWCASTLE JOURNALISTS

THE journalists of Newcastle who flourished in the sixties, being many of them masters of the craft, and worthy men besides, deserve a special chapter.

Richard Welford exchanged journalism for commerce in 1862. Though I was too late to become his colleague, I was fortunate to become his friend. First secretary, then manager, and finally managing director of an important shipping company, Mr. Welford devoted his leisure to local history and antiquities. So he has enriched the literature of Tyneside and Northumberland with many valued and learned volumes. My immediate colleagues on the leading paper of the district were two—James Clephan and James Hay. Mr. Clephan, who had been editor of the *Gateshead Observer* in its palmy days, was a painstaking writer, something of a poet and a philosopher, an antiquary of repute, and much respected in all the serious circles of the town. Towards the end of his long life he deliberately took to his bed and waited for death. He lived in bed, worked in bed, received his visitors in bed–all for months and months before the end came. Nor did he select the most comfortable position, for he lay with his head in the darkest corner of the room, and no persuasion on the part of his friends could induce him to change it. Mr. Hay removed early, first to Plymouth and then to Portsmouth, where, having acquired an expert knowledge of naval affairs, he was for years the correspondent of the *Times*. Latterly he purchased a paper at Melton Mowbray, which he conducted till his death in 1901. It was in 1863 that the present writer added his farthing candle to the general illumination. Soon there came three other colleagues, still in the same decade, who are entitled to separate paragraphs.

Sidney Milnes Hawkes was a barrister-at-law, and had been a man of means. I understood from himself that he had lost his fortune in some unlucky venture with his friend James Stansfeld, afterwards Sir

James Stansfeld, and a member of various Liberal Governments. Devoted to Mazzini, he had assisted in some of the revolutionary enterprises that had startled Europe a few years before. Further, he had been brought in contact with many of the most eminent people of the time, recollections of whom he long subsequently embodied in a series of lectures. Mr. Hawkes was a clever, but not a ready writer. As he never really liked the work, he exchanged a few years later the duties of a pressman for those of a publican. The Marsden Inn and the Marsden Grotto, situated on the picturesque coast between Shields and Sunderland, came under his control as the successor of the Allan family, an earlier member of which had carved a dwelling-house and a dancing-room out of the solid rock. Mr. Hawkes's tenancy commenced just about the time that the Whitburn Colliery was opened. The pitmen and quarrymen who patronised the Grotto and the Inn–the one on the sea shore the other high up on the cliffs–were sometimes an unruly lot. Mr. Hawkes, however, who was as gentle as a girl and as amiable as an angel, exercised a wonderful command over them even in their cups. There was not a more popular or a more highly respected man in the whole district than the landlord of Marsden Grotto. Mr. Hawkes had a large family. One of his sons, Mervyn Hawkes, having first tried his pinions as a contributor to the "Notes and Queries" of the *Newcastle Weekly Chronicle*, became attached to the London Press, wrote a political novel of considerable merit, and would probably have won a place of distinction in journalism and literature if he had not died young. It was Mervyn Hawkes who, standing as a candidate for Eye against Mr. Ashmead Bartlett, challenged one of the supporters of his honourable opponent to run a race for the honour of representing the constituency!

William Stowell belonged to a clerical family. His father was the Rev. Dr. Stowell, related to the celebrated Hugh Stowell; his brother became a clergyman of the Church of England; and one of his sons entered the Congregational ministry. Our colleague himself was pastor of an Independent Church at Ryton. He preached and wrote equally well. His capacity for writing was immense. He could write at any length on any subject, whether he understood it or not, though he generally did understand it. I used to think that he could make more bricks without straw than anybody I ever knew. But there was this to be said for him–that he wrote about nothing that he did not make attractive. Mr. Stowell had some strong tastes–for strong tea and strong tobacco particularly. The tobacco was black: so also was the tea (which he brewed himself) as it came from the pot. One day, when some carpenters were employed in making alterations in the office, Stowell mislaid his pouch. Whereupon, the carpenters having gone home, he went crying along the corridor that the "working classes" had stolen his tobacco! A smart repartee of his is also worth recalling. The members of the staff were taking tea at the office when John Lovell, then manager of the Press Association, was introduced to the company. "Mr. Stowell!" said Lovell: "any relation of Lord Stowell?" "No–o," slowly replied Stowell: "any relation of Lord Lovel?" Our colleague had the best of that deal. When he died in the prime of life, he was buried in the picturesque churchyard of Ryton, where troops of friends assembled from all the district round to testify their respect for his memory.

Perhaps the best known member of the staff was Thomas Nelson Brown, who came from Dunfermline, but who had previously earned a good reputation as a platform speaker in Glasgow. More than thirty years later I met in Madeira a retired and wealthy manufacturer (Mr. John Leckie, of Walsall) who had been in far-away days a sort of disciple of his on the banks of the Clyde. Mr. Brown's prodigious memory was the wonder of his colleagues, as was his marvellous fund of anecdote. His mind was a veritable storehouse of poetry. I believe he could recite the whole of Pollok's "Course of Time," besides hundreds of other poems. And he knew more of Scotch theology than half the professors put together. Moreover, he talked so well that I often thought he missed his vocation when he took to the press instead of the pulpit. But the worst of it was that he did not quite know when to stop talking, especially if he chanced to meet a friend in the street. Brown and Clephan were in the habit, at the close of the night's work, of seeing each other home. Usually they fell into such enthralling discussions that the process lasted till far into the morning. Once, when the whole town was sleeping, they were overtaken by a shower of rain, and took refuge in a doorway. Here they were seen by a new policeman, who ordered them off the premises, hinting that they could be up to no good purpose at that hour and in that place. Brown, of course, remonstrated; but Clephan, appreciating the humour of the situation, retired quietly to his virtuous couch. But the midnight rambles of the two friends did not cease with this *contretemps*. I believe they were continued till the elder of the two, as recorded above, took to his bed to wait for death.

The office of sub-editor was held for many years by a careful and painstaking pressman–William Duncan. Being a Scot, and an Aberdonian at that, he was as cautious as the policeman in Callander who (as previously recorded) declined to say which was the best hotel in the place because he was a person in authority. Mr. Duncan was a Latin scholar, and was, indeed, so saturated with the speech and style of the ancient Romans that they coloured almost all he said or wrote. When he retired from the active pursuit of journalism, his colleagues presented him with an illuminated address. Thereafter he had sufficient employment as official reporter for the Town Council. William Duncan and James Hornsby were two of the oldest members of the staff in 1863.

Hornsby reported the inquests and the policecourts. If information was wanted, he was the man to get it. Of course he met with many rebuffs. One was administered by Mr. L. M. Cockcroft, then coroner for South Northumberland. News of a certain inquest was required. The coroner declined to supply it. Late at night James–we all called him James–"tried him again." The coroner answered the door in his dressing gown. "What!" he exclaimed, as he caught sight of the reporter, "you here again!" and he slammed the door in his face. The insult did not disturb the reporter in the least: it was, he said, all in the way of his work. Mr. Hornsby was an enthusiast in phonography. Besides teaching classes in England, he went on a phonographic mission to America. Horace Greeley received him courteously, and next day printed a paragraph in the *New York Tribune*, announcing that "Professor Hornsby from Europe" had arrived to enlighten the citizens of the Great Republic on the subject of shorthand!

We had two rivals in 1863. One is dead. It claimed, I think, to be the first penny daily paper established in the North of England. A printer named John Watson started it in Darlington in 1855, bringing it to Newcastle just before the other newspaper proprietors converted their weeklies into dailies. The paper was owned at the time I mention by a wholesale grocer, and had just previously been edited by a clever but unscrupulous journalist of the name of James Bolivar Manson. The editor had got himself into so many escapades that the proprietor presumably thought it was better he should return to Scotland. At any rate he had just left Newcastle in 1863, though he still continued to write the leading articles. But one of his escapades showed his smartness so much, and yet had such ludicrous consequences, that some of the particulars may be considered interesting.

A municipal election in one of the wards of the town had given rise to a good deal of bigoted feeling on account of one of the candidates being a Roman Catholic–a highly respected gentleman of the name of Dunn. The French consul at the time was the Comte de Maricourt. And M. de Maricourt was accused of interfering in the election on behalf of Mr. Dunn. Shortly before the contest, Newcastle society had been greatly scandalised by the doings of a notorious Frenchwoman. This woman, owing to the action of the police, had been expelled the town. The paper took up the cry against the consul; the editor wrote a furious article on the subject; and the article concluded with a frightful sting "Monsieur must follow Madame." It was clever, but it was outrageous. The conjunction in the same sentence as deserving of the same treatment of a respectable nobleman with a disreputable procuress naturally excited great indignation. The consul's son, the Vicomte de Maricourt, a young officer in the French army, happened to be on a visit to his father. Him the insult aroused to fury. The young man presented himself at the editor's house with a revolver, demanding a written apology. Mr. Manson was compelled to accompany his visitor to the office, where he wrote the declaration the Vicomte de Maricourt required. Then came proceedings in the police-court. The affair was compromised in some way. But the editor followed the consul.

Mr. Manson left a flavour of romance behind him. From the circumstance about to be related one would conclude that he was what our American cousins used to call a "festive cus." It chanced that I needed to rent a house. The house that I thought would suit me, situated at the corner of two streets, was owned and once occupied by a chemist who was on intimate terms with the journalist. The chemist was proud of the connection. Manson and Marley were bosom friends–neighbours too. Often had the one held high revels in the other's house. When Marley was showing the prospective tenant over the house, he pointed to the parlour window as he gleefully said, "Many's the time Manson has smashed that window as he has been going home hilarious." The smashing of the window seemed to be regarded by the owner as a token and evidence of affection on the part of his friend.

About this house I have another story to tell. It was situated, I have said, at the corner of two streets. A little grass plot ran round the two sides. The mother of the family, being new to Newcastle, was anxious for the safety of her children: so she used to padlock the gate in order to prevent them from wandering away. As for myself, I was always late at the office; moreover, when I returned home in the early hours of the morning, it was my custom to sit up reading for an hour or two. These things were noted by a neighbour on the opposite side of one of the streets. The neighbour put two and two together and built up a beautiful theory. It chanced that he was acquainted with a friend of mine. To this friend he one day imparted his suspicions. "We have some queer folks living opposite to us," he said. "The man is at home all day; there is a light burning all night ; and the gate is always padlocked. I fancy they are coiners!" Such was the reputation the writer had acquired in the neighbourhood till his friend had the opportunity of explaining that the mysterious and nocturnal habits of the journalist were due to the exigencies of work on a daily newspaper.

Clever stories are apt to be attributed to all sorts of different people, especially if the said people should happen to be noted for saying smart things. It is likely, therefore, that the rather profane story which was ascribed to Manson may have been told of other wits. Anyhow, it is good enough for anybody. Manson, having returned to Edinburgh, was in conversation with an acquaintance, who remarked as a curious circumstance that he had been mistaken for the Duke of Argyll. "That's nothing," said Manson; "I was taken for a bigger card than the duke." "Ay, and who was that?" "Well, as I was crossing the North Bridge, a man I had not seen for years stepped right in front of me and exclaimed, 'God Almighty! is that you?' "

Mr. Manson's immediate successor was a young Scotchman–James Macdonell. I had but a slight acquaintance with him, for he tarried in Newcastle only a year or two. Almost all I remember was that he was tall and slim, and wore his hair long. Mr. Macdonell became afterwards a famous journalist in London–first as a coadjutor of Thornton Hunt's on the *Daily Telegraph*, and then as a coadjutor of J. T. Delane's on the *Times*. Most of the best articles on foreign affairs that appeared in the *Thunderer* from 1876 to 1879 were credited to him. Unfortunately, his brilliant career was of short duration. When he died, many of his brother journalists wrote touching and beautiful things to his memory. Even as late as 1885 Mr. Escott published a panegyric in the *Chicago Times*, and at a still later date his biography was written by Dr. Robertson Nicoll. Mr. Macdonell was succeeded by Mr. R. N. Worth, who came from Plymouth, and returned thither, after a few years in the North. Mr. Worth was the author of a "History of Devonshire," and of some other works of a topographical and historical character. The hand of the syndicate was upon the unfortunate property by this time. The syndicate entertained the strange delusion that opinion, or what was supposed to be opinion, if poured into a given mould in London, would be gratefully received in Newcastle and in Plymouth and in many other places between. The false estimate that had thus been formed of the weakness and ductility of the public mind of England was fatal to the paper. The candle flickered and guttered for some years longer, but went out at last, almost without anybody knowing that it had ceased to smoulder.

The other daily contemporary had in earlier days been a fierce and somewhat scurrilous party organ. It had once suggested that John Bright, who had been announced to visit Alnwick at the beginning of the Anti-Corn Law agitation, should be dipped in a horse-pond.

And it had made some insulting observations about the wife of a Newcastle alderman which caused a considerable rumpus in the town. For this outrage the editor was publicly horsewhipped by the son of the injured lady. The young man who had thus avenged his mother became in after-years the Mayor of Newcastle, besides being decorated by the Crown for his services to the Volunteer movement. But he had broken the law in his generous anger: so he had to suffer–perhaps one ought rather to say enjoy–a period of imprisonment. The detention was rendered pleasant and agreeable by the visits and commendations he received the while from his friends. But the paper in 1863 had ceased to play the scurvy tricks which brought indignity upon its former editor. It was still a Tory organ, but a Tory organ that knew how to behave decently.

The staff of the paper in the sixties included three gentlemen who need not be nameless. One was the son of an Independent minister in the town. Leaving Newcastle, he was first the editor of the *Leeds Mercury*, and then literary director of the great printing and publishing firm of Cassell, Petter, and Galpin. For some years past he has been familiar in the world of politics and literature as Sir T. Wemyss Reid, founder of *The Speaker*, and author of "Gladys Fane " and a memoir of Charlotte Brontë. Mr. Reid, I believe, was both reporter and occasional leader-writer. The chief of the reporting staff was John W. Lowes, reputed to be the fastest note-taker in the North of England, equal even to taking a verbatim note of Sir George Grey, who rattled away like a Gatling gun. Mr. Lowes, the author of a system of shorthand of his own, was a native of Durham, whither he retired, and where he died a long time ago. Among the junior reporters was Thomas Lawson, who, when John H. Amos was appointed to the secretaryship of the River Tees Commissioners, was elected to an important and confidential office in the Corporation of Newcastle.

Newspaper success depends even more upon skilful management than upon skilful writing. One of the most skilful managers of the time of which I am writing, and long afterwards, was Richard Bagnall Reed. No shrewder intellect than his, I think, was ever connected with the press. If he did not write much himself, he knew how to instruct and inspire others to write. And his energy was amazing. Nothing in any department of the paper escaped his watchful eye. Added to untiring zeal was a marvellous capacity for gauging the tastes and requirements of the reading public. Mr. Reed was a newspaper genius who, had his lines been cast in other walks of life, would have attained distinction wherever he sought it. To him must be ascribed the credit of raising the press of the North of England from the parochialism of an earlier day to the rank and dignity it has ever since enjoyed.

CHAPTER XLIX

JOSEPH COWEN

BUT the ablest journalist of them all was Joseph Cowen. The rest were pigmies beside him. The real journalist, like the real poet, is born, not made. The qualities which come to others as the result of laborious effort come to him by instinct. So it was with Mr. Cowen. Having a passion for public service, a faith to preach, and an object to accomplish, he made of the paper he owned and controlled an organ of illumination and beneficence.

Joseph Cowen
(1829-1900)

Mr. Cowen, however, was a journalist and something more. Journalism, indeed, was only an incident. No better business man was probably to be found in the North of England. But business was only an incident too. It was merely a means to an end, just as the newspaper was. A propagandist from his earliest youth, Mr. Cowen had something to say, and sought all sorts of opportunities of saying it. Then the press became the adjunct of the platform. It was when a regular channel of conveying his ideas to the public had been acquired that the natural aptitude of the born journalist discovered itself. Nobody knows so well the difficulty of gauging the public wants and forecasting the public sentiments as the man engaged in conducting a newspaper. In Mr. Cowen's case the knowledge of how to do it seemed to come by intuition. Thus the press in his hands became, as I have said, a machine for spreading enlightenment and effecting progress. But Mr. Cowen was more than a great journalist: he was a great man–great in every variation of human activity–a great politician, a great orator, a great instructor of the people, with sympathies that embraced all the races of the earth. What he did for the struggling nationalities of Europe, when kings and emperors were banded together to keep down the natural aspiration for freedom, will never be known. Yet some of the results of his labours and sacrifices may be seen to-day in the emancipation of Italy from the thraldom of petty despots and foreign oppressors.

For years and years Mr. Cowen was the Tribune of the North. No man in our time spoke as he spoke for the Northern race. The characteristics, the ideas, the idiosyncrasies, even the prejudices of the people among whom he had been born and bred, were more truly represented by him than were those of any other district by any other prominent figure in public life. Mr. Cowen was a Tynesider from top to toe–"native and to the manner born." Few men better understood or better appreciated the brusque and sturdy race of which in its higher traits he was himself a type. And he was "hail fellow" with the proudest and the humblest–with lord and lordling, keelman and puddler. The tastes of the common people were to some extent his tastes–as, for instance, in the countenance he gave to aquatics in the palmy days of Clasper and Chambers. It was generally his custom, too, before the Races were removed from the Town Moor, to share in the exhilaration of the scene when the favourite won the Pitman's Derby. The amusements of the people, though he had practically none of his own, always interested him. And then his native Doric–it was never changed, and never sought to be changed. What was good enough for Hotspur was good enough for him. Thick of speech, as Shakspeare says of Hotspur, indeed he was; but the glowing periods in which he denounced the enemies of liberty from the platform of the Lecture Room or the Town Hall obtained an added force from the deep and mystical burr. Nor did it prevent him from electrifying the House of Commons as he had many a time and oft electrified vast gatherings of his own townsfolk.

Most of the commentators in the London press at the time of his death, on Feb. 18th, 1900, alluded to the early difficulty which some of the members of the House of Commons experienced in understanding all that Mr. Cowen said. But this difficulty, greatly exaggerated by envious critics, was soon overcome. The overcoming it was itself a triumph for the orator. Had there not been matter behind the unusual pronunciation of the speaker, the House would never have filled as I have seen halls and theatres and circuses filled in the North when Mr. Cowen was delivering an address. (Who that was present can ever forget the scenes of wild enthusiasm that occurred in the Town Hall every time he appeared before the electors during his parliamentary contests?). While all the commentators spoke in one emphatic tone of the power of his eloquence, some of them ventured the opinion that Mr. Cowen lacked the ready skill of the debater. This was a mistake. It was Mr. Cowen's custom, at the close of his great harangues, to submit himself to the examination of his constituents. All sorts of questions–dozens of them, scores of them, almost hundreds of them– were put and answered in a night. And I used to think that these impromptu replies were sometimes more effective, because less polished, than the well-studied speech that had preceded them. Readiness and promptitude in answering a question, stating an argument, explaining a policy, expounding a principle, or exposing a fallacy–these are qualities that go to the making of an accomplished debater, and Mr. Cowen had them all to perfection. But the critics and observers in Parliament had only rare opportunities of seeing and hearing Mr. Cowen, and not even then perhaps at his best. We in Newcastle, who had seen and heard him so often that we knew every trick and mood and attitude, the expressive turn of the head, the impressive tone of the voice, the significant wave and shake of the finger—we in Newcastle knew infinitely better than any gentleman in London to what heights of power and oratory our great tribune was capable of ascending. I have heard most of the famous speakers of the last fifty years, and I venture to declare that never a speaker among them had anything like the same power of moving and inspiring a vast audience as Mr. Cowen had.

The speeches of great speakers will not always bear reproduction in unimpassioned type. Some of us will remember Henry Vincent. He spoke like a whirlwind, and like a whirlwind swept his audiences before him. But his best efforts, if reported word for word, would have been but tawdry stuff mere sound and fury, signifying little. It was much the same with other famous speakers. Mr. Cowen saw this default, and determined to evade it in his own case. Hence the preparation he gave to his set deliverances—the thought and study and information he put into them. Never in any contest before or since was so masterly a series of speeches delivered as those which Mr. Cowen addressed to the electors of Newcastle in 1874, and again in 1885. To read them even now, when the subjects discussed have become mere matters of history, is to get a new view of the dignity and grandeur of the English language.

I have said already that the speeches of Mr. Cowen are classics. Take down the volume in which Major Evan R. Jones collected some of them together, open it where you like, and see whether you can resist the desire to read to the end. They will stand the test of time as well as Burke's, and perhaps even better than Canning's. Every word is a stroke, every sentence a poem or a sermon, every speech a lesson and an exposition. A Parliamentary reporter asked his editor what he was to do with a speech of Robert Lowe's. "Cut it down," said the editor; "give only the points." "You forget," replied the reporter; "a speech of Lowe's is all points." Much the same may be said of Mr. Cowen's, which are studded with gems as well as points—all brilliant and all genuine. Even as you read, you are constrained to pause if you mean to drink in all the beauty of diction or all the richness of thought–to pause as long and as often as when reading an essay of Emerson's or a chapter from Ruskin. A popular novelist, who is as skilful with words and as inventive in ideas as any of her contemporaries, assured me months before the catastrophe of Feb., 1900, that it was her habit, when she felt in want of an intellectual stimulant, to refresh her jaded spirits with a draught from one of Mr. Cowen's speeches. Since Major Jones's volume was published, many other brilliant performances were added to the public store. All have been issued in isolated form. One could wish for nothing better than the issue of a new and complete collection.

There were many sides to Mr. Cowen's character–so many that the most intimate of his friends probably did not know them all. Few outside his own circle, for instance, knew that he at one time practically managed a great theatre when fortunes were made in it. Business, finance, journalism, stagecraft–Mr. Cowen was expert at them all. Had his inclinations lain in the direction of office, had he been endowed with the pliability which seems to be necessary to statecraft, he would have made a brilliant Chancellor of the Exchequer or a still more brilliant Secretary for Foreign Affairs. But he was content with moulding and influencing the opinions and affairs of his own people. For the rest, he had but one recreation–books. It was his hobby to buy books, the best and choicest in the market. But he also read them. And all he said and wrote bore evidence, not only of deep and original thought, but of wide and absorbent reading. Gifted with a splendid memory, versed in all sorts of knowledge, and thoroughly acquainted with almost all branches of literature, he was able to illuminate every question he discussed or expounded with examples and precepts from ancient and modern writers–from classic and recent history–from the philosophers of the pagan world or the poets and essayists of our own dear land.

It is recorded in the "Life and Letters of Dean Lake" that that eminent divine consulted Mr. Cowen before he launched his great scheme for the establishment of the Durham College of Science. And the same thing happened whenever any other important project connected with the North of England was under consideration. Mr.

Cowen's counsel was always invaluable in these matters. Nor was the help of his influence less useful or less esteemed. Besides the moral support that he gave to great enterprises, the material support which followed it was ever most liberal and generous. But far more numerous than his public were his private benefactions. Many a struggling acquaintance and many a troubled entertainer owed their rescue from despondency to his ready assistance.

Mr. Cowen, when the political party with which he had previously acted became estranged and embittered, was accused of inconsistency. No hollower accusation was ever made. Mr. Cowen was no more enamoured of a "foolish consistency" than Emerson was. A given policy is only applicable in the same circumstances. But circumstances, changing from year, and often from month to month, are seldom the same. It was the policy of the British Government at the time of the Russian invasion of Turkey that caused the rupture between Mr. Cowen and his former political friends–this and the attempt to introduce "machine politics" into England. Russia, however, though she then seemed to pose as a liberator, had no more altered in character than a leopard could change its spots. She still stood for despotism. Mr. Cowen once likened her to a huge iceberg, which, sailing into summer seas, caused everything to freeze or shiver around it. Russia had dismembered Poland and crushed Hungary. These things, forgotten by the politicians of the period, could not be forgotten by Mr. Cowen. Where, then, was his inconsistency? But the estrangement had a disastrous effect. It led the one masterly politician of the district to retire from Parliament and ultimately from public life. The loss to Tyneside has never since ceased to be deplored. Rarely afterwards did Mr. Cowen entrance his townsmen with his eloquence. But when for special reasons he emerged from his retirement, the public interest in his addresses, all models and all classics, showed the abiding affection of the people for the greatest among them.

The last words of eminent men are always interesting. The last words of Mr. Cowen were pathetic and gratifying as well. Before he closed his eyes in what proved to be his final sleep, he said to his daughter: "I am very comfortable." Truly his end was peace.

CHAPTER L

TERRORS AND SINGULARITIES OF THE PRESS

THE linotype machine is an ingenious invention. Like the Chassepot at Mentana, it has done wonders. But it is also responsible, I am afraid, for many of the dismal errors that so often appear in the press, the reason being that the whole process of type-setting, or rather of type-casting, is now almost purely mechanical. Added to this there is the difficulty of correcting the mistakes the printers have made, inducing people in charge of newspapers who know the value of time to abstain from correcting them at all. The thing is unfortunate, because the blunders, besides being liable to mislead the ignorant or half-educated reader, are calculated to cause confusion in his mind as to the real meaning of words.

"Literals," mistakes of mere letters, were common enough in the old days. Now the errors of the press take the form of substituting a wrong word for the right one. Blunders of this more serious kind were formerly rectified in a paragraph devoted to errata, as in the celebrated case of the American editor who had reported that a Baptist minister was "spanked in infancy," and who inserted a correction in his next issue—"for 'spanked,' read 'sprinkled.'" But no attempt is made to explain such matters now. Indeed, if it were made, a considerable space would be required for the purpose. Hence, unless there should be a libel in the case, blunders remain blunders. Once for a few weeks I went to the trouble of making a collection of the errors I had seen in newspapers. Here are a few of them:—"Described" was printed for "descried;" "received" for "reviewed," "bloated" for "floated," "recognised" for "reorganized," "transmitted" for "transmuted," "immunity" for "impunity," "affected" for "afflicted," "denoted" for "devoted," "denied" for "deprived," "comprised" for "compressed," "converged" for "conversed," "wonder" for "winter," "invitation" for "initiative," "glister" for "glitter," "warrior" for "wanderer," "masked" for "marked," "stained" for "strained," "disposed" for "disputed," "animal spirits" for "annual sports," "infernal agreement" for "informal agreement," and "devil to play" for "devil to Pay"! When Dr. Johnson was asked by a lady how he came to make a certain mistake in his dictionary, he is said to have replied, "Pure ignorance, madame." Pure ignorance would perhaps be the rightful explanation of many of the errors that appear in newspapers—pure ignorance on the part of reporters or sub-editors, compositors or printers' readers. What but pure ignorance could make any body speak of "poems by Dante, Gabriel, and Rossetti"? The cause of the great majority of errors, however, is the haste which all engaged in the production of newspapers display to be first on the market. [27]

Errors of the press have furnished food for mirth to many generations—ever since the early printers printed the first Bibles. Dismissing all the old standards—such as the substitution of the word "sauce" for the word "sense" in Ross's translation of Lessing's "Laocoon"—a few recent examples that have not been collected before may amuse the reader. A controversialist wrote of Irishmen that they couldn't tell "whether they would like to cuddle maidens on Mars or have England pitch Ulster," etc.; but the ingenious printer made him say that Irishmen couldn't tell whether they wanted to cuddle "maidens or mars"—maidens or mammas! The report of an application for contempt of court against a newspaper stated that the said newspaper had accused a party to a suit then pending of "mailing Tory misstatements to the country." What the newspaper had said was that he had been "nailing Tory misstatements to the counter"! And then there was the report of an inquest in which it was twice stated that the deceased had died of "inflammation of the bowls." Which rather reminds one of the quack doctor who, explaining the anatomy of the human frame, said that the principal organs were "the heart, the liver, and the bowels, of which there are five—a, e, i, o, u, and sometimes w and $y!$"

One of the most exasperating misprints that ever appeared in a newspaper, though it is amusing enough now, occurred in the report of an address which the Rev. T. Harwood Pattinson, now a professor in a Theological College at Rochester, U. S., delivered in Newcastle in 1872. The effect of an eloquent appeal in favour of peace was entirely destroyed, so far as the report was concerned, by a misprint in the word "save." For the audience was urged to take its place in that increasing host—

> Along whose front no sabres shine,
>   No blood-red pennons wave,
> Whose banner bears the simple line,
>   "Our duty is to shave."

Here the mistake was a single word; but many words were misprinted in a passage from Byron's "Siege of Corinth" which Mr. Joseph Cowen quoted in a speech at Blaydon in 1876. The poet's lines, describing the work of dogs on a battlefield, were weird and magnificent:—

> From a Tartar's skull they had stripp'd the flesh,
> As ye peel the fig when its fruit is fresh;
> And the white tusks crunch'd o'er the whiter skull,
> As it slipp'd through their jaws when their edge grew dull,
> As they lazily mumbled the bones of the dead,
> When they scarce could rise from the spot where they fed.

But the printer made them ludicrous:—

> From the Tartar's skull they had stripped the flesh
> As ye *feed the pig* when the fruit is fresh;
> And their white tusks crushed o'er the whiter skull
> As it slipped thro' their jaws when their edge grew dull,
> As they *largely resembled* the bones of the dead,
> When they scarce could rise from the spot where they fed.

Reporters, when they "let themselves go," as we say, sometimes play strange pranks with the King's English. One whom I knew wrote of an actor who was playing the Ghost in "Hamlet" that he had a "semi-resurrectionary voice." Another was guilty of curious carelessness. Reporting a speaker who related the origin of a recreation ground, he made him remark that "a cabbage garden was taken in hand by some enterprising gentlemen who lived in the neighbourhood, most of whom, he was sorry to say, were now dead, and converted into a park." But these feats were pardonable compared with that of the reporter who, in an account of a notable man's funeral, got off the following:—"It was a boisterous winter's day, with fitful showers of rain and hail; and as the polished coffin was borne into the church the lid was sprinkled with rain, like dew-drops on a laburnum leaf, which was a great contrast to wreaths of flowers, as the deceased did not approve of them!"

There was a time when even the editorial articles of a leading London daily were strewn with rare specimens of gush and bathos. The "young lions" of the *Daily Telegraph* produced every morning columns of fantastic literature that made the hair of staid old journalists stand on end. The staid old *Standard*, indeed, allowed itself to print at irregular but frequent intervals clever parodies of the style of the *Gaily Bellograph*. Elderly people will recollect the wonderful meteoric visitation of 1866. Thomas Aird wrote a famous line that extorted the admiration of George Gilfillan describing the sky in a storm as "like a red bewilder'd map with lightning scribbled o'er." It was not lightning, but meteors, that "scribbled o'er" the sky on two or three November nights in that year. Myriads of rockets seemed to be darting noiselessly hither and thither all over the heavens. Not a second passed without innumerable meteors of varying sizes and brilliancy coming into view. Sometimes it appeared as if all the stars in the firmament were seized with a mad impulse to rush into each other's arms. People woke up their children—I did mine—to show them the great wonder. Hundreds of writers tried to picture the entrancing sight. Some succeeded fairly well; others utterly failed. As a matter of fact, it was a spectacle that could not with any approach to accuracy be described in words. But the "young lions" of the *Telegraph* were equal to the occasion. One of them—Godfrey Turner or Jefferey Prowse most likely, for George Augustus Sala had cut his wisdom teeth by that time—called the meteors "baby stars that had died in teething"! The earthly leonid who had ventured on this daring metaphor was probably the same youthful spirit that had spoken of the New Year "as a new volume for which Time's scythe would serve as paperknife"!

Journalists, like actors, are exposed to the temptation of playing to the gallery. Some of them played to the gallery when they accepted gutter stories—stories that were based on the horrible crimes of Burke and Hare or the perhaps still more infamous career of Charles Peace. The policy of pandering to the lowest taste of the lowest section of the populace in the matter of fiction was not pursued for long. It was pursued long enough, however, to get at least one young lad into trouble. The lad was tried in 1888 before the Recorder of a provincial town on a charge of housebreaking. When asked what he had to say for himself, he replied that he had been reading the story of Charles Peace in a weekly newspaper, and that this had led him to commit the robbery. Earnest appeals were made to newspapers which professed to be intended for family reading not to "run the very filth of gutters and sewers through our kitchens, our parlours, and even our nurseries." The appeals had a good effect in at least one instance; for a Cardiff paper, which had begun the horrible and demoralising narrative, announced that it intended to publish no more of the vile trash. Stories of a less reprehensible character, but still of a low and vulgar type, were then, and long afterwards, offered to weekly journals by a gentleman who boasted that his serials raised the circulation of the papers which published them by thousands a week. This ingenious author had three or four stories, or alleged stories, which he used to adapt to different localities according to the orders he received. The title of one of the tales, which had, he said, been printed no nearer than Bedford, and which he proposed to refurbish for the Northern market, might have stood for that of a penny dreadful of the Edward Lloyd period—"Newcastle's Lovely Lady Martyr; or, Doomed to Fire and Faggot: A Northumberland Romance of the Middle Ages." If this would not suit, he intimated that he had other tales of blood and murder and mystery which he could localise at a cheaper rate. Even "Newcastle's Lovely Lady Martyr," however, would have been less degrading to the press, and less demoralising to the public, than the dishing up of Peace's revolting crimes in the shape of fiction.

It was a passing danger, that which beset the press in 1888. A more serious danger seems to be threatened by an organization that has lately sprung into existence. If the members of the Institute of Journalists should succeed in making journalism a strict and exclusive profession, they will do the press an infinite injury. One of the great merits of the journalistic craft is that it is free and open to everybody who can justify his claims to admission, whether he has been trained in a newspaper office or not. "Gentlemen of the Press," as Mr. Disraeli called them, are recruited from all ranks and callings in the country. Some, I know, have been blacksmiths, others tailors, others factory-workers. In fact, there is scarcely a pursuit in the land that is not represented among the people who manage and write for our newspapers. And it is this catholicity of selection that helps to give to journalism its unique character and position. But it would be otherwise if, unfortunately, through the action of the Institute of journalists or in any other way, the ranks should be closed to all but such as had passed through a restricted form of indenture or apprenticeship. The tendency of the times, however, is to create a system of castes. Let journalists beware how they encourage that tendency. We know what the caste system has done for India. There the man who carries water is not permitted to fetch coals, and the man who fetches coals is not permitted to sweep a carpet. Thus progress, in consequence of the stereotyped regulation of society, has been utterly impossible for centuries. The same deplorable condition is creeping into our workshops; for there men are trained to do certain work, and are not allowed to do any other—trained, as Emerson says, to be mere spindles and needles, and nothing else. Once admit the fatal system into journalism, and it is simply a matter of time when reporters will not be permitted to become editors, nor editors managers, nor anybody anything but that which he has paid a handsome premium for becoming. It is probably this question of premium much more than any interest in the profession that inspires the sordid part of the movement. Of all the errors of the press no greater could be committed than that of yielding to the suggestions of the fussy and pedantic gentlemen who are as proud as peacocks when they are able to write strange initials after their names.

CHAPTER LI

ECCENTRIC AND CRAZY PEOPLE

CRAZY people are nearly always sure, sooner or later, to put themselves in communication with the press. When a mad shoemaker murdered a tax-collector in Newcastle, he remarked to the policeman who arrested him, "This will be a grand thing for the penny papers." Usually the connection is much closer than that implied in providing material for sensational news. For more than thirty years, to my own knowledge, there never was a time when one or more lunatics, not including poets, were not in direct and almost constant communication with the editor of the *Newcastle Weekly Chronicle*. Some sent indecipherable prose, others indecipherable verse. Some were crazy about the shape of the earth, others were crazy about being buried alive. But there was a bee in the bonnet of them all. Sometimes the correspondent was not known even by name, sometimes only by name, at other times personally known. The correspondence would sometimes continue for months, sometimes for years, and then suddenly cease. In either case we knew quite well that the unfortunate correspondent was either dead or had become helpless. It was of course the crazy people who were personally known, and who insisted on seeing the editor, that gave the most trouble.

An afternoon alone with a madman, or one akin to a madman, is not a pleasant experience. I once went through it. Mr. William Bewicke, of Threepwood Hall, near Haydon Bridge, "a gentleman of considerable property, ancient family, and Herculean frame, but unfortunately gifted with a violent temper, and of eccentric habits," made use of his power as a magistrate to unlawfully arrest a poor woman of the neighbourhood. For this the woman's husband subsequently obtained damages, while the Lord Chancellor struck the name of the offender off the roll of justices of the peace. Mr. Bewicke, refusing to pay the expenses of his own solicitors, was served by them with a writ. One morning in January, 1861, a sheriff's officer from Hexham proceeded with several assistants to execute the writ. Mr. Bewicke, armed with a rifle, locked his doors and parleyed with the party from a window. The bailiffs, however, took possession of the stables. Here two of them remained in possession. But during the night, they alleged, Mr. Bewicke fired at them from the house. Then followed his arrest for feloniously shooting at the bailiffs. The prisoner defended himself at the Assizes in Newcastle, with the result that he was convicted and sentenced to four years' penal servitude. Mr. Bewicke was the victim of a dastardly plot. The housekeeper at Threepwood set herself to prove it. As the consequence of extraordinary efforts on her part, three of the witnesses for the prosecution, just a year after the original trial, were found guilty of conspiracy. It was their turn to suffer penal servitude, while Mr. Bewicke was, of course, released. The whole case was so strange and romantic that the editor of the *Weekly Chronicle*, in an unguarded moment, determined to retell the story. The narrative was published in 1875. Mr. Bewicke took exception to some of the details, and demanded an interview with the editor, which was readily granted. There was nothing really wrong with the narrative; but Mr. Bewicke insisted on going through every sentence with the editor. The two were alone in an upper room of the office. Every now and then, as the reading proceeded, the visitor, who was accurately described as a man of "Herculean frame," would rise in a rage, storm about the room, and almost terrify the other out of his wits. All the arts the editor knew had to be employed to pacify the furious gentleman. Scarcely a statement in the story failed to stir up angry recollections. There was just a fear that the excitable visitor would associate the editor with his wrongs, in which case the unhappy man expected to be throttled in his chair or hurled into the street below. The time of terror lasted all a summer's afternoon, with no help at hand either. No man was more thankful than the editor when the interview ended. The corrections Mr. Bewicke required were printed in the next issue. And as these happily appeased the wrath of the injured and eccentric laird of Threepwood, nothing more was heard of the affair.

The scientific articles which Mr. R. A. Proctor was contributing to the *Newcastle Weekly Chronicle* in 1883 aroused the ire of another eccentric gentleman, who, however, luckily limited his attentions to the writing of scurrilous and abusive letters from Balham. Mr. John Hampden was a flat-earth fanatic who had offered a large sum of money—£500, I think—to anybody who could prove the curvature of the globe. The challenge was accepted by Mr. Alfred Russel Wallace, the celebrated naturalist who is associated with Darwin in suggesting the theory of the origin of species. Experiments were made on the Bedford Canal, and the verdict of the arbitrator was given against Mr. Hampden. The result of the litigation that followed was, I think, that Mr. Hampden got himself cast into prison. Many of Mr. Hampden's letters on the subject were printed in the *Weekly Chronicle*. But many others could not be printed on account of their violent and offensive character. Specimens of the rejected contributions have been preserved. A few of them may serve to amuse a later generation of readers:—"If, instead of dishonourably suppressing two-thirds of my letters, you would leave out the same proportion of the infamously false statements contained in Mr. Proctor's articles, it would be much more to your credit. The shameful lies which this man is publishing every week, both in your paper and in his own, are a disgrace to the journalism of England. He is openly spoken of as a lying charlatan all over the kingdom. He may depend upon my thoroughly exposing him, and the contemptible cur shall be taught now to speak the truth." This is not bad. The following, however, seems to go one better:—"The most conclusive argument in favour of myself with respect to the survey to which Mr. Proctor makes allusion (the Bedford Canal experiment) is to request that gentleman to inform Mr. Alfred Russel Wallace, of Grays, in the county of Essex, that I am still, at the expiration of eight years, advertising him as a cheat, a swindler, and a defaulter; if the degraded cur dares to take any notice, or can justify his conduct by repeating the experiment in the presence of honest men, he can sue me for slander and libel. Mr. Proctor is the only man in England who has degraded himself by defending the swindler Wallace." Mr. Proctor had written something about the origin of whales; whereupon Mr. Hampden wrote to him direct:—"If you would endeavour to describe the origin of liars and impostors, you would find they came into the world when the Pagan lunatics devised the shape of the world. If whales are derived from pigs, according to your theory, you must have been foaled by an ass!"

Mr. Empson E. Middleton, a disciple of the same school as Mr. Hampden, was also a frequent correspondent of the *Weekly Chronicle*. Who and what else he was Mr. Middleton explained in a pamphlet which he printed in 1876. There he described himself as "the Poet, Geometrician, Metaphysician, Lecturer, and Patentee in Yacht and Ship Building, E. E. Middleton, Esq., member of the Royal Canoe Club, London; the Royal Albert Yacht Club, Southsea; and the Naval and Military Club, London." "There is not," he adds, "the smallest question as to my right to the title of Esq. My father was Boswell Middleton, Esq., born in Yorkshire. His father was Empson Middleton, Esq., a more or less wealthy landowner in Yorkshire." A further explanation is given in some verses which somebody is said to have written "on seeing Popsy Middleton asleep on board the Swift packet on her passage from Falmouth to Barbadoes." One of the verses reads thus:—

> Sleep, and while slumber weighs thine eyelids down,
> May no foul phantom o'er thy pillow frown,
> But brightest visions deck thy tranquil bed,
> And angels' wings o'er-canopy thy head!
> Sleep on, sweet boy; may no dark dreams arise
> To mar thy rosy rest, thou babe of Paradise!

Mr. Middleton had gone to Canterbury to lecture on the shape of the earth, and had there got into a squabble with the proprietor of St. George's Hall. It was out of this squabble that a case arose in the county court. "I would not tolerate," said Mr. Middleton, speaking to the judge, "the proprietor addressing myself in a flippant and democratic manner, and I refuse to tolerate any such address, not only because I am a bona-fide gentleman, but because I am a man of exceeding talent—in fact, a very great genius." Nor could he tolerate, as he says in the same pamphlet, "that an under-bred hall-keeper should dictate his slovenly and insulting method of doing business to an exceeding highly polished and artistic, and also scientific, gentleman; one of the most able racing yachtsmen of England, a classical poet, a geometrician, metaphysician, lecturer, and patentee in yacht and ship building."

Less eccentric, though not less egotistical, than the "babe of Paradise," was another correspondent and lecturer—a clergyman of the Church of England, the Rev. W. D. Ground. While holding a curacy at Newburn-on-Tyne, Mr. Ground, who claimed to be "at least a philosopher," " near akin to a prophet," wrote a book which, besides demolishing the philosophy of Herbert Spencer, ought, he thought, to have been "a passport to a bishopric, not to say the Primacy." It was a great and burning grief to him that he never rose higher in the Church than the vicarages of Alnham and Kirkharle. Once he delivered—this was 1881—a lecture on the "Dynamical Force of Thought, a Newly-Discovered Law of Nature." The new law, he said, which had cost him twenty years to work out, would accomplish "hardly anything less than an intellectual revolution." The philosophy of Herbert Spencer was by common consent one of the greatest systems of thought that had appeared in any age. Yet the lecturer boasted that he had "written papers which, in the judgment of competent men, overthrew it." But "he did not intend to stop until the system had been battered to pieces and converted into a logical ruin." And when this destructive work had been effected, "he purposed fashioning a system of philosophy of his own." Mr. Ground did not speak without book when he claimed for himself an intellectual superiority even over Shakspeare, for he had put the matter to "veritable scientific proof" in a series of experiments with a borrowed spirometer. "One morning," he said, "he tested the spirometer, which registered 242, 244. He then read Act III. in the play of 'Hamlet,' after which he tested the spirometer, which registered 222,213, carrying him down very low indeed. He next read a composition of his own, and then tested the spirometer, which registered 262,253, carrying him, as would be seen, 40 cubic inches." Forty cubic inches higher than Shakspeare! "My own consciousness," innocently observed Mr. Ground, "agreed with this test." Sad to say, the great discoverer of the "dynamical force of thought" died, not a bishop nor a primate, nor even a canon of the Church, but the vicar successively of two remote parishes in Northumberland. [28]

But a genuine madman was numbered among the correspondents of 1885. There had occurred about twenty years before a horrible murder in the North of England. The victim was a little girl, and the crime was of such a character that nobody but a lunatic could have committed it. The murderer was sentenced to be confined in the criminal asylum at Broadmoor. Thence he wrote a series of astonishing letters. "I am undoubtedly," he declared, "the lawful heir of the present King of Bavaria." But he had received "warnings from Providence of the rancorous opposition of Windsor Castle." In consequence of this opposition, "I have decided upon deposing the present Queen Alexandria Victoria d'Este Guelph, dispossessing her and the rest of the Guelphs of all their riches, except so much as will enable them to live in comfort without luxury." Then he asserted that two of the leading ladies of the operatic stage at that time— Madame Marie Roze and Madame Alwina Valleria—were sisters. For the latter the poor lunatic designed a high distinction. "I have resolved," he wrote, "to get myself and my betrothed wife, Emily Jaques of Osmotherly, commonly known as Alwina Valleria, appointed conjoint and equal King and Queen of Great Britain and Ireland. Emily Jaques shall be wed to me under the same name as she had when we were betrothed; and the survivors of her former schoolmates and companions will be delighted beyond measure when they learn that the merry, gracious, and amiable little maiden, who in her puce mantle and frock used to diffuse joy and gladness in the upper part of High Felling, has become their Queen. Instead of bearing water-cans balanced on her head, she shall wear her own special tiara and sceptre; and instead of singing for the public in music halls, she shall sing for the private delectation of the most illustrious in the land." A vast deal more of the same inconsequential maundering was written from Broadmoor in 1885 and 1886. And then there was silence—the silence of the grave. The unhappy madman was no more.

CHAPTER LII

POPULAR DEMONSTRATIONS

NEWCASTLE has always done its share, and even more than its share, in the way of popular demonstrations. Every just cause has received its support, and every great patriot has received its homage. To it belongs the honour of being the only town in England to recognise the heroism of Garibaldi after the memorable defence of Rome. Advantage was taken of the visit of the patriot to the Tyne as the captain of a merchant trader to present him with a sword of honour. This event took place in 1854, and the principal part in it was played by Mr. Jos. Cowen, then and always the friend of the struggling and the oppressed. Ten years later, when Garibaldi had achieved his marvellous victories in Sicily and Naples, preparations were made to give him a great public reception in Newcastle.

This second reception of Garibaldi on the Tyne, had it not been frustrated by intrigues and occurrences in London, would have been a magnificent affair. No foreigner, save Kossuth, had ever met with heartier or more general acclamations on British soil than the hero of Marsala. It was a popular triumph, spontaneously offered by the people themselves, that was accorded to the illustrious visitor in Southampton and in the Metropolis. All the other large towns in the country desired to testify in much the same manner their appreciation of the services which Garibaldi had rendered to the cause of liberty. As, however, it was manifestly impossible that the gallant patriot could accept even a tithe of the invitations with which he was overwhelmed, he resolved, out of respect for his old friend Mr. Cowen and out of gratitude for the kindness he had received ten years before, not to disappoint the people of Newcastle. A committee was therefore appointed, with Mr. Cowen as chairman and Mr. Thos. Pringle and myself as secretaries, to make the necessary arrangements. Suddenly, however, it was announced that Garibaldi would almost immediately, without visiting the provinces at all, return to his home in the island of Caprera. The mystery surrounding this startling change in the General's plans has never been fully explained; but there is little doubt now, nor was there much doubt in 1864, that the enthusiasm which had been aroused in this country on behalf of the liberation of Rome and Venice, coupled with the visit of Garibaldi to his "friend and teacher, Joseph Mazzini," had excited the jealousy and alarm of the Continental despots. To avert complications, the Government of Lord Palmerston appealed to the General to save it from embarrassments by quitting the country. Garibaldi complied; the Governments of Europe were satisfied; and Newcastle was deprived of the opportunity of once more demonstrating its attachment to the cause of the nationalities. [29]

Another famous soldier, from whose progress through the country and popularity with the people no complications were likely to arise, visited Newcastle thirteen years later. Ulysses S. Grant, as commander-in-chief of the Federal armies, had by his dogged perseverance and masterly combinations done more than any single man save Abraham Lincoln to re-establish the Republic of the United States. Further, he had, as President of the Republic, helped to solve in a peaceful fashion the dangerous difficulty that had arisen between England and America in consequence of the depredations of the *Alabama*. When, therefore, General Grant, taking a tour round the world, came within hail of Newcastle, he was invited to pay it a visit. The American Government was at that time represented in the North of England by a popular and energetic Consul—Major Evan R. Jones, who had himself served through the four years of the Civil War. It was due to the appeal of his old companion in arms that General Grant consented to accept the invitation. The September of 1877 was made memorable by the circumstances and ceremonies of the General's presence. The distinguished stranger was entertained at a banquet, held a reception in the Town Hall, and was presented with an address on the Town Moor. The proceedings on the Town Moor, which were preceded by a procession through the streets, took the form of a demonstration of respect for General Grant and of amity towards the United States. Vast numbers of working men and others, accompanied by bands and banners, escorted the visitor and his friends to the Moor. There a hustings had been erected, and there in the presence of an enormous and enthusiastic concourse of citizens the General was presented with the address that had been prepared. It was said of some celebrated person that he was silent in six languages. General Grant was silent in one. But another American soldier—General Lucius Fairchild, who had lost an arm in the service of the Republic—made eloquent amends for his comrade's reticence. A few words were all that the conqueror of Donelson and of Vicksburg ever said in public at any one time. Short speeches, however, had to be delivered so often on Tyneside that he expressed his doubt at the banquet whether the people of the United States, when they read the report of the proceedings, would believe that he had ever spoken them!

The demonstration in honour of General Grant had been preceded some years before by demonstrations in favour of political reform. The first of these, organized by Mr. Cowen and the society of which he was the life and spirit, was held on Jan. 29th, 1867. John Bright— or was it Richard Cobden?—had said a few years before, referring to the apathy of the public, that nothing would be done in the way of the further enfranchisement of the people "till the old men died." The "old men" were those members of the Liberal Party who, like Lord John Russell, considered that the Reform Bill of 1832 was a final measure. Chief of the "old men" was Lord Palmerston. Lord Palmerston died in harness in 1865. Hardly had he been buried before the new men of the Liberal Party justified the prophetic statement. An attempt was made to solve the Reform Question on the old lines of a rating suffrage. The £10 franchise was to be reduced to £5. This was the proposal of the new Government, with Mr. Gladstone at its head. But the scheme was defeated by the narrow majority of five on an amendment proposed by Lord Robert Grosvenor, the author of the Sunday Bill that led to the Hyde Park riots. Back came the Tories to office. The populace was now thoroughly aroused. Imposing demonstrations, unexampled in enthusiasm and in numbers, were one after the other held in all the chief centres of population—Manchester, Birmingham, Glasgow, Newcastle, etc. Many thousands of workmen, preceded by a carriage containing Lord Teynham, the elder Mr. Cowen, and other veterans of the agitation of 1832, marched to the Town Moor, there to show that the demand for political reform could no longer be safely ignored.

These immense demonstrations, not in one part of the country, but in all, convinced even the Tories that something would have to be done now. Mr. Disraeli, leader of the House of Commons at last, was the first to see it. There would have to be a Reform Bill of some sort. But of what sort? The imagination of Mr. Disraeli, always equal to the demands upon it, was not at fault in the existing emergency. It occurred to him that the old Whig method of taking a few pounds off the rental qualification was humdrum, commonplace, lacking in ingenuity and statecraft. The Tories must go further down to the bed-rock of the household. There was no principle in a pound more or less; there was, however, a clear and captivating principle in declaring that every householder was entitled to the suffrage. So he set himself to "educate his party." "Household suffrage! Good heavens! was the man mad?" Yes, but he would surround it with restrictions and hindrances, checks and counterpoises. And then, see how the principle would enchant the multitude! The Tory party yielded—not, however, without a good deal of squirming. Honest old Tories, too, saw that they were going to take "a leap in the dark." But as they had to take a leap somewhere—well, they would just have to follow their leader. Besides, there was, as Lord Derby, the old Rupert of Debate, said, the temptation of "dishing the Whigs." Again, was it not possible, if you dug down deep enough, that you would come even among the masses upon a substratum of Toryism—the Tory Democracy about which Mr. Disraeli had written in his early novels? It is certain at any rate that the Whigs were "dished."

When Mr. Disraeli's Reform Bill was produced in 1867, it was received with amusement tinctured with disdain on the part of the Opposition, with surprise tinctured with doubt on the part of the supporters of the Government. The whole thing, said the Liberals, was a sham. It pretended to accede to the popular wishes, but in reality frustrated them. Mr. Disraeli was not a statesman, but a juggler. His scheme was both a delusion and a snare. What he offered the country was a feast of Dead Sea apples—fair to look upon, but ashes in the mouth. Mr. Bright riddled and ridiculed what he called the "fancy franchises," as indeed they were. There was, it was contended by the chiefs of the Opposition, only one course to pursue with this preposterous measure, and that was to reject it with scorn and contumely. But certain Radicals in the House were wiser than their leaders. The elder Mr. Cowen, who was by this time one of the members for Newcastle, was prominent among the Radicals. They met in the Tea Room of the House of Commons. And the conclusion they came to was that the principle of the Bill was worth accepting. As for the restrictions and counterpoises, they could be modified or even swept away afterwards. The Tea Room party settled the fate of the measure. The action of the little party settled more than the fate of Mr. Disraeli's Reform Bill—it practically settled the Reform Question itself from that time to our own.

But there were earnest men in the North who were not satisfied even with an unadulterated Household Suffrage Bill. They held to the old doctrine of Manhood Suffrage. So another demonstration was promoted—the last of its kind, but the greatest. Again were Mr. Cowen's superb powers of organization brought into play. The trades unions mustered as before with their banners and insignia. But the most numerous and the most imposing part of the procession was composed of miners from all parts of Northumberland and Durham. Fifty thousand of these hardy sons of toil, each colliery with its band and its banner, marched into Newcastle on that memorable day—April 12th, 1873. Accurate and exhaustive returns showed that at least 80,000 persons took part in the splendid array, while it was computed that from first to last fully 200,000 must have followed the appointed speakers to the Town Moor. Almost every railway in England and Scotland was laid under contribution for carriages and conveyances. The North-Eastern Company alone borrowed 550 carriages, equal to 60 ordinary trains. Between 80 and 90 bands of music accompanied the procession, and upwards of 150 banners and flags, most of them of a costly and beautiful description, beside bannerettes, emblems, and devices of every conceivable kind, were carried with the different contingents. The whole procession, walking four deep and in quick order, took exactly two hours and twenty-five minutes in marching past. The length of it could not be measured, for the proceedings at the six platforms on the Moor, although they lasted an hour and a half, were entirely concluded when the first part of the last section of demonstrators appeared in sight of the people on the hustings.

Never before had so many orderly men paraded the streets of Newcastle. It was a spectacle that brought tears to the eyes. The writer marched with the miners, whom he best knew, for he had been much among them when lecturing in the colliery villages on the subject of American slavery and the American war. Many and fervent were the ejaculations of pride and encouragement from the spectators as the magnificent procession tramped through miles of streets towards the trysting place. But there were other ejaculations too. Mr. Cowen was at that time idolised by the people, but cordially disliked by the caddish section of society. As he walked with his friends at the front of the procession, a tradesman in Grey Street expressed the friendly hope that the demonstrators when they reached the Moor would hang him from one of the platforms! It was an evidence of the intense feeling of resentment that had taken possession of the privileged classes and their supporters.

As I have said, this was the last of the great demonstrations. It was, too, as I have also said, the greatest. Whether because the people are satisfied with the measure of liberty since enjoyed, or because they are now much more interested in other things than politics, it is certain that the lethargy which Mr. Bright lamented in 1864 has once more spread over England.

CHAPTER LIII

"THE MORPETH HUBBUBBOO"

THE expectations of the Tea Room party that the hindrances to emancipation contained in Mr. Disraeli's Reform Bill could and would be removed were in due course completely realised. The credit of removing such of them as related to the residents of colliery villages and the occupants of colliery houses belongs to the miners of Northumberland. How this came about forms an interesting episode in the history of the borough of Morpeth. The secretary of the Northumberland Miners' Association, Thomas Burt, soon after his election to that office in 1864, showed so much ability in the management of the society's affairs, and endeared himself so much to his fellow-workmen by reason of his personal qualities, that there arose a strong desire to see him in the House of Commons. But household suffrage, pure and simple, was not yet the law of the land. Of the thousands of miners in Northumberland only a few hundreds were numbered among the electors of the county. As occupiers of colliery houses, and so not paying rates directly to the overseers of the poor, they were considered not entitled to have their names inscribed on the rate-books or on the register of voters. But some ingenious people in the neighbourhood of Choppington and Bedlington conceived the idea that the occupants of colliery houses, since they stood in respect to rates in about the same position as compound householders in towns, had equal claims with the said householders to the suffrage. To press this idea upon the authorities the Miners' Franchise Association was formed in the early part of 1872.

The inception of the movement, undoubtedly one of the most successful ever set on foot in the North of England, was due, I think, to Thomas Glassey, then a miner at Choppington, but for some years now a leading member of the Parliament of Queensland, and at this date a member of the Senate of the Commonwealth of Australia. Mr. Glassey, a native of the North of Ireland, had not been long in the district, nor had he always been associated with the Radical party.

Indeed, he had until shortly before been a rampant Orangeman. When he did take sides with the Radicals, however, he went with them heart and soul. Being a man of resource, too, he soon made the whole coalfield ring with the claims of the miners. Associated with Mr. Glassey were two other notable men. One was Robert Elliott, author of a vernacular poem which created some stir at the time, entitled "A Pitman Gan te Parliament." It was thought by many of his friends that justice was hardly done to his services and abilities when he failed to secure the nomination for a neighbouring constituency to Morpeth. The other member of the triumvirate was Dr. James Trotter, one of four or five brothers, natives of Galloway, all pursuing the practice of medicine at the same time in Northumberland. James was also an Orangeman at the beginning of his public career. Like Glassey, moreover, he threw himself with ardour and enthusiasm into the Radical movement.

The Franchise Association aimed at two things—the extension of the suffrage to all householders in the villages included in the borough of Morpeth, and the return of Thomas Burt as the first working-man member of the House of Commons. Both objects were achieved, but not before the district had become the scene of exciting events. Once, when Mr. Walter B. Trevelyan, the revising barrister, sitting at Morpeth, gave a decision hostile to the claims of the association, Mr. Glassey, rising in great wrath, called all his friends outside the court. It seemed as if a revolution was going to begin there and then. I recollect assisting to throw oil on the troubled waters, with the result that the standard of rebellion was neither then nor later unfurled. Greater still was the excitement when a poem entitled "The Morpeth Hubbubboo" made its appearance. The name of no author was attached to the piece, nor did anybody at the time know whence it had emanated; but it was supposed to represent the feelings of the tradesmen and respectable classes of Morpeth. As the verses have become historical, I give some of them here:—

> Come, all ye jolly freemen,
>   And listen to my tale,
> How Morpeth served the Howkies,
>   And made them turn their tail.

And you, ye Howky beggars,
　We dare you to come down!
And though you come in thousands,
　We'll kick you from the town.
You dirty sneaking cowards,
　Come back to Morpeth, do,
And we'll kick your Burt to blazes,
　And stop your Hubbubboo

The rascals, how they spouted
　On sham gentility,
And swore the dirty Howkies
　Were just as good as we.
They wanted rights of voting,
　The law had ordered so:
What right to Rights have Howkies
　Is what I'd like to know.
We'll let them drink our beer, sir,
　The worst that we can brew,
It's good enough for Howkies
　To raise a Hubbubboo.

Hurrah for Champion Robberts
　That damned the Howky dirt,
The boy that thrashed the traitors
　Who wished to vote for Burt,
That stood up for Sir Georgy,
　And cursed the Howkies well,
And damned them and the Trotters
　To trot right off to hell!
He showed them like a man, sir,
　What brandy schnapps can do,
And soon smashed up the Templars,
　And spoiled the Hubbubboo.

Nine groans for both the Trotters,
　Confound the ugly quacks;
When next they show their faces,

We'll make them show their backs,
  Nine groans for Irish Glassey;
  If he comes here again,
We'll pelt him out with murphies,
  And get the rascal slain.
Nine groans for Poet Elliott
  And his North-Country crew,
Aud ninety for the Howkies
  That raised the Hubbubboo.

Nine groans for Burt the Howky;
  And if he ventures here,
His dry teetotal carcase
  We'll soak in Robberts' beer.
We'll put him in the stocks, too,
  And pelt him well with eggs;
We'll black his Howky eyes, boys,
  And kick his bandy legs.
He would unseat Sir Georgy,
  He would be member, too;
We'll hunt him out of Morpeth,
  And spoil his Hubbubboo.

The effect of the publication was instantaneous. Not only did the pitmen round about refuse to enter a public-house where "Robberts' beer" was sold, but the pitmen's wives drove back home the tradesmen's carts that travelled round the pit villages laden with provisions. Dr. Trotter himself described the state of affairs in a letter I received from him a few days after the appearance of the "Hubbubboo." It will be seen that the letter was partly in reply to a suggestion of mine that nothing foolish or indiscreet should be done to bring discredit upon the movement. Here, then, is Dr. Trotter's account of matters :—

BEDLINGTON, THURSDAY.

My dear Sir,—The whole district is in a blaze. The tradesmen of Morpeth are like to be ruined.

A great meeting was held at Morpeth, on Tuesday night, to take the crisis into serious consideration. A reward of £150 is offered by the tradesmen for the publishers and authors of the squibs which are setting the miners into so desperate a state of excitement.

All the inns and beer-shops in the district have orders to receive no more ale or spirits from Morpeth on pain of instant extinction, and all here have complied with the demand. The pitmen made an entrance into every public-house, took down all the Morpeth spirit advertisements framed on the walls, trampled them under foot, and sent the fragments to the owners carefully packed and labelled.

You can have no idea of the sensation here at present. It is to be proposed, and has every likelihood of being carried unanimously, that Choppington pits be at once laid idle should a single tubful of coals be sent to the town of Morpeth, and every colliery in the county is to be invited to join issue to the same effect. So you see that Morpeth people will not only be starved as regards food, but as respects fuel also, if things go on at this rate much longer.

I believe we could have 10,000 men into Morpeth at a week's notice. However, I will follow your advice in the matter and keep things as quiet as possible; but if the men get determined, the devil himself will hardly be able to prevent them making an inroad.

I will excuse our deputation to the collieries to which we were invited as you suggest. Besides, Mr. Burt will as surely be M.P. for the borough of Morpeth as that I am

Very sincerely yours,

JAMES TROTTER.

The shopkeepers of Morpeth were indeed in serious straits. In this extremity they got up a meeting to repudiate the "Hubbubboo." Peace, however, was not restored till the Franchise Association was invited to hold a conference in the sacred precincts of the borough itself. It was suspected at the time, though it was not positively known till long afterwards, that the poem which set the district on fire was the production, not of an enemy, but of a friend. Things were getting dull, it was thought, and so it was deemed advisable to invent something that would fan the embers of the agitation into a blaze. And the blaze produced then has certainly never in the same district been equalled since. Dr. Trotter was fond of practical jokes, and the "Hubbubboo" was one of them [30]—quite of a piece with another which set the inhabitants of his own town of Dalry by the ears. The "Clachan Fair," a long descriptive poem, satirising everybody in the place, including the author's father, was printed and posted to persons concerned. And then the incorrigible joker took a holiday, and went back to his old home to enjoy the fun!

The franchise movement never flagged after the excitement about the "Hubbubboo." It even attracted attention in distant parts of the country. Archibald Forbes, in an interval of his war reporting, was sent down to describe for the *Daily News* the position of matters in the North. Writing of a "Miners' Monstre Demonstration," held at Morpeth on Sept. 28th, 1872, he fell into a curious confusion in respect to a leading spirit of the movement, assigning to him the name of the colliery village in which he resided. One of the speakers at the meeting, said Mr. Forbes, was "an Irish pitman, Thomas Glassey, known to fame as the Choppington Guide Post"—"a fine, ardent young fellow, with yellow hair, and a brogue broader than the platform. And then," he added, "Mr. Glassey lapsed into revolutionary utterances, and began to talk about tyrants and despots and other matters of a like sort, which seemed to indicate him as rather an unsafe guide post for Choppington or any other loyal community." But the upshot of the whole business was that the revising barrister, when he came his rounds in 1873, admitted the whole of the pitman claimants to the franchise, thus increasing the constituency of Morpeth at one bound from 2,661 to 4,916.

The rest was easy. Sir George Grey, the Home Secretary in many successive Whig Ministries, who had represented Morpeth since 1852, retired into private life. Mr. Cowen presided over a great meeting at Bedlington Cross on Oct. 18th, 1873, at which a requisition was presented to Mr. Burt inviting him to stand as a candidate for the borough. The invitation was of course accepted. A committee constituted as follows was chosen to conduct the election:—Robert Elliott, chairman; Thomas Glassey, vice-chairman; James Archbold, treasurer; James Trotter, secretary; general members—Joseph Cowen, M.P., the Rev. Dr. Rutherford, George Howard (now Earl of Carlisle), W. E. Adams, Matthew Pletts, and Ralph Young. Although the return of Mr. Burt by an overwhelming majority was absolutely certain, a rival candidate was found in Captain Francis Duncan, who, as Colonel Duncan, the author of a "History of the Royal Artillery," rose to distinction both in Parliament and in the military service, and died later while serving his country in Egypt. The contest which followed was unique.

Captain Duncan was everywhere respectfully received by the miners. When he addressed a meeting at Choppington, not a murmur of opposition was heard from the crowded audience; but when a vote of approval of his candidature was proposed, every hand was held up against it. And the proceedings closed with a vote of thanks to Captain Duncan for his lecture! Both candidates on the day of the polling visited the different towns and villages comprising the constituency of Morpeth. Mr. Burt's tour was a triumphal procession. The arrival of the candidate and his friends at Bedlington, I recollect, led to an extraordinary scene. The main street of the town was crowded, for of course the pits were all idle. First there was much cheering; then arose an irrepressible desire to do something unusual. The horses were taken out of the conveyance, dozens of stalwart miners seized the shafts, and the electoral party was rushed up and down the thoroughfare at a furious and hazardous pace amidst the wildest excitement. It was even proposed to run the carriage all the way to Morpeth: nor was it without some difficulty that the jubilant crowd was dissuaded from its purpose. Not less astonishing was the reception accorded to Mr. Burt at Morpeth itself, where both candidates—such was the friendly character of the contest—addressed the multitude, which literally filled the Market Place, from the same platform and from the windows of each other's committee rooms!

The ballot box revealed the fact, or rather emphasised the fact, that the old order had indeed changed. The miners' candidate had received 3,332 votes as against his opponent's 585. So was Thomas Burt returned the first veritable working man that had ever entered the House of Commons. [31]

CHAPTER LIV

THE LAWS OF THE WORKSHOP

WORKMEN, now that they make their own laws, have the power to make the workshop a place of pleasure or a place of torment. It is to be feared that the policy of modern days is calculated to bring about the latter result. And the reason for this policy is the false and wrong-headed conception that all labour is degrading, to which there has latterly been added the equally false and wrongheaded doctrine that the less the labourer produces the more the labourer will profit.

The fundamental error of the workman lies in disparaging his own calling. He should leave disparagement to snobs and idlers and loafers—to those slugs and scums of the earth who have never done an honest day's toil in their lives. If work is degrading, how, then, about the workman? As one cannot touch pitch without being defiled, so one cannot do a degrading thing without being degraded oneself. To this complexion the modern doctrine must bring the whole working world at last. A leader of the new school—he was a member of Parliament, too, at the time—once advised the blast-furnacemen of Cleveland to do as little work as possible, adding that he himself never did any work at all if he could help it! French adherents of the same school have gone even further. The ideal of one of them—M. Jules Guesde, a member of the Chamber of Deputies—was, as I recollect writing in 1892, not so much a "fool's paradise" as a "pig's paradise." But a comrade of his—M. Godefroy, described as "an anarchist of local celebrity in one of the lower quarters of Paris," that same year put the doctrine into practice in a singularly audacious way. M. Godefroy, so it was recorded at the time, went into a fashionable restaurant, ordered a sumptuous repast, consumed all the luxuries that were placed before him, and then refused to pay the bill. He had no money, he said, because he did no work, and he did no work because work was degrading!

The older and infinitely better conception was comprised in the desire to elevate labour, and so elevate the labourer. "Work is worship." Never was truer aphorism put into words. Work has redeemed the world. It is the salvation of man: for those who don't work die of weariness or debauchery. Every great thinker has acclaimed the old doctrine—none more powerfully than Thomas Carlyle. "For," says he, "there is a perennial nobleness, and even sacredness, in Work. Were he never so benighted, forgetful of his high calling, there is always hope in a man that actually and earnestly works: in idleness alone is there perpetual despair." Again, "Blessèd is he who has found his work; let him ask no other blessing." And again, "All true Work is sacred; in all true Work, were it but true hand-labour, there is something of divineness. Labour, wide as the earth, has its summit in heaven. Sweat of the brow; and up from that to sweat of the brain, sweat of the heart; which includes all Kepler calculations, Newton meditations, all Sciences, all spoken Epics, all acted Heroisms."

But Carlyle has preached in vain; for a canker is eating into the very soul of the worker. "Ca' canny" is an ugly term; but it is not nearly so ugly, so ineffably repulsive, as the policy it represents—a "policy of skulk," a policy of demanding a good day's wage and doing in return for it a bad day's work. And yet it is a policy that received in 1896 the open approval of certain prominent leaders connected with the International Federation of Ship and Dock Workers—not Dock Workers, but Dock Skulkers, if the policy were carried out. Everybody can understand what happens when workmen demand higher wages; everybody can understand, and even appreciate, what happens when the workmen enter upon a strike to enforce their demands; but what cannot be understood, what certainly cannot be appreciated, is a course of procedure which, if persistently and successfully pursued, must inevitably end in the utter demoralization of the artizan classes. Honesty, according to the new doctrine, is not the best policy. Trick, deceit, sloth—these are to take the place of industry, integrity, and honour. Such a scheme of behaviour would have surprised most people if it had been proclaimed by men of the gutter. That it should have been advocated by persons in the position of leaders of workmen was simply astounding. The mere fact that the base proceeding should have even been discussed gave the world a shock.

Consider for a moment. If dishonesty be good for ship and dock workers, it must be good for all other workers. And what then? Bad workmanship will be the order of the day. Our ships will be made, not to swim, but to sink; our houses, not to stand, but to fall; our clothes, not to wear, but to wear out. And who will fare worst from the general collapse of things—who but the sailors who go to sea in the rotten ships the labourers who live in the jerry houses, the poor who buy the shoddy clothes? Dreadful calamities have happened often enough from criminal negligence and botchery—the bad workmanship put into ships, into bridges, into dwelling-houses, into public buildings. I write as a victim; for my health was permanently injured, and my life was nearly lost, through the conduct of workmen who deliberately mislaid the drains in a new house. And the terrible catastrophe that befell the Forth Bridge and the train that was crossing it in a storm was presumably due to the faulty castings that were used in the structure.

Our workmen are yet too honest, too proud of their skill, too mindful of their character and reputation, to sanction the disgraceful policy of skulk. Out upon the evil counsellers who persuade them to dishonour themselves! But ominous reports are current that the odious system is creeping, or has crept, into the laws of the workshop; that workmen who do their best, if that best is better than the restrictions laid down allow, are penalised, worried, and assaulted; and that agents and spies are appointed to watch that the restrictive rules are not infringed. Fancy the shame and degradation of being obliged to refrain from doing an honest day's work! The effect is disastrous, not only to the character, but to the comfort of the workman. The labour problem will never be really solved till means have been found to make every man feel an affection for his work and a desire to excel in it. "A man's joy in his work," the late Mr. Cowen once wrote, "is the best of all human feelings and the greatest of all human pleasures." The great aim ought, then, to be the realisation of a state of industry in which men will pursue their callings with the same love and the same ardour as they pursue their hobbies and amusements. Secure such a condition of industry as this, and you make the world happier than it has ever been before— happier than it ever can be in other and differing circumstances. The policy of the workers, or of some of them, is to get themselves regarded as so many machines. There is no policy more calculated to make the working life of mankind unendurable. "A man can do his best thing easiest," says Emerson. And when he is doing his best he is happy. The happiest time is the busiest time (so long as the worker is not over wrought), whether in factory, field, or office. It is the idler and the loafer who find the hours drag heavily. To ordain idling and loafing, therefore, is to ensure that the workman's life shall be dreary and miserable. But human nature itself will revolt against the general application of so tyrannous a practice—unless, indeed, the British workman should become a mere slave to his own agent, the petty despot of the workshop.

The doing of less than they can do, less than they ought to do, and less than they contracted to do, was a ground of just complaint against the men who were employed to plant some of the belts of trees that surround the Town Moor of Newcastle. There was a great stagnation of trade during the winters of 1892-93 and 93-94. To relieve the distress the Town Council resolved to provide work in the shape of trenching the ground for the trees. The work was satisfactorily done the first winter. But before the second winter came round the ca' canny cancer had eaten its way into the conduct of the suffering people. The annual report of the City Engineer, dated March 25, 1894, contained this significant passage:—"The result of the efforts made to provide work for the unemployed during the last winter have not been encouraging. The work has cost more than double what similar work, done under the same conditions and the same supervision, cost the year before." What was done for 2½d. one year cost 6¼d. the next! The loss was the town's, but the benefit was nobody's. The loss was the workman's too, since he lost his character for honesty.

Curious reasons—sometimes silly and sometimes tyrannical—are occasionally given for strikes. Miners at one colliery struck because the management had discharged men for dishonest practices; those at a second because the management had closed a pit which had ceased to pay; those at a third because some of their fellows were not in the union. This latter form of strike, common in all trades of late years, is symptomatic of the growth of arrogance and despotism in the workshop. And in some trades the employers are compelled to carry out the unlawful and unwarrantable behests of the employed. Was ever position so humiliating? I remember how we old Radicals fought tooth and nail against employers who denied to their workmen the right of combination. It is the right to abstain from combining that is now denied. Moreover, if workmen insist upon exercising that right, they are expelled from the workshop altogether. This is the new unionism as once expounded in a document circulated in Tyneside factories:—"The non-unionist should be treated as a social leper, avoided as the plague." But the old unionism as expounded by Thomas Burt was this:—"While asserting and resolutely maintaining our own rights and liberties, we should respect the rights and liberties of others." Those who fought against the tyranny of capital, not because it was capital, but because it was tyranny, have now to fight against the tyranny of labour, not because it is labour, but because it also is tyranny. But Abraham Lincoln was right:—"Men who deny freedom to others deserve it not for themselves, and under a just God cannot long retain it."

The laws of the workshop sometimes help to make the worker's life a burden. They do so, I think (for I have had personal experience of both systems), when they insist on time-work instead of piece-work. Drearily drag the hours in the one case, but rapidly and happily they pass in the other. As Earl Grey once said, "the man who takes no interest in his work is apt to become morose, peevish, and discontented—a pest to the society in which he lives, and a sort of human mosquito, carrying a microbe which spreads the malaria of unhappiness." Not less effective in the same direction is the system of castes which the laws of the workshop are establishing. The dominant idea of working men, or rather of working men's societies, is that nobody should be allowed to do anything outside his own trade. Once a scavenger always a scavenger. "A man," says Emerson, "should not be a silkworm, nor a nation a tent of caterpillars." Yet, under the new caste system, men and women will be reduced to the condition, not so much of spiders and ants, as of slugs and worms. The life of the wretched exiles in Siberian mines is scarcely more weary, monotonous, and despairing than that to which some of our modern trades unionists would condemn all mankind. Without hopes, aspirations, or even the desire for anything better, our workmen will have to drag out their lives in rounds as dismal as a horse in a grinding-mill, or a squirrel in a cage, or a criminal on the tread-wheel. But Englishmen will never consent to become or remain mere cogs in a machine. The attempt to make them or keep them in that condition, however, may bring infinite mischief—such mischief as will inevitably result from the elimination of character and spirit from even a small section of the working classes.

Workmen are now invested with so vast a power that they can, if they will, reform and renovate the world. But first they must set their faces against practices in the workshop that are a disgrace to all concerned. Men are often so much like monkeys and school-boys that they find pleasure in tormenting and ill-using each other. These petty tyrannies, rendering existence intolerable in the case of victims who are capable of defending themselves, are mean and contemptible in the case of helpless and inoffensive companions. I know of a poor half-wit in a London workshop who seldom comes home without some tale of outrage done to him. Once he was smothered with lime which nearly cost him his eyesight. The men who do these things are scoundrels, and the men who permit them to be done are cowards. If workmen would exercise a moral censorship—send sots to Coventry and wife-beaters out of the pale—they would do more than has ever yet been done to purge and elevate society.

And now I will finish with a story. A great strike for an advance of wages was in progress in one of our chief coal-fields. It had been raging for fourteen or fifteen weeks, and nearly a quarter of a million men were still idle, their families of course being in dire distress. The Government of the day (Mr. Gladstone's Government), desiring to end the disastrous strife, commissioned a discreet person to sound the president of the union as to the willingness of the miners' leaders to meet Lord Rosebery and the coalowners to discuss terms of settlement. The president had gone to bed when the discreet person reached the headquarters of the society on Saturday night. Next morning the president was interviewed. "No, sir," said he, "I won't talk about it. I'm a member of the Lord's Day Observance Society. Do you think I'm to be bothered about worldly affairs on the Sabbath?" But the discreet person had already seen the other officers of the society—the vice-president and secretary—and had obtained their assent. So a conference was held, which resulted in an agreement to pay the old rate of wages for a time, and then refer all matters in dispute to a Board of Conciliation. Whereupon the miners' delegates passed resolutions congratulating the president on the victory he had won! Lord Rosebery, then Foreign Minister, delighted with the story of the Sabbath, said to Sir William Harcourt, then Home Secretary: "Splendid fellow that! Wish I had him in my department."

CHAPTER LV

DYNAMITE AND DAGGER

MICHAEL BAKUNIN, the Russian giant whom I saw at the funeral of Dr. Bernard after his escape from Siberia, is accorded the credit of having inspired the Anarchist movement. Proudhon had been before him in teaching the doctrine that "property is robbery," and Blanqui had been before him in fighting and conspiring against society. But Bakunin had more to do than either with fomenting an agitation that has resulted in incredible crimes. "Neither God nor master," was one of Bakunin's mottoes; "destruction for destruction's sake," was another. From this horrible teaching, and the evil spirit it evoked, there have issued such a series of assassinations and murders as have appalled the world.

It was not, however, till after Bakunin's death that anarchism was scientifically formulated. This was done at a conference held in Berne in 1876. The propositions then adopted, partly positive and partly negative, cleared the ground of all possible misconception as to the meaning of the Anarchists. The negative doctrine was thus set forth: —

All things are at an end.

There is an end to property. War to the knife against capital, against every description of privilege, and against the exploitation of one man by another.

There is an end to all distinctions of country. There shall be no such thing as frontiers or international conflicts.

There is an end of the State. Every form of authority, elected or not, dynastic or parliamentary, shall go by the board.

Equally precise and unmistakable was the affirmative part of the doctrine: —

The social revolution, if it is to escape being a fresh exploitation of the individual, must have no other aim than to create a community in which the individual shall enjoy absolute independence, obeying simply and solely the behests of his own will, and fettered by no obligations imposed upon him by the will of his neighbour; for any restraint of this latter description would undermine the very foundations of the system. Hence are deduced the two propositions which comprise the whole positive creed of the Anarchist—

1. Do what you choose.

2. Everything is everybody's; that is to say, the entire wealth of the community is there for each individual to take from it what he requires.

Even before the tenets of the Anarchist had been put into formal and precise language, as if the authors were stating a mathematical proposition, they had been practised and exemplified by the Paris Commune. The Communards, when they were at last defeated, destroyed for the sake of destroying. It was well for Paris that they had at their command petroleum instead of dynamite. Dynamite was a later weapon that was employed with deadly and dastardly effect by the furies of another race. There was perhaps some excuse for the Communards, who were caught like rats in a trap, and who fought like rats in a pit. Despair and madness accounted for the flames with which the desperate and maddened insurgents endeavoured to reduce Paris to ashes. It may, however, be doubted whether any similar excuse can be urged for miscreants who, beginning with the dagger, calmly planned and executed the most villainous and yet most useless outrages.

Broken down in health, in consequence of the criminal negligence, or rather the deliberate rascality, of certain workmen who had prepared a death trap for the first occupants of a new house, I was in the spring of 1882 on my way to America to recruit. Our ship was the *Germanic*, one of the fleet of the White Star Line. We were nearing New York in a dense fog, with icebergs round about us. The situation was unpleasant, but perhaps not unusual on Atlantic liners. Nevertheless, we landsmen were greatly relieved when the yellow sails of a pilot boat were seen looming though the mist. A few minutes more and the pilot was on board. Almost instantly the whole ship's company—officers, crew, and passengers—was in a state of commotion. The pilot had brought copies of the latest papers, and these papers contained particulars of the assassination of Lord Frederick Cavendish in Phoenix Park. The crime had been committed more than a week before—the day after we had left Liverpool. It was the one subject of excited conversation on board the Germanic, among Britons and Americans alike, till our ship was moored at the landing stage.

The murder of Lord Frederick and his companion, who were cut to pieces with knives in broad daylight and in a public park, was the beginning of a series of even more diabolical and purposeless atrocities. The Fenians who did these things, many of whom came from America to do them, had probably not needed the incitements of Anarchist apostles to initiate a propaganda of bloodshed. But they preached and put into operation the same ferocious doctrines. The midnight use of torch and dagger in England was openly and almost incessantly advocated in New York and other cities of the United States from 1881 onwards. The mysterious sinking of the British ship *Doterel* with the loss of all on board was claimed as a triumph for the dynamite party. "It is the duty of every Irish citizen," cried an Irish orator in 1883, "to kill the representatives of England wherever found. The holiest incense to Heaven would be the smoke of burning London." Emergency Clubs and Crusader Clubs were established to wreck and ruin England. One of these took the name of one of the murderers of Lord Frederick Cavendish—the Joe Brady Emergency Club. A meeting of the members was held in March, 1884, whereat Frank Byrne, who had been concerned in the Phoenix Park crime, but who then ran a liquor saloon in New York, advised the general use of "dynamite, the torch, and the knife."

But the great fire-eater of the day was Jeremiah O'Donovan, otherwise known as O'Donovan Rossa. The Americans called him a blatherskite, but he called himself a madman. "I am not a fool," said he at a meeting in Columbia Hall, Brooklyn, on Dec. 30, 1883; "I am not a fool, but I admit I am a madman." Rossa published a paper called the *United Irishman*. This paper announced that a "verdict of murder" had been returned against Mr. Gladstone, and that "four Irishmen had volunteered to carry out the verdict." Gladstone was doomed, but London was doomed also. "The wrongs and injuries of seven centuries of oppression," it was declared, "may yet be avenged by the conflagration of London. It has been repeatedly asserted that London is perfectly combustible. It is built of such wretched materials, and contains such mountains of coal, wood, cotton, and cloth, such oceans of spirituous liquors, such immeasurable quantities of inflammable materials, that the Irish inhabitants might easily wrap London in crimson conflagration. Not London alone. Liverpool might blaze like another Moscow, or Manchester redden the midnight skies like another Chicago." Rossa was for practical work, he said at the Brooklyn meeting:–"I go in for dynamite. Tear down English cities; kill the English people. To kill and massacre and pillage is justifiable in the eyes of God and man." One need not, after this, contest the accuracy of Rossa's description of himself.

Yet there were other madmen in the field then—three at least. One was Robert Blissert, another William Bourke, the third Professor Mezeroff, "the dynamite apostle." Mr. Blissert declared that it would be "an act of humanity to lay all England in ashes." Mr. Bourke was a little more particular. "Scientists teach us," he said, "that gunpowder will blow a man up at the rate of 6,000 miles a minute; but, thank Heaven, these same scientists have given us dynamite, which would send the city of London—yes, all England— flying at the rate of 73,000 miles a minute. If we educate a thousand men in the science of chemistry, they can blow every city in England four miles above heaven in less than six months." It was to teach them chemistry that Professor Mezeroff (apparently an Irishman with a Russian name) desired to set about establishing dynamite schools—a dynamite school in every ward of New York. Bourke asked for a thousand men. Mezeroff thought a tenth of that number would do. "One hundred men educated in scientific warfare," he proudly proclaimed, "could lay every town and city in England in ashes."

Madness was in the air in the eighties and far into the nineties. Nor was it confined to one country or one race. It was rampant in England as much as in America, and in France and Spain as much as in either. There were German madmen, English madmen, French madmen—all thirsting for blood, like so many ghouls or vampires. Johann Most, who, like Bakunin, wished to "destroy everything," advised every labourer to select a victim: "He will seek him at his house, in his office, in his factory, at the counter, at the store, or in the church. Then he will bludgeon him, or stab him, or poison him." The German was not more sanguinary than the English Anarchist. "If," said Mr. Champion, "I thought the miserable system under which we live could be done away with by cutting the throats of the million and a quarter of people who hold among them three-fourths of the wealth of England, I would do it with my own hand this minute." Even the champion pig-killer of Chicago could hardly with his own hand cut a million and a quarter of throats in a minute; but this was a difficulty that did not occur to the English Anarchist. Champion, however, was scarcely more bloodthirsty than some of his comrades. One Nicoll, representing the "Commonweal Group," declared that all means were lawful to the Anarchist, "whether the knife, the pistol, or the running noose," and that everything that stood in his way was to be destroyed, "from God to the meanest policeman." During a time of distress in 1894, one Williams, an organizer of the Social Democratic Federation, set himself to incite the suffering people of London to violence and outrage. "The unemployed," he said, "were morally justified in helping themselves to the accumulations of wealth created by their own toil." And the police who interfered with them should be "sent to heaven by chemical parcels post." Quite a facetious person, Mr. Williams!" With a piece of explosive the size of a penny, which could be carried in the pocket," he added, "the whole of two lines of police could be removed." And a comrade of Williams's said he was prepared to start at once the pulling down and burning business. Compared with these ferocious sentiments, the advice of one Shaw Maxwell, who came down from London to suggest that the unemployed people of Newcastle should "sack the bakers' shops," was commendable for its moderation. The French Anarchists were not behind the rest in truculence. The massacre of the bourgeoisie was openly advocated in Paris in 1884; Citizen Eudes, a general of the Communards, lamented that the Commune had not "slaughtered, burned, and destroyed to the end"; and Louise Michel, the crazy Frenchwoman whom the Anarchists thought inspired, exultantly exclaimed in 1886, when a Socialist mob had robbed the jewellers' shops in Pall Mall, that "the English people were at last aroused, and would choke the Thames with the corpses of the capitalists."

But Anarchism did not confine itself to threats. Diabolical outrages were of frequent occurrence from 1890 to 1894—now in France, then in Italy, anon in Spain. Ravachol, a low thief and murderer before he became an Anarchist, startled the world with a fiendish crime. Worse atrocities followed. Auguste Vaillant, a gaol-bird and the companion of thieves and burglars, threw a bomb into the midst of the Chamber of Deputies of France, causing terrible injuries; Emile Henri, selecting the happiest crowd he could find, did the like in a Paris restaurant; and Salvador Franch, who seems to have never done an honest day's work in his life, exploded an infernal machine in a crowded opera house at Barcelona, killing twenty-three innocent people and wounding twice as many more. And the deeds of these demons were hailed with acclamations in the Anarchist circles of London. "If," said one Turner at a meeting in Wardour Street, "if the working classes were to do any good for themselves, they must do as Ravachol did." H. B. Samuels, the editor of a bloodthirsty print called the *Commonweal*, declared at a meeting in the Grafton Hall, Fitzroy Square, that "their comrade in Barcelona had done a great and good act." Writing later of the same event in his own publication, he expressed the pleasure he felt "because of the death of thirty rich people and the injury of eighty others"! The Anarchists had other heroes besides Ravachol and Franch. One was Hermann Stellmacher. This man was executed in Austria for the murder of a policeman. But he had been guilty of still more despicable crimes. Two men, one evening in January, 1883, entered the office of a money-changer named Eisert, situated in a principal street of Vienna. Herr Eisert was first blinded with sand, and then so brutally assaulted that he died shortly afterwards. This done, the miscreants penetrated to an inner apartment of the house, where they attempted to murder the two children of their victim and an aged lady who was giving them some lessons. One of the children subsequently died. The murderers ransacked the office, and stole all the money they could find. Some brewery shares which fell into their hands were sold to a bank in Pesth, the proceeds being distributed between Stellmacher and two Anarchist newspapers. The memory of this common thief and assassin, who was described as the "Hero of the Proletariat," was commemorated a few months later by the Anarchists of New York, Most and a man, named Kennel glorifying his crimes and extolling him as a martyr!

The homicidal maniacs who constitute the extreme section of the Anarchical party are alleged to be all consumed with vanity. The behaviour of most of them in court and prison warrants this assumption. When Ravachol was condemned to death, he wrote an abominable song which he hoped to sing before a great crowd on the way from the prison to the place of execution. But his calculations were upset by the arrangements of the Prefect of the Loire. When he found, says M. Lepine, that he was to be deprived of an audience, his bravado forsook him, and he collapsed so utterly that he was half-dead before he reached the guillotine.

CHAPTER LVI

BLANQUI

THE mention of Blanqui in the last chapter induces me to turn aside for the purpose of recording particulars of the career of one of the most remarkable revolutionary characters even France has ever produced. That career was strange and stormy—perhaps the strangest and stormiest of the nineteenth century. It came to a close on New Year's Day, 1881. Louis Auguste Blanqui, whose name had been familiar to every democrat in Europe for fifty years before, ceased that day to trouble the world more. "After life's fitful fever, he sleeps well." Never were words so appropriate as in Blanqui's case. His life, indeed, was one long "fitful fever." From the time that he was wounded on a barricade in 1827, down to the agitation in which he was concerned a few days before he died, he had been conspicuous in every revolution and in almost every disturbance that had taken place in Paris. Blanqui was nothing if not a revolutionist. One half of his long life was spent in prison; the other half was spent in conspiring or agitating against the various Governments of France. Not untruly did his friends describe him as "the martyr of every reaction." The type of a class which is not even yet extinct, and which will perhaps never be extinct till society has been transformed, all that was kindly and amiable in the old revolutionist was at the time of his death revived to his credit. Whatever was fierce or repellent about Blanqui perished with him. Enemies and admirers alike said little but what was good of the dead.

Garibaldi and Blanqui were born in the same city—Nice. The one attached himself to Italy, the other to France. Garibaldi made a nation; but Blanqui left little behind him except an austere and turbulent fame. Blanqui's father, a deputy for Nice in the great French Convention, had two sons. Both became eminent, though in totally different walks of life. The elder brother, a pupil of Jean Baptiste Say, acquired great distinction as a writer on political economy. Louis Auguste himself was at first a private tutor; then he studied both law and medicine in Paris; lastly, he became alternately a political propagandist and a political prisoner. It was while studying law in 1827 that he was wounded in a political disturbance. Three years later the Revolution of July overturned the throne of the elder Bourbons. For his share in that memorable event Blanqui was rewarded with a cross of honour. But Louis Philippe was naturally no more acceptable to Blanqui than was Charles the Tenth, whom he had helped to dethrone. Associated with his friends Armand Barbès and Martin Bernard, he planned the insurrection which broke out in May, 1839. The rising was abortive; Barbès was condemned to death; and Blanqui, after being concealed for some time in the house of the famous sculptor, David, was awarded the same sentence. Victor Hugo, making powerful use of a birth and a death in Louis Philippe's family, appealed for mercy in a pathetic poem—"Mercy in the name of the tomb, mercy in the name of the cradle." This touching appeal was successful. Barbès and Blanqui, their lives spared, were ordered to be imprisoned for the rest of their days. The treatment of the prisoners was so frightful—it resembled the treatment of Pellico in Spielburg and Poerio in Naples—that Blanqui nearly died under it. But the Revolution of 1848 restored him to liberty. Lamartine appealed to him to serve instead of harassing the Republic. Blanqui, impressed by the poet's arguments, seemed inclined to yield, but he was soon afterwards engaged in a plot to overthrow the Provisional Government. The demonstration he had organized, which was discountenanced by Barbès, Cabet, and Louis Blanc, came to nothing. A later attempt to invade the National Assembly, which was frustrated by Ledru Rollin, resulted in Blanqui's condemnation to ten years' imprisonment. Some time after his release he set himself to propagate his doctrines among the refugees in London. Visiting Paris in 1861, he was incarcerated again—this time for a term of four years. When the Empire was beginning to reel, Blanqui concocted a scheme to capture the arms of the Pompiers Barracks. For this he was condemned to death in default. The fall of the Empire, annulling the judgment, enabled him to reappear in Paris. But the Government of National Defence was as little to his liking as the Provisional Government of 1848. A rising of his adherents took place on October 31, 1870; the new Ministers were captured; and Blanqui was actually for a few hours installed in the Hotel de Ville. It was this incident which inspired Bismarck with the hope that internal dissensions would enable the invaders to dictate terms of peace within the walls of Paris. When the capital, after an unavailing resistance, surrendered to the Germans, Blanqui retired to the provinces. During his absence, two events of moment occurred: he was elected a member of the Commune, and he was condemned to death for the third time. The sentence was afterwards commuted to imprisonment in a fortress for life. Old and infirm, the veteran revolutionist, who was for once well treated in prison, devoted his time to the study of astronomy. The result of his studies was a speculative work entitled "Eternity in the Stars." Blanqui, it was thought, was now too advanced in years to be any longer a danger to the State; wherefore he was once more released. But he was still vigorous enough to commence a new paper, to which he gave the characteristic name *Ni Dieu ni Maitre* (*Neither God nor Master*). The paper, however, which had a very small circulation, practically expired before its author. Blanqui died as he had lived— irreconcilable to the last.

The extraordinary career whose salient features I have here summarised was remarkable even in France. It is doubtful whether the whole history of revolutionary enterprises can furnish another such example of romantic endurance, of inveterate hostility to established systems, of sincere and persistent attachment to impracticable ideas. Blanqui was extreme in all things. He was not only a Republican, but a Red Republican—not only a Democrat, but a Social Democrat—not only a Communalist, but a Communist. No form of Government yet established appeared to satisfy him. He was as much the enemy of the Republic of Jules Grévy as he was of the Empire of Louis Bonaparte. The circumstance that the people were free to work out their own emancipation never seemed to concern him. What was the value of liberty so long as there were any poor in the land? The only use of liberty was to enable those who enjoyed it to agitate and conspire for social equality. There was a touch of eccentricity or extravagance in almost everything he did. Even when a tutor, "he eschewed wine, spirits, and coffee, lived on fruit and vegetables, dispensed with a fire in the depth of winter, and slept composedly with the snow falling on his counterpane."

Though he appears to have been sincerely attached to his wife, a rich banker's only child, who died while he was suffering his first incarceration, he was almost devoid of family affection. For a long time he would not allow his son to be taught to read, declaring that he would do better without that accomplishment. The son, brought up a peasant, was so little under his father's influence that he identified himself with the party of Reaction. As to his own brother, the political economist, Blanqui repudiated the relationship. "My brother," said he, "is a *bourgeois*, and consequently a *canaille*." But his sister, Madame Antoine, attended him in his last days.

Blanqui had never any clear idea of what he wanted to accomplish, or of how he meant to accomplish it. It was necessary to destroy everything in order to place something else in its stead. "We must begin," he observed to a gentleman who visited him in prison, "by making a *tabula rasa* of existing abuses. What exists is so bad that what is put in its place will always be better than what exists." It was as a destructive and an anarchist that he claimed the approbation of the populace. He had neither system nor programme. Indeed, he had a horror of the people who concocted them. M. Ranc related in the *Voltaire*, the Radical paper of Paris, that the surest way to exasperate Blanqui was to ask him what he would do if the people next day placed supreme power in his hands. "I shall act," he would reply with evident irritation, "according to circumstances." So it would seem that the old revolutionist was himself an Opportunist. That he saw the ludicrousness of hoping to transform society of a sudden is clear from another statement of M. Ranc's. Blanqui, Ranc, and Regnard were projecting a new journal in 1869. Ranc was to write on politics, Regnard on philosophy, Blanqui on the social question. "The subject assigned to me," said Blanqui, "is difficult. Do you not see that Socialism is in the stage of criticism?" The same doubts found expression in a speech which he delivered in Milan, only a few weeks before his death, on the occasion of the unveiling of a monument to the heroes who had fallen at Mentana. "Citizens," said he, "I put no faith in those who pretend to solve the social question in a few hours. When, in prison, I worked out an intricate problem of mathematics or astronomy, I only discovered its solution after the lapse of many months. Often I could not solve it at all; I waited, and resumed my task years after. And for the solution of such a problem as the social question, it is not months or even years that will suffice, for one must reckon by centuries. Those who assert the contrary are seeking to lead you astray."

It was natural that a man of Blanqui's temperament and antecedents should live in an atmosphere of suspicion. He suspected everybody, and, in turn, he was himself suspected. During the excitement which followed the Revolution of February, Blanqui was the president of a club which demanded as a first instalment the heads of three hundred thousand citizens! This was the moment chosen for revealing the fact that he had played false to his friends Barbès and Bernard after the affair of 1839. The statements then published would have been incredible but for the circumstance that Barbès, the Bayard of the Democracy, is said to have believed them. The two revolutionists never acted together afterwards. It is difficult, for all that, to reconcile the accusation with the other incidents in Blanqui's career. A man who could spend thirty-seven years of his life in prison for the sake of his opinions must have been sincere. It was the sincerity of fanaticism, if you will, but it was infinitely more worthy of respect than the falsehood which is true only to itself. "Liberty and the Republic," says M. de Girardin, "never had a more fatal friend than Blanqui." The fault of his life was precisely the fault which Irreconcilables have always been bent upon committing.

CHAPTER LVII

DEGENERACY

OLD people are apt to institute invidious comparisons between the days of their youth and the days of their decline. Maybe the reason is that youth is the season of optimism and age the season of pessimism, though optimism is not invariably a sign of youth nor pessimism invariably a sign of age. But the world cannot always be getting worse, else some day it would come to deserve the fate of Sodom and Gomorrah. My own opinion is, trying to recollect the state of things in the thirties and comparing it with the state of things in the new century, that there has been decided improvement in some directions, but decided retrogression in others. The worst complaint one has to make against the later generations is that they have failed to make the best use, or indeed any use at all, of the enormous advantages they enjoy over the generations that preceded them.

Let us begin with education. The masses of the people were entirely ignorant when I was a lad; indeed, as I have said before, it was a distinction to be able to read and write. Now the masses of the people are at least partly educated—not only able to read and write, but able to do many other clever things besides. There are evidences of intellectual improvement beyond a doubt; but where are the evidences of moral improvement? As a matter of fact, we are in no respect better, but in some respects worse, than our grandfathers were. We have greater freedom, but less inclination to turn it to the best advantage; more knowledge, but less desire to use it for the best purposes. Nothing is more disappointing to early reformers than the comparatively little benefit that has accrued to society from the millions of money that have been spent and that are being spent on School Boards and Board Schools. A dear old friend of mine—the late Alderman Lucas, of Gateshead, whose whole public life was devoted to disinterested efforts for the welfare of the community— put into words, a few years before his lamented death, the thoughts of all his reflective contemporaries. "We were assured," he wrote, "that when compulsory education became general we should see Paradise restored. Social and political questions would be considered on their merits; every man would have liberty to think out all questions concerning his welfare without molestation; crime would gradually disappear before the light of education; and a general transformation of the people (for the better of course) would speedily take place." Some of these anticipations I put myself into a pamphlet published in 1860.

But what has been the result? Let Alderman Lucas answer:— "Intolerance of the worst description is to be found in all directions; brutality in its most horrible forms is still going on; cruelty to the weak and helpless abounds far more than we can estimate; and disregard of authority, if not general, is found almost everywhere. The great object of the lives of multitudes is how to minister to their self gratification and love of pleasure. One of the main causes of this deplorable state of things is the insufficiency of modern education. The mind is crammed, but the sentiments are left uncultivated." Hence it is that the manners of the people have not improved, that the intelligence of the people has not increased, that the respect of the people (or those who call themselves the people) for the rights of others has almost ceased to exist. Suffering people are pushed to the wall, agéd people into the gutter, while our very pavements testify to the disgusting habits of the time. These and other evils come of cultivating the intellect, while neglecting the conscience. To complete the catalogue of popular faults and foibles which popular education has failed to correct, the masses of the people are as prone to fall victims to plausible delusions or sophisms as they were in more ignorant ages.

The effect on the Press, or on a large portion of the Press, has been disastrous. When few people could read, the matter provided was mostly of an elevating character—rarely of a debasing character: for the few in all ages have invariably been more refined than the many. But since our children have been taught to read without being taught to think, and since everybody can read, whether able to think or not, the general quality of popular reading has distinctly deteriorated. Newspapers find it necessary to play to the groundlings and the gallery, pandering to the lowest tastes because the lowest tastes pervade the biggest multitudes. And so vulgar sensationalism has taken the place of sober earnestness. Instead of being the instructors of the people, many of our newspapers have become mere ministers to the passions of the people. Some of them that profess to be intended for family reading even descended a few years ago to the level of the "penny dreadful," publishing stories that were founded on the most atrocious crimes of the age. A daily paper that was established in London to advance the interests of a great political party—its chief promoter was a university professor—borrowed from the American Press one of its worst features. All the news of the day was furnished with vulgar headings. Even sad and sorrowful news was made the occasion of coarse jests. It seemed as if the scholarly gentlemen who had set out to exalt a great party had set out also to degrade the general multitude.

Periodicals did not escape the lamentable infection. The most popular of the new periodicals owed its early success to an ingenious method of picking and stealing from all and sundry. It soon had imitators no better than itself. And so the superior publications of Chambers and Cassell were to a large extent superseded by a series of slangy and superficial serials which could not support themselves by their own merits, for they made no pretence to originality or skill, and which had to be bolstered up by evasions of the Lottery Act, and such panderings to the gambling propensities of the people as the missing word competitions. Worse than these publications were others that came as near to the vilest indecency in print and illustration as the law will allow. The taste that was thus encouraged was further sustained by some of the new magazines, which rival each other in the publication of stories of rapine and outrage, supplemented by pictures of abortions and similarly repulsive subjects.

The disease that has eaten into the vitals of the Press has shown itself also in Fiction and the Drama. It is recorded that Sir Walter Scott, shortly before he died, consoled himself with the reflection that he had done nothing with his pen that any upright or pure-minded man might regret. "I have been perhaps," he said, "the most voluminous author of my day; and it is a great comfort for me to think that I have tried to unsettle no man's faith, to corrupt no man's principles, and that I have written nothing which, on my death-bed, I should wish blotted out." Some of the "voluminous authors" of our day—they are not numerous, perhaps, but they are sufficiently repugnant—may hereafter, when in the same straits as the great novelist, wish that they, too, had tried to corrupt no man's principles. There are books now on the shelves of our libraries, with noted (though I will not say distinguished) names attached to them, which Sir Walter Scott would have gone to the pillory or the gallows rather than have written. Sarah Grand, herself by no means squeamish, said of one of them that the author seemed "to want us to return to the customs of the poultry yard." And then we had an English Zola who revelled in the details of a lying-in hospital. And then—most repulsive of all—the novelist who laid down the abandoned doctrine that the father of a woman's child was no more anybody's concern than the cut or fashion of her under-garments. If the people—for women as well as men have been connected with the work of pollution—if the people who have produced these books should be remembered at all in the annals of literature, they will have to be classified with the creatures who, in past ages, prostituted their talents to pander to the vices of their time.

The plea of realism which is sometimes put forward on behalf of odious authors is a paltry plea. It is not even real itself. "If," says an American critic, "there is any greater humbug and hypocrisy than 'realism' can be, I do not know what it is. Take, for instance, the single detail of profanity in the 'conversation' of a story. Is there a living realist who would be willing to put down in cold black and white to the extent of a foolscap page the habitual language of certain types with which he deals in fiction? And if he did so, would he be willing to keep that piece of paper over-night even under lock and key?" When Henry Vizetelly—our old acquaintance of the *Illustrated Times*—published translations of some of Zola's realism, which in this case was simply another name for mere beastliness, he was prosecuted for misdemeanour, fined a hundred pounds, and ordered to be of "good behaviour" afterwards. Yet not long subsequently "gentlemen of the Press" entertained Zola himself at a public function in London! More recently, one of the most eminent of American authors, writing in a leading American magazine, set himself to exalt the French writer on the ground that there is nothing immoral in his obscenity! Fine literary people, women as well as men, seem to be afflicted with a paralysis of the moral sense when they can note nothing offensive in indecency, just as those unfortunate people who can smell nothing evil in a cesspool or a pig-sty are afflicted with a paralysis of the physical sense. There is filth enough in real life which one cannot avoid seeing without going to books for it. We know that sewers and stenches exist; but some of our modern writers have sought to introduce them into our kitchens and our drawing-rooms. The race of authors must indeed have degenerated when they actually itch for the opportunity of embalming in literature the unthinkable blasphemies of the stews.

The stage has no more escaped the contagion of decadency than has literature. Patrons of theatres have been nauseated with the loathsome suggestiveness of the problem play. Harlots and strumpets have been made the heroines of dramas, and accomplished actresses have not hesitated to represent these disreputable characters behind the footlights. Why, it is not so long ago that three or four plays idealising the adventures of a courtesan of the most dissolute period of English history were running in our theatres at the same time. But perhaps the most odious production of all—a production which had not even the saving grace of literary merit—came from America. It was the work of an obscure playwright of that country; it was founded on a story by an obscene French writer; and it was produced by a leading actor at a leading theatre in London. As brutal an incident as it is possible to conceive as occurring among the vilest people on earth was actually presented on the stage. We may judge of the nature of the play by the statement of one of the critics that the "revolting details" of the plot could not be described in print without outraging decency and offending the reader. Yet there were women writers who could not or would not see the gross immorality of the production, and who spoke of the disgusting incident on which the plot turned as a "strong situation." Nor was it till many remonstrances had been addressed to him that the manager withdrew the hideous thing.

But, after all, we are not so depraved in theatrical matters as some other countries. One hears of plays and performances in France and Belgium which are fit only for satyrs. As for America, one of the principal members of a band of thieves and murderers known as the James Boys actually appeared on the stage in scenes that depicted his own atrocious exploits. More recently the news was considered sufficiently important to be telegraphed from New York to Cincinnati that a star actor was "about to bring out a play founded on the Whitechapel murders," he himself appearing in "the dual *rôle* of Jack the Ripper and a clergyman"!

Impartially reviewing the circumstances of the present and the past, I venture to say that the penny dreadful of my young days did far less harm to the morals of the people than the disgusting rubbish that finds a place in the plays and novels of our own time. Nor is it to be less deplored that critics and pressmen, even those of the highest standing, pass without censure books and dramas of the worst character, precisely as though they had no duty to condemn the gross and repulsive foulness that is cast before the public.

CHAPTER LVIII

THE DECLINE OF MAN

MEN who have done the best for the world have the best right to be disappointed with the result of their efforts. "With few exceptions," wrote Mazzini to Mathilde Blind, "I despise the present generation, and only in humanity as it will be in the future do I find any consolation." Kossuth concurred in the sentiment of Mazzini, for he wrote on his ninetieth birthday:—"I do not believe in humanity as now developed. As for society, it is a vile beast." It is not a little curious that Napoleon entertained much the same disparaging opinion of our race. "Mankind," he said to Gourgaud, at St. Helena, "must be very bad to be as bad as I consider it." And Marie Corelli clenches the austere indictment:—"Humanity has cursed and killed every great benefactor it ever had, including Christ." For the rest, it will not be easy for those of us who have lived long on the earth to dispute this further judgment of the same writer:—"No beast of the field is so beastly as man at his worst."

The records of crime and the circumstances of society go far to justify these harsh and unpalatable verdicts. We have never for any length of time been without a favourite miscreant since Probert, Hunt, and Thurtell were tried for the murder of William Weare. This was in 1824. Four years later—I am taking into account only the princes of crime—the populace was greatly interested in the murder of Maria Martin and the yet more horrible misdeeds of Burke and Hare. Greenacre came next—Greenacre, who carried about in public conveyances the head of his victim wrapped in a paper parcel. The baleful procession was continued by Courvoisier in 1839; Daniel Good in 1842; Tawell and Hocker in 1845; Mrs. Manning and James Bloomfield Rush in 1849; Palmer, the Rugeley poisoner, in 1856; Madeleine Smith in 1857; George Victor Towneley in 1863; Muller in 1864; Dr. Pritchard, Charlotte Winsor, and Constance Kent in 1865; Mary Anne Cotton in 1873; Wainwright in 1875; Peace in 1879; Lefroy in 1881; the Phoenix Park assassins in 1882. And then came the Whitechapel fiend, followed by many other monsters. But some of these crimes indicated less cowardly brutality on the part of the criminals, besides bringing less shame and disgrace on society, than the despicable assaults on women that occupy, every working day, the attention of our police-courts.

The editor of the *Newcastle Weekly Chronicle* took the trouble in 1884, in the hope of shaming the brutes who make us disgusted with our own species, to compile a record of a week's wife-beating. The cases were thirty in number. Yet it was from a few of the leading newspapers only that the list was compiled, and it was pointed out, as is well known, that but a small proportion of the most infamous cases find their way into such journals. If it had been possible to prepare a complete catalogue of these brutal offences, there is no doubt that the number would have risen to hundreds. Hundreds of wife-beatings every week! Nothing shows the degeneracy of the British race so much as the cowardice displayed in the ill-treatment of the weaker sex. Has there been any improvement since 1884? A blackguard who had deserted his wife in Sunderland told the magistrates in 1899 that the "only enjoyment a working man had was getting drunk." But a still more contemptible specimen of manhood turned up at Teddington the same year. The prisoner in this case was charged, not with deserting, but with assaulting his wife. The poor woman stated that "he had always been in the habit of knocking her about." When asked by the magistrates what he meant by such conduct, the ruffian replied in an injured tone" that "it was the only recreation he had." Foreigners, when they read such cases as those of Sunderland and Teddington, may be almost excused if they put us down as a nation of sots and savages.

Some of us are sots and dastards, and some are dastards without being sots. The new century has supplied many examples of both forms. A woman was being murdered on Yarmouth sands. Her cries for help were heard by a young man (the man in this case must be understood in a quite restricted sense) who was passing. But the prudent young man went on his way, not only without rendering, but without seeking, assistance. An equally scandalous case of indifference was disclosed at the Norwich Assizes. The widow of a soldier who had died for his country in South Africa, lived alone with her baby in a cottage at the village of Stokesby. The poor woman's sorrow and loneliness might have been expected to ensure pity and protection. Instead, they seem to have inspired a brutal youth of seventeen to attempt a criminal assault. The attack was made while the widow was calmly sleeping with her baby. There was a fierce struggle, and then the knife. The woman's screams were heard by a man living in the adjoining cottage. Here again no assistance was rendered or sought. While the murderer resumed his work next morning as if nothing had happened, his victim remained without aid all night, and died the following day. The jury, with that strange tenderness for criminals which has lately become a fashion, recommended the murderer to mercy, though it is not recorded that they had anything to say about the cowardly neighbour.

A still worse case of poltroonery occurred on the first day of the new century. It took place at Broomhill Colliery, in Northumberland. There a ruffian miner named Craig struck and kicked his wife in such a way that she died a few days later. And part of the striking and kicking took place in the very presence of three other miners—John Joicey, Richard Grey, and John Richardson—whose only excuse for permitting it was that they had been "first-footing." Joicey, indeed, had listened behind a door for half an hour to the beating and kicking before he and the others ventured into the house where the murderer had already half-killed his victim. The sickening story told by this man and the other witnesses at the trial must have made the people who heard or read it ashamed of their own species.

Drink was the cause of the Broomhill atrocity, as, indeed, it is of most of the other crimes committed in this country. Yet drunkenness is no longer a matter of shame. On the contrary, it is sometimes a matter of pride. The sots who can drink the most or get drunk the oftenest consider themselves heroes and heroines, and are even so considered by others. The drunkard was once a disgrace, but we have got past this squeamish notion now. Workmen, it is alleged, will work no longer than they can earn money enough for a three days' booze. And social clubs and political clubs are being established in all our industrial villages to enable them to drink all day and every day, Sundays included. Three youths of sixteen, seventeen, and eighteen years of age, in a case heard at the Moot Hall Police Court, Newcastle, admitted having drunk in the space of three hours nine or ten glasses of beer each. We talk of swine. Why, swine are almost gentlemen alongside such swill-tubs as these.

While there has been shown in recent years a marked decline in mortality from ordinary diseases, the deaths from intemperance rose from 45 per million in 1878 to 77 per million in 1897. The North of England has probably contributed more than its share to this loss of life; for to Durham, Northumberland, and Lancashire belong the distinction of being the three most dissipated counties in the kingdom. As compared with soberer districts, they stand convicted of producing more than a thousand drunkards as against less than 150. Though the national drink bill for 1900 (£160,891,718) was a million and a quarter less than the corresponding expenditure in 1899, it was yet equal to an outlay of £3 18s. 8d. for every unit of the population. The rents of all the farms and houses in the country fall short of the money we spend annually on intoxicants. We are indeed a drunken nation. And the effect of our evil habits on the future of our race must be calamitous. If we do not want to become a nation of degenerates, we must cease to become a nation of drunkards.

Since drink, taken to excess, makes either demons or imbeciles of its victims, it may fairly be held accountable for part at least of that alarming increase of insanity which has been recorded in late years. Lunatics have increased in proportion to the population far faster than the population itself. The total number of lunatics in England and Wales in 1899 was 105,086, being an increase of 3,114 over the corresponding number for 1898. Mr. H. H. Asquith informed a meeting held in this present year, 1903, that besides the 110,000 persons actually confined in lunatic asylums, "he believed there were at least 100,000 more in what was known as the outer zone of lunacy." It is calculated that the growth of mad people in the administrative County of London alone is at the rate of 500 a year, requiring the erection every four years of a new asylum, at the cost of £600,000. The progression of madness was steady from the middle to the end of last century. Thus in 1859 there was one official lunatic to every 536 persons; in 1869 one to 418; in 1889 one to 337;

and in 1899 one to 302. It is easy for a statistician to calculate how long it will be, at this rate, before the whole population is liable to be confined in lunatic asylums.

Mr. Arnold White has more than once called attention to what he calls the multiplication of the unfit. "Our higher civilization," he says, "is multiplying from its lower specimens, and our voters are being propagated increasingly from idle, unthrifty, and unemployable invalids. Scientific men declare that there are nine sorts of idiots and six sorts of madmen. All these fifteen kinds of idiots and madmen are cheerfully multiplying with impunity. [32] Yet the dogma is still current among religious and kindly souls that a man who cannot maintain himself possesses an inalienable right to engender degenerate offspring, to whom no parental responsibility is due." A professor of the University of Bonn traced the progeny of a woman named Jurke, a drunken and thievish vagabond who died in 1740. There was 834 altogether—106 of them bastards, 142 of them beggars, 181 of them prostitutes, 76 of them criminals, and 7 of them murderers. And it is a grievous charge against some of our charitable institutions that they contribute to the maintenance and multiplication of persons who are so mentally and morally diseased that they must always be a burden on others.

There is a sort of degeneracy again in the everlasting craving for excitement. We make a business of pleasure, not a pleasure of business. Seriousness has gone out of fashion. All we seem to want is amusement or indulgence. And our amusements are not always elevating. Intellectual pastimes are but little patronised, while brutal sports are always sure of a large following. Chess-masters have to be content with modest prizes of a hundred or two hundred pounds; but two pugilists fought in America for stakes amounting to £9,000! Glove fights in England are often as brutal as the old prize-fights. It was said of the Chartists of Swalwell that they got up a boxing-match for the benefit of the Chartist prisoners. Much the same spirit prevails yet. During the election for 1892, the proceedings at a political meeting were suspended in order to watch a fight between two supporters of the rival candidates, and a member of Parliament, after the fight had concluded, called for "three cheers for the Morley man!" Blood sports are still as popular as ever, where the law allows them. Nor would the sports of the bull-ring, with all their horrible accompaniments, lack patrons among us if permission could be obtained for introducing them. Even football, splendid pastime as it is, is being ruined by the introduction of the professional and gambling elements. Hence the rowdyism which sometimes takes place when the favourite team gets beaten.

Gambling is a species of insanity that takes possession of all classes—rich as well as poor, women as well as men. The cases of three wastrels who had reduced themselves from affluence to bankruptcy (in one case beggary) by betting and extravagance were investigated in 1898. One had wasted £11,000 in four months, and was then in prison for obtaining money under false pretences; another had got rid of £30,000 in three years, was in debt to the tune of between two and three thousand pounds, and had no assets save a punt of the value of £10; the third, a peer of the realm, who had inherited an annual income of £15,000 eight years before, and whose debts amounted to £166,000, with assets nil, confessed that he had in one season lost as much as £20,000 on horse-racing alone. As gambling and the society of gamblers conduce to loose morals and loose conversation, society is increasingly demoralised by the growth of the gambling spirit. And so we get evil habits and evil conversation—coarseness and vulgarity all round.

While the conditions of life have vastly improved during the last seventy years, greater efforts than ever being made by society and the Legislature to add to the comforts of the people, I am sorry to have to confess that I see no evidence of any moral progress whatever. There was far less drunkenness when I was a boy than there is now. People were more thrifty, less given to scamp or shirk their work, and more disposed to rely on their own efforts than on the efforts of others. On the other hand, there is better teaching now than there was then, fewer class distinctions, less cause for discontent among the poor, and more social and political freedom. One must not therefore despair. Mazzini had hope in humanity as it will be in the future. We should be false to our faith in the destinies of the human race, if we did not believe that degeneracy is only a passing symptom, and that the onward march of mankind will one day be resumed—all the more reliantly and resolutely resumed because of the present retrogression.

CHAPTER LIX

APROPOS

A CHAPTER of good stories, though I have told some of them before in another place, may be *àpropos* here. As far as I know, only two of them were Joe Millers, except as gossip among friends, when I first put them in print. However, whether new or not—chestnuts or tinker's news—they will perhaps be amusing.

Let us begin with a lawyer's story—told to me by a lawyer, too. There lived in Newcastle a good many years ago a clever attorney of the name of Philip Stanton. Mr. Stanton had for one of his clients a well-known Quaker bachelor of that time. During a consultation, the client complained of the useless verbiage employed in legal documents. The man of law explained, however, that precise and elaborate expressions were really necessary in all such instruments. "For instance," he said, "if an earthquake were to occur in Newcastle, the ordinary newspaper report would probably read as follows:—'Mr. Bachelor and his housekeeper were thrown out of bed.' But a lawyer, drawing up a legal account of the occurrence, would say : 'Mr. Bachelor and his housekeeper were thrown out of their respective beds!'"

Another lawyer, John Clayton, was Town Clerk of Newcastle and a gentleman of great wealth. So far as the public knew, he did not dispense much in charities: for, as he was said to have remarked himself, he was "never an ostentatious giver." Mr. Clayton was a bachelor, and the heir to all his wealth was his nephew, Nathaniel George Clayton. When a collector for one of the institutions in the town called upon him to solicit a subscription, he was handed a sovereign. "Oh, but, Mr. Clayton," said the collector, "I would not like to see your name to so small a sum. Mr. Nathaniel George is down for five pounds." "Ah!" replied Mr. Clayton, "my nephew has great expectations: I have none."

Ralph Park Philipson succeeded John Clayton as Town Clerk of Newcastle. He was a shrewd lawyer, too, and for many years the chief adviser of the Whig party in the town. Among the members of the Town Council at the time was Ralph Dodds. Ralphy Dodds, as he was generally called, was a curious customer. He was also a magistrate, an alderman, and chairman of the Town Improvement Committee. One day, during a discussion in committee on some legal subject, a member quoted the opinion of Baron Martin. "Wey, ma man," interposed the chairman, as he patted Mr. Philipson on the back, "here's wor Baron Martin."

Mr. Dodds in his early days obtained the contract for the plastering work at Ravensworth Castle. The contractor was not known to the then Lord Ravensworth, nor was the then Lord Ravensworth known to the plasterer. While the work was in progress, the two met in the new building. Seeing a stranger, the noble lord asked him rather haughtily who he was. The reply was startling: "Aa's Ralphy Dodds the plaisterer: whe the h- are ye?"

Harking back to the lawyers, there is another story of Ravensworth Castle. But first as to the etiquette of visiting. "If," says an authority on the subject, "you go to a house in response to a card of invitation, you may take it for granted that the maid knows you are expected, or should know; you walk in, and merely wait in the hall while she asks you your name and announces you. To do otherwise might convey an impression that you are not an expected guest." A Newcastle lawyer who did "otherwise" met with a most unpleasant experience. The lawyer practised in a Court of Petty Sessions over which a later Lord Ravensworth frequently presided. One day his lordship, wandering about his estate, fell in with a hunting party (the lawyer being of the number), whom he invited to dine with him the next evening. The lawyer, like the rest of the hunters, presented himself at the castle. All the other guests had arrived, and, in fact, were already seated. The legal gentleman, however, instead of acting as an invited guest should have done, inquired if Lord Ravensworth was at home. "Yes," said the butler, "but his lordship is at dinner. If you will give me your card, I will take it to him." The card was presented. "Oh!" said the noble lord, looking at the name, but not recognising that the owner was one of the party he had invited to dine, "tell Mr. Parchment I will see him at the Court in the morning." And so the poor lawyer, through failing to understand the etiquette of visiting, had to trudge back to town, some three or four miles distant, without his dinner.

And now for a small story, not of lawyers, but of the law. A poor woman applied to the Registrar of a County Court in the North of England for a longer time to pay a debt she had been ordered to discharge in instalments. "But I can only do this," said the Registrar, "for one of two reasons—illness or unavoidable accident. You do not look ill, and you have not, I suppose, met with an unavoidable accident." "Oh, yes, I have, sir," replied the debtor, "I've had a baby!"

It was fear of the law, or of the public inquiry which the law enforces in the case of a sudden or violent death, that led a servant girl to act strangely. The members of a Newcastle family—I shouldn't be far wrong if I said it was my own—were sitting down to the Sunday's dinner. The joint was just served, and the diners were on the tiptoe of expectation. But there's many a slip, etc. Crash! Down came the ceiling with its heavy plaster ornament. The chandelier was smashed: so was the table: so was everything on the table. Joint and vegetables, bread and salt, water jug and cruet-stand, plates, dishes, glasses, knives, forks, spoons—all were piled in a heap on the floor. The ladies screamed, the children shrieked, the gentlemen shouted. The noise of the falling debris was hardly so loud as the cries of the disappointed bairns. For that day's dinner the family had to make the best of pudding and cheese. Notwithstanding the uproar, it was noticed that the servant girl did not put in an appearance. "Why, Susan," said the mistress of the house, "did you not hear the noise?" "Hear it, mum?" replied Susan; "aa shud think se." "Why, then, did you not come to see what was the matter?" "Not me, mum," was Susan's answer: "aa didn't want te be caalled te ne coroner's inquests!"

It happened not so long ago that a candidate for a Northern borough fell in with an old friend who belonged to the opposite party. Liberal and Conservative adjourned to the club, where they fraternised heartily. There was much political excitement at the time. The excitement or something else made the old friends hilarious. As the Conservative was the least incapable of the two, he volunteered to see the candidate home. When the door was opened and the lady of the house appeared in the hall, the Conservative pointed to his helpless companion. "Look there, Mrs. H-hicks," he hiccupped; "see what them d— —d Radicals have done for your hus-husband!"

Of this same Conservative another story was told years before. He was the son of a wealthy coal-owner, and became in the end a wealthy coal-owner himself. But he was kept under restraint in his youth, and was, until he succeeded to his father's estate and fortune, allowed only a moderate amount of pocket-money. It was during this period of subservience that he met some other golden youths in a bar-room. Told there that the father of one of his friends had just died, he exclaimed as he dejectedly thrust his hands deep into his pockets, "Ugh! everybody's father dies but mine!"

Two friends, journalists, who had been to see a boat-race on the Tyne, were returning up Dean Street, when they saw the announcement that a fat woman was on exhibition in a shop. "Let us go in," said one, and the other assented. The interview over, they retired. As they reached the door into the street, they heard the showman bawling to the crowd: "Mark the character of the haristocracy as they leave the pavilion!" I need not say that the aristocracy hastened to hide themselves among the common people.

A good story was picked up in Shields by a dear old colleague, the late Robert Sutherland. During one of the periodical depressions in the shipping trade, a farmer in the neighbourhood, who had lost heavily on shipping shares, came home one day after a shareholders' meeting, called for his gun, and began firing away at the ducks on his pond. When asked what he was doing this for, he angrily muttered, "Ne mair floatin' property for me ; ne mair floatin' property for me!"

Of Irish stories there is no end. Two were told me by a friend, who avowed that the incidents occurred in his own presence. A tourist on a jaunting car, seeing an angler in a Wicklow stream, asked the driver whether he was getting any sport. "Sport!" exclaimed the driver: "shure he'd have got more bites if he'd kept in bed!" The scene of the second story was New York. An Irish labourer, watching some Italians at what they called work, said to a bystander: "D'ye see thim apologies for min, sor? And yet they make Popes of thim in Italy." Now for one of my own. I was travelling with some friends in the vicinity of the Devil's Bit Mountain—the mountain which gets its name from the legend that the fiend, finding himself surrounded by old women, cut his way to the sea by making a gap in the hills. The legend was duly related by the driver of the jaunting car. "Do you believe it?" inquired one of the party. "Bedad!" returned Pat, "but he's left his marrk annyhow!"

The late Alexander Shannon Stevenson brought from Scotland a triad of good stories a few months before he died. Mr. Young, the famous paraffin oil man, was approached by a neighbour with the suggestion that a missionary should be appointed to look after the spiritual welfare of his workpeople. "It's no a bit o' guid," said Young; "aw paid a missionary mysel' a hunnerd a year for twa years, and he didna save a dom'd soul!" A pious old lady was invited to pay a visit to a friend. "Varra weel," she replied, "aw'll come if aw'm spared; but if aw'm no, ye'll no expect me." Mr. Balfour should include the third story in the next edition of his treatise on the "royal game." It is the keeper of one of the best golf courses in Scotland who speaks. "The Awmighty," said he, "must hae had a guid heed for goaf when He made yon green!"

John Lawrence Toole was always playing tricks at somebody's expense before he unhappily became helpless from paralysis. One of his tricks, when he was acting Paul Pry, was to introduce the names of his local friends to the company on the stage. Thus on a certain occasion, knowing I was in the theatre, for I had just seen him in his dressing room, he said he had "just popped in" to say that he had that very morning seen a big cabbage or a big gooseberry in "Mr. Adams's garden." It was the only time I was ever in an actor's dressing-room. Mr. Disraeli is credited with the caustic saying that when royalty is concerned you have to lay on flattery with a trowel.

Mr. Toole, I thought, had found it necessary, when making up for Paul Pry, to lay on paint with the same implement. Miss Eliza Johnstone and Miss Kate Carlyon were leading ladies of Mr. Toole's company when he went touring in the provinces. It was upon these and others (as Miss Carlyon told me) that he once played this pleasant trick. "My dear," said Toole to Miss Carlyon, "I want to make you a little present. But keep it quite secret from the rest. I know how jealous you ladies are of one another." The present was a brooch, I believe. And then he went to the other ladies in turn, presenting a similar trinket to each, and laying the same injunction in every case. But the secret couldn't be kept—J. L. knew that well enough. Great was the confusion of the recipients when, confiding to their bosom friends the marks of favour they had received from their chief, they discovered that precisely the same favours had been distributed all round!

The district of Tyneside was visited in 1886 by two lecturers who represented opposite schools of thought. One was a Russian exile who advocated anarchy; another was a member of a noble family who advocated individualism. The two met at the same table, when the talk turned on methods of propagandism. Did the anarchist, asked the individualist, believe in dynamite? "No," he responded, as calmly as if he had been answering a question about the sort of soup he preferred "no, I do not pelieve in dynamite." The individualist, one of the gentlest men that ever lived, rubbed his hands, and said he was delighted to hear him say so. "No," the anarchist went on in the same impassive tone, "dynamite does not do what is expected. It killed soldiers and servants at the Winter Palace, but not the Czar. Pesides, it makes people dislike the party which uses it. No, dynamite is not goot. Ze dagger is petter!"

Another lecturer who for fifty years and more has often been heard in Newcastle and all parts of the country had chambers in London conveniently provided with gas fires. One day he locked up his chambers and went on a three months' tour, and when he came back in the dog days his gas fire was still burning!

An absent-minded beggar of a different sort was the custodian of an editor's sanctum who absented himself with the keys. The editor was Frederick Guest Tomlins, author of a "History of England," whose acquaintance I made when he came to beg a copy of the "Tyrannicide" pamphlet for the purpose of making it the subject of one of his weekly contributions to a London newspaper. One morning, when Tomlins was editing *Douglas Jerrold's Newspaper*, he found his office door locked and no office-boy on the premises. The boy appeared at length, and explained that he had been up all night. "It's this way, sir," he said: "my uncle was hung at the Old Bailey this morning, and although we weren't on speaking terms with him, I thought, as one of the family, I ought to go and see the last of him." "Quite right," replied Tomlins, "never neglect your family duties; but when another of your relations is to be hanged, please to leave the office key under the mat."

Mr. Tomlins at the time I knew him supplemented his literary labours by keeping a shop for the sale of rare old books near the British Museum. But he loved his books so well that he once roundly abused a customer who wanted to buy one. It is George Agustus Sala who tells the story. The customer called at the shop, and asked for a particular volume marked in the catalogue. The bookseller mounted a ladder, picked out a book from the upper shelves, and began reading it. And he stood reading it for so long a time that the other had to remind him that he was waiting below. Then Tomlins replaced the book, descended the ladder, and told the customer that it was like his impudence to want to rob him of such a treasure!

My last story is also about an editor. During a great industrial crisis—I think it was the Nine Hours Strike—his paper had taken strong views on the side of the working people. One day a deputation of capitalists called to remonstrate with him on the subject. The deputation hinted that he would damage his paper. This stirred him up. "Well, gentlemen," said he, "the working man's penny is as good as yours, and there's a d——d sight more of 'em!"

CHAPTER LX

PEOPLE OF SOME IMPORTANCE IN THEIR DAY

WHEN Mr. Bradlaugh once announced a lecture on "Dead Men I have Known," I pointed out the solecism in the title; whereupon he altered it to "Dead Men whom I Knew when Living." The new title was clumsier, but more correct, than the old. I have already mentioned in the course of this narrative some of the dead men whom I also knew when living. These recollections may now be supplemented by references to a few others—some dead, some still living—whom I have seen, or heard, or known.

First as to public speakers. Immense interest was taken in the affairs of Italy from 1849 down to the time when the unity and independence of the country were accomplished. It was in 1849 that Garibaldi made that heroic defence of Rome which first gave him a European reputation. Conspicuous in the defence, as an orator inspiring the populace, was an Italian priest, Father Gavazzi. Father Gavazzi came to England in 1850, where he lectured for many years—first in Italian and then in English—first on political subjects and then on subjects connected with the Church. I heard him in Italian the year he came. The melodious language and the striking attitudes of the orator were most impressive. More impressive still was the use which he made of a long cloak that he wore. Gavazzi turned this long cloak to as much advantage as Dr. Parker in his younger years used to turn his long hair. Another famous orator of the same period was John B. Gough. He came from America, and he advocated temperance. Gough thrilled his audiences as he depicted the drunkard's doom. It was impossible to listen without admiration to his impassioned appeals. But there was one exquisite passage about water introduced into some of his addresses which he is said to have borrowed from somebody else. For all that, John B. Gough was really a great orator. George Thompson was as famous at that time for his denunciations of slavery as Gough for his denunciations of drink. Unfortunately, having no resources but his eloquence, he had to become the paid advocate of the movements to which he gave his assistance. John Arthur Roebuck was an incisive speaker, rather than an orator. But his speeches were marred by egotism. I have preserved the report of one in which the personal pronoun appears in almost every line, and sometimes twice or thrice in the same line. Mr. Roebuck once likened himself to a watch-dog, Tear 'Em, and ever afterwards the populace gave him that name. Mr. Disraeli was a clever debater—the inventor, too, of many clever phrases. It was not given to him, however, to sway the multitude. When he was visiting Manchester on the occasion of a great Conservative gathering in Pomona Gardens, he was invited to distribute the prizes that had been won at an educational institution in the town. The long address he then delivered, I recollect, was intolerably dull. Mr. Gladstone, his great rival, was sometimes verbose and often obscure, but he knew how to illuminate the driest of subjects. Perhaps his versatility was never better shown than in 1880, when, on his way to Midlothian, he delivered fervent speeches at every railway station on the road. The crowd at the Central Station, Newcastle, was enormous. It surged from side to side of the platform alongside the train in a manner that threatened perilous consequences. The appearance of Mr. Gladstone at the window of his carriage was the signal for immense cheering. I heard the single word "Gentlemen," and then was swept to another part of the platform. The rest was dumb show, except to the porters and reporters on the top of the carriage. Dr. Parker has just been mentioned. It was at Cavendish Chapel, Manchester, that he made so effective (albeit so theatrical) a use of his hair. The hair, dark and abundant then, was grey and scanty when I heard him at Bournemouth forty years later. All his somewhat pompous mannerisms notwithstanding, the old Hexham boy was a powerful preacher. Very different was the style of the old Newcastle boy, Thomas Binney, whose little treatise on the possibility of making the best of both worlds had an immense vogue in the middle years of the century. A long tramp I made one Sunday morning at that time to the Weigh House Chapel, in the very centre of the City of London, was not unrewarded, though Mr. Binney's sermon was devoted to the not very attractive theme of Church Government and Discipline. While Mr. Binney was preaching near the Monument, Robert Montgomery was ministering to a congregation in the neighbourhood of Tottenham Court Road.

Montgomery had also published a notable book—the poem entitled "Satan." Macaulay scarified it in a famous review, and the title attached itself to the name of the author, so that he is known to this day as "Satan Montgomery." I recollect nothing of the poet's sermon save a dainty phrase or two that occurred in it. [33] Henry Ward Beecher was a more powerful preacher than any of those yet named. I crossed over from New York to Brooklyn to hear him in 1882—it was before the great Brooklyn Bridge had been built. The church outside was about as handsome as a barn. Inside, however, the seats were so conveniently arranged that everybody faced the preacher. There was no pulpit, but, instead, a broad platform, at either end of which was a huge spittoon, something of the shape and size of a washing-tub. Mr. Beecher paced up and down the platform as he delivered himself of many fine passages—many humorous passages, too, which set the congregation "teetering on the precipice of a laugh." A more eccentric preacher than Beecher was Peter Mackenzie, who used to make his congregation laugh outright. When Peter occupied the pulpit at Jesmond Wesleyan Church, Newcastle, the performance was almost as good as a play. It was less a sermon than an entertainment. All the same, the preacher was terribly in earnest, for he perspired like a race-horse. Other eminent preachers have been lecturers also. Mr. Spurgeon, lecturing on the use of anecdote in the pulpit, kept a large audience in the Town Hall, Newcastle, amused and delighted for more than an hour as he told story after story. The Town Hall was crammed on another occasion when Dr. Morley Punshon enchained and enchanted the crowd with his eloquence. Dr. Punshon was a Wesleyan; so is Mr. Fred. W. Macdonald, an ex-President of the Conference, and an uncle of Rudyard Kipling's. No pleasanter lecture was ever delivered in my hearing than that which Mr. Macdonald gave in Newcastle on his experiences in America.

Novelists have quite as much claim to attention as preachers and lecturers. The great novelist of the sea, the legitimate successor of Captain Marryat, is undoubtedly William Clark Russell. Mr. Russell began his literary life as a journalist. For some time he was a member of the staff of the *Newcastle Chronicle*. When he left to join the staff of the *Daily Telegraph*, he was followed to London by the esteem and regret of all his colleagues. Alas! he was soon afterwards seized with paralysis, and has now for many years been compelled to take the air in a bath chair at Bath. But his physical helplessness has not impaired his intellectual productiveness. Twice a year or so he adds to the gaiety of nations by a new novel of the sea. All the moods of the changeful waste are described in his books with wonderful fidelity. Not less wonderful is the fertility of an imagination that can work out one exciting plot after another within the comparatively narrow scope afforded by a brig or a schooner. Many of Hall Caine's stories have had a comparatively narrow field too—the Isle of Man. It was while he was writing "The Bondman" that he came to Newcastle to get local colouring for a little story he contributed to one of the Christmas numbers of the *Weekly Chronicle*. He did not remain long; but he remained long enough to leave the impression, strengthened by subsequent correspondence, of a genial gentleman without pride or pretence of any sort. Joseph Hatton, whose pleasant novels, numerous enough to fill a library, are fit for anybody's reading, is as genial, as accessible, and as devoid of humbug or assumption as Hall Caine. And so with John Strange Winter, who, relieved by her husband of the care and worry of business, devotes the major part of a happy married life to the production of tales that are as popular as they are short. Mrs. Stannard (to give her her real name) deserves credit for a great public service when she scotched and crushed a threatened revival of the crinoline.

Both Literature and the Press owe a deep debt of gratitude to the men who in earlier days fought and struggled to remove the taxes on knowledge. This object was completely accomplished at the end of a twelve years' agitation. Collet Dobson Collet, who was educated for the law, but who became a musician, acted as secretary to the Society for the Repeal of the Taxes on Knowledge from its inception to its dissolution. Mr. Collet, in the first or second year of the movement, came on a mission to Cheltenham, bringing with him, I remember, what might have been his own swimming bath. Not long before he had been deputed with W. J. Linton to visit Paris and congratulate the French Republic in the name of the Reformers of London on the downfall of Louis Philippe. Lloyd Jones, Edward Truelove, and

George Jacob Holyoake were more or less intimately associated with the knowledge movement. As a popular lecturer on social and political questions, Lloyd Jones spent much of his time among the Durham miners; yet the miners of one of the divisions of that county rejected his advances when he offered them his services as a candidate for Parliament. I don't think he ever recovered from the disappointment he then suffered, for he died soon afterwards. Edward Truelove, who lived to the age of ninety, had two great heroes—Robert Owen and Thomas Paine. Other heroes he had too—Mazzini, Kossuth, Comte, Bradlaugh. Never a revolutionist appeared in any part of the world, provided he had for his object the elevation or liberation of the oppressed, without finding in Edward Truelove a warm sympathiser and helper. Neither did any cause of advancement, political or social, economic or intellectual, present itself for approval without finding in the same quarter an earnest and enthusiastic adherent. I cannot call to mind a popular movement of his time in which Mr. Truelove did not bear a hand. But, as I have said, Owen and Paine were his leading lights. Relics of both were among his most cherished possessions. It was on Paine's own writing-table that Moncure Conway wrote in Truelove's house at Hornsey the opening sentences of his biography of the great needleman. A man of absolute sincerity, pure as a girl and unselfish as a saint, Edward Truelove was as defiant as Danton when the occasion needed. And he needed all his fortitude and endurance when, for publishing a philanthropic pamphlet by Robert Dale Owen, son of the old Socialist, he had, at the age of seventy and over, to submit for months to the treatment of the lowest criminal. George Jacob Holyoake, long connected with Truelove in many enterprises for the welfare and improvement of mankind, published in the *Newcastle Weekly Chronicle*, and subsequently in two stately volumes, his reminiscences of an agitator's life. Now considerably over eighty years of age, though he was never at any time a strong or a robust man, he can look back at many triumphs which he had a share in achieving.

Enthusiasts are sometimes the salt of the earth. One I knew was William Maccall, the apostle of Individualism. A big and brawny Scot, he never lost, nor cared to lose, the traces of his nationality: for his dialect was broad as his shoulders, and his speech as picturesque as the highlands of his native country. Henry George, the author of "Progress and Poverty," was an enthusiast of a different quality. When he came to Newcastle to propagate his ideas, he was confident of his ability to revolutionise society; nor did this confidence desert him when he returned to America. What he might have accomplished, if he had been elected Mayor of New York, as he had some prospect of being when he died suddenly in the midst of the contest, will now never be known. The movement he initiated died with him. George Crawshay was an enthusiast of a still different calibre—an enthusiast for many things, for the Charter at one time, for the repeal of the Corn Laws at another, for the Poles, the Danes, and the Turks. A scholar and a philanthropist, he entertained Emerson when that great thinker visited Newcastle. Though he had command of great wealth throughout his early and middle life, the vicissitudes of industry swept it all away, and he died without a penny. But he never repined. During his last days, while confined to what proved, to be his death bed, he wrote many notable things for the *Weekly Chronicle*, all marked by dainty taste and rare culture. A love-story of his—a record of reality, not a figment of imagination—was the most beautiful piece of the kind I ever read. It is sad to know that, when he left the town he and his firm had so long and so bountifully served, and left it penniless, he departed, as Joseph Cowen wrote, "without a sign of sympathy or a syllable of regret."

CHAPTER LXI

SCRAPINGS OF MEMORY

AFTER all has been said, there is always something more to be said. Let us gather up the fragments that remain.

Place to the ladies! This is only polite. But one must expect to be called a brute if one speaks one's mind on some of their manners and fashions. Time was when ladies, taking to heart the admonitions which the old parsons gave to the poor, were "content with the condition of life in which God had placed them." But this was before the advent of the "new woman"—before the advent of the "girl of the period" even. Everybody must lament the decay of that old-fashioned courtesy which lent so great a charm to social and public intercourse. But ladies themselves are perhaps not altogether blameless for the change. Some of them, as we know, show such entire contempt for the comfort of others—as, in theatres, for instance, when they refuse to remove their obstructive hats—that they arouse a not unnatural indignation. Moreover, the "new woman" has set up claims which must in the end prove fatal to all the ancient privileges the sex enjoyed. If women want to stand on the same footing as men, they must of course be prepared to submit to the same buffetings. Besides, it sometimes happens that ladies are deficient in manners themselves, especially when travelling in public vehicles. A lady enters a tramcar, and a gentleman resigns his seat to her. "I beg your pardon?" says the gentleman. "I did not speak," says the lady. "Oh," returns the gentleman, "I thought you said 'Thank you'!" A rebuke of this sort does not often need to be administered. But it ought not to be needed at all. It is only when ladies show consideration for the comfort of others that they can expect the deference and attention that were almost invariably extended to them in my young days.

Fashions are continually changing. The man of seventy who endeavours to recall their peculiarities, or even the order of their succession, will soon find himself in a difficulty. But there is one fashion that nobody who lived in the early sixties is likely to forget. I mean the crinoline. That dreadful arrangement was responsible for hundreds of miserable deaths. Rarely a week passed while our women were wearing it without a fatality due to its use being recorded. But neither danger nor inconvenience—not even inevitable exposure in a high wind or a narrow passage—deterred our women from retaining the hateful structure for many years. When a lady in a crinoline wanted to sit down, she had to lift up the hinder hoops of which it was composed and sit on them. I once went with a party of ladies and gentlemen for a drive into the country, when the crinolines had all to be surreptitiously taken off and stuffed under the seat. It was a tiresome time for everybody then. Many a man, sitting near the door of an omnibus on a rainy day, had his shirt-front and even his face smeared by the dirty skirts of the ladies who entered the vehicle after him. We may know from this that the fashion was—well, anything but decent. [34]

The chignon flourished at the same time as the crinoline. If you take a look at Leech's drawings in *Punch* at the period, you will see how hideous both looked. Even the Pope denounced the chignon; for in the March of 1869 Pius the Ninth invited all "Christian mothers and daughters of Mary" to form a league against it. "The doing up of chignons and the arranging of tresses several times a day," his Holiness declared, "occupy the time which should be devoted to religious duties, pious works, and family affairs." The chignon, a huge excrescence fixed to the back of the head, was accompanied by pads—resembling polonies in shape and size—which were hung on each side of the face. These pads were of course concealed under the hair—except at night, when they were hung (like Kilkenny cats on a clothes line) over the back of a chair. It must be admitted that the chignon, encased in a chenile net, had its uses when Belinda happened to have a back fall on the ice. But no use that anybody ever knew could be claimed for the polonies.

The fashions just mentioned were dirty and dangerous. But they were followed by others that were perhaps even more reprehensible—trailing skirts, and the wearing of the carcases of birds as millinery decorations.

Trailing skirts were a fearful nuisance; for anybody who walked behind a lady on a dusty day in town was certain to get smothered. What condition the lady herself was in can only be imagined. Our women were all Dorothy Draggletails then. They swept up and carried home in their garments much of the nameless filth of the streets. Investigations made by an Italian doctor indicate that the microbes thus introduced into the household might easily have been fatal to an ailing child. The skirt had always to be dusted in dry weather, but in wet weather it had to be scraped. Yet women submitted to this foul fashion for several years. [35]

"Of all the forces that regulate human society," it has been said, "fashion is one of the most irresistible, the most irresponsible, and the least intelligent. Inscrutable in its origin, impalpable in its authority, it is independent alike of humanity, taste, and sense." And fashion for nearly thirty years has proved more than a match for humanity. The craze for wearing first the feathers and then the wings and bodies of birds was in full flood in the middle of the seventies. It was in 1876 that Professor Newton, protesting against the barbarous custom, wrote that "feathers on the outside of any biped but a bird naturally suggest the association of tar." But neither ridicule nor remonstrance has availed to stay the cruelty. Millions and millions of birds have been destroyed to gratify a vanity which does not differ in its essence or its outward show from that of a Red Indian. Some species, once numerous, have been practically extirpated, while rarer and more beautiful species will soon be known no more on earth. It is women—the so-called gentle sex—that have worked this awful havoc. If they cannot be shamed into tenderness, one could almost wish that they could be stoned into it.

Men have their fashions as well as women. The shape of the hat, for instance, is continually changing, as is the cut of the coat and the trousers. Middle-aged people will recollect when the latter articles were so fashioned as to make the wearer look like a peg-top. Even in the matter of tobacco-smoking there have been changes. The habit is now almost universal—boys and even children, owing to the introduction of cigarettes, having acquired it. Unfortunately, it has induced another habit—the disgusting habit of spitting always and everywhere. But in my young days, smoking, though common, was by no means general. Perhaps the difficulty of getting a light before the invention of the lucifer match had something to do with the slender patronage of the weed. Working men smoked clay pipes, and carried their tobacco in brass boxes. The clay pipe is still in vogue, but the brass box is now a curiosity. Churchwardens were an evening luxury, and meerschaums appurtenances of richer folk. And now briarwood pipes and india-rubber pouches have taken the place of the older conveniences.

But of the habit itself, what shall one say? As a pretty old smoker— off and on I have smoked for more than fifty years—I have this to say, that smoking is merely a habit, pleasant enough when you have acquired it, but not indispensable to human happiness if you haven't. Much has been said about the slavery of the habit. It is fascinating rather than enslaving. I once abandoned it altogether, and only took to it again when I began to write for the press. Since then I have had no desire to discard the practice, and see no reason for discarding it. The experience of others may be different. There is, for example, the story of Max Müller and Alfred Tennyson. The talk turned on tobacco. The professor confessed that he had formerly been the slave of the pipe, but had asserted his independence by entirely renouncing it. "Well," said the poet, "anybody could do the same." Forthwith out of the window went his whole stock of pipes. The next day he was complacent, the day after he was moody, the third day he was miserable. Tennyson was then seen in the garden collecting his precious gods, never to be discarded again till the day he "crossed the bar." Similar was the experience of a Newcastle friend—a town councillor now dead. One evening he made a compact with another devotee of the soothing weed that neither should smoke again without his friend's consent. Next morning, immediately after breakfast, both were hunting all over the town for each other!

Diseases and accidents are common to us all. I have had experience of both. Once an attempt to protect a poor woman from a pack of dastardly boys led to weeks in bed from a sprained ankle. The boys were pelting the old dame with stones. She was so deaf that she did not hear the stones rattling around her head. I made a pretence of chasing the assailants, turned suddenly round, wrenched my foot on the curb-stone, and then—agony! Sick and faint and unable to walk, I crawled to a main street where I could hail a cab. While I was propped against a wall, waiting in awful pain for a cab to come along, the poor creature whom I had perhaps saved from fatal injuries, totally unconscious of her danger or mine, passed on her way home. Inscrutable indeed are the ways of Providence. Of another accident, though I was the subject, some one else was the victim. It arose from a telegraphic blunder. Not being able to keep an appointment, I instructed one of my children to send a telegram. The message, as prepared, ran thus:—"Don't expect any one to-night; father is in bed." As delivered, however, it ran thus: "Don't expect any one to-night; father is dead." When the telegram was received, the lady of the house went into hysterics, remained in a distressing condition for several hours, and did not recover from the shock for many days afterwards. "Whenever, in telegraphic or telephonic circles, curious mistakes are discussed," wrote the chief of the department in Newcastle, "this is one of the worst that can be recalled." As the false report somehow got abroad in the town, people seemed to feel, I thought, that I had no right to be seen in the streets after all they had heard. Blood-poisoning, the result of scamping work in a new house, was not only nearly fatal, but the parent of a whole crop of diseases. Sydney Smith once remarked: "I have gout, asthma, bronchitis, and seven other maladies, but am otherwise very well." James Payn, the novelist, shortly before he died, wrote in a similar strain: "I have had a fine old time with many disorders. For extreme agony, there are few things to beat rheumatic fever. As regards intolerant discomfort, there is nothing to vie with eczema; but for helpless, hopeless misery, with a struggle for life every five minutes—a night with bronchitis." Well, asthma is pretty bad too. Dr. Horace Dobell relates the case of a gentleman who, travelling from Leeds or Manchester to Bournemouth, had to spend the time of the journey on his knees at the bottom of the railway carriage, gasping for air. A lady of my acquaintance had to sleep in a chair for months on end because she could not breathe in bed. Another patient could not rest in any bedroom in his house, and had at last to fix his couch in a sort of coal-hole, among pots and pans and other kitchen utensils. Such are the dreadful peculiarities of asthma. When the disorder is complicated with bronchitis, as it often is, a new misery is added to life. The wheezing and whistling in the sufferer's throat, comparable sometimes to the droning of a foghorn, sometimes to the wail and yelp of a ship's syren, disturb the household, wake up the sufferer from a fitful sleep, and rob even death of its terrors. But for excruciating agony there is nothing equal to sciatica. It is curious, though, that every form of painful disease seems preferable to every other form when you are free from all but one. When I am writhing from sciatica, I think I would prefer asthma; and when I am gasping from asthma, I think I would prefer sciatica. But the happy discoveries of modern days have given relief from many intolerable ailments. The effects of morphia are wonderful. First the pain begins to subside; then it disappears altogether; and then ensues a feeling of perfect peace—not sleep, nor the desire for sleep, but absolute and ecstatic enchantment. Such was my experience at heavenly intervals when enduring for months the torments of sciatica.

Yet there are vile complaints, the fruit of the lowest vices, which the public opinion of the day will not allow the faculty to prevent. I attended a meeting which was called in the sixties to consider the extension of the Contagious Diseases Act. The chairman of the meeting was the Mayor of Newcastle, Mr. Henry Angus. Most of the principal practitioners of the town were present—Dr. Charlton, Dr. Embleton, Dr. Arnison, Dr. Brady, Dr. Gregson, Dr. Hardcastle, Dr. Philipson, Dr. Russell. So were some of the leaders of the religious world—Archdeacon Prest, the Rev. Clement Moody (Vicar of Newcastle), and the Rev. Dr. John Collingwood Bruce. Indeed, the movement, judging from the people who took a prominent part in promoting it, seemed to be of a religious and philanthropic character. Nevertheless, it provoked one of the most unpleasant agitations of the century—almost as unpleasant as that which arose later from the publication of the "Maiden Tribute." The opposition which the proposal of the Newcastle philanthropists brought out had the effect in the end of stopping all legislation of the nature indicated.

CHAPTER LXII

MORE SCRAPINGS

NEWCASTLE, since the present scribbler knew it, has been the scene of many exciting public meetings in the Town Hall. One of the earliest he recollects was called to consider a subject on which there was great division of opinion. The meeting was divided too. Sir John Fife occupied the chair. The gallant knight, after vainly endeavouring to obtain a hearing for the speakers, stepped down from his seat, strutted across the platform, and exclaimed at the top of his voice, as if he had been dispersing his regiment of volunteers, "I dissolve you as a disorderly meeting."

During the agitation for the disestablishment of the Irish Church, a ticket meeting was called by the Church party. A great gun was there from Dublin—the Rev. Tresham Gregg. There had been other meetings in the neighbourhood, called in the same way, at which the resolutions adopted were represented to embody the opinions of the inhabitants. As soon as the proceedings in the Town Hall had been opened, the late Dr. Rutherford ascended the platform, and demanded an assurance from the promoters that no attempt would be made to pass off that meeting as a meeting of the inhabitants of Newcastle. Immense hubbub and excitement followed. Dr. Rutherford, however, was encouraged to persist by a small but determined section of the audience. The result was that the meeting was dissolved. As the gathering dispersed, a reverend gentleman was seen on the stairs holding out a ticket to the crowd, and exclaiming in a voice broken with anger and emotion, "They have come here with a lie in their right hand to disturb the proceedings." From that time to this, ticket meetings have never been popular in Newcastle.

No meetings in the Town Hall have ever been so crammed or so enthusiastic as those which Mr. Cowen addressed when he was seeking the suffrages of the electors or giving an account of his stewardship. Once there was a fearful crush to hear him when it was announced that he was going to address his constituents. The hon. member was himself so crushed and injured that there was no address at all. The time was critical, and some of Mr. Cowen's good-natured friends suggested that the whole thing was a feint; yet from the injuries he sustained he never completely recovered. On that occasion or some other the seats in the body of the hall had been removed so as to give room for a larger gathering. The consequence was disastrous. The pressure from both ends of the floor was so terrible that the audience seemed to bulge up in the middle. Many people in the midst of it had to be rescued in a fainting and exhausted condition by the occupants of the side elevations. I have witnessed many exhilarating scenes, but never any that equalled the delirium Mr. Cowen produced by a magnificent peroration about Arnold of Winkelreid and the gallant Greeks who leapt from Suli's rock.

During the short time he was member for Newcastle, Mr. Ashton Dilke had some exasperating experiences. One was when he called his first meeting after he had been elected. Infuriated Irishmen came from all parts of Tyneside, prevented the hon. member from speaking, and eventually stormed and captured the platform. It was not a meeting—it was a pandemonium. Irishmen on a later occasion were just as much infuriated against Michael Davitt. For some reason or other, Mr. Davitt had incurred the displeasure of the Fenians, and the Fenians had planned an organized attack upon their fellow-countryman and his friends. When the platform was invaded by a hostile and threatening mob, Mr. Davitt drew a revolver from his pocket to defend himself. Fortunately, he had no occasion to use it: else the audience in the Town Hall, as an Irish Chief Constable of Newcastle said of another meeting that was broken up in the same place, might have been "floating in blood."

Besides disorderly meetings, party politics sometimes produce ludicrous things—party poetry, for instance. It is sad rubbish generally—a shade worse, perhaps, than the common run of comic songs of the day. When Mr. Surr William Duncan was Conservative candidate for the Wisbech Division of Cambridgeshire in 1892, the Hon. Mrs. Brand was said to have sung with great success at Liberal gatherings, a song which contained the following couplet:—

We have kept Surr William Duncan out,
And shoved the Tories up the spout.

Conservative poets have been equal to the occasion also. Here are some sample lines from a ditty that was chanted with much amusement at a banquet in Edinburgh:—

The G.O.M. will rise,
        By and by,
To a mansion in the sky,
        By and by,
Unless—oh! tale of woe!—
He unfortunately go
To the regions down below,
        By and by.

But worse is in store for the country if the party spirit should be allowed to ride rough-shod over it. The formation of a society of political agents is bringing us nearer and nearer to that system of "machine politics" which has produced so much corruption in the United States. As matters have looked in recent years, it seems likely that we shall not be long before there is a Tammany Hall in England—an institution which will make the ballot a fraud and popular government a scandal. One of the casuistic questions which election agents, who would appear to be qualifying themselves for Jesuit priests, have been asked to answer is this:—"What form of words would you advise for the use of a candidate anxious to pledge himself to the Temperance party without losing the support of the liquor interest?" If this be a specimen of the examination which professional politicians are expected to go through, we may bid farewell to what honesty and sincerity yet pertains to our political life. Nobody knows better than Mr. Bryce, whose great work on the "American Commonwealth" is a standard and a warning, the rascality and rottenness which the "spoils system" has introduced into the body politic of the United States. Yet, when he was Chancellor of the Duchy of Lancaster in 1893, he actually followed, in respect to the appointment of magistrates, very nearly the same policy as that which has had demoralizing results on the other side of the Atlantic.

But politics afford a pleasant occupation to people who are socially inclined. The House of Commons has been described as the best club in London. I became for the time being a convert to that opinion when I once spent a night in it. We were the guests of the late John Candlish, then one of the members for Sunderland. Mr. Candlish showed us everything and everywhere—the legislative chamber, the library, the dining-room, the smoke-room. We practically sat in the House itself, though the business in hand was neither important nor very interesting. I recollect recognising many of the members from the struts and attitudes I had seen caricatured in the cartoons of *Vanity Fair*. But the strangest thing I saw there was an Irish member who was born without arms or legs. This was Mr. Kavanagh. We saw him in the smoke-room. Nothing particular was noticeable about him as he sat smoking and drinking and chatting with his friends, for he had been fitted with a contrivance which enabled him to hold his cigar and lift his glass. But the division bell rang. Then all was commotion. And the last we saw of Mr. Kavanagh was a figure with a dark skirt hurriedly disappearing on the back of another member. The agility of the hon. gentleman in mounting his friend's shoulders was less astonishing than the fact we were told that he was in the habit of riding to hounds. That night in the House of Commons was an agreeable finish to a short holiday. One would perhaps think less highly of the performance, however, if one had to sit it out every night, and sometimes all night, for six months of the year.

Legislators who have every facility for getting drunk themselves— facilities that are not always neglected, for even Mr. Disraeli, according to Mr. Gladstone, had his "midnight manner"—can hardly be expected to put too tight a rein on other people. So temperance legislation, at all events until lately, made slow progress. Not that any legislation will do much to correct a habit that has long been reckoned one of the worst foibles of the English race. Dr. Johnson told Boswell that he remembered the time "when all decent people in Leicester got drunk every night, and were not the worse thought of." Decent people, or people who thought themselves decent, got drunk long after Johnson's time. A circumstance will illustrate the point. The drinking glasses we now call tumblers seem to owe their name to a new fashion that was introduced into this country at the close of the eighteenth century. They were then called "tumbling glasses," for the reason that they were so made (somewhat after the shape of soda-water bottles) that they tumbled over unless held in the hand. Indeed, the object of these "tumbling glasses" was apparently to make the persons who used them drink more than they probably would have done otherwise. A correspondent of *Notes and Queries*, writing on this subject, quoted from an old diary kept by a great-uncle of his in the year 1803, in which occurred the following entry:—"Had a few friends to dine; tried my new 'tumbling glasses'; very successful—all got drunk early." But people in the "hupper suckles" got drunk early at the end as well as the beginning of the century—early in the day even. There was a fashionable wedding in Northumberland in 1896. Two days before the marriage a reporter was sent out to glean particulars at the ancestral mansion of the bride. The bride's father was found drunk at noon. "Can you tell me," he was asked by the reporter, "anything about the bridegroom?" "Bridegroom?" came the dazed reply: "well, they call him Archie, but d—d if I know what else they call him!"

The origin of other names besides that of "tumbler" is apt to get obscure unless fixed before it is too late. Take as an example the name Jingo, meaning a sort of national swashbuckler. According to the "National Dictionary of Biography," the late Professor Minto, a member of the staff of the *Daily News*, claimed that he was the first to give the word "the currency of respectable print." But let the facts be fairly stated. During the excitement occasioned by the Russo-Turkish war, a music-hall performer named MacDermott obtained a great amount of kudos by singing a war-like song, the chorus of which ran something like this:—

We don't want to fight;
   But, by Jingo, if we do,
We've got the men, we've got the ships,
   And we've got the money too.

The song, in spite of its absurdity, took hold of the public mind, so that the refrain was heard and chanted everywhere. It came to pass that Mr. Bradlaugh and Mr. Auberon Herbert called a peace meeting in Hyde Park on Sunday, May 10th, 1878. The park, however, was invaded by a boisterous crowd, who roared the music-hall song, marched to the Turkish Embassy, and kept things lively for the rest of the day. Thereupon my old friend George Jacob Holyoake wrote to the *Daily News* suggesting that the war party should take the name of the patron saint of the music-halls, St. Jingo, and so he headed his letter, "The Jingoes in the Park." The suggestion was adopted at once; advocates of a war policy became known as Jingoes; and the designation has since been appropriated by many foreign countries. This statement of the origin of the name is not invalidated by the fact that Sir George Otto Trevelyan (then Mr. Trevelyan, member for the Border Burghs) quoted the musichall song in a speech at Selkirk in the January previous. The song was one thing; the proposal that the war party should be baptised Jingoes another thing.

There is no obscurity about the origin of Primrose Day and of the political organization called the Primrose League. The anniversary and the association were so christened because the primrose was supposed to be the favourite flower of Lord Beaconsfield, the Mr. Disraeli of an earlier period. But the assumption about the flower is alleged to have been due to a mistake. James Payn explained the matter. When Lord Beaconsfield died, Queen Victoria sent a huge wreath of primroses, bearing the inscription, "His favourite flower." The fashionable world at once jumped to the conclusion that the Queen meant the deceased statesman, whereas Payn declares that "his" in the royal mind always signified something belonging to the Prince Consort. The explanation is plausible. Throughout Disraeli's novels it appears there is only one mention of primroses, and that is in "Lothair," where Lord St. Jerome remarks that "they make excellent salad." Payn was of opinion that nothing could have been conceived more out of character for Lord Beaconsfield than a preference for a simple flower. The peacock was his favourite bird. Reasoning from analogy, one would therefore suppose that the peony or the sunflower would have been more in harmony with his gaudy taste.

The weaknesses and follies of our people notwithstanding, we are all proud of our native land. It was Robertson of Brighton who said or wrote:—"Blessings on thee, my dear old blundering country: she never long mistakes an actor for a hero or a hero for an actor." Two sailors were talking about their respective countries. "If I were not a Frenchman," said one, "I would like to be an Englishman." "If I were not an Englishman," said the other, "I would like to be an Englishman." And so say all of us! England is not always right; but she is oftener right than any other country in the world. It is true that she occasionally conquers new territories; but the territories that are thus conquered, thanks to an enlightened policy that has seldom varied, are not exploited simply and solely for her own advantage. She does not shut up her possessions, as France has shut up Madagascar or as Russia would shut up China. There is little need, therefore, for any Englishman to raise the cry of some foolish Americans—"Our country, right or wrong." The influence and prospects of the British race can only be ruined by the vices and stupidities of the British race itself. The pursuit of narrow and sordid interests in preference to broad and patriotic interests— solicitude for the advantage of a class instead of the welfare of the nation at large—would sooner or later be fatal to us all. So also would be the sacrifice of the general prosperity to the gross indulgences of the individual. Thrift and industry, probity and sobriety, will ensure the salvation of any race on earth. They will prove the salvation of ours. For the rest, there is the idea of obligation. Thomas Drummond laid down the doctrine that property has its duties as well as its rights. When we have learnt the still better lesson of Joseph Mazzini—that the duties of man are as divinely ordained as the rights of man—we may march on our way, defiant and rejoicing.

FINIS.

FOOTNOTES.

1.This was written before a correspondence on the subject took place in the *Newcastle Weekly Chronicle* in 1902, Major A. C. Cunningham, writing from Cheltenham, therein stated that he had "read the epitaph many years ago in the old cemetery in the High Street, Cheltenham," and that his brother, "now the Vicar of Marnham, Notts," also read it, and remembered having done so. Here was the first positive assertion I ever saw in print of anybody having seen the lines on a tombstone. The "old cemetery in the High Street" was the new cemetery when I was a boy. For twenty years I was as familiar with it as I was with any part of the town; yet I never saw or even heard of the epitaph till long afterwards. Major Cunningham, in a later communication, submitted that the inscription had been erased, since it could not now be found. So the matter stands pretty much where it stood before. Early recollections are not always to be trusted, unless they are supported by documentary or other evidence. For example, in regard to this very epitaph, I know a clergyman in the North of England who is, or rather was, as positive on the subject as Major Cunningham—only he had seen the doggerel, not in the cemetery, but in the parish churchyard! And the witness in this case even recollected the location of the gravestone!

2.The Archbishop of Armagh (Lord John George Beresford) was also called "the beauty of holiness."

3.Mr. Douglas Sladen, writing in *Harper's Magazine*, records the fact that the names of the foremost representatives of the college in sports and athletics are inscribed on the walls of the gymnasium. Thus we are reminded that the William Conyngham Plunket, who was a silver medallist in 1845, became Archbishop of Dublin, the Right Hon. Lord Plunket; that R. T. Reid, who figures as a scholar of the college, is now Sir R. T. Reid, K.C., member for the Dumfries Burghs; and that Mr. John Morley, member for Montrose, and Mr. R. E. Francillon, the novelist, have also left their names on the college walls.

4.Hallam, Lord Tennyson, refers to this incident in the "Life of the Poet Laureate":—"My father would say: 'The first time I met

Robertson I felt that he expected something notable from me, because I knew that he admired my poems, that he wished to pluck the heart from my mystery: so for the life of me from pure nervousness I could talk of nothing but beer."'

5. It was in Cheltenham, I think, that an acquaintance would keep on assuring the poet that it was the greatest honour of his life to have met him. Tennyson's answer was—Don't talk d——d nonsense.

6. Tennyson writes from Cheltenham in 1845 to his friend Rawnsley;—"Here is a handsome town of thirty-five thousand inhabitants, a polka-parson-worshipping place, of which the Rev. Francis Close is Pope, besides pumps and pump-rooms, chalybeates, quadrilles, and one of the prettiest countries in Great Britain."

7. G. L. Jessop, the famous cricketer, is, I believe, a grandson or great-grandson of the old nurseryman.

8. Samuel Smiles, now more than ninety years old, is, of course, the author of "Self-Help" and many other well-known books.

9. There is a story of a Leicester journalist who, when an accident had occurred on the eve of publication, went to press with a column of pie, preceded by this intimation—"Our Dutch mail has just arrived. Having no time to translate the despatch, we give it in the original."

10. A clerical friend suggests that I may have made a mistake here. Horde, he says, was the name of a showman who regularly visited Taunton and the neighbourhood in the forties. It is just possible that my friend's showman and mine were one and the same person.

11. The "enthusiastic disciple" was Mr. John Lea, a gentleman of independent means, who, when he died in 1899, was described as "probably the oldest stenographer in the kingdom."

12. While these pages were going through the press, I read with great sorrow of the death of Henry Solly. This venerable friend of my youth died in March, 1903, at the residence of his son-in-law, the Rev, P. H. Wicksteed.

13.Mr. Foxton was also, I think, the author of another work of note, "The Gospel according to Mrs. Grundy." "Popular Christianity" was published by John Chapman along with Froude's "Phases of Faith," and Newman's "Soul, its Sorrows, and its Aspirations." It is recorded in the "Life of Lord Tennyson" that Mr. Foxton had been "Carlyle's companion and caretaker during a journey on the Continent." I was personally grateful to the reverend gentleman, because he had encouragingly written on the manuscript of the essay which gained the first prize—"The author will have an admirable style when he has written more?" When a year or so later some of us had plunged into the great democratic whirlpool, we had the temerity and conceit to approach Mr. Foxton, he being, as we knew, a scholar of advanced ideas, with the view of asking him to join our movement! We were kindly received, attentively heard, and placed in a row with our faces to the light, so that we could be seen to the best advantage. Mr. Foxton did not despise us because we were young and audacious; but he did not join our movement.

14.This extraordinary fanatic, who came from America and attracted immense crowds by throwing handfuls of half-dollars among them, called himself Ecce Homo also, declared himself to be Christ, dressed himself in a white robe, and claimed to have been the cause of the potato blight! A Chartist meeting in Sandford Fields, addressed by Ernest Jones and R. G. Gammage, attracted an enormous multitude, mainly because a report had been circulated that Shiloh was to take the chair!

15.John Temple Leader, the last survivor of the twelve politicians who initiated the People's Charter, died at Florence in March, 1903, at the advanced age of 93. Mr. Leader, once member for Westminster, was as well known in his day as Mr. Labouchere is in ours; yet he had so long outlived his fame that few papers announced his death, and fewer still could recall anything about him.

16.Edward Sharland, now nearing ninety years of age, is still living at Cheltenham.

17.The juvenile orator was a nine days' wonder—at least he thought he was. Just about that time we used to read in the newspapers of the exploits of "the boy Jones," a pertinacious imp who could not be kept out of the Queen's apartments in Buckingham Palace. It was suggestive of similar notoriety, though of a less undignified sort, that a section of the people of Cheltenham for the space of a week or more talked of "the boy Adams."

18.John West was a comrade in the Chartist agitation.

19.Macready, the celebrated tragedian, described Bunn at this time as living on the price of his wife's infamy. The poet's wife, it was alleged, was loaned to the peer for a handsome consideration.

20.Grantley Berkeley's blackguardism is another story. The facts of the matter, or some of them, have been pieced together in a letter from an old friend in Chicago—Mr. James Charlton, the doyen of American passenger agents. What follows is a mere re-arrangement of Mr. Charlton's narrative.

William Maginn, the Captain Shandon of Thackeray's "Pendennis," and peradventure the "most protean genius that ever appeared in literature," was a writer in *Fraser's Magazine,* as well as one of the largest contributors to the "Noctes Ambrosiana" in *Blackwood.* It was in the former capacity that he came into conflict with the Hon. Grantley Fitzhardinge Berkeley.

Grantley wrote a novel entitled "Berkeley Castle," which was reviewed and scarified by Maginn in No. 123 of *Fraser's Magazine.* The author of the novel took his revenge on the publisher of the magazine. Fraser was physically weak, while his assailant was physically powerful. The result was that Fraser never recovered from the shock of that brutal assault, and finally died of it. An action at law cost Berkeley £100, and a cross-action, Berkeley v. Fraser, ended in a verdict for forty shillings.

The legal proceedings were followed by a duel. Maginn acknowledged the authorship of the article in *Fraser.* Then came "coffee and pistols for two," Honour was satisfied when the heel of Maginn's boot and the collar of Berkeley's coat were both grazed.

Failing to shoot his critic, Grantley Berkeley did his best and wickedest to blast the reputation of an innocent girl. Years after, when he came to write his "Reminiscences," he wove together a tissue of falsehoods and misrepresentations relating to Maginn and Miss Landon, the unfortunate L. E. L.

The story of L. E. L. is one of the saddest in English literature. Miss Landon was at one time engaged to John Forster, the biographer of Dickens. As Forster "never hesitated to correct Dickens, or anybody else, about almost everything, and as he knew everything and a great deal more, and had absolute faith in his own point of view and in nobody else's," it is doubtful whether the gentle poetess would have had a happy life with him. Anyway, affected by the slanders which "spiteful scoundrels" like Grantley Berkeley had circulated about her, Miss Landon declined the offer of Forster's hand. Afterwards she went to Cape Coast Castle. The mystery of her death there has never been satisfactorily solved.

Ernest Jones, subsequent to his release from prison, published several poetical pieces in his "Notes to the People." One was entitled "The New World," which, during the Indian Mutiny, he re-issued under the more attractive title of "The Revolt of Hindostan." In the original publication the following four lines occur: —

> Pale rose an anxious face from Niger's wave,
> And murdered Park one groan of anguish gave;
> While distant ocean, starting at the knell,
> Washed from its sands the letters L. E. L.

Grantley Berkeley died on February 23rd, 1881, at the age of eighty-one. Ten years before, Mortimer Collins published a novel, "Marquis and Merchant," which he dedicated "to the Hon. Grantley Fitzhardinge Berkeley, who, both in Life and Literature, shows the true meaning of the adage—'Whom the gods love die young.'" To appreciate the force and sting of the dedication one has to remember that the Honourable Grantley was even then more than seventy years old.

21. Grief and humiliation resulted from one order given to a Coniston tradesman. It was an order for a pair of boots—Bluchers

they were called, after the German general who fought at Waterloo. Heavy, clumsy, shapeless, they were as much like boats as boots. Unfortunately, they were taken to London. There it was intended to use them as office shoes. But they were early discovered. Forthwith they were carried from frame to frame till every compositor in the establishment had had an opportunity of wondering at the monstrous specimens of "clod-hopper fashion." The horrid things could not be disowned, but they were very promptly discarded. If the shoes were a curiosity, so was the shoemaker. It was his custom to physic his apprentice whenever he felt ill himself!

22. Shortly after the Coup d'État, Richard Chevenix Trench, then Dean of Westminster, but afterwards Archbishop of Dublin, published a little volume on the "Study of Words." Therein he discussed the word "tyrant," pointing out that a tyrant in the ancient Greek sense meant a usurper, one who had "attained supreme dominion through the violation of the laws and liberties of the State," whereas in the modern sense a tyrant is a ruler who uses his power for base and hateful purposes. And then he added:—"The present ruler of France, in the manner in which he obtained his power and in the manner in which he wields it, throws the fullest light on the meaning of this word." But the passage—the policy of the British Government having in the meantime made the usurper and tyrant respectable—was expunged from subsequent editions of the book.

23. Mr. Harold Johnson, who used to write in Secular periodicals over the signature of "Anthony Collins," stated in the *Radical* for August, 1887, that an agent from the Home Office was sent in 1858 to search among his papers at Blackburn for the manuscript of "Tyrannicide." This curious proceeding he explained thus:—'When Mr. Truelove was arrested, Mr. Johnson instructed him by telegraph to print the pamphlet entire in the next number of the *Investigator*, a periodical which he then edited and which Mr. Truelove published. A copy of the telegram, he surmises, must have been communicated to the Home Office. At all events, an agent from that department waited on Mr. Johnson for the purpose stated. Among the contributors to the *Investigator* was a gentleman named J. P. Adams. Confusing one

Adams with another, the authorities appear to have got the notion that the document they wanted to obtain would be found in the possession of the editor of the *Investigator*.' Such was Mr. Johnson's story. While sorting some old papers more than forty years after the publication, I came upon the original essay that had formed the foundation of the prosecuted pamphlet.

24. Mr. Pope was the eminent Parliamentary barrister who died in 1901 at the age of seventy-five.

25. An amusing story may be told of this old friend. He was very dark, bearded like the pard, and somewhat free and easy in his attire. When he donned a big black slouch hat and hung it over his left ear, he looked very much like a corsair or a cowboy. For some such reason we gave him the name of Dirk Hatteraik. It chanced that a fellow-compositor—he was working in the office of the *Manchester Guardian* at the time—had been tormented by the trespasses and depredations of a neighbour's fowls among his flower-beds. To get rid of the nuisance he conceived the dangerous project of scattering poisoned grain in his garden. A chemist had told him that he could have what poison he required, provided he brought a witness to certify that the drug would be used for no unlawful purpose. Would Dirk be his witness? Certainly he would. Forth the pair sallied into Market Street. I think it was to Jewsbury's—the same family as Geraldine Jewsbury, Carlyle's Geraldine. A bland young chemist came to the counter. "I have called for that poison," said the customer; "this is my witness." The bland young chemist's face assumed various expressions—curiosity, anxiety, suspicion, doubt. Without saying a word, he retired behind a screen. There was a sound of whispering; then heads appeared above the screen, peeping at the customer and the witness; and then the bland young chemist returned with an apologetic air. "Sorry to say, sir," he said, "but we are quite out of poisons just now!" Dirk—his real name was Doughty, and he had been associated with Edwin Waugh in his early days at Wakefield—Dirk was never happier than when telling this tale against himself.

26. Mr. Gaskell encouraged his students to write essays on such subjects as pleased them, and submit the papers to him. The essays,

having been read and corrected in the meantime, were criticised at the next meeting of the class. I tried my hand more than once. One of the essays dealt with the republican idea. Protesting against the notion that the American Republic was to be considered a genuine republic, the daring essayist hazarded the statement that the people of the United States were "far on the way to become Red Indians themselves." Yet the astounding assertion was not so bad a shot after all; for, more than thirty years later, the following paragraph went the round of the English papers:—Considerable sensation has been caused in the United States by a lecture given by Professor Starr, a well-known anthropologist of Chicago University. In the course of his remarks, the professor declared that, if intermarriage with immigrants were to be stopped, Americans would soon become Indians again."

27.It was no doubt to this cause that we must ascribe a recent feat of a Plymouth daily. The name of my old friend the member for Morpeth was therein given as "Mr. Durt, M.P."

28.It was this same divine who astonished a diocesan conference in Newcastle by declaring that dynamite and the dagger, in the eyes of the judge of all the world, were "only an impassioned prayer"!

29.Confirmation of the statements in the text may be found in the "Memoirs of an Ex-Minister." The Ex-Minister was the Earl of Malmesbury, who twice held the seals of the Foreign Office in the Cabinets of Lord Derby. Lord Malmesbury made the following entry in his diary on April 20th, 1864:—"Garibaldi leaves England on Friday. Lord Clarendon, who has just returned from Paris, has informed the Government that the Emperor has made that a condition of his joining with us in the conference (Danish-German affairs); and certainly there must be some intrigues, as Mr. Ferguson, the surgeon, writes a letter to the Duke of Sutherland—which is published—saying that it would be dangerous to Garibaldi's health if he exposed himself to the fatigue of an expedition to Manchester, etc. On the other hand, Dr. Basile, Garibaldi's own doctor, says he is perfectly well and able to undergo all the fatigue of a journey to the manufacturing towns. The publication of this letter in contradiction to Mr. Ferguson's must have been done with Garibaldi's consent; it shows he is angry, and does not leave England willingly."

30.Mr. Elliott thinks I am wrong in this statement. The "Hubbubboo," he says, was the production of Dr. Robert Trotter, then of Choppington, but now of Perth, the author of "Galloway Gossip" and a host of other things.

31.Mr. Burt often afterwards dined at the same table as Mr. Gladstone—often, therefore, heard the great statesman tell interesting stories. Here is one that I have not seen in print before. An old admiral lay on his death bed. The fact did not seem to concern him. So the clergyman of the parish endeavoured to prepare his mind for the impending change. The dying man was reminded of the privileges that belonged to the household of faith. Wonderful was the happiness that awaited the repentant and believing spirit. Eye hath not seen, ear hath not heard, neither hath it entered into the heart of man to conceive, the glories of the realms above. "Aye, aye," piped the old salt, "it may be as you say,—but," feebly waving his nightcap around his head, "Ould England for me! Ould England for me!"

32.Sir James Crichton Browne lately quoted a case in which the ten children of a half-witted father were all imbeciles.

33.Sir John Bowring, in some autobiographical reminiscences that were published after his death, says:—"Montgomery's real patronymic was Gomery—the son of the clown of that name—but he sought to aristocratise his designation, and wished to be called 'The Poet Montgomery,' an ambition which gave no little offence to James Montgomery, the veritable poet, who stands in the first rank of devotional minstrels."

34.Àpropos of the crinoline, which was a cage-like arrangement of wires and tapes, the following little story may be appreciated:— When the ceremony of laying the foundation-stone of the proposed new docks on the Black Middens at North Shields was performed by Sir Joseph Cowen, chairman of the Tyne Commissioners (the stone was laid in the sixties, but the docks were never made), the latter part of the proceedings, as I well remember, was marred by a drenching shower. Among the gentlemen who assisted at the ceremony was Chevalier Brightman, the Austrian Consul, whose official uniform was a gorgeous affair—duck trousers, scarlet coat, cocked hat, white plumes, etc. Mr. Brightman got drenched like the rest of us. On his way home he called at a cottage in search of a change of raiment. But the only change the poor woman could offer him was a crinoline!

35.Written in 1901. And now (1903) the foul fashion is rampant again.

Lightning Source UK Ltd.
Milton Keynes UK
UKOW051649051211

183233UK00002B/35/P